Hermann August Hagen, Philip Reese Uhler

Synopsis of the Neuroptera of North America

Hermann August Hagen, Philip Reese Uhler

Synopsis of the Neuroptera of North America

ISBN/EAN: 9783744666510

Printed in Europe, USA, Canada, Australia, Japan

Cover: Foto ©ninafisch / pixelio.de

More available books at **www.hansebooks.com**

SMITHSONIAN MISCELLANEOUS COLLECTIONS.

SYNOPSIS

OF THE

NEUROPTERA

OF

NORTH AMERICA.

WITH A LIST OF THE SOUTH AMERICAN SPECIES.

PREPARED FOR THE SMITHSONIAN INSTITUTION

BY

HERMANN HAGEN.

WASHINGTON:
SMITHSONIAN INSTITUTION.
JULY, 1861.

ADVERTISEMENT.

The present "Synopsis of North American Neuroptera" has been prepared by Dr. Hermann Hagen of Königsberg (one of the highest living authorities on this subject), at the special request of the Smithsonian Institution, from materials in considerable part supplied by the collections of the Institution, or furnished for the purpose, by correspondents, at its request. It is hoped that the publication of this work and its distribution throughout the country will call attention to the insects of this order, and result in the collection of fuller materials, to be used hereafter in the preparation of a more perfect report.

For the purpose of making the present work serve the purpose of a report on the Neuroptera of the New World, a list of the names of the known South American species has been added. Some of these have not yet been published, but descriptions of them will shortly be presented to the world by Dr. Hagen in some one of the German scientific journals.

The manuscript of this work was furnished by Dr. Hagen in Latin, and it has been translated into English by Mr. P. R. Uhler of Baltimore. To him, and to Baron R. Osten Sacken, the Institution is under obligations for the careful examination and correction of the proof sheets.

JOSEPH HENRY,
Secretary S. I.

SMITHSONIAN INSTITUTION,
WASHINGTON, June, 1861.

ACCEPTED FOR PUBLICATION, NOVEMBER, 1860.

PHILADELPHIA:
COLLINS, PRINTER.

PREFACE.

The following Synopsis of the Neuroptera of North America has been prepared in accordance with the desire of the Smithsonian Institution, and contains all the known species found hitherto in the United States, in the English and Russian colonies, Mexico, Central America, and the West Indies. Many species described originally as belonging to the last-named countries, may hereafter be found in the southern parts of the United States.

The materials upon which the Synopsis has been based are the following:—

1. Species furnished by the Smithsonian Institution, chiefly Odonata, collected by Capt. J. Pope, U. S. A., on the Pecos River, Western Texas (lat. 32°, long. 104°), by Dr. Berlandier and Lt. Couch, U. S. A., at Matamoras, and by Dr. Engelmann at St. Louis.

2. The very numerous species collected by Baron Osten Sacken in different parts of the United States, particularly at Washington, at Trenton Falls, at Savannah and Dalton in Georgia, at Berkeley Springs in Virginia, in Florida, in Cuba, on the St. Lawrence River, and at Chicago.

3. A considerable number of Odonata, collected by Mr. Abbot in Georgia, and furnished by the late Mr. Escher-Zollickofer of Zurich.

4. A considerable number of Odonata, collected by the late Mr. Guex at Bergen Hill in New Jersey, and communicated by Prof. Schaum of Berlin.

5. A considerable number of Neuroptera from California, Maryland, Illinois, and North Red River (from Mr. Robert Kennicott), furnished by Mr. P. R. Uhler of Baltimore.

6. Some species collected in Florida by Mr. Norton, and at New York by Mr. Calverly.

7. Other species collected in South Carolina by Mr. Zimmermann, and furnished by the late Prof. Germar of Halle.

8. A considerable number of Neuroptera collected in Cuba and furnished by Prof. Poey of Havana.

9. A considerable number of Neuroptera collected in Mexico and supplied by Mr. de Saussure of Geneva.

10. My own collection, containing the types of Winthem, described by Prof. Burmeister, and some species furnished by the late Mr. Say.

11. Many species collected in the Russian colonies and in California, communicated by Mr. Menetries from the Imperial Museum of St. Petersburg, and by Colonel Motschulsky.

12. The Neuroptera of North America of the Museum at Berlin, furnished by Dr. Gerstaecker.

13. The Neuroptera of North America of the Museum at Vienna, communicated by Mr. Kollar.

14. The Neuroptera of North America of the collection of the Baron Selys Longchamps at Liege, with the types described by Messrs. Rambur, Latreille, Palisot de Beauvois, contained in Serville's collection, and some supplied by Mr. Asa Fitch.

15. Some types, chiefly from Labrador, described by Mr. Burmeister, and contained in the collection of Mr. Sommer at Altona.

16. The very great number of Neuroptera of the British Museum in London, described by Mr. Fr. Walker, chiefly from Canada and the polar regions, which I examined at London in 1857, with the kind permission of Dr. J. E. Gray.

I have endeavored to cite the literature of the subject as completely as possible. Besides the printed works, I have taken advantage of written communications made by Mr. Haldeman and Mr. Uhler on those species, which had been described by them. The rare memoir of the late Mr. Say, "Godman's Western Quarterly Reporter, Vol. II," could not be procured, except in a manuscript copy kindly communicated by Baron Osten Sacken.

An exclamation mark (!) has been added to every species contained in my own collection, or described by me from actual examination.

Where an (!) has been added to the name of the author, I have seen the types which he described.

The foregoing statements show that the Synopsis has been principally composed from species which I myself have examined, and which can be considered as undoubtedly fixed. There are, however, some, especially from the British Museum, which are not entirely certain, the time I could spend at London not being sufficient to determine all the species. The number, however, of species mentioned in the Synopsis not examined by myself is but small.

I have added a Catalogue of all the species of South American Neuroptera hitherto described, and of the new species contained in my collection. All the yet undescribed species have been added to the present Catalogue, as their publication, which has already partly been effected (Gomphidæ), will soon be terminated.

There can be no doubt that the species named in the Synopsis and in the Catalogue constitute only a fraction of the Neuropterous Fauna of America; may its incompleteness be soon shown by a multitude of new discoveries.

DR. H. HAGEN.

KOENIGSBERG, 8th April, 1860.

Note.—The measurements given are in millimetres. A millimetre is equal to .039 of the English inch, or about .04 ($= \frac{1}{25}$). Multiplying, then, any number of millimetres by four, and setting off two places of decimals, will at once give us the inches and fractions.

TABLE OF CONTENTS.

Advertisement	iv
Preface	v
Table of Contents	ix
Authorities	xi
North American Neuroptera	xi
South American Neuroptera	xvi
Analytical tables	xix
Synopsis of North American Neuroptera	1
PSEUDONEUROPTERA	xix, 1
Fam. I. TERMITINA	1
Fam. II. EMBIDINA	7
Fam. III. PSOCINA	7
Fam. IV. PERLINA	14
Fam. V. EPHEMERINA	38
Fam. VI.* ODONATA	55
Tribe I. Agrionina	56
Sub-fam. I. Calopterygina	56
Sub-fam. II. Agrionina	62
Legion I. Pseudostigmata	62
Legion II. Agrionina	65
Tribe II. Aeschnina	98
Sub-fam. III. Gomphina	98
Sub-fam. IV. Aeschnina	117
Tribe III. Libellulina	132
Sub-fam. V. Cordulina	132
Sub-fam. VI. Libellulina	141
NEUROPTERA	xix, 187
Fam. VII. SIALINA	187
Fam. VIII. HEMEROBINA	196
Fam. IX. PANORPINA	240

* Erroneously given as Fam. V. on p. 55.

Fam. X. Phryganina	249
Sub-fam. I. Phryganides	249
Sub-fam. II. Limnophilides	253
Sub-fam. III. Sericostomides	270
Sub-fam. IV. Leptocerides	275
Sub-fam. V. Hydropsychides	284
Sub-fam. VI. Rhyacophilides	295

List of South American Neuroptera.

PSEUDONEUROPTERA.

Fam. I. Termitina	299
Fam. II. Embidina	301
Fam. III. Psocina	302
Fam. IV. Perlina	302
Fam. V. Ephemerina	304
Fam. VI. Odonata	305
Tribe I. Agrionina	305
Sub-fam. I. Calopterygina	305
Sub-fam. II. Agrionina	307
Tribe II. Aeschnina	312
Sub-fam. III. Gomphina	312
Sub-fam. IV. Aeschnina	314
Tribe III. Libellulina	315
Sub-fam. V. Cordulina	315
Sub-fam. VI. Libellulina	315

NEUROPTERA.

Fam. VII. Sialina	321
Fam. VIII. Hemerobina	322
Fam. IX. Panorpina	327
Fam. X. Phryganina	328
List of genera of North American Neuroptera	330
Distribution of species of do.	333
List of genera of South American Neuroptera	334
Summary	336
Glossary	337
Index	345
Corrections and additions	347

AUTHORITIES.

NORTH AMERICAN NEUROPTERA.

Bartram, John.—Observations on the Dragon-Fly, or Libellula of Pennsylvania. Philos. Transact. 1750, XLVI, 323. Observations upon the metamorphosis of the Odonata in general.

Blanchard, Emile.—Histoire naturelle des Insectes, etc. Paris, 1840, 1841, etc. 3 vols. 150 pl. Contains description of some typical forms from N. America, but no new species.

——— Les planches dans Cuvier règne animal, edit. Masson, 1836—1846, 8vo. *Corydalis cornuta* and *Chauliodes pectinicornis* are figured in this work.

Browne, Patrice.—The Civil and Natural History of Jamaica. London, 1789 (1756), fol. pp. 437. Four species of Odonata are mentioned: "1. Tota viridis; 2. Fusca tennis, ad oculos et anum coeruleo-nitens; 3. Maxima rufula, pectore crassiori; 4. Tenuior tota coerulea. These insects are very common in Jamaica."

Burmeister, Hermann.—Handbuch der Entomologie. Neuroptera, II, Part I. Berlin, 1839, 8vo. 60 species from N. America are described in this work; 36 of them are new.

——— Zoologischer Hand Atlas. Berlin, 1836—1843. Fol., 41 pl. *Termes flavipes* and its nympha are figured. (I have examined the types of Mr. Burmeister.)

Coquebert, Ant. Joh.—Illustratio iconographica insectorum quæ in museis parisinis observavit J. C. Fabricius. Paris, 1799—1804. Fol., 30 pl. *Libellula eponina* figured.

Curtis, John.—Description of the Insects brought home by Commander James Clark. Ross's Second Voyage. App. Nat. Hist. 1831, 4to. — pl. *Tinodes hirtipes* described.

Drury, Drew.—Illustrations of Natural History, etc. London, 1770 —1782, 4to. 3 vols. (ed. Westwood, 1837). Several species are figured and described.

Duncan, J.—Introduction to Entomology. London, 1840. 8vo., — pl. *Libellula axillena* figured by Mr. Westwood.

Erichson, Fr. W.—Beitraege zu einer Monographie von Mantispa. Germar's Zeitschrift f. Entomologie, 1839, 8vo. I, Part I, 147—173, 1 pl. Contains three species.

——— Insekten in Schomburgk's Reise in Guyana, 1848, 8vo. III. Contains several species from the West Indies.

Fabricius, J. C.—Entomologia Systematica et Supplementa. Hafniæ, 1792—1798, 8vo. 5 vols. Seventeen species are described, nine of them are new. (The same are contained in the works previously published by this author, viz: Systema Entomologiæ, 1775; Species Insectorum, 1781; and Mantissa Insectorum, 1787.)

Fabricius, Otto.—Fauna Groenlandica. Hafniæ, 1780, 8vo. Contains *Libellula virgo* (erroneously), *Phryganea rhombica, Termes divinatorium.* See Schioedte.

Fitch, Asa.—First Report on the Noxious, Beneficial, and other Insects of the State of New York. Albany, 1855, 8vo. Thirty-six species of *Chrysopina* and *Hemerobina* are described, mostly new.

——— Winter Insects of eastern New York, from Dr. Emmons' Journal of Agriculture and Science, 1847, vol. v, p. 274. Contains two species of *Boreus* and two of *Perla* new to science.

De Geer, Charles.—Mémoires pour servir à l'histoire des insectes. Stockholm, 4to, 1752—1778, 7 vols. Four species are described, two of them new.

Giebel, C. G.—Fauna der Vorwelt, etc. Leipzig, 8vo. 1856. T. II, P. I, Insecta. *Termes debilis* included in gum Animé, described by Prof. Heer, erroneously, as a succinic insect.

Gosse.—Canadian Naturalist. I have not seen this work, which contains two new *Pteronarcys*.

Gray, G. R.—In E. Griffith's Animal Kingdom. London, 1824—1833. 8vo. 16 vols. Contains some new species.

Guérin-Meneville, F. E.—Iconographie du Règne animal. I have not seen this work, which contains one new *Palingenia*.

Guilding, Landsdowne.—The generic characters of Formicaleo, with the description of two new species (from the West Indies). Trans. Linn. Soc. Lond. 1829, vol. xvi, p. 47.

Hagen, H.—Monographie von Termes in Linnæa, X, XII, XIV. 1855—1860.

——— Revue des Odonates; Monographie des Calopterygines; Monographie des Gomphines. (cf. Selys Longchamps.)

Haldeman.—Description of the *Agrion veneri-notatum;* Proceed. Acad. Philad. 1844. *Termes nigriceps,* ibid. 1853, June.

——— *Corydalus cornutus.* Journ. Acad. Boston, 1848, with plates.

Harris, Dr. T. W.—A Treatise on some of the Insects of New England, which are injurious to Vegetation. Boston, 1852. I regret much not to have seen this excellent work. Contains one *Chrysopa*.

Heer, O.—Die Insectenfauna der Tertiaergebilde von Oeningen und

Radoboj. Leipzig, 1849, 4to. T. II. Contains *Termes debilis* as succinic insect (included in Gum Animé).

Kirby, W.—Fauna boreali-Americana, etc. Norwich, 1837, 4to. Contains a List of arctic Insects, *Libellula virgo* and *Phryganea rhombica* from O. Fabricius, and *Tinodes hirtipes* from J. Curtis; besides p. 252 the descriptions of four species taken in lat. 65—68. *Agrion puella* probably erroneously determined, and three new species, *Perla bicaudata* (erroneously), *Limnephilus nebulosus* and *femoralis;* the descriptions are very incomplete.

Klug, Friedr.—Monographie der Panorpatae. Act. Acad. Berolin. 1836, 4to., 1 plate. Contains five species, three new ones from N. America.

Kolenati, F.—Genera et Species Trichopterorum. Part I. Prague, 1848, 4to. Contains three species from Greenland, Labrador, and N. America, one of them new.

—— Systematisches Verzeichniss der dem Verfasser bekannten Phryganiden und deren Synonymik. Wien. Entom. Monatschrift, T. III, 1859, p. 15. Contains the names of six species from N. America, four of them new.

—— Genera et Species Trichopterorum. Part II. Nouv. Mémoir. de la Soc. Impér. des Naturalistes à Moscou. 1859, T. XI, 4. I have not seen this work, which contains the descriptions of the species mentioned in the foregoing work.

Kollar, V.—Naturgeschichte der schaedlichen Insekten. Wien, 1837, 4to. Contains *Termes flavipes*, injurious in the warmhouses of Schoenbrunn and Vienna. This description has been omitted in the translation of this work by Mr. Loudon.

Latreille, P.—Histoire naturelle, etc. des Insectes. Paris, 8vo. 1792 —1805, vol. xiv.

—— Genera Crustaceorum et Insectorum. Paris, 4to. 1806—1809, vol. iv. Some species from N. America are described, but none of them are new.

Leidy, J.—Internal Anatomy of *Corydalus cornutus* in its three stages of existence (with Haldeman).

Lichtenstein.—Catalogus musei ditissimi (Holthuisen). Hamburg, 1796, 8vo. Part III. Contains one new Ephemera.

Linne, C.—Systema Naturæ ed. XII. 1767, 8vo. Contains three species from N. America, two of which are described previously in Centuria Insector. 1763, 4to., or in Amoenit. Acad., vol. vi. The ed. xiii, by Mr. Gmelin, contains several species described by different authors.

v. Motschulsky, V.—Two species of Termes from N. America are mentioned in the Etudes Entomologiques, T. IV. I find mentioned Etudes VIII, p. 11, two species of Phryganina from N. America, *Leptocera flexuosa* Haldeman, and *Leptocera 8-maculata* Haldeman. I do not know if, or where, these species are described.

Newman, E.—Several species, chiefly Perlina, are described in Entomological Magaz., vol. v, and in Annals of Nat. History, vol. xiii, by this author.

Newport, G.—On the Genus Pteronarcys. Trans. Linn. Soc. Lond., vol. xx, and Annals of Nat. Histor., vol. xiii, contains, moreover, some species of Perlina.

Olivier, G.—Encyclopédie méthodique, vol. vii, 4to. Some species of N. America are described by this author.

Palisot Beauvois.—Insectes recueillis en Afrique et en Amérique. Paris, 1805—1821, fol. Three species are described by this author.

Perty, M.—Delectus animalium articulatorum, etc. Monachiæ, 1830, 4to. One species of Termes from the West Indies has been described.

Pictet, F.—Histoire naturelle, etc. des insectes Neuroptères. Part I, Perlides; Part II, Ephémérines. Genève, 1841—1845, 8vo., with pl. color. Numerous species are figured and described in this first-rate work.

Reichenbach.—Volks-naturgeschichte. *Termes flavipes* has been figured in this work.

Rambur, P.—Histoire naturelle des Neuroptères. Paris, 1842, 8vo., with plates (forms a part of the Suites à Buffon, published by Roret). Numerous species are perfectly described, mostly new.

Say, Th.—Descriptions of insects belonging to the order Neuroptera Linn. Latr., collected by the expedition authorized by J. C. Calhoun, etc. under the command of Major S. H. Long, in Godman's Western Quarterly Reporter, 1823, vol. ii, No. 2, article iv, pp. 160, 165. This very rare work contains four species of Phryganina, three Ephemerina, one Myrmeleon, one Bittacus, and four Perlina, well described.

——— Nine Species of Neuroptera (three Ephem., one Ascalaphus, two Hemerob., one Chauliodes, two Phrygan.), in Keating's narrative of an expedition to the source of St. Peter's River, etc., under the command of Major Long. Philadelphia, 1824, 8vo., vol. ii, p. 205.

——— American Entomology, vol. ii, 1825, 8vo. Contains six figures (two Mantispa and four Phryganea), described and figured.

——— Descriptions of new N. American Neuropterous Insects, and observations on some already described by (the late) Th. Say. Journ. Acad. of Nat. Sci. of Philadelphia, 1839, vol. viii, Part I, p. 9—46. Contains the descriptions of forty-nine species (ten Aeschna, twenty-one Libellula, three Calopteryx, three Lestes, four Agrion, four Baetis, one Ephemera, two Formicaleo, one Chrysopa), mostly new to science. Unfortunately the work of Prof. Burmeister was published at the same time and contains some species described by Mr. Say under different names.

Savigny, J. C.—Description de l'Egypte. Paris, 1825, fol. Contains the figure of one species of Libellula (*L. flavescens*), found in N. America.

Schioedte, J. C.—Arthropoden Groenlands, in Rink, geographischer, etc., Beschreibung Groenlands and in Berlin Entom. Zeitschr., 1859, t. III, p. 134. Contains four species (one Ephem., one Hemerob., two Phrygan.).

Schneider, W. G.—Symbolæ ad Monographiam generis Chrysopæ Leach. Vratislaviæ, 1851, 8vo., with plat. color. Contains seven species, well described and figured.

De Sélys Longchamps, E.—Revue des Odonates ou Libellules d'Europe avec la collaboration de H. Hagen. Paris, 1850, 8vo. (Mémoir. Soc. R. Science de Liége, vol. vi). Two species, *Lib. hudsonica*, p. 53, and *Agrion Doubledayi*, p. 209, are described in this work.

—— Synopsis des Calopterygines. Bullet. Acad. Bruxelles, 1853, t. xx.

—— Monographie des Caloptérygines avec collab. H. Hagen. Paris, 1854, 8vo. (Mém. Soc. R. Science de Liége, vol. ?). Fourteen species from N. America are described in this work.

—— Synopsis des Gomphines. Bullet. Acad. Bruxell. 1854, t. xxi.

—— Monographie des Gomphines, avec collab. H. Hagen. Paris, 1857, 8vo. (Mém. Soc. R. Science de Liége, vol. ?). Thirty-four species from N. America are described in this work.

—— Additions au Synopsis des Caloptérygines. Bullet. Acad. Bruxell. ser. 2, 1859, T. VII, No. 7.

—— Additions au Synopsis des Gomphínes. Bullet. Acad. Bruxell., ser. 2, 1859, T. VII, No. 8.

—— Neuroptères de l'isle de Cuba, de la Sagra Hist. Cuba, 1857, fol., T. VII, p. 183—201, or in Poey, Ins. Cuba, 8vo., p. 435—473. Contains thirty-nine species from the West Indies, chiefly Odonata; several of them are new to science.

Sloane, H.—A voyage to the islands Madeira, Barbadoes, Nieves, St. Christopher's, and Jamaica, with the natural history, etc. of insects. London, 1707—1725, fol., 2 vols. Ten species of Libellula from Jamaica have been described in this work: 1. Libellula rufa major (an *L. abdominalis?*); 2. L. rufa minor (an *L. simplex?*); 3. L. maxima cœrulea aut viridis (an *Aeschna ingens?*); 4. L. purpurea (*Lib. discolor*); 5. L. cœrulea minor (*Agrion* spec.).

Stephens, J. F.—Illustrations of British Entomology. London, 8vo., 1835. Mandibulata, vol. VI. Some species of European Neuroptera mentioned in this work have been found in N. America.

Swederus, N. S.—Two species of Panorpa have been described by this author, Vetensk. Acad. nya Handl. Stockholm, 1787, T. VIII.

Uhler, P. R.—Contributions to the Neuropterology of the United States. Proceed. Acad. of Nat. Sc. Philad., 1857, March, p. 87. Seven species of Odonata are described.

Walker, F.—Catalogue of the Specimens of Neuropterous Insects in the Collection of the British Museum. London, 8vo., Part I, 1852 (Phryganides, Perlides), p. 1—192; Part II, 1853 (Sialidæ—Nemopterides), p. 193—476; Part III, 1853 (Termitidæ—Ephemeridæ), p. 477—585; Part IV, 1853 (Odonata, Calopteryginæ), p. 586—658. In this work 234 species from N. America are described; numerous of them are new, chiefly from Canada and the Arctic regions.

Wesmael, C.—Sur les Hemerobides de Belgique. Bullet. Acad. Bruxell., 1841, vol. viii, p. 203. One species of Europe described here has been found in N. America.

Westwood, J. O.—Monograph of the genus Panorpa. Trans. Entom. Soc. Lond., vol. iv, with plates. Contains fourteen species from N. America, some of them new.

——— On the genus Mantispa. Trans. Ent. Soc. Lond., new ser., vol. i, with plates. Contains three species from N. America.

——— Introduction to the modern Classification of Insects. London, 1840, 8vo., vol. ii. Contains Termes flavipes, figured.

Zetterstedt, J. W.—Insecta Lapponica. Lipsiæ, 1840, 4to. Some species from Lapland have been found in the Arctic regions of N. America.

SOUTH AMERICAN NEUROPTERA.

(The authorities mentioned above for North American Neuroptera are omitted.)

Blanchard, E.—Insectes du voyage dans l'Amérique méridionale de M. Alcide d'Orbigny. 4to. pl.

——— Insectes dans C. Gay historia fisica de Chili. Paris, 1851, 4to. I have not seen this work; a few Neuroptera are described and figured.[1]

Fischer von Waldheim, G.—Notice sur quelques Orthoptères et Neuroptères du Brésil. Bullet. Acad. Moscow, 1834, T. VII, p. 322, 1 pl. col. Two Mantispa are described and figured.

Hagen, H.—Neuroptera von Mossambic in Peters Reise, T. II. Written and printed 1853, but not yet published. Two Termes from Brazil are described.

——— Monographie der Gattung Oligoneuria. Stettin, Entomol. Zeit. 1856, T. XVI, p. 262.

——— Description of *Mantispa chilensis*, in Stettin. Entom. Zeit., 1859, T. XX, p. 408.

Kirby, W.—Description of the *Agrion brightwelli* in Trans. Linn. Soc. London, 1825, T. XIV.

---

[1] Twenty-six new species are described, and most of them figured. (Osten Sacken.)

Kollar, V.—Brasiliens vorzüglich lästige Insecten in Dr. Pohl's Reise in Brasilien. Wien, 1832, 4to. Two species of Termes are described and figured.

Pictet, F. J.—Description de quelques nouvelles espèces de Neuroptères du Musée de Genève. Mém. Soc. Phys. Genève, 1836, T. VII, p. 299. *Bittacus blanchetti* and *Macronema lineatum* are described and figured.

Percheron, A.—Genera des Insectes, with pl. Paris, 1831, 8vo. (with M. Guérin). One species of Palingenia has been described.

Retzius, A.—C. De Geer genera et species insectorum ex auctoris scriptis extr. Lipsiæ, 1783, 8vo.

Rengger, J.—Reise nach Paraguay. Aarau, 1835, 8vo. Some species of Termes have been described in this work.

Seba, A.—Locupletissimi rerum naturalium thesauri accurata descriptio et iconibus expressio. Amsterdam, 1734—1764, fol., 4 vols. Few species of Odonata are figured.

Serville, A.—Les Neuroptères, dans le t. X d'Encyclopedie méthodique de M. Olivier. (*Mantispa semihyalina.*)

Thunberg, C. P.—Fauna Surinamensis. Upsalia, 1822, 4to.

——— Fauna Cayennensis. Upsaliæ, 1823, 4to.

——— Fauna Brasiliensis. Upsaliæ, 1823, 4to.

——— Fauna Americæ meridionalis. Upsaliæ, 1823, 4to., 3 parts. I have not been able to use this work, which contains the complete list of all the species described. (cf. Stett. Entom. Zeit. XVIII, p. 202.)

Weber, F.—Observationes entomologicæ. Kiel, 1801, 8vo. (*Ephemera atrostoma.*)

Westwood, J. O.—Characters of Embia. Trans. Linn. Soc. Lond., 1837, T. XVII, with pl.

ANALYTICAL TABLE.[1]

SECTIONS.

SECTION I.—PSEUDONEUROPTERA ERICHS.

Mandibulate insects with an incomplete metamorphosis (active pupa); lower lip mostly cleft; four membranaceous, reticulate wings (rarely with rudimentary wings or apterous); antennæ either subulate, and then the tarsi three- to five-articulate, or setiform, or filiform, in which case the tarsi are two- to four-articulate.

 FAMILIES.—*Termitina, Embidina, Psocina, Perlina, Ephemerina, Odonata.*

SECTION II.—NEUROPTERA ERICHS.

Mandibulate insects with complete metamorphosis (inactive pupa); lower lip entire; four membranaceous, more or less reticulate wings rarely with rudimentary wings or apterous); antennæ setiform, filiform, clavate, capitate, or pectinate; tarsi five-articulate.

 FAMILIES.—*Sialina, Hemerobina, Panorpina, Phryganina.*

FAMILIES.

Four or two distinct wings;
 Antennæ inconspicuous, subulate, short and slender.
  Anterior and posterior wings nearly of the same length; tarsi triarticulate.   Fam. VI. ODONATA.
  Posterior wings either smaller or wanting; tarsi four- or five-articulate.   Fam. V. EPHEMERINA.
 Antennæ mostly conspicuous, setiform, filiform, clavate, capitate, or pectinate.
  Tarsi two- or three-articulate;
   Wings equal.   Fam. II. EMBIDINA.

---

[1] These tables, prepared by Baron Osten Sacken at the request of the Institution, are to be considered as merely provisional in their nature, and as not aiming at a natural arrangement of the families.

Wings unequal.
    Posterior wings smaller.   Fam. III. Psocina (in part).
    Posterior wings broader, or at least of the same size with the anterior ones.   Fam. IV. Perlina (in part).
Tarsi four-articulate; wings equal.   Fam. I. Termitina (in part).
Tarsi five- (sometimes apparently four-articulate).
    Posterior wings with no anal space; not folded.
        Mouth more or less rostrated.   Fam. IX. Panorpina (in part).
        Mouth not rostrated (at the utmost only conical).
                       Fam. VIII. Hemerobina.
    Posterior wings with a folded anal space.[1]
        Wings reticulate.   Fam. VII. Sialina.
        Transverse veins rather few.   Fam. X. Phryganina (in part).
Apterous, or with rudimentary wings;
    Mouth rostrated.   Fam. IX. Panorpina (in part).
    Mouth not rostrated.
        Tarsi five-articulate.   Fam. X. Phryganina (in part).
        Tarsi four-articulate.   Fam. I. Termitina (in part).
        Tarsi three-articulate.
            Apterous, or with two rudimentary wings of a leathery substance.
                       Fam. III. Psocina (in part).
            Four rudimentary wings, still with distinct neuration.
                       Fam. IV. Perlina (in part).

---

[1] The anal space is absent in a few *Phryganina*.

NEUROPTERA

OF

NORTH AMERICA.

Section I. PSEUDONEUROPTERA.

FAM. I. TERMITINA.

Body depressed, ovate; head free; wings equal, membranaceous, deciduous; tarsi 4-articulate.

CALOTERMES Hagen.

Head small, two ocelli; prothorax large, transverse, oblong; costal area veined; tarsi furnished with an apical plantula.

1. **C. castaneus!**

Termes castaneus Burm.! II. 764, 3.—*Termes anticus* Walk.! Catal. 523, 31.—*Termes guatimalæ* Walk.! Catal. 528, 38.—*Caloterm. castaneus* Hag.! Linn. XII, 38, 1; tab. ii, fig. 2; tab. iii, fig. 2.

Chestnut-color, beneath, antennæ and feet luteous; the wings tinged with brown, margin and costal veins infuscate; head elliptical; prothorax quadrangular, anteriorly a little sinuated; median nervule approaching the subcostal one, its apex bifurcated.

Var. Smaller, pale, wings hyaline. (Cuba, St. Domingo.)

Length to tip of wings 13—20 millimetres. Length of body 6—8 millim. Expanse of wings 23—36 millim.

Hab. San Francisco, California (Chamisso); Honduras (Miller); Guatimala (Deby); Cuba; Porto-Rico; St. Domingo, Port-au-Prince (Ehrenberg); Columbia, Venezuela (Moritz, Appun); Brazil (Olfers); Rio (Schott); St. Leopoldo; Chile; Isle of France (?). Collection of de Selys Longchamps.

Note.—An exclamation point after the specific name at the head of an article shows that the description has been made by the author from a specimen. When placed after a reference, it shows that the author has seen the type of the description.

2. C. marginipennis!

Termes marginipenne Latr.! Humboldt, Recueil, II, 111; tab. xxxix, fig. 8.—*Term. mexicanus* Walker! Catal. 528, 39.—*Caloterm. marginipennis* Hag.! Linn. XII, 47, 6; XIV, 100.

Fulvous, beneath, antennæ and feet luteous; wings whitish, margin and costal veins yellowish; head square; prothorax square, anteriorly emarginate; median and subcostal veins separated.

A smaller specimen from San Diego does not differ in coloring.

Var. Smaller, fuliginous, beneath, antennæ and feet fuscous; wings dirty-fuscous, margin and costal veins infuscate. (California.)

Length to tip of wings 18—19 millimetres. Body 7—8 millim. Expanse of wings 31 millim.

Hab. Mexico (Humboldt, Muehlenpford, Deppe); Cuantla (Saussure); San Francisco and San Diego, California.

3. C. posticus!

Calotermes posticus Hag.! Linn. XII, 67, 15.

Piceous, base of the antennæ and feet bright yellow; wings ——; head square; prothorax oblong.

Length of body 4½ millim.

Hab. St. Thomas (Moritz).

4. C. brevis!

Termes brevis Walk.! Catal. 524, 33—*Term. indecisus* Walk.! Catal. 524, 32.—*Term. flavicollis* Walk.! (in part) Catal. 502, 1 (Imago), 503 (Soldier).—*Term. lucifugus* Walk. (in part)! Catal. 505, 3.—*Caloterm. brevis* Hag.! Linn. XII, 68, 16; tab. ii, fig. 6; tab. iii, fig. 5. Linn. XIV, p. 101.

Fulvous, beneath, antennæ and feet pale; wings hyaline, costal veins yellowish, linear, head square; prothorax large, oblong, anteriorly emarginate; median nervure distant, curved before the apex, united to the subcostal one.

Length to tip of wings 9 millim. Body 4 millim. Expanse of wings 16 millim.

Hab. Mexico (Deppe), Vera-Cruz (Sallé); Central America; Jamaica (Gosse); Cuba (Poeppig, Osten Sacken); St. Thomas (Moritz), St. Fe de Bogota; Brazil (Olfers, Schott, Natterer, Kuemmel).

The variety from Mexico has the median nervure, sometimes not curved, nor joined to the subcostal one. Is it a distinct species?

TERMOPSIS Heer.

Head large; ocelli absent; prothorax small; costal area veined; tarsi with an apical plantula.

1. T. angusticollis!

Termes castaneus Walk.! Catal. 506, 4.—*Termops. angusticollis* Hag.! Linn. XII, 75, 1; tab. ii, fig. 1; tab. iii, figs. 6, 41. Linn. XIV, 101.

Rufous, beneath paler, mouth infuscate; wings dusky hyaline, costal veins rufous; head oval, flat; prothorax small, semicircular.

Length to tip of wings 26 millim. Body 11 millim. Expanse of wings 46 millim.

Hab. Louisiana (Pfeiffer); San Francisco, California (Hartweg); Ft. Steilacoom, Puget Sound (Dr. Suckley).

2. T. occidentis!

Termes occidentis Walk.! Catal. 529, 41.— *Termops. occidentis* Hag.! Linn. XII, 77, 2; tab. i, fig. 8. Linn. XIV, 101.

Soldier. Fulvous, broad, head thick, rounded; prothorax anteriorly strongly emarginate; meso- and metathorax with the posterior angles produced.

Length of body 14 millim.

Hab. West coast of Central America (Wood).

The genus of this species is doubtful; it may, perhaps, be *Termopsis angusticollis* Hagen.

TERMES Linn.

Head large, rounded, two ocelli; prothorax heart-shaped, small; costal area free; plantula absent.

1. T. flavipes!

Termes flavipes Kollar! Naturgesch. schädl. Ins. 411. Burm. II, 768, 14. Burm. Zoolog. Hand-atlas, tab. xxvii, figs. 9, 10. Westw.! Introduct. II, 14; tab. lviii, figs. 12, 14, 15. Hag.! Linn. XII, 182, 26; XIV, 107. Reichenbach Volksnaturgesch. fig. col. Latr. Diction. d'hist. nat. XXII. *Termes frontale* Haldem.! (teste Osten Sacken), Proc. Acad. Philad. 1844, II, 55.

Chestnut color; head and prothorax black-brown; antennæ brownish, annulated with pale; mouth, tibiæ and tarsi yellow;

wings whitish, a little roughened, costal veins yellowish; head quadrangular, flat, with a distinct fovea in the middle, ocelli distant, prothorax cordiform.

Length to tip of wings 9 millim. Body 5 millim. Expanse of wings 16 millim.

Hab. U. S. (Bosc, Beauvois, Schaum); Cleveland, Ohio (Le Conte); Cincinnati; Paduca (Motschulsky); Pennsylvania (Haldeman); Maryland (Uhler); Washington (Osten Sacken); Carolina (Zimmerman); Eutaw, Alabama; Florida (Osten Sacken); Mexico, Matamoras, Tamaulipas (Couch); Europe (Plant-houses of Schönbrunn, Kollar).

Specimens from Florida are smaller and paler, but not distinct.

2. T. morio!

Termes morio Latr.! Hist. Nat. XIII, 69, 3. Dict. d'hist. nat. XXII, 3. Burm.! II, 767, 11. Hagen! Linn. XII, 201, 34; tab. iii, fig. 29. Linn. XIV, 122.—*Termes cornigera* Motschulsky! Études Entom. IV, 10.

Pitchy-black; antennæ, mouth, feet and venter yellowish; wings opaque, blackish-gray, costal veins black-brown; head flat, quadrangular, a bifid impressed line upon the middle; ocelli large, distant; prothorax small, semicircular.

Length to tip of wings 12—14 millim. Body 5 to 6 millim. Expanse of wings 22—25 millim.

Hab. Guatimala (Sivers); Panama (Motschulsky); St. Domingo (Ehrenberg); Porto-Rico (Moritz); Martinique; Venezuela (Moritz, Appun); Santarem, Brazil (Bates).

Nasuti and workers from Matanzas, Cuba (Osten Sacken), seem to belong here.

3. T. debilis!

Termes debilis Heer! Insektenfauna der Tertiärgebilde II, 35, 19; tab. iii, fig. 6 (contained in gum copal). Giebel, Fauna der Vorwelt, II, 295.—*Termes morio* Burm. (in part) II, 767, 11.—*T. debilis* Hag.! Linn. XII, 205, 38; tab. iii, fig. 30.

Brownish-black, antennæ annulated with white; mouth, feet and middle of the venter yellowish; wings opaque, blackish-gray, costal veins fuscous; head convex, square, an impressed point upon the middle; ocelli small, approaching the eyes; prothorax small, rounded.

Length to tip of wings $8\frac{1}{2}$ millim. Body $3\frac{1}{2}$ millim. Expanse of wings 16 millim.

Hab. Porto-Rico (Moritz); Brazil, Congonhas (Burmeister). Frequently found in gum copal.

4. T. Rippertii!

Termes Rippertii Ramb.! Neuropt. 308, 15.—Walk.! Catal. 520, 4; Hagen! Linn. XII, 218, 47; tab. ii, fig. 13; tab. iii, fig. 32. Linn. XIV, 118.—*Termes destructor* Perty! Delect. 127; tab. xxv, fig. 9.

Ferrugineous, head piceous, fulvous in front; the antennæ, feet, prothorax and abdomen beneath in the middle luteous; wings opaque, yellowish-gray, costal veins rufous; head flat, with an impressed line; eyes very prominent, ocelli close to the eyes; prothorax semicircular, short.

Length to tip of wings 14—18 millim. Body 5—7 millim. Expanse of wings 27—35 millim.

Hab. Havana, Cuba (Rippert); Trinidad (Osten Sacken); Jamaica (Gosse); Columbia (Moritz); Brazil (Spix); Ypanema (Natterer); New-Freiburg (Beschke); Isle of France? (Collect. de Selys).

A damaged specimen from Vera Cruz (Sallé) seems to belong here.

5. T. lividus!

Termes lividus Burm.! II, 767, 12. Walk. Catal. 515, 13. Hagen! Linn. XII, 221, 49; tab. iii, fig. 33.

Testaceous, the mouth, middle of the prothorax, antennæ, feet, and margins of the abdominal segments luteous; wings opaque, yellowish gray, costal veins rufous; head small, flat, a small yellow line upon the middle, ocelli large, approaching the eyes; prothorax almost orbicular.

Length to tip of wings 14 millim. Body 6 millim. Expanse of wings 27 millim.

Hab. Port au Prince, St. Domingo (Ehrenberg).

6. T. armiger!

Termes armiger Motschulsky! Étud. Ent. IV, 10. Hagen! Linn. XII, 228, 52; tab. i, fig. 1.

A nasute soldier. Rufous; thorax and feet a little paler; head pear-shaped, large, anteriorly porrected into a long nose; mandibles ensiform; prothorax small, anterior lobe narrow, recurved, anterior angles prominent, depressed, posterior margin rounded.

Length of body 6¼ millim.

Hab. Panama, Obispo (Motschulsky).
Imago unknown.

7. T. tenuis!

Termes tenuis Hagen! Linn. XII, 231, 57; tab. iii, fig. 35.

Pale yellow; head and prothorax a little brownish; wings opaque, pale whitish-yellow, the costal veins luteous; head oblong, convex, a salient point in the middle; ocelli absent; prothorax quadrangular.

Length to tip of wings 10 millim. Body 3 millim. Expanse of wings 20 millim.

Hab. St. Domingo, Port au Prince (Ehrenberg); Columbia (Moritz); Brazil (Helm).

The ocelli, which are present in the other species, are absent in this. In other respects it belongs to the genus.

8. T. simplex!

Termes simplex Hag.! Linn. XII, 238, 60; tab. iii, fig. 23.

Fulvous, antennæ and feet yellowish, wings hyaline, a little roughened, costal veins yellowish; head rounded, convex, a distinct fovea upon the middle, ocelli small, closely approximate; prothorax flat, semicircular; wings with the median nervure absent.

Length to tip of wings 10 millim. Body 5 millim. Expanse of wings 17 millim.

Hab. Cuba (Poeppig).

An anomalous species. Only a single, very much damaged, specimen seen.

9. T. nigriceps.

Termes nigriceps Haldeman, Proceed. Acad. Philad. 1853, June, VI, 365.—Hag. Linn. XII, 230, 55.

Workers and soldiers nasute; head blackish-brassy, pyriform, nasute, antennæ, feet and body yellow.

Length of body 3 millim.

Hab. Western Mexico (Leconte). Unknown to me.

10. T. strenuus!

Termes strenuus Hagen! Linn. XIV, 105.

Fuscous, villose; mouth, antennæ, feet and margins of the

abdominal segments fulvous; wings opaque, brown, costal margin yellow, subcostal and basal veins blackish-brown; head rather large, opaque, rounded, flat, impressed in the middle, brassy, ocelli rather small, distant; prothorax semicircular, opaque.

Length to tip of wings 22—25 millim. Body 8—10 millim. Expanse of wings 42—47 millim.

Hab. Vera Cruz, Mexico (Sallé).

11. T. fumosus!

Termes fumosus Hagen! Linn. XIV, 123.—Perhaps imago of *Termes nigriceps*.

Blackish-brown, brassy; antennæ blackish-brown annulated with pale; mouth, venter and feet yellowish-brown, tibiæ a little obscure; wings opaque, dark-smoky, costal veins blackish-brown, the rest fuscous; head flat, rounded, anteriorly bi-impressed; ocelli rather large, distant; prothorax hardly narrower than the head, semicircular.

Length to tip of wings 14 millim. Body 6 millim. Expanse of wings 24 millim.

Hab. Vera Cruz, Mexico (Sallé).

I have seen similar specimens, badly preserved, from Matamoras, Tamaulipas. They may be distinct.

Fam. II. EMBIDINA.

Body depressed, linear; head free; wings equal, membranous; tarsi triarticulate.

I have seen a specimen (perhaps a larva) without wings, not well preserved, from Cuba (Gundlach, Berlin Museum). Pale fuscous. Length of body 4 millim. Belonging to the genus *Olyntha?* It is probably a new species.

Fam. III. PSOCINA.

Body oval; head free; prothorax small, obtected; wings unequal, sometimes wanting; tarsi two- or three-articulate.

CLOTHILLA Westwood.

(*Lepinotus* von Heyden; *Paradoxenus* and *Paradoxides* Motsch.)

Ocelli absent; wings incomplete, coriaceous; tarsi triarticulate.

1. C. picea!

Paradoxenus piceus Motschulsky! in lit.

Entirely piceous, with a brassy reflection.
The specimen seen was imperfect; the wings were wanting.
Length of body 1 millim.
Hab. California.

ATROPOS Leach.

Ocelli and *wings* absent; tarsi triarticulate.

1. A. divinatorius.

Termes divinatorius O. Fab. Fn. Grœnl. 214, 181.

Pale, mouth fuscous, eyes black, anus obscure (Descript. from Fab.)
Length 1 millim.?
Hab. Greenland. In old books. Perhaps it is *A. pulsatorius* Leach.

PSOCUS Latr.

Three ocelli; wings membranaceous, rather unequal; tarsi two- or three-articulate.

† *Tarsi three-articulate.*
* Discoidal cellule closed, quadrangular.

1. P. sparsus!

Psocus sparsus Hagen!

Fuscous, varied with yellow and white; nasus lineated with grayish-fuscous, front yellow, punctured and lineated with black; antennæ rather slender, pale; the two basal joints thicker, yellow, black at base; thorax fuscous, varied with yellow; femora fuscous, annulated with pale before the apex, tibiæ and tarsi pale, with the apex fuscous; anterior wings opaque, fuscous, densely varied with yellow and gray, veins yellow, spotted with fuscous; pterostigma triangular; posterior wings a little smoky, costal margin at the apex interruptedly fuscous and yellow.

Length to tip of wings 6 millim. Expanse of anterior wings 11 millim.

Hab. Washington (Osten Sacken, 1858); Baltimore (Uhler).

2. P. lugens!

Psocus lugens Hagen!

Fuscous, varied with white; nasus fuscous, lineated with gray; front fuscous, occiput striated with whitish; antennæ rather slender, brownish, two basal articulations thicker, apex pale, setæ with the apical articulations whitish; thorax fuscous, margined with white; femora fuscous, annulated with pale before the apex; tibiæ and tarsi paler, at the apex fuscous; anterior wings opaque, fuscous, densely varied with gray, margin and veins marked with white points; pterostigma triangular; posterior wings a little smoky, costal margin at the apex interruptedly white and fuscous.

Length to tip of wings $4\frac{1}{2}$ millim. Expanse of anterior wings 8 millim.

Hab. Washington (Osten Sacken, 1857).

** Discoidal cellule open, absent.

3. P. signatus!

Psocus signatus Hagen!

Blackish-fuscous; eyes globose, distant, prominent; nasus blackish-fuscous, lineated with gray; front each side anteriorly with an oblique band, and a whitish yellow point upon the occiput; thorax margined with yellow; abdomen luteous; feet luteous, tarsi blackish-fuscous; wings hyaline, veins fuscous, pterostigma narrow, linear, blackish-fuscous, posterior margin at base fuscous; cellule at the posterior margin free, elliptically triangular.

Length to tip of wings 5 millim. Expanse of anterior wings 9 millim.

Hab. New York.

It is very much like *Psocus immunis* Stephens (*naso*, Rambur), but differs a little in the reticulation of the wings. Is it distinct?

4. P. pumilis!

Psocus pumilis Hagen!

Pale luteous; nasus brassy-fuscous, obsoletely lineated with gray; front with a medial, longitudinal, blackish-fuscous stripe, two incurved fuscous lines at the eyes; thorax marked with fuscous; the feet pale luteous; anterior wings pale grayish hyaline, pterostigma, interrupted basal band and the margin behind the base fuscous, veins fuscous; pterostigma short, rounded; cellule of the posterior margin free, elliptical.

Length to tip of wings 3½ millim. Expanse of anterior wings 6 millim.

Hab. New York.

†† *Tarsi two-articulate.*

* Discoidal cellule closed, quadrangular.

5. P. venosus!

Psocus venosus Burm.! II, 778, 10; Walk. Catal. 484, 9.—*Ps. magnus* Walk.! Catal. 484, 10.—*Ps. microphthalmus* Ramb. Neur. 321, 6.—*Ps. aceris* Fitch! MSS. Collection of de Selys Longchamps.

Fuscous; head brassy, antennæ blackish-fuscous (in the male rather thicker, pilose), the two basal articulations luteous; thorax margined with yellow; the feet luteous, tarsi fuscous; anterior wings fuscous or blackish-fuscous, pterostigma triangular, yellowish; basal veins yellowish, apical ones fuscous; posterior wings smoky-hyaline.

Length to tip of wings 6—8 millim. Expanse of anterior wings 12—15 millim.

Hab. New York (Winthem, Asa Fitch, Uhler); Washington (Osten Sacken, 1858); Mount Pleasant, Ohio; Mexico (Deppe); Cuba (Riehl, Poey); Maryland (Uhler).

Specimens communicated by Baron Osten Sacken are a little smaller, blacker, with the apex of the tibiæ black; but they belong to this species.

6. P. contaminatus!

Psocus contaminatus Hagen!

Fuscous; nasus yellow, scarcely lineated with obscure brown; the front luteous, two occipital spots, two at the nasus and two at the ocelli black; antennæ rather slender, fuscous; thorax black, margined with yellow; the feet luteous, knees and tarsi fuscous; wings hyaline, pterostigma triangular, blackish-fuscous; apical margin with a large band attaining to the inferior angle of the pterostigma and a spot upon the middle of the posterior margin, cloudy-fuscous; posterior wings hyaline.

Length to tip of wings 7 millim. Expanse of anterior wings 13 millim.

Hab. New York; Maryland (Uhler); Washington (Osten Sacken); Vera Cruz, Mexico (Sallé).

7. P. novæ scotiæ!
Psocus novæ scotiæ Walk. Catal. 485, 12.—*Psocus crataegi* Fitch. Collection of de Selys Longchamps.

Blackish-fuscous; head pale yellow, two spots upon the occiput and two at the eyes black; front fuscous in the middle; antennæ black; thorax black, margined with yellow; feet testaceous, tibiæ at apex and tarsi pitchy; wings hyaline, anterior ones with four fuscous spots, one at the pterostigma, another at the apex, the rest at the posterior margin, the basal one joined to an obscure spot; veins black.

Length to tip of wings 6 millim. Expanse of anterior wings 12 millim.

Hab. Nova Scotia (Redman); New York (Asa Fitch).

8. P. moestus!
Psocus moestus Hag.!

Brownish-black, spotted with yellow; nasus yellow, lineated with fuscous, and fuscous in front; occiput yellow, varied with fuscous, antennæ rather slender, pale, the two basal articulations fuscous; apex yellow; thorax and abdomen brownish-black; femora fuscous, knees yellow, tibiæ pale, their apex and the tarsi fuscous; wings milky-hyaline, densely spread with small fuscous points, veins fuscous, basal ones yellow; pterostigma triangular, the internal angle yellow.

Length to tip of wings $4\frac{1}{2}$ millim. Expanse of anterior wings 8 millim.

Hab. Dalton, Georgia (Osten Sacken).

9. P. striatus!
Psocus striatus Walk.! Catal. 486, 16.

Pallid; nasus yellow lineated with black; front yellow, a band upon the middle and punctiform lines at the eyes black; eyes of the male globose, prominent, rather approximate; antennæ fuscous, two basal articulations pale; antennæ of the male thicker, the seta hairy; thorax black marked with yellow; abdomen yellow, a black fascia upon the middle; feet pallid, femora fuscous above, tarsi fuscous; wings hyaline, pterostigma large triangular, acute, fuscous, internal angle paler; posterior margin at base and a discoidal nebula fuscous; posterior wings hyaline.

Length to tip of wings 6¼ millim. Expanse of anterior wings 2 millim.

Hab. Nova Scotia (Redman); New York, Washington (Osten Sacken, 1857); Pennsylvania (Zimmerman).

10. P. quietus!
Psocus quietus Hag.!

Luteous; the nasus luteous lineated with black, a spot at base and two anteriorly black; front luteous varied with black; antennæ pale; thorax black; feet pale luteous, tibiæ at base and apex obscurer; wings hyaline, veins luteous, pterostigma triangular, inferior angle rounded, obscure.

Length to tip of wings 5 millim. Expanse of anterior wings 9 millim.

Hab. New York; Dalton, Georgia (Osten Sacken).

* * Discoidal cellule open, absent.

11. P. mobilis!
Psocus mobilis Hag.!

Pale brown, hairy; wings hyaline, pterostigma narrow, ovate; cellule at the posterior margin free, elliptical.

Length to tip of wings 2½ millim. Expanse of anterior wings 4¾ millim.

Hab. Cuba (von Winthem). Described from a single damaged specimen.

12. P. madidus!
Psocus madidus Hag.!

Pale luteous; nasus brassy fuscous, lineated with obscure gray, two spots upon the occiput and a third upon the front black; antennæ pallid; tibiæ obscurer at base; wings pale gray, with two paler obsolete bands, the veins luteous; pterostigma narrow, ovate; no posterior marginal cellule.

Length to tip of wings 3¼ millim. Expanse of anterior wings 6 millim.

Hab. New York; Dalton, Georgia (Osten Sacken).

13. P. abruptus!

Psocus abruptus Hag.!

Brown, hairy; head and thorax brassy; antennæ very slender, whitish, the apical joints infuscate at their tip; posterior femora fuscous, whitish at apex; anterior wings brown with a brassy reflection, a narrow, transverse, hyaline band before the apex, veins ciliated: pterostigma elongated, ovate; no cellule at the posterior margin; posterior wings grayish-hyaline. (Female.)

Length to tip of wings 4 millim. Expanse of anterior wings 7 millim.

Hab. Washington; Dalton, Georgia (Osten Sacken).

14. P. corruptus!

Psocus corruptus Hag.!

Pale brown, hairy; head and thorax brassy; eyes rather prominent, globose, front narrower than in the preceding; antennæ thicker, hairy, seta fuscous; all the articulations pale at base; feet pale; anterior wings shining brassy-brown, pterostigma brown; a spot before the apex, upon the costal margin and a discoidal cloud, grayish-hyaline; veins with fuscous cilia; posterior wings grayish-hyaline. (Male.)

Length to tip of wings 4 millim. Expanse of anterior wings 7 millim.

Hab. Washington (Osten Sacken, 1858); Dalton, Georgia (Osten Sacken).

Reticulation of the wings as in the preceding. Is it the other sex of that species?

The reticulation in *Ps. abruptus* and *Ps. corruptus* is abnormal, and may constitute a distinct subgenus, or rather genus.

15. P. salicis!

Psocus salicis Fitch! Collection of de Selys Longchamps.

Very small, brown; head and thorax brassy; mouth yellow; eyes very small, front broad; antennæ very slender, villose, apex obscurer; feet pale; wings hyaline, veins brown; pterostigma hyaline, anteriorly truncated; posterior marginal cellule elliptical.

Length to tip of wings 1½ millim. Expanse of wings 3 millim.

Hab. New York (Asa Fitch).

16. P. aurantiacus!

Psocus aurantiacus Hag.!

Orange-colored, shining; head bright orange, occiput in the middle dusky; antennæ pale, brownish-black at the apex; thorax orange with four cloudy spots upon the dorsum; feet yellow, tarsi fuscous at the apex; abdomen yellow; wings yellowish-hyaline, pterostigma bright yellowish green; veins yellow, apical ones fuscous; cellule of the posterior margin orbicular. (Female.)

Length to tip of wing $3\frac{1}{2}$ millim. Expanse of wings 6 millim.

Hab. Dalton, Georgia (Osten Sacken).

Fam. IV. PERLINA.

Body depressed, elongated, parallel; prothorax large; antennæ long, setaceous; wings unequal, posterior ones broader; tarsi three-articulate.

† *Two abdominal setæ.*
* Wings charged with many irregular transverse veins.

PTERONARCYS Newman.

Wings densely net-veined; palpi setaceous; mandibles membranaceous. This genus is very abnormal on account of its imago being furnished with external branchiæ.

1. P. proteus!

Pteronarcys proteus Newman! Entom. Mag. V, 177, 3. Walk.! Catal. 139, 1. Gosse, Canadian Naturalist, fig. —, p. 232.

Fuscous, head broader than the prothorax; antennæ paler at base; sides of the prothorax emarginate, a little broader posteriorly, an interrupted yellow line upon the middle. (Is it so always?) Feet yellowish-fuscous, knees yellow; abdomen beneath yellowish; the caudal setæ luteous, paler at base; ♂ last ventral segment yellowish, narrower, sparsely punctured; ♀ ? antepenultimate segment truncated, armed with two distant, conical, yellowish appendages; wings pale grayish-hyaline, veins fuscous, clouded.

Length to tip of wings 38—48 millim. Expanse of wings 73—90 millim.

Hab. Trenton Falls, New York (Doubleday); Mackenzie River district (Richardson); North Red River (Robt. Kennicott).

2. P. regalis!

Pteronarcys regalis Newm.! Entom. Mag. V, 176, 1. Newm.! Annals Nat. Hist. XIII, 21. Pictet, Perlides, 134. Ann. Sci. Nat. I, 183. Newport! Trans. Linn. Soc. XX, p. 425; tab. xxi, fig. 1—11; 14—17. Froriep, Notiz. XXX, 179. Walker! Catal. 140, 3. *P. proteus* Pictet, Perl. 128, 1; tab. xxix, fig. 1—6. Ramb. Neuropt. p. 449.

Fuscous, head as broad as the prothorax; antennæ pitchy; sides of the prothorax emarginate, not broader behind, a narrow, yellow line upon the middle; feet fuscous; abdomen fuscous, apex yellowish; caudal setæ fuscous, at base yellowish; ♂ last ventral segment yellowish; ♀ antepenultimate segment produced, in the middle a broad, quadrangular excision; wings grayish-hyaline, before the apex a little clouded with fuscous, veins fuscous.

Length to tip of wings 44—48 millim. Expanse of wings 76—84 millim.

Hab. Canada; Mackenzie and Slave River districts (Richardson); St. Martin's Falls, Albany River, Hudson's Bay (Barnston); Philadelphia.

3. P. biloba!

Pteronarcys biloba Newm.! Entom. Mag. V, 176, 2. Pictet, Perl. 135. Walk.! Catal. 140, 3.

Brownish-black; head narrower than the prothorax; prothorax not emarginated at the sides, posteriorly a little broadened, a line upon the middle yellow; feet brownish-black; abdomen brownish-black, beneath in the middle with a broad, yellowish band; caudal setæ brownish-black; ♀ antepenultimate ventral segment blackish-brown, produced, incised in the middle; wings grayish-hyaline, before the apex a little clouded with fuscous, veins fuscous.

Length to tip of wings 46 millim. Expanse of wings 84 millim.

Hab. Trenton Falls; St. Martin's Falls, Albany River, Hudson's Bay (Barnston); Minnesota (Osten Sacken).

I have seen the typical specimens in the British Museum; but I am not certain whether the female from Minnesota belongs here.

4. P. nobilis!

Pteronarcys nobilis Hagen!

Black, head broader than the prothorax; antennæ black; prothorax quadrangular, sides straight, a yellow line narrowed in the middle; feet black; abdomen black, beneath with a broad orange band; caudal setæ black, piceous at base; ♂ last ventral segment deep black; ♀ antepenultimate one truncated, orange, two short setiform appendages? (they cannot be clearly seen); wings grayish-hyaline, clouded with fuscous, veins fuscous.

Length to tip of wings 31—34 millim. Expanse of wings 55—66 millim.

Hab. New York.

Does the "smaller, new species" from Sherbrooke, Lower Canada (Gosse, Canadian Naturalist), belong here?

5. P. californica.

Pteronarcys californicus Newp.! Trans. Linn. Soc. XX, 450. Proceed. Linn. Soc. I, 388. Walk.! Catal. 140, 5.

Fuscous; labrum, clypeus and front rufous; prothorax with an interrupted, yellow line upon the middle; abdomen orange-yellowish, the sides fuscous, the last ventral segment broad, pilose, the apex deeply incised; caudal setæ at base yellow; antennæ and feet black; wings with obscure black veins, pterostigmal spot absent.

(Description taken from that of Mr. Newport.) (Male.)

Almost the size of *P. proteus.*

Hab. California (Hartweg).

I saw the species in the British Museum, but I am not now able to furnish a more accurate description.

6. P. insignis.

Kollaria insignis Pictet, Perl. 123; tab. iv, fig. 1—8. Walker, Catal. 138, 1.

Fuscous; head equal in width to prothorax; prothorax quadrangular, on middle a yellow line; abdomen black, segments margined behind with yellow; feet yellowish-brown, knees yellowish; caudal setæ fuscous, yellow at base; ♀ antepenultimate ventral segment truncated, two very short setiform appendages? (from the figure); wings grayish-hyaline, before the apex clouded with fuscous; maxillary palpi very long.

(Description taken from the description and figure of Pictet.)

Length to tip of wings 53 millim. Expanse of wings 86 millim.

Hab. The locality unknown. Vienna Museum. It has the *habitus* of an American insect. I have not seen the typical specimen: from the figure and description of Pictet it seems to be a *Pteronarcys.* The generic character is derived from the length of the maxillary palpi: it is, however, of doubtful importance. The species, perhaps, is *P. biloba.*

** Wings with few, but rather regular, transverse veins.

PERLA Geoffroy.

Wings veiny, transverse veins few, very regular; posterior wings with the anal space large, plicated; palpi setaceous; two caudal setæ.

○ The submarginal, apical space of the anterior wings with some transverse veins. Subgenus *Acroneuria* Pictet.

1. P. abnormis!

Perla abnormis Newm.! Entom. Mag. V, 177. Pict. Perl. 180, 12. Walker! Catal. 147, 21.—*P. arenosa* Pict.! Perl. 178, 11; tab. x, fig. 1—2. Walker, Catal. 147, 19.—*P. pennsylvanica* Ramb.! Neuropt. 456, 13. —*P. internata* Walker! Catal. 152, 41.—*P. trijuncta* Walker! Catal. 153, 43.—*P. sonans* Barnston, Newport, Linn. Trans. XX, 447.

Yellowish-fuscous; the head broader than the prothorax, luteous, obscure in the middle; the antennæ fuscous, the second articulation and sometimes the following ones luteous; prothorax narrower posteriorly, the angles acute, sides straight, surface rugulose, the middle line scarcely more distinct; the feet luteous, knees fuscous; abdomen beneath yellowish, setæ fuscous, densely pilose; ♂ last ventral segment large ovate, with a round, polished spot; ♀ antepenultimate ventral segment slightly rounded, produced; wings subhyaline, veins clay-yellow; the vein accessory to the subcosta four-forked, some transverse veins.

Length to tip of wings, ♂ 27; ♀, 35 millim. Alar expanse, ♂ 50; ♀, 60 millim.

Hab. St. Lawrence River (Barnston); Philadelphia, Pa. (Pictet); Trenton Falls (Osten Sacken); Georgia (Abbot); South' Illinois (Robt. Kennicott); Maryland (Uhler).

I have seen a specimen from Mexico (Muehlenpford, in the Berlin Museum), which was paler, with many transverse veins, and the antepenultimate segment produced elliptically. Is it a distinct species?

2. P. ruralis!

P. ruralis Hagen!

Testaceous; head broader than the prothorax, a curved fuscous line in front; antennæ fusco-testaceous, the second articulation and some of the following ones luteous; the prothorax quadrangular, short, equal, rugulose, angles rather obtuse; feet testaceous, knees fuscous; abdomen beneath yellowish, setæ yellowish, behind the base banded with fuscous, hardly pilose; ♀ antepenultimate ventral segment a little rounded, produced, before the apex a linear transverse tubercle; wings sub-hyaline, the veins luteous; anterior wings with the subcostal accessory veinlet five-branched, transverse veins very numerous. (Female.)

Length to tip of wings 31 millim. Alar expanse 57 millim.
Hab. St. Louis.

3. P. arida!

Perla arida Hagen!

Yellowish-fuscous; head broader than the prothorax, yellowish, clouded with fuscous anteriorly; antennæ fuscous, second articulation yellowish; prothorax narrower posteriorly, angles acute, sides straight, rugulose, middle line yellowish; the feet luteous, knees fuscous; the abdomen beneath luteous; setæ pilose, yellow, articulations of the tip fuscous at their apex; ♂ last ventral segment large, ovate; ♀ antepenultimate ventral segment with a middle lamina narrow at base and at the apex two-lobed; wings sub-hyaline, veins fuscous; anterior wings with the subcostal accessory vein three-branched, transverse ones few.

Length to tip of wings 23 ♂, 28 ♀ millim. Alar expanse 43 ♂, 53 ♀ millim.

Hab. New York, Philadelphia.

Is this not *P. arenosa* Pictet, tab. x, fig. 2, from Philadelphia?

○ ○ Submarginal space of the anterior wings not charged with transverse veins.

a. Subcostal accessory veinlet of the anterior wings with four incurved branches. Subgenus *Isogenus* Newm. *Nephelion* Pict.

4. P. frontalis!

Isogenus frontalis Newm.! Entom. Mag. V, 178. Mag. Nat. Hist. III, 25.— *Nephelion frontalis* Pict. Perl. 172, 8; tab. viii, fig. 10—11. Walk.! Catal. 144, 10.—*Perla bicaudata* Kirby, Fn. Bor. Am. 252.

Blackish-fuscous; head hardly broader than the prothorax, an occipital spot and a frontal one in the shape of a V, yellow; prothorax quadrangular, rugulose, sides straight, a yellow stripe upon the middle, angles acute; feet yellowish-fuscous, knees blackish-brown banded with yellow; abdomen fuscous, apex beneath yellowish; the setæ pilose, luteous; ♀ antepenultimate ventral segment slightly, but broadly excised; wings hyaline, anterior ones with a medial costal, hardly conspicuous, fuscous cloud; veins blackish-brown. (Female.)

Length to tip of wings 24 millim. Alar expanse 42 millim.

Hab. St. Martin's Falls, Albany River, Hudson's Bay (Barnston); Latitude 68° (Richardson); Trenton Falls, and Ohio (Schaum).

I possess a ♀ specimen, taken at the same place, Ohio, most resembling this, but the incisure of the antepenultimate segment differs a little; being narrower and longer. Perhaps distinct.

5. P. clio.

Isogenus clio Newm. Mag. Nat. Hist. new ser. III, 86, 7. Walker Catal. 146, 17.

"Fuscous, head laterally around the eyes yellowish; prothorax with a median, longitudinal, yellow line; abdomen testaceous."— *Walker.*

Hab. Georgia (Abbot).

Unknown to me.

6. P. drymo.

Isogenus drymo Newm. Mag. Nat. Hist. new ser. III, 86, 6. Walker Catal. 146, 18.

"Fuscous, head testaceous, clypeus and a quadrate spot behind it fuscous; prothorax fuscous, marked with two large bright testaceous spots; base of the femora paler."— *Walker.*

Hab. Georgia (Abbot).

Unknown to me.

7. P. aurantiaca !

P. aurantiaca Hag.!

Orange-luteous; head with two ocelli; prothorax narrower behind, sides straight, surface rugulose, angles acute; last ventral segment short, produced in the middle; wings subhyaline, orange-yellowish, veins orange; accessory veinlet three-branched.

Length to tip of wings 18 millim. Alar expanse 35 millim.
Hab. Mexico. The unique type is very defective.

a a Accessory subcostal veinlet of the anterior wings, two-branched. Subgenus *Perla* Pictet. (Apical costal space with some transverse veins.)

8. P. dorsata.
Sialis dorsata Say, Godman's Western Quart. Rep. 1823, II, 164, 1.

"Black varied with rufous; head blackish, with about six blacker spots; beneath pale yellowish, labrum pale; palpi black; prothorax blackish, with impressed blacker lines, anterior and posterior incisures and dorsal vitta rufous, angles rather prominent, a pale obsolete line from the base of the thorax to the abdomen, beneath yellowish, disk of the segments black; trochanters yellowish; abdomen black, segments above with yellow posterior margins, venter pale yellow; nervures of the wings deep black."—*Say* (amended, *Uhler*).

Length to tip of wings 50 millim. (1¾ inches). Alar expanse 80 millim.?

Hab. Ohio River, Pittsburg; "common in May."—*Say.*
Unknown to me.

9. P. Coulonii.
Perla Coulonii Pictet, Perl. 212, 22; Pl. x, fig. 4. Walk. Catal. 150, 32.

"Black; head broad, the sides and occiput luteous; beneath luteous; the prothorax large, fuscous, very rugulose, the disk obscurer; abdomen paler fuscous; setæ rather short, fuscous; wings fusco-hyaline, veins fuscous, stout."—*Pict.*

Length to tip of wings 46 millim. Alar expanse 77 millim.
Hab. United States. Unknown to me. Perhaps *P. dorsata?*
Is it different from Walker's species, captured at the "Mackenzie and Slave Rivers?"

10. P. immarginata.
Sialis immarginata Say, Godman's West. Quart. Rep. II, 164, 2.

"Black varied with yellow, or yellow varied with black; eyes deep black-brown; prothorax transversely quadrangular, posterior angles a little rounded, disk a little rugose, with impressed irregular lines, an impressed dorsal line, and each side of it a slightly arcuated one; beneath yellow; wings obscure, veins fuscous, immarginate.

"It varies very much in coloring, being generally entirely yellow beneath, and sometimes upon the tergum. The thorax has sometimes a yellow dorsal line, and sometimes a black one."—*Say.*

Length to tip of wings ♀ 30 millim. ("more than one inch"). Male smaller.

Hab. Ohio River: "common in May" (Say). Unknown to me.

Perhaps a unique male from Washington (Osten Sacken) belongs to this species.

11. P. lurida!

Perla lurida Hag.!

Testaceous, varied with yellowish; head hardly broader than the prothorax, yellowish, a broad fuscous stripe upon the middle excised in front and drawn out into a semilunar form posteriorly; antennæ testaceous; prothorax quadrangular, narrower posteriorly, testaceous, rugulose, sides a little incurved, anterior angles acute, posterior ones a little rounded; feet testaceous, knees fuscous, underneath yellowish; body beneath yellowish, setæ testaceous-yellow, base of the venter pale yellow; antepenultimate ventral segment a little produced, triangularly emarginate in the middle; wings testaceo-hyaline, veins fusco-testaceous. (Female.)

Length to tip of wings 33 millim. ♀ Alar expanse 62 millim.

Hab. New Orleans (Pfeiffer).

12. P. lycorias!

Perla lycorias Newm. Mag. Nat. Hist. ser. 2, III, 85. Pict. Perl. 214. Walk. Catal. 152, 40.

Testaceous-yellow; head broader than the prothorax, orange-yellow, a transverse, trilobed, brownish-testaceous band; anteriorly and posteriorly clouded with fuscous; antennæ brownish-testaceous, base yellowish, first articulation brownish-black; prothorax quadrangular, hardly narrower posteriorly, sides straight, angles acute; its color orange-yellow, with fuscous rugulæ, a middle line brownish-black; feet testaceous, knees and the tibiæ externally, fuscous; beneath yellowish, setæ fusco-testaceous, pilose; ♂, last ventral segment larger, rounded, furnished with a transverse, ovate, flat, polished tubercle; ♀, antepenultimate segment with an elliptical middle lobe; wings subhyaline, veins fusco-testaceous.

Length to tip of wings 21—28 millim. Alar expanse 42—52 millim.

Hab. New York (Trenton Falls). Is this the true *P. lycorias* Newm. ?

13. P. tristis!
Perla tristis Hag.!

Fusco-piceous; head broader than the prothorax, fusco-piceous, two points anteriorly and two upon the middle yellow; antennæ piceous, base beneath and second articulation paler; prothorax quadrangular, posteriorly narrower, fusco-piceous, rugulose, shining, sides a little oblique, posterior angles hardly rounded, anterior ones acute; the feet luteous, exteriorly fusco-piceous; abdomen piceous, base beneath yellow; setæ fuscous; ♂ last ventral segment larger, triangular, incurved; ♀ antepenultimate segment truncated; wings smoky brownish, costal margin obscurer, veins fuscous. (Male small.)

Length to tip of wings 17—25 millim. Alar expanse 32—44 millim.

Hab. Trenton Falls, New York; Washington (Osten Sacken).

14. P. capitata.
Perla capitata Pict. Perl. 214, 23; tab. xviii, fig. 4, 5. Walker Catal. 150, 31.

Fuscous; head broader than the prothorax, luteous, the disk and anterior portion black; prothorax quadrangular, narrower behind, rugulose, fuscous; abdomen luteous, obscurer at the apex; setæ luteous, apex fuscous; feet luteous, exteriorly and tarsi fuscous, knees with a black band; wings fusco-hyaline, veins black-brown. ♂ (The diagnosis is from the figure and description of Pictet.)

Length to tip of wings 20 millim. Alar expanse 29 millim.

Hab. United States. Unknown to me.

15. P. annulipes!
Perla annulipes Hagen!

Brown varied with yellow; head a little broader than the prothorax, brown, occiput, two median spots and a transverse fascia in front yellow; antennæ dusky, two basal articulations pale yellow; prothorax quadrangular, narrower behind, sides oblique, angles acute; brown, rugulose upon the surface, shining, anteriorly margined with yellow; feet yellow, a fuscous ring upon the femora at base, knees, tibiæ externally and tarsi fuscous; abdomen above brown, segments margined with yellow; beneath yellow, middle of the base obscure; setæ yellow at base (the remainder is broken off); ♀ antepenultimate ventral segment, middle lobe, short, broad, rounded, infuscated; wings grayish-subhyaline, costal margin a little yellowish, veins testaceous. (Female.)

Length to tip of wings 18 millim. Alar expanse 34 millim.

Hab. Washington (Osten Sacken, 1857). Is this *P. capitata* Pictet?

16. P. postica!

Perla postica Walker Catal. 144, 11.

Black; head equal to the prothorax, black, a spot upon the occipital middle, which is hastiform and sometimes two anteriorly orange-yellow; antennæ black; prothorax transverse, quadrangular, short, black, rugulose, an orange stripe upon the middle, sides straight, angles acute; feet brownish-black; abdomen black, beneath in the middle yellowish; setæ black; ♂ last ventral segment larger, ovate, fuscous; ♀ antepenultimate segment large, triangularly ovate, fuscous; wings grayish-subhyaline, veins fuscous.

Length to tip of wings 15—20 millim. Alar expanse 28—34 millim.

Hab. Louisiana (Schaum); Mackenzie River (Richardson).

I do not know whether this is the same with Walker's species or not. It is some time since I examined his specimens in the British Museum.

The words in Mr. Walker's diagnosis, "prothorax produced into an acute angle, or short horn on each side by the foreangle," are erroneous, and they are accordingly omitted here.

17. P. olivacea!

Perla olivacea Walk. Catal. 144, 12.

Fuscous; head hardly broader than the prothorax, fuscous, fulvous in front with a large occipital, trilobed, transverse spot; antennæ fuscous, fulvous at base; prothorax transverse, quadrangular, shorter, fuscous, rugulose, a broad, yellow middle stripe; sides straight, anterior and posterior margin a little rounded; the feet fuscous, beneath and tibiæ luteous; abdomen fuscous; setæ luteous, pilose; ♂ with last ventral segment luteous, larger, oval; wings small, shorter than the abdomen, subhyaline, veins fuscous.

Length of body 9 millim.

Hab. Arctic America. St. Martin's Falls, Albany River (Barnston). Is this Walker's species?

18. P. media.

Perla media Walker Catal. 145, 13.

Black; head broader than the prothorax, black, the sides, posterior margin and two spots yellowish-brown; prothorax quadrangular, black, rugulose, with a middle sulcus; narrower posteriorly, anterior angles acute, posterior ones rounded; wings subcinereous, veins black.

Length to tip of wings? 20 millim. Alar expanse 36 millim.

Hab. St. Martin's Falls, Albany River, Hudson's Bay (Barnston). Unknown to me. Is it not *P. immarginata*?

19. P. æthiops.

Perla æthiops Walk. Catal. 154, 45.

Black; head hardly broader than the prothorax, black; prothorax quadrangular, narrower behind, black, subrugulose, subsulcated, sides convex, angles subacute; wings blackish-fuscous, veins black. (The diagnose is taken from that of Walker.)

Length to tip of wings? 24 millim. Alar expanse 40 millim.

Hab. Mexico (Hartweg). Unknown to me. Is it not *P. tristis*?

20. P. cincta.

Perla cincta Pict. Perl. 229; tab. xx, fig. 5. Walk. Catal. 156, 50.

Black varied with yellow; head broader than the prothorax, black, in front yellow; antennæ black, the basal article fuscous; prothorax transverse, angles rounded, sides straight, surface subrugose, black, margined with yellow, the anterior margin broader, upon the middle a yellow stripe; abdomen and setæ fuscous; the feet luteous, streak of the femora, and the knees black, tibiæ at base and tarsi black; wings tinged with yellowish, semihyaline, veins orange-yellow. (From the figure and description of Pictet.)

Length to tip of wings 30 millim. Alar expanse 50 millim.

Hab. Vera Cruz. Unknown to me.

21. P. nigrocincta!

Perla nigrocincta Pict.! Perl. 236, 34; tab. xxii, fig. 5—8. Walker, Catal. 158, 56.

Yellow varied with fuscous; head as wide as prothorax, yellow, disk brownish-black, only two ocelli; antennæ fuscous; prothorax yellow, rugulose, externally the half each side fuscous, sulcus upon the middle fuscous; posteriorly narrower, in front and sides rounded, anterior angles subacute, posterior ones rounded; feet yellow, knees, tibiæ and tarsi externally fuscous; abdomen yellow; setæ yellow; ♂ last ventral segment large, ovate; wings fusco-subhyaline, costal margin somewhat yellowish, veins testaceous. (Male.)

Length to tip of wings 18 (—22) millim. Alar expanse 33 (—41) millim.

Hab. Mexico (Koppe); Cordova (Saussure).

22. P. dilaticollis!

Perla dilaticollis Burm.! II, 880, 7. Pict.! Perl. 240, 36; tab. xxiii, fig. 5—10. Walk. Catal. 158, 58.

Yellow varied with brown; head wide as the prothorax, yellow, in front clouded with fulvous: ocelli only two, black; the antennæ brown, the base luteous; prothorax narrower behind, anteriorly rounded, rugulose, brown, a broad, yellowish middle vitta, sides oblique, anterior angles rounded; feet yellowish, knees and tibiæ externally a little infuscated; abdomen and setæ yellowish; ♂ last ventral segment large, ovate; ♀ antepenultimate ventral segment truncate? wings testaceo-subhyaline, veins testaceous, accessory subcostal vein incurved.

Length to tip of wings 10—13 millim. Alar expanse 20—27 millim.

Hab. Mexico; Columbia; Brazil; North America (Museum Vienna). I have not seen the Mexican specimens.

23. P. litura.

Perla litura Pict. Perl. 242, 37; tab. xxiv, fig. 1—3. Walk. Catal. 159, 59.

Yellow varied with brown; head as wide as the prothorax, brown, margined with black, only two ocelli, antennæ blackish; prothorax brown, rugulose, a broad middle yellow stripe; broad, narrower behind, in front rounded, anterior angles rounded, sides oblique; feet yellowish, knees, tibiæ externally and apical ring, and tarsi fuscous; abdomen and setæ yellow; wings grayish-subhyaline, costal margin obscurer, veins fuscous. (Taken from the figure and description of Pictet.)

Length to tip of wings 11 millim. Alar expanse 20 millim.
Hab. Mexico. I have not seen it. Is it not *P. dilaticollis?*

24. P. similis!

Perla similis Hagen!

Fuscous varied with fulvous; head as wide as the prothorax, fuscous, sides fulvous, antennæ blackish-fuscous; prothorax quadrangular, transverse, rugulose, fuscous, a broad fulvous stripe upon the middle, sides straight, anteriorly and posteriorly somewhat rounded, angles subacute; feet fuscous; abdomen fuscous, apex above bright fulvous; yellowish-brown below; setæ blackish-fuscous; ♀ antepenultimate ventral segment truncated; wings smoky-hyaline, costal margin obscurer, veins deep fuscous. (Female.)

Length to tip of wings 14 millim. Alar expanse 23 millim.
Hab. Pennsylvania and Maryland (Uhler).

25. P. xanthenes.

Perla xanthenes Newm. Entom. Mag. V, 178. Mag. Nat. Hist. 2d ser. III, 35, 3. Pict. Perl. 245, 38; tab. xxi, fig. 3, 4. Walker, Catal. 159, 60.

Body entirely pale yellow; head hardly broader than the prothorax, with a fuscous spot, ocelli black; prothorax quadrangular, rugulose, posteriorly a little narrower, angles subacute; apex of the femora hardly annulated with fuscous; apex of the abdomen fuscous; wings pale yellowish, subhyaline; veins pale yellow. (Taken from the figure and description of Pictet.) (Female.)

Length to tip of wings? 27 millim. Expanse of wings 47 millim.
Hab. Pennsylvania; Georgia (Abbot).

26. P. annulicauda.

Perla annulicauda Pict. Perl. 249, 40; tab. xxii, fig. 1—4. Walk. Catal. 160, 64.

Lurid; head as wide as the prothorax, lurid, disk obscurer, anteriorly a pale sinuated nebulous stripe, ocelli (two?) posterior ones banded with black, prothorax short, rugulose, lurid, rugulæ paler; sides and angles rounded; the abdomen luteous, the setæ luteous annulated with black; the feet luteous, femora above, knees, base and apex of the tibiæ and apex of the tarsi fuscous; wings yellowish-gray, semihyaline, apex of the costal margin obscurer, veins luteous. (Taken from the figure and description of Pictet.)

Length to tip of wings 22 millim. Alar expanse 29—38 millim.
Hab. Mexico; Brazil. Unknown to me.

27. P. costalis.
Perla costalis Pict. Perl. 264, 48; tab. xxiv, fig. 4. Walk. Catal. 162, 70.

Fuscous; head broader than the prothorax, fuscous, in front rufescent; antennæ black; prothorax quadrangular, black, middle reddish-rugulose, angles rounded, behind narrower; abdomen yellowish-fuscous; the setæ fuscous, at base luteous; feet yellowish, apex of the femora, tarsi, black, tibiæ exteriorly fuscous; wings fuscous, veins black, costal one golden-yellow. (Taken from the figure and description of Pictet.)

Length to tip of wings? 18 millim. Alar expanse 27 millim.
Hab. Vera Cruz. Unknown to me.

28. P. occipitalis!
Perla occipitalis Pict. Perl. 254, 43; tab. xxvi, fig. 1—3. Walker, Catal. 160, 65.

Yellow varied with brown; head broader than the prothorax, ocelli black, only two in number, surface between the ocelli blackish-brown, remaining surface yellow, in front clouded with fulvous; antennæ brown, their base luteous, with the basal articulation blackish-fuscous at base, and at its apex luteous; prothorax brown, rugulose, posteriorly narrower, anteriorly somewhat rounded, sides a little oblique, anterior angles acute; feet yellow, exteriorly fuscous; abdomen and setæ yellowish; ♀ antepenultimate ventral segment truncated; wings testaceo-subhyaline, costal space yellowish, veins testaceous; accessory vein direct. (Female only seen.)

Length to tip of wings 15 millim. Alar expanse 27 millim.
Hab. Philadelphia; New York; Washington (Osten Sacken); Maryland (Uhler).

Very similar to *P. dilaticollis*. In the specimen from Maryland the prothorax has a middle yellow stripe, anteriorly and posteriorly broadened.

29. P. picta.
Perla picta Pict. Perl. 261, 47; tab. xxvii, fig. 3, 8.

Yellowish-fulvous; the head broader than the prothorax, luteous, a spot upon the middle triangular, and another irregular, between the ocelli black, ocelli three; antennæ yellowish, apex fuscous; prothorax at sides black, with a luteous medial line or broader fascia; quadrangular, sides almost straight, angles somewhat rounded; abdomen and setæ luteous; wings hyaline, hardly obscured, veins fuscous. (Taken from the figure and description of Pictet.)

Length to tip of wings 16—18 millim. Alar expanse 27—32 millim.

Hab. North America. Unknown to me and a somewhat doubtful species.

30. P. placida!
Perla placida Hag.!

Yellowish-fulvous; the head a little broader than the prothorax, luteous, in front clouded with fulvous, a large discoidal, quadrangular black spot, three ocelli; antennæ fuscous, base yellow, basal article fuscous above; prothorax rugulose, brown, posteriorly a little, anteriorly somewhat rounded, sides a little oblique, anterior angles acute; the feet luteous, knees subfuscous; the abdomen and setæ luteous; ♂ last ventral segment larger, ovate; ♀ antepenultimate one truncate; wings pale testaceo-hyaline, costal space yellowish, veins testaceous.

Length to tip of wings 10—12 millim. Alar expanse 17—23 millim.

Hab. New York; Washington (Osten Sacken, 1857). Very similar to *P. occipitalis.*

31. P. ephyre!
Chloroperla ephyre Newm.! Mag. Nat. Hist. 2d ser. III, 87, 5. Pictet. Perl. 283, 3. Walk.! Catal. 168, 91.

Yellowish fulvous; head broader than the prothorax, yellowish-fulvous, ocelli three, joined together by a V-shaped brownish-black line, antennæ fuscous, base hardly yellow, basal articulation obscurer; prothorax yellowish-fulvous, rugulose, hardly narrower behind, anteriorly somewhat rounded, sides almost straight, anterior angles acute; feet yellowish, knees exteriorly a little dusky; abdomen yellowish; setæ yellowish, at apex fuscous; ♀ antepenultimate ventral segment truncated; wings pale testaceo-hyaline, veins luteous, costal space slightly yellowish.

Length to tip of wings 15 millim. Alar expanse 25 millim.

Hab. Georgia (Abbot); New York; New Orleans; Berkeley Springs, Virginia (Osten Sacken).

32. P. clymene.

Chloroperla clymene Newm. Mag. Nat. Hist. 2d ser. III, 87, 4. Pict. Perl. 283, 4. Walk. Catal. 167, 87.

" Head yellow, eyes and ocelli black; wings lightly tinged with fuscous, nervures all fuscous."—*Newman.*

Alar expanse 26 millim.

Hab. Georgia (Abbot). Unknown to me. Does it belong here?

Subgenus *Chloroperla* Pictet. (Costal, apical space with one transverse vein.)

33. P. Guerinii.

Perla Guerinii Pict. Perl. 279, 55; tab. xxx, fig. 6—8. Walk. Catal. 164, 77.

Black; head as wide as the prothorax, black, a stripe upon the occiput yellow; prothorax quadrangular, anteriorly narrower, rugulose, a stripe upon the middle yellow; feet brown, femora and tibiæ with a longitudinal line, and tarsi, black; abdomen black, the last segment whitish-gray; setæ fuscous, pilose, base whitish; wings dusky subhyaline, veins dusky. (From the figure and description of Pictet.)

Length to tip of wings 15 millim. Alar expanse 27 millim.

Hab. New Orleans. Unknown to me.

34. P. maculata.

Perla maculata Pict. Perl. 280, 56; tab. xxx, fig. 9. Walker, Catal. 164, 78.

Black; head as wide as the prothorax, yellow, disk broadly black; prothorax black, with a yellow middle line, posteriorly narrower, sides rounded; wings dusky, costal space obscurer, veins black. (From the figure and description of Pictet.)

Length to tip of wings 11 millim. Alar expanse 20 millim.

Hab. Philadelphia. Unknown to me.

35. P. decolorata†

Perla decolorata Walker, Catal. 170, 98.

Pale testaceous; head a little broader than the prothorax, pale testaceous, with an irregular, discoidal, black spot; prothorax quadrangular, subrugose, a large fuscous spot each side, sides straight, angles subacute; wings hyaline, veins black, testaceous at base. (From the description of Mr. Walker.)

Alar expanse 27 millim.

Hab. Great Bear Lake (Richardson). Unknown to me.

36. P. decisa.

Perla decisa Walker, Catal. 170, 99.

Ferrugineous, shining; head broader than the prothorax, testaceous, antennæ fuscous; prothorax square, rugulose, angles subacute; wings gray, veins black.

Alar expanse 25 millim.

Hab. St. Martin's Falls, Albany River, Hudson's Bay (Barnston).

37. P. bilineata!

Sialis bilineata Say, Godman's Western Quarterly Reporter, II, 165, 4.— *Chloroperla transmarina* Newm.! Mag. Nat. Hist. ser. 2, III, 87, 3. Newm.! Ent. Mag. V, 499. Walk. Catal. 161, 89. Pictet. Perl. 283, 2. *Perla picta* Walk. Catal. 161, 169.

Pale fuscous, varied with yellow; head broader than the prothorax, with three ocelli; surface yellow, two, anteriorly conjoined, semicircular, fuscous lines upon the disk, two straight fuscous lines before the discal ones; antennæ yellowish, apex fuscous, basal articulation dusky; prothorax quadrangular, yellow, rugulose, each side with a broad fuscous stripe, sides straight, posteriorly hardly narrower, angles acute; the feet luteous, knees, and exteriorly obscurer; the abdomen and setæ luteous, ♀ antepenultimate ventral segment rounded at apex; wings grayish-hyaline, exteriorly tinged with yellow, veins testaceous. (Female.)

Length to tip of wings 12 millim. Alar expanse 21 millim.

Hab. Canada; Trenton Falls, New York; Ohio (Schaum); "Cincinnati, 15th May: not rare" (Say).

38. P. severa!

Perla severa Hag.!

Pale yellow; head hardly broader than the prothorax, pale yellow, three black ocelli; antennæ pale yellow, apex obscurer; prothorax quadrangular, rugulose, pale yellow, a narrow brown stripe upon the middle, sides straight, angles obtuse, rounded; feet yellowish, exteriorly obscured, tarsi blackish fuscous; abdomen ——; wings hyaline, veins fuscous, base and disk partly pallid.

Length to tip of wings 13 millim. Alar expanse 23 millim.

Hab. Island of Unga, Russian America.

39. P. citrinella.

Perla citrinella Newp. Proc. Linn. Soc. I, 388, 6. Newp. Trans. Linn.
   Soc. XX, 540, 1. *P. citrinella* Walk. Catal. 169, 97.

Pale luteous; the head as wide as the prothorax, ocelli fuscous; antennæ fuscous, pale at base; prothorax not broader behind, luteous, subrugulose, the anterior margin and middle line blackish, angles obtuse, sides incurved; wings hyaline, veins pale. (From the description of Mr. Walker.)

Length to tip of wings(?) 13 millim. Alar expanse 23 millim.

Hab. St. Martin's Falls, Albany River, Hudson's Bay (Barnston); Nova Scotia (Redman.)

Unknown to me. The description of Mr. Newport differs a little: "antennæ entirely black." The description of Mr. Walker was drawn from the typical specimen. Is it an *Isopteryx*?

40. P. imbecilla.

Sialis imbecilla Say, Godman's West. Quart. Rept. II, 165, 3.

Pale green, immaculate; head with three fuscous ocelli, antennæ rather obscurer, pilose; prothorax transversely oval, rugulose; wings greenish-white. (Taken from the description of Mr. Say.)

Length to tip of wings 9 millim. Alar expanse 16 millim.

Hab. Ohio River at Cincinnati. Common in the middle of May (Say). Unknown to me. Is it an *Isopteryx*?

ISOPTERYX Pict.

Wings with the transverse veins rare, almost absent; no basal space to the posterior wings; palpi setaceous, last articulation shortest.

1. I. cydippe!

Chloroperla cydippe Newm. Mag. Nat. Hist. ser. 2, III, 88, 8. Pict. Perl.
   · 317. Walk. Catal. 168, 88.—*Chl. sulphurea* Fitch! (Collection of de Selys Longchamps.)

Pale yellow, immaculate; head hardly broader than the prothorax, three black ocelli; antennæ nigro-fuscous, base pallid; prothorax transversely oval, subrugulose, angles rounded; feet pale, tarsi nigro-fuscous; wings greenish-hyaline, veins pale.

Length to tip of wings ♂ 7 ♀ 9 millim. Alar expanse ♂ 13 ♀ 16 millim.

Hab. Georgia (Abbot); Trenton Falls, New York; Washington (Osten Sacken, Asa Fitch). Is it not *P. imbecilla?*

CAPNIA Pictet.

Wings veiny, transverse veins very few and very regular; anal area of the posterior wings large, plicate; palpi filiform, last joint ovate, longer than the preceding one; two setæ.

1. C. pygmaea!

Semblis pygmaea Burm.! II, 874, 1.(♂)—*Capnia pygmaea* Pictet! Perl. 324, 2; tab. xl, fig. 1—3. Walk. Catal. 175, 2.—*Perla nivicola* Fitch! Winter Insects of E. New York, 5, 3.

Black, shining, with gray hairs; articulations of the antennæ long; prothorax rounded, subrugulose, in front with an impressed, curved line; feet black, tibiæ brown, at the apex pitchy, tarsi fuscous; abdomen black; setæ with somewhat near 20 articulations, black, apex fuscous; ♂ wings rudimentary; ♀ wings pale, veins fuscous; penis of the male long; to the back of the abdomen two tubercles, placed before the apex of the penis.

Length to tip of wings 4½ ♂, 9 ♀ millim. Alar expanse 16 ♀ millim.

Hab. Pennsylvania (Zimmerman); Newfoundland. "New York, common in February."—*Dr. Fitch.*

Is not *Capnia vernalis* Newport, this same species?

2. C. necydaloides!

Capnia necydaloides Pict.! Perl. 326, 3; tab. xl, fig. 4—5. ♀; Walker, Catal. 175, 3.

Black, shining; articulations of the antennæ long; prothorax rounded, subrugulose, anteriorly an impressed, curved line; feet black, tibiæ brown, piceous at the apex, tarsi fuscous; the abdomen luteous, the apex black; setæ black, with 13—18 articulations, the apex fuscous; ♂ wings rudimental; ♀ wings a little longer than the abdomen, pale, the veins stout, black; penis shorter than in the preceding species; abdomen having one dorsal tubercle before the apex of the penis.

Length to tip of wings ♂ 4, ♀ 6½ millim. Alar expanse 11½ millim.

Hab. North America (Pictet); Washington, 20th December (Osten Sacken).

3. C. minima!

Perla minima Newp.! Proc. Linn. Soc. I, 388, 2. Trans. Linn. Soc. XX, 450, 2. Walk.! Catal. 183, 19.

Black, shining; antennæ moniliform; prothorax narrower than the head, subquadrate, sides straight, angles acute; feet blackish-fuscous; abdomen black (setæ with 13 articulations, Newp.); ♂ wings rudimental; ♀ wings pale, veins black; penis ♂ very short; abdomen having no dorsal tubercle before the apex of the penis.

Length to tip of wings ♂ $2\frac{1}{2}$; ♀ 6 millim. Alar expanse, 7 millim.

Hab. St. Martin's Falls, Albany River, Hudson's Bay; April (Barnston).

I possess only the male; the remainder of the description is from Newport and Walker.

4. C. vernalis!

Capnia vernalis Newp. Proc. Linn. Soc. 388, 3. Trans. Linn. Soc. XX, 451, 3. Walk. Catal. 176, 8. *Nemoura tenuis* Walk.! Catal. 182, 13.

Black, shining, sparingly pilose; antennæ moniliform; prothorax narrower than the head, rounded, rugulose; feet, abdomen, and setæ blackish-fuscous; setæ with somewhat near 20 articulations; wings pallid, veins fuscous; wings with the form and reticulation of *Nemoura* (subgenus restricted); penis rather long; no dorsal tubercle before the apex of the penis.

Length to tip of wings 6—7 millim. Alar expanse 10—12 millim.

Hab. St. Martin's Falls, Albany River, Hudson's Bay (Barnston).

I possess a male and female from the British Museum; they are certainly *N. tenuis* Walker, but I do not know whether the specimens described in the same place and taken in New York, belong here. Nor have I quoted here Newport's species *C. vernalis*, without some doubt. But not finding his typical specimens in the British Museum, I am rather inclined to believe that Mr. Walker has erroneously united them to *N. tenuis*. *N. tenuis* Pictet is very different.

†† No abdominal setæ.

* Second articulation of the tarsi equal to the others.

TAENIOPTERYX Pictet.

Wings a little involuted, veined, transverse veins very scarce, rather regular; anal area of the posterior wings large, plicated; palpi filiform, the last article ovate; no abdominal setæ; tarsi with three long, equal articles.

1. T. fasciata!

Semblis fasciata Burm.! II, 875, 6. Pict.! Perl. 359, 5, tab. xlvi, fig. 4, 5. Walker, Catal. 179, 5.

Black, with gray pile; head hardly broader than the thorax, in front and at the eyes rufous, tubercles flat, polished, anteriorly with two parallel grooves; antennæ fuscous, the basal articulation black; prothorax broader behind, rugulose, sides oblique, posterior margin rounded, anterior angles subacute, tubercles a little shining, near the anterior margin a transverse, biarcuated sulcus, two closely approximated, linear, parallel discoidal tubercles, at the posterior margin a transverse sulcus; feet yellowish-brown, femora exteriorly, tibiæ at base and the tarsi blackish-brown; abdomen black, shining, ♀ appendix broad, yellow, triangular, beneath excavated, the apex narrow, rounded, incurved; ♂ appendix yellow, lanceolate; wings subhyaline, a gray transverse band upon the middle and another at the apex; veins fuscous.

Length to tip of wings 11—13 millim. Alar expanse 23—25 millim.

Hab. Philadelphia, Pa.; Washington, April (Osten Sacken).

2. T. similis!

Tæniopteryx similis Hagen!

Black, shining; head broader than the prothorax, shining, hardly rufous anteriorly, antennæ black; prothorax short, broad, sides oblique, posterior margin rounded, anterior angles rounded, posterior ones acute, anterior margin subreflexed, very rugulose; feet brown, femora exteriorly and the tarsi blackish-brown; abdomen black, shining; the last ventral segment truncated; wings subhyaline, with three broad gray bands, the extreme one is apical, veins fuscous. (Female.)

Length to tip of wings 8 millim. Alar expanse 14 millim.

Hab. Washington, May (Osten Sacken).

I possess males from Washington, April (Osten Sacken), with the femora unarmed, the ventral appendage narrow, oval, concave, and with the sculpture of the front, anteriorly, a little different. Is it a new species?

3. T. frigida!
Tæniopteryx frigida Hagen!

Black, grayish-pilose; head hardly broader than the prothorax, in front fuscous, tubercles flat, polished; anteriorly with two parallel furrows; antennæ black; prothorax hardly broader posteriorly, sides straight, anterior and posterior margin subrotund, anterior angles rounded, posterior ones square, with a few flat, polished tubercles, near the anterior margin a transverse biarcuated sulcus, at the posterior margin a transverse one; feet yellowish-brown, femora exteriorly, tibiæ at base and the tarsi blackish-brown; abdomen black, shining; wings subhyaline, a gray band upon the middle and another at the apex, veins fuscous.

Length to tip of wings 15 millim. Alar expanse 25 millim.

Hab. Maryland (Uhler).

Is this not *N. nivalis* Fitch, Winter Ins. 6, 4. Walk. Catal. 190, 48? It is certainly a *Tæniopteryx*, and perhaps *T. fasciata* Burm.?

4. T. maura!
Tæniopteryx maura Pict.! Perl. 361, 6; tab. xlvi, fig. 6.

Black, opaque; head equal to the prothorax, rugulose, occiput punctated, antennæ blackish-brown; prothorax broader behind, sides sinuated, oblique, anterior angles rounded, posterior ones subacute, the anterior and lateral margins a little recurved, tubercles very few, polished; feet whitish-pilose, femora black, tibiæ luteous; abdomen black; wings grayish-hyaline or fuscous, veins fuscous; male with shorter wings, the ventral appendage oblong, concave. The same sex has a robust tooth upon the middle of the femora beneath.

Length to tip of wings, ♂ 9; ♀ 15 millim. Alar expanse ♀ 27 millim.

Hab. Philadelphia, Pa.; Washington, April (Osten Sacken). Common.

5. T. glacialis!

Nemoura (Brachyptera) glacialis Newp.! Proc. Linn. Soc. I, 389, 4. Trans. Linn. Soc. XX, 451. Walk.! Catal. 192, 53. *N. maura* Walk.! Catal. 179, 7. (Female.)

Allied to *T. maura;* differs in having the occiput verrucose, and the prothorax smoother; the wings in the males rudimentary, the femora unarmed, the ventral appendage quadrangular, flatter.

Length to tip of wings 9—15 millim. Alar expanse 27 millim.

Hab. St. Martin's Falls, Albany River, Hudson's Bay (Barnston).

* * The second article of the tarsi small, shorter than the others.

NEMOURA Pictet.

Wings veiny, flat, transverse veins few, very regular, veins of the pterostigma forming an X; anal area of the posterior wings large, plicate; no setæ; the second articulation of the tarsi short.

1. N. completa.

Nemoura completa Walk. Catal. 191, 52.

Black, shining; head broader than the prothorax, upon the disk a luteous spot; prothorax quadrangular, equal, sides straight, angles subacute, surface subrugulose, a smoother sulcus upon the middle; feet ferruginous; wings hyaline; anterior ones with a band upon the middle and another at apex fuscous, veins fuscous. (From the description of Mr. Walker.)

Length to tip of wings 8? millim. Alar expanse 14 millim.

Hab. Nova Scotia (Redman). Unknown to me. May it not belong to *Tæniopteryx?*

2. N. albidipennis!

Nemoura albidipennis Walk. Catal. 191, 51.

Piceous, shining; head broader than the prothorax; antennæ fuscous; prothorax quadrangular, sides straight, angles subacute, anterior margin a little recurved, disk with a few tubercles; feet pale luteous, apex of the femora and base of the tibiæ fuscous; abdomen yellowish-fuscous; wings hyaline, veins fuscous, a little margined with fuscous.

Length to tip of wings 9 millim. Alar expanse 16 millim.

Hab. Washington (Osten Sacken); Nova Scotia (Redman) Is not the ferruginous-colored species of Mr. Walker distinct from this?

3. N. perfecta!
Nemoura perfecta Walk.! Catal. 191, 51.

Black, shining; head broader than the prothorax, antennæ black, prothorax narrower behind, sides oblique, anterior angles rounded, the anterior margin a little recurved, disk with a few tubercles; feet testaceous, femora exteriorly and the tarsi brownish-black; wings clouded with fuscous, broadly margined with fuscous, veins fuscous.

Length to tip of wings 8 millim. Alar expanse 14 millim.

Hab. Trenton Falls (Osten Sacken); Nova Scotia (Redman). It may be different from Mr. Walker's species.

I possess an individual of the European *N. variegata*, labelled "Philadelphia," but the label is very doubtful.

LEUCTRA Stephens.

Wings veiny, involuted when in rest, transverse veins very few, very regular, veins of the pterostigma simple (*i. e.*, not forming an X); anal area of the posterior wings small, plicate; caudal setæ absent; the second articulation of the tarsi short.

1. L. tenuis!
Nemoura tenuis Pict.! Perl. 375, 10; tab. xlix, fig. 1—3.

Fuscous, opaque, head a little broader than the prothorax; antennæ fuscous; thorax quadrangular, sides straight, angles subacute, disk with three elevated lines, the middle one straight, the others subincurved; feet fulvous, abdomen fuscous; wings subhyaline, a little ciliated, veins fulvous.

Length to tip of wings 7 millim. Alar expanse 12 millim.

Hab. Philadelphia; Washington (Osten Sacken); Sharon Springs, New York, in August (Osten Sacken).

2. L. ferruginea!
Nemoura ferruginea Walk.! Catal. 183, 18.

Fusco-ferruginous, somewhat shining; head a little broader than the prothorax; antennæ ferruginous; prothorax a little broader in front, quadrangular, sides a little convex, anterior angles somewhat rounded; disk with three straight elevated lines, the outer ones shorter; feet and abdomen ferruginous; wings subhyaline, a little ciliated, veins ferruginous.

Length to tip of wings 8 millim. Alar expanse 14 millim.

Hab. Nova Scotia (Redman).

Fam. V. EPHEMERINA.

Body elongated, conical; prothorax of moderate size; antennæ small, subulate; parts of the mouth rudimentary, connate; caudal setæ two or three, long, slender; wings unequal, posterior smaller, or sometimes absent; transverse veins few or numerous; tarsi four- or five-articulated.

EPHEMERA Linn.

Three long and equal caudal setæ; wings four, transverse veins very numerous; eyes remote, in the males simple.

1. E. decora!

Ephemera decora Walk.! Catal. 537, 7. Male Imago.

♂ *Imago.* Rather luteous, apex of the antennæ black; the head, thorax, and abdomen each side with a fuscous fascia, that of the abdomen broader, exteriorly serrated; beneath yellowish, abdomen bilineate; anterior feet very long, luteous, the apex of the femora, base and apex of the tibiæ and apex of the tarsal articulations fuscous; posterior feet (partly destroyed) luteous; setæ luteous, long, the articulations fuscous; wings yellowish-hyaline, veins fuscous, partly margined with fuscous, anterior ones with some discoidal fuscous spots. Female paler, feet shorter, wings more hyaline.

Length of body 11 millim. Alar expanse 26 millim. Setæ 25 millim.

Hab. New Haven; Canada (Barnston); Chicago (Osten Sacken).

Does *E. guttulata* Pictet. Ephem. 135, 4, tab. iv, fig. 4, belong here? I have never seen it, and the locality is unknown. The figure and description agree, but yet, the wings are more spotted.

2. E. simulans.

Ephemera simulans Walk.! Catal. 536, 5.

Piceous; feet fulvous, anterior ones obscurer; setæ pale piceous, pubescent, longer than the body; wings subcinereous, the anterior ones maculated and subfasciated with fuscous, the apex and posterior margin not maculated; veins cloudy. (From Mr. Walker's description.)

Length of body 12 millim. Alar expanse 31 millim. Setæ 14 millim.

Hab. St. Lawrence River.

Is it not a female subimago? I have seen the specimen described and noted "that it was allied to *E. vulgata*, but smaller."

3. E. hebes.

Ephemera hebes Walk. Catal. 538, 8. ♀ Subimago.

Piceous; antennæ black; feet testaceous, anterior ones fuscous; setæ fusco-testaceous; wings cinereous, veins black. (From Mr. Walker's description.)

Length of body 9 millim. Alar expanse 22 millim.

Hab. St. Johns, Newfoundland.

The specimen described is in the British Museum.

4. E. natata!

Palingenia natata Walk.! Catal. 551, 13. ♀ Subimago.

Fusco-testaceous; antennæ black; abdomen interruptedly bivittated with fuscous; setæ pilose, fulvous, banded with fuscous, a little shorter than the body; feet testaceous, tibiæ and tarsi fuscous; wings subcinereous, veins black and black-banded, except at the apex and posterior margin; the anterior ones with three or four discoidal fuscous spots.

Length of body 15 millim. Alar expanse 38 millim. Setæ 15 millim.

Hab. St. Martin's Falls, Albany River, Hudson's Bay (Barnston); Chicago (Osten Sacken).

5. E. pudica!

Ephemera? pudica Hagen! ♀ Subimago.

Luteous; thorax spotted with fuscous; abdomen with the posterior margin, exteriorly, of the middle dorsal segments black; feet luteous, the knees and a ring upon the middle of the femora fuscous; wings grayish-hyaline, longitudinal veins yellow, transverse ones fuscous, banded with gray; transverse discoidal veins a little irregular.

Length of body 12 millim. Alar expanse 40 millim.

Hab. Washington (Osten Sacken, 1858).

Are there three setæ? The unique specimen is very much mutilated; but it has the *facies* of an Ephemera.

PALINGENIA Burm.

Three setæ, the middle one short, in the males sometimes, almost absent; wings four, transverse veins very numerous; eyes remote, simple.

1. P. hecuba!

Palingenia hecuba Hagen! ♀ Imago.

Luteous, spotted with fuscous; head blackish-fuscous, apex of the antennæ pale; prothorax shining fuscous, broad, narrower anteriorly; abdomen luteous, above blackish-fuscous; setæ thick, whitish-gray, the middle one of equal thickness with the others (partly destroyed); base of the feet luteous (the feet are wanting in the specimen); wings large, opaque, grayish-rosy, the costal margin a little obscurer, veins gray.

Length of body 22 millim. Alar expanse 78 millim.

Hab. Vera Cruz (Sallé). Collection of de Selys Longchamps.

The largest species yet known. The wings are opaque, but yet it is an imago; and it has a mass of eggs in the vulvar aperture.

2. P. alba!

Bætis alba Say, Long's Narrative, Appendix, II, 305, 3.

Milk-white; vertex fuscous; prothorax transverse, quadrangular, in front truncated, yellowish-white; anterior feet grayish-fuscous, the others white; wings whitish, anterior margin grayish.

Length of body 11 millim. Alar expanse 22 millim.

Hab. North Red River (Robt. Kennicott); Winnipeg River (Say).

"This insect appears in immense numbers;" for a more particular account see Long's Narrative, as quoted above. I have seen only a mutilated specimen.

3. P. puella.

Palingenia puella Pictet, Ephem. 145, 2; tab. xi, fig. 4.

Milky-whitish; ocelli black; prothorax transverse, short, anteriorly produced in the middle; apex of the feet brownish, femora pale; wings whitish, costa a little obscurer. (From the figure and description of Pictet.)

Alar expanse 26 millim.

Hab. New Orleans. Not seen by me. Is it *P. alba* Say?

4. P. bilineata!

Bætis bilineata Say, Long's Exped. II, 303, 1. *P. limbata* Pictet, Ephem. 146, 3; tab. xii.

Imago ♂. Fulvous, antennæ pale, basal articulation obscurer; head dusky in front, beneath yellow; prothorax compressed in the middle, above triangularly tuberculated, each side with a fuscous stripe; abdomen fulvous, spotted with fuscous; each side with a medial fuscous stripe composed of oblique striæ, margins of the segments fuscous; anterior feet fuscous, basal articles of the tarsi yellow, posterior feet yellow, unguiculi fuscous; setæ yellowish, long, apex of the articles annulated with fuscous; intermediate seta very short; anal appendages yellow, the apex fuscous; penis two-parted, fuscous, apex incurved, oval; wings hyaline, anterior ones with the costal margin fulvous, veins black, some transverse blackish-banded veins; posterior wings with the apex hardly clouded, transverse discoidal veins banded with blackish-fuscous. Imago ♀. Pale yellow; tarsal unguiculi fuscous; abdomen with a fuscous apical band in the middle and interrupted ones on both sides; wings yellowish-hyaline, costal margin yellowish, longitudinal veins yellowish, transverse ones black.

Subimago ♀. Similar to the imago, the abdomen above obscurer, wings opaque.

Length of body, ♂ 16; ♀ 18. Subimago, ♀ 22 millim. Alar expanse, ♂ 34; ♀ 40. Subimago, ♀ 48 millim. Length of caudal setæ, ♂ 46. Subimago, ♀ 25 millim.

Hab. St. Peters River, "common" (Say); N. Red River (Robt. Kennicott); Maryland (Uhler); Philadelphia; Washington (Osten Sacken); St. Louis. The specimens from Washington are yellower.

5. P. limbata!

Palingenia limbata Serv. Guér. Icon. Regn. Animal. Ins. tab. lx, fig. 7.
Ephemera limbata Ramb. Neuropt. 295, 4. Walker, Catal. 548, 3.
Pal. viridescens Walk.! Catal. 550, 11. Fem. Subimago. *Bætis angulata* Walk.! Catal. 564, 28. Male imago.

♂ Imago. Fulvous, spotted with fuscous; antennæ gray, basal article brownish-black; head dusky in front, beneath yellow; prothorax narrowed in the middle, above triangularly tuberculated, each side with a fuscous stripe confluent upon the disk; abdomen brownish-black, dorsum each side with an interrupted yellow stripe; anterior feet entirely fuscous, posterior ones brownish-yellow, unguiculi fuscous; setæ long, fuscous, the apex of the articles with a very small whitish annulus; intermediate seta very short; anal appendages fuscous; penis two-parted, fuscous, apex unguiculated, recurved; wings subhyaline, anterior ones with the costal margin fuscous; veins black, some transverse ones bounded with black; posterior wings margined exteriorly with fuscous, discoidal transverse veins covered with black.

♂ Subimago. Like the imago, but with the body opaque, grayer, the feet obscurer, the wings opaque gray, the anterior ones hardly colored upon the costal margin, the posterior ones more broadly margined.

♀ Imago. Similar to the male; the whole body paler, more fulvous, setæ and feet paler; the intermediate seta very short; the anterior wings have the costal margin paler.

♀ Subimago. Similar to the imago, the body opaque; brownish-gray, feet and setæ brownish-black, wings opaque gray, the anterior ones with the costal margin of the same color, the posterior ones with a brownish-black margin.

I possess another female subimago, a younger specimen. The body, feet, and setæ are much diluted and pale-colored, the margin of the posterior wings is of the same color, pale. It is hardly different.

Length of body, ♂ 17. ♂ ♀ Subimago, 21. ♀, 29 millim. Alar expanse, ♂ 34. ♂ ♀ Subimago, 42. ♀, 46 millim. Length of setæ, ♂ 42. ♂ ♀ Subimago, 18. ♀, 20 millim.

Hab. New Orleans (Pfeiffer); Ohio (Schaum); St. Louis; Chicago (Osten Sacken); St. Martin's Falls, Albany River, Hudson's Bay (Barnston); Canada (*id.*)

Male imagines from Chicago seem to differ a little, the colors are much paler, the apex of the penis is incurved, the basal half of the antennæ is black, the setæ yellowish and the apex of the articulations has a fuscous ring. *P. bilineata* from Washington and *P. limbata* from New Orleans certainly are distinct species; the species from Chicago is colored very much like *P. limbata*, but the penis is incurved. *P. bilineata* Say, from N. Red River (determined by Mr. Uhler), is colored more like *P. limbata* from Chicago; Mr. Walker's species require a new examination.

6. P. occulta.
Palingenia occulta Walk.! Catal. 551, 12. ☿ ♀, Imago.

Testaceous; antennæ black, the base testaceous; sides of the mesothorax fuscous; abdomen obscurer, interruptedly bivittated with fuscous; setæ not longer than the body, testaceous, a little hairy; tarsi and anterior feet fuscous; wings subcinereous, veins black, basal ones testaceous; anterior wings yellowish at base, with the costal margin brownish. (From the description of Mr. Walker.)

Length of body 21—25 millim. Alar expanse 41—50 millim. Setæ 19 millim.

Hab. Arctic America, Lakes Winnipeg and Superior (Richardson).

The typical specimens are similar to *P. viridescens*, but smaller, and the posterior wings are scarcely margined exteriorly.

7. P. bicolor.
Palingenia bicolor Walk.! Catal. 552, 15. ♀ Subimago.

Ferruginous; thorax each side below, with a black spot; abdomen fuscous, beneath paler; setæ long, hairy, testaceous; feet yellow, anterior ones brownish testaceous, base of the tarsi whitish; wings cinereous, the margin pilose, the veins black, margined with fuscous.

Length of body 12 millim. Alar expanse 27. Setæ 24 millim.

Hab. St. Martin's Falls, Albany River, Hudson's Bay (Barnston).

8. P. decolorata!
Palingenia decolorata Hagen!

Luteous; head brownish-black, antennæ pale; prothorax narrower anteriorly; anterior feet blackish, posterior ones luteous; mesothorax yellowish-fuscous; abdomen luteous, sides striped with obscure fuscous, setæ luteous, intermediate very short; wings yellowish-hyaline, veins luteous, the subcosta fuscous. (Imago.)

Length of body 16 millim. Alar expanse 30 millim. Setæ 30? millim.

Hab. Mexico; Matamoras, Tamaulipas. Common.

I have seen many specimens, but all of them in alcohol and mutilated, and the colors were probably a little changed.

I have had a large species from New Grenada in alcohol, but the specimen is very much damaged.

BAËTIS Leach.

Abdomen furnished with two setæ; wings four, transverse veins numerous; eyes simple; in the male approximate, large.

1. B. interpunctata!

Baëtis interpunctata Say, Jour. Acad. Philad. VIII, 41, 1. Walker, Catal. 562, 23.

Yellowish white tinged with green; head yellowish, vertex with a lateral black point, front with an arcuated black line; ocelli with a black ring around each, apex of the antennæ black; prothorax with a black line each side: mesothorax tinged with brown; feet greenish, the four anterior femora with a black ring upon the middle and apex, apex of the posterior ones fuscous; abdomen with the apex ferruginous, the posterior margin of the dorsal segments black; setæ pale; wings hyaline, the anterior margin greenish, the transverse veins black, an abbreviated, submarginal, medial black line. Imago and subimago, male and female.

Length of body 8 millim. Alar exanse 18—26 millim. Setæ ♂ 20, ♀ 14.

Hab. Indiana (Say); Washington, Trenton Falls (Osten Sacken); Chicago, Alleghany Mountains, Va. (Osten Sacken).

2. B. flaveola!

Baëtis flaveola Pict. Ephem. 186, 12, tab. xxiii, fig. 4. Walker! Catal. 559, 12.

Yellow, eyes black; wings yellowish-hyaline, transverse veins black; posterior femora with a black point; abdominal segments margined with black; setæ yellowish. (From the figure and description of Pictet. (Female imago.)

Length of body 8 millim. Alar expanse 22 millim. Setæ 9 millim.

Hab. Tennessee (Pœppig, Museum of Vienna); St. Martin's Falls, Albany River, Hudson's Bay (Barnston).

I have seen a specimen (♀ Imago) from the Vienna Museum; it may be the one described by Pictet (although the setæ are longer, 14 millim.). As that female pertains, undoubtedly, to *B. interpunctata*, probably, therefore, *B. flaveola* is nothing but a female *B. interpunctata* Say. On account of a slight fold in the anterior margin of the wings the submarginal line is seen with difficulty.

I have seen a mutilated, smaller, female subimago from Tennessee (with the wings expanding 18 millim.), which may be a distinct species.

3. B. obesa.

Baëtis obesa Say. Journ. Acad. Philad. VIII, 43, 4. Walk. Catal. 563, 26.

Subimago. Black, livid; wings brownish-black, with many small, transverse hyaline spots or abbreviated lines, a large, hyaline, oblique semifascia about the middle on the anal margin; posterior ones, with many transverse, abbreviated, hyaline lines not attaining to the apical margin; feet pale yellow, incisures of the tarsi black; abdominal segments margined with rufous; setæ very short, pilose, annulated with black. (From Say's description.)

Length of body 8 millim.

Hab. Indiana (Say).

4. B. fusca!

Baëtis fusca Walker! Catal. 568, 38.

Imago ♂ ♀. Piceous, beneath ferruginous; antennæ black; abdomen ferruginous, beneath fulvous; setæ testaceous, subannulated with fuscous, three times the length of the body; feet testaceous, the anterior ones fuscous; wings hyaline, anterior ones with the costal margin at the apex fuscous. (From Mr. Walker's description.)

Length of body 8 millim. Alar expanse 20 millim. Setæ 25 millim.

Hab. St. Martin's Falls, Albany River, Hudson's Bay (Barnston).

I saw the specimen in London, and noted at that time that it was closely allied to *B. flaveola*; the specimen from Nova Scotia belongs to *P. concinnus* Walk. Perhaps a male imago, from Washington (Osten Sacken), and one from Chicago, belongs here.

5. B. debilis.

Baëtis debilis Walker, Catal. 569, 39.

Ferruginous; abdomen obscurer; setæ testaceous, much longer than the body; feet pale testaceous; wings subhyaline, veins testaceous. ♀. (From the description of Mr. Walker.)

Length of body 6 millim. Alar expanse 17. Length of setæ 8 millim.

Hab. Nova Scotia (Redman).

6. B. arida.

Baëtis arida Say, Jour. Acad. Philad. VIII, 42, 2. Walk. Catal. 562, 24.

Reddish-brown; head whitish, varied with ferruginous, vertex each side, with a small black point; eyes rufous, with a whitish vitta; incisures of the abdomen much obscurer; setæ and posterior feet greenish-white; wings immaculate. (From the description of Say.)

Length of body 10 millim.

Hab. Indiana (Say). A female imago, from Washington, may belong here; the specimen is mutilated.

7. B. verticis!

Baëtis verticis Say, Jour. Acad. Philad. VIII, 42, 3. Walk. Catal. 562, 25.

Yellowish-white; vertex ferruginous; thorax with two ferruginous vittæ, which are confluent anteriorly, but obsolete posteriorly; setæ a little longer than the body, the incisures black; feet whitish, anterior femora at the apex ferruginous, apex of the anterior tibiæ and incisures of the tarsi fuscous; wings hyaline, veins exclusive of the marginal ones, black. (From the description of Say.) ♂ Imago.

Length of body 8 millim. Alar expanse 21 millim. Setæ 24 millim.

Hab. Indiana (Say); Maryland (Uhler).

Two specimens from Maryland agree with the description, except in the color of the veins of the wings; the marginal ones are black, or rather fuscous. Is the description good? It should be observed that the species of *Baëtis* are very difficult to separate, and perhaps some species heretofore described may be only synonyms of others. A further acquaintance is necessary. A male and female from Dalton, Georgia (Osten Sacken), and Washington (*id.*)

are possessed by me, perhaps the true *B. verticis:* is it not *B. flaveola* Pict.?

8. B. canadensis!

Baëtis canadensis Walk. Catal. 569, 40.

Testaceous; vertex and disk of the thorax ferruginous; abdomen with the margins of the segments piceous; feet pale, femora fuscous, incisures of the tarsi black; wings hyaline, costal margin at the apex fuscous, veins black. (From Mr. Walker's description.)

Length of body 6 millim. Alar expanse 16 millim.

Hab. Canada (Barnston); Trenton Falls (Osten Sacken).

I have seen mutilated male and female imagines from Trenton Falls; are they the true *B. canadensis* Walker? A larger female, expanding 30 millimetres, is pale yellow, wings hyaline, veins yellow; the head and abdomen are wanting. In London I noted nothing about Mr. Walker's species, except that it was "allied to *B. flaveola;*" the variety there described is perhaps a female.

9. B. ignava.

Baëtis ignava Hagen. *Baëtis?* subimago, Walk. Catal. 571, 45.

Rufous; eyes broad, very prominent; thorax rufous; abdomen pale, reddish-gray; setæ thick; feet rufous; wings gray, opaque, the anterior ones narrow at base, veins bordered with fuscous.

Alar expanse about 25 millim.

Hab. Newfoundland.

Certainly a female subimago: the species is very doubtful; Walker assigns Madrid as the locality. I found the typical specimen labelled Newfoundland.

10. B. fuscata.

Baëtis fuscata Walk. Catal. 570, 41.

♀ Imago. Piceous, beneath ferruginous; antennæ black; sides of the thorax spotted with yellow; feet ferruginous, anterior ones piceous; wings hyaline, veins pale.

♀ Subimago. Obscure testaceous, setæ much paler, longer than the body; wings gray, opaque. (From Mr. Walker's description.)

Length of body 4—5 millim. Alar expanse 12—16 millim.

Hab. St. Martin's Falls, Albany River, Hudson's Bay (Barnston).

11. B. invaria.

Baëtis invaria Walk. Catal. 568, 37.

♂ Imago. Pale ferruginous, beneath fulvous; antennæ black, at base ferruginous; feet testaceous; wings hyaline, transverse veins pale-whitish. (From Mr. Walker's description.)

Length of body 5—6 millim. Alar expanse 14—18 millim.

Hab. St. Martin's Falls, Albany River, Hudson's Bay (Barnston). Perhaps the male of the preceding species?

12. B. annulata.

Baëtis annulata Walk. Catal. 567, 34.

♂ Imago. Ferruginous, beneath testaceous; antennæ fuscous, base ferruginous; thorax with two testaceous stripes; abdominal segments with a testaceous, triangular spot each side; setæ whitish, the incisures black; feet whitish, banded with black; wings hyaline, veins black. (From Mr. Walker's description.)

Length of body 10 millim. Alar expanse 26 millim.

Hab. Trenton Falls, New York.

The mutilated specimens from Trenton Falls, cited under *B. canadensis*, may belong here, only they are of smaller size.

13. B. vicaria!

Baëtis vicaria Walk. Catal. 565, 30.

Imago. Ferruginous; antennæ black; sides of the thorax marked with yellow; segments of the abdomen banded with fuscous; setæ pale testaceous, subannulated, more than twice the length of the body; feet testaceous, femora with two black bands, anterior feet obscurer, wings hyaline, anterior ones with the costal and discoidal veins brownish-black, costal margin at the apex dusky, obscurer farther in. Imago and subimago, male and female.

Length of body 12 millim. Alar expanse 30 millim. Setæ 20—30 millim.

Hab. St. Lawrence River; Chicago; Washington; Savannah (Osten Sacken). Is it distinct from *B. canadensis*?

14. B. femorata.

Baëtis femorata Say, Godman's West. Quart. Rep. II, 162, 1.

♂. Fuscous, abdomen beneath whitish, setæ double the length of the body; femora with a middle and apical reddish-brown band;

wings snowy hyaline, veins clouded with fuscous, especially the basal, discoidal and apical ones.

♀ Fuscous, thorax yellowish, venter whitish; feet pale fuscous, a reddish-brown band upon the middle and apex; setæ nearly the same length as with the male; wings whitish, veins fuscous, clouded with fuscous. (From Say's description.)

Length of body 12 millim. Setæ 24 millim.

Hab. Cincinnati, Ohio (Say). Not common. Similar to the preceding species; it may be the same or *B. annulata.*

15. B. alternata!

Baëtis alternata Say, Long's Expedition II, 304, 2.

Fuscous; head in front and at sides whitish; thorax pale fuscous, in front yellowish, sides varied with yellow; feet pale ochraceous, an apical fuscous ring upon the femora; abdomen above fuscous, segments at base whitish, the two last with two whitish lines; venter whitish, each segment with two oblique lines and two intermediate points black; setæ whitish, regularly pointed with fuscous; wings hyaline, veins not margined. (From Say's description.)

Length of body 12 millim.

Hab. Northwest Territory (Say).

I would believe that a male imago and subimago and a female subimago from Maryland, communicated by Mr. Uhler, belong here, but the femora have a medial and apical band.

The ♂ subimago is paler; wings gray, opaque, veins a little clouded with fuscous. ♀ subimago obscurer, feet uniform fuscous; wings blackish-fuscous, posterior ones yellowish at base, veins not clouded.

Length of body 12 millim. Alar expanse 30 millim. Setæ ♂ 27 millim. Male and female, subimago, setæ 15 millim.

I saw subimagines like the female, from Washington (Osten Sacken).

16. B. luridipennis.

Baëtis luridipennis Burm. II, 801, 7. Pict. Ephem. 192. Walker Catal. 563, 27.

Fuscous; abdomen banded; wings lurid, veined with fuscous (Burm.) ♀ and subimago fulvous; antennæ fuscous; margins of the abdominal segments fuscous; setæ whitish, covered with short pile, a little longer than the body; feet whitish, femora with a medial and apical fuscous band; wings hyaline, veins fulvous; anterior ones with the apex of the costal margin fulvescent.

Length of body 8 millim. Alar expanse 24 millim. Setæ 24 millim.

Hab. North America (Zimmerman); St. Martin's Falls (Barnston).

The specimens described by Mr. Walker are a female and subimago, not males as Walker contends, and, perhaps, belong to a different species; Burmeister's species is perhaps a subimago, and it may be of the preceding species.

17. B. basalis.

Baëtis basalis Walk. Catal. 565, 31.

Pitch-black; antennæ whitish; abdominal segments margined with testaceous; setæ whitish, the incisures annulated with black, twice as long as the abdomen; anterior wings hyaline, the costal veins clouded with fuscous, a middle marginal fuscous nebula; posterior wings fuscous, their apex hyaline. (From Walker's description.)

Length of body 12 millim. Alar expanse 28 millim. Setæ 22 millim.

Hab. Lake Winnipeg (Richardson). Is it not *B. luridipennis?*

18. B. noveboracana.

Ephemera noveboracana Lichtenstein, Catal. Mus. Holthuisen 1796, III, 193, 52.

Bisetous; wings fuscescent, the hind ones smallest; the abdomen fuscous, margined with luteous. (From the description of Lichtenstein.)

Hab. New York. Is it not *B. luridipennis?*

19. B. tessellata!

Baëtis tessellata Hagen!

Luteous; mesothorax each side with a fuscous line; abdomen, upon the segments, superiorly each side, with two fuscous triangular spots; setæ —? feet luteous, tarsi at the apex fuscous; wings opaque, gray, ciliated, veins lurid, many quadrangular, hyaline spots, posterior wings very small. Female, subimago.

Length of body 16 millim. Alar expanse 26 millim.

Hab. Puget Sound, Washington Territory.

I have examined one specimen, in alcohol.

I saw a species of *Baëtis* from Mexico (in the Berlin Museum), but the only specimen, a female, was very much mutilated.

POTAMANTHUS Pictet.

Three setæ; wings four, transverse veins numerous; eyes, in the male, double, large, approximate.

1. P. cupidus.

Ephemera cupida Say, Godman's West. Quart. Rep. II, 163, 1.

♂ Black; thorax blackish-gray, a broad dorsal stripe and each side an impressed line black; eyes large fuscous; abdomen black, the segments having the posterior margin pale, a dorsal line and each side an oblique obsolete line, whitish; setæ longer than the body; feet pale fuscous, tarsi black, anterior feet black; wings obscure, posterior ones palê, at tip obscurer.

♀ Like the male, but the eyes are small, remote; the abdomen black, ventral incisures pale; setæ a little longer than the body.

Length of body, ♂ 11, ♀ 8 millim. Length of setæ, ♂ 5, ♀ 10 millim.

Hab. Cincinnati, Ohio; 15th of May. Common (Say).

The form of the eyes demonstrates Mr. Say to have wrongly determined the sexes; therefore I have changed his female to male and his male to female. It will be observed that the length of the setæ given by Mr. Say disagrees with his description.

2. P. concinnus!

Palingenia concinna Walk.! Catal. 553, 17. (♂ Imago.) *Palingenia pallipes* Walk.! Catal. 553, 16. (♀ Imago and subimago.) *Baëtis tessellata* Walk.! Catal. 566, 32. (♀ Subimago.)

♂ Imago. Pitchy black; beneath partly ferruginous; antennæ black; setæ double the length of the body; intermediate one much shorter, luteous, incisures black; feet luteous, tarsi fuscous, anterior feet entirely piceous; wings hyaline, veins luteous, the apical veins much obscurer; costal margin of the anterior wings fuscous at the apex.

♀ Imago. Obscure ferruginous, beneath paler; disk of the

head piceous, antennæ black; sides of the thorax spotted with fulvous; setæ a little longer than the body; intermediate one shorter, luteous, incisures obscurer; feet luteous, anterior ones ferruginous; wings hyaline, veins fuscous, costal margin of the anterior ones lurid at the apex.

♀ Subimago. Whitish-testaceous, marked with fuscous; antennæ fuscous, testaceous at base; abdomen fuscous above; setæ testaceous, almost double the length of the abdomen; feet testaceous, femora banded with black, tarsi fuscous; wings subcinereous, opaque, veins testaceous, clouded with fuscous. (From Mr. Walker's description.)

Length of body 10 millim. Alar expanse 22—28 millim. Setæ, ♂ 27, ♀ 14 millim.

Hab. Nova Scotia (Redman); Washington, April (Osten Sacken).

Although I have examined the specimens described by Mr. Walker, the length of the setæ in the description of *B. tessellata* strikes me now as doubtful, as they should be shorter than those of the imagines.

3. P. nebulosus.

Palingenia nebulosa Walk.! Catal. 554, 18.

♂ Imago. Black; abdomen piceous, beneath fulvous; setæ testaceous, banded with fuscous; more than double the length of the body, intermediate one shorter; feet fulvous, anterior ones much obscurer; wings hyaline, veins fuscous, the anterior wings with a broad, longitudinal, fuscous band. (From Mr. Walker's description.)

Length of body 9 millim. Alar expanse 18 millim. Length of setæ 24 millim.

Hab. St. Martin's Falls, Albany River, Hudson's Bay (Barnston).

CLOË Leach.

Two setæ; four wings (sometimes the posterior ones are wanting), transverse veins few; eyes, in the males, double, large, approximate.

1. C. bioculata.

Cloëon bioculata Walk. Catal. 572, 1. (Complete synonymy.)

Eyes of the male obscure; mesothorax yellow; base and apex of the abdomen obscure; wings hyaline. (From Mr. Walker's description.)

Length of body 8 millim. Alar expanse 18 millim. Length of setæ 11—15 millim.

Hab. St. Martin's Falls, Albany River, Hudson's Bay (Barnston), Europe.

Further comparison will be necessary to show whether this be really the European species.

2. C. undata!

Cloë undata Pict. Ephem. 264, 10; tab. xli, fig. 6. Walk. Catal. 575, 10.

Pale luteous; feet yellowish, apex of the tarsi obscurer; setæ whitish, annulated with black; wings hyaline, anterior ones with the costal margin fuscous, marked with round, hyaline spots; clouded with fuscous upon the disk and posterior margin. ♂ Imago.

Length of body 7 millim. Alar expanse 15—19 millim. Setæ 10 millim.

Hab. Mexico; Cuba (Pictet); New York (Calverly).

I have seen but a single very much mutilated specimen.

3. C. mollis.

Cloë mollis Asa Fitch in de Selys Longchamp's collection.

Hab. United States. Unknown to me.

4. C. posticata.

Cloëon posticata Say, Godman's Western Quart. Rep. II, 162, 1.

♂ Imago. Greenish-white; eyes reddish-brown; thorax black, opaque; abdomen greenish-blue-hyaline, three apical segments fuscous; setæ long, white; feet white, anterior ones obscure at base; wings hyaline. (From Say's description.)

Length 8 millim. Length of setæ 19 millim.

Hab. Shippingsport, 21st May. Common (Say).

5. C. unicolor!

Cloë unicolor Hagen!

Entirely brassy-brownish; feet pale luteous; setæ white; wings hyaline. ♀ Imago.

Length of body 4 millim. Alar expanse 10 millim. Setæ 10 millim.

Hab. Washington (Osten Sacken). I have seen a female specimen from Porto-Rico, similar to this, with the thorax fulvo-aeneous: is it a different species?

6. C. pygmaea!

Cloë pygmaea Hagen!

Body brownish-gray; feet and setæ white; wings hyaline. ♀ Imago.

Length of body 3 millim. Alar expanse 6 millim.

Hab. St. Lawrence River, Canada (Osten Sacken).

7. C. vicina!

Cloë vicina Hagen!

Whitish-hyaline; thorax fulvous; eyes rufous; abdomen with the three apical segments fuscous above; setæ whitish; feet whitish, anterior ones fulvous at the base; wings hyaline. Male Imago.

Body yellowish-white; setæ and feet whitish; wings hyaline. Female Imago.

Length of body 4 millim. Alar expanse 10 millim. Length of setæ, ♂ 10, ♀ 6 millim.

Hab. Washington (Osten Sacken).

Schiœdte, Berlin Ent. Zeit. J. III, p. 143, reports *Ephemera culiciformis* Linn., from Greenland; I have not seen the specimens.

CAENIS Stephens.

Setæ three; wings two, transverse veins few; eyes in the male very simple, remote.

1. C. hilaris.

Ephemera hilaris Say, Jour. Acad. Philad. VIII, 43. Walk. Catal. 583, 13.

Small, whitish; eyes black; thorax pale fulvous, beneath and sides with abbreviated obscure lines; apex of the abdomen, each side, with three fuscous points; setæ long; wings whitish, the costal margin obscure. (From Say's description.)

Length of body 3 millim.

Hab. Indiana, 4th September (Say).

2. C. diminuta.

Caenis diminuta Walk.! Catal. 584, 14.

Fulvous; abdomen pale testaceous, setæ long, white; feet white, anterior ones banded twice or thrice with black; wings whitish, veins white, the costal margin blackish. Male. (From Mr. Walker's description.)

Length of body 3 millim. Alar expanse 6 millim. Length of setæ 12 millim.

Hab. St. John's Bluff, E. Florida (Doubleday).

This species is allied to *C. lactea* of Europe.

3. C. amica!

Caenis amica Hagen!

Head and prothorax fulvous, banded with black; antennæ whitish; mesothorax brassy-fulvous; feet whitish, anterior ones much longer, cinereous, the femora obscurer, posterior femora with a spot above upon the apex, black; abdomen pallid, varied with gray upon the back, segments with the apex and sides marked with black; setæ white; wings opaque, whitish-gray, the two costal veins black. (Male Imago.)

A male, taken at the same place, differs in its colors; the head is yellow banded with black; the thorax yellow; the feet white; the anterior femora and tibiæ have the apex gray; the abdomen is whitish-yellow. ♂ Imago. It may be a distinct species.

Length 2 millim. Alar expanse 4 millim. Length of setæ 6 millim.

Hab. Pennsylvania (Zimmerman, Berlin Museum).

Is it *C. hilaris?* Say?—he describes the eyes as double: are they really so? The genus *Caenis* has the eyes simple; nevertheless the description best suits *Ephemera hilaris* Say.

Fam. V. ODONATA.

Antennæ short, setiform; mouth not furnished with palpi; wings flat, reticulated; tarsi with three articles; second ventral segment of the male furnished with accessory genital organs; abdomen with anal appendages; body elongated, narrow.

Tribe I. AGRIONINA.

Antennæ four-jointed; eyes distant; wings equal; abdomen cylindrical, slender; accessory genital organs, with the anterior hook connate, penis and vesicle separated; genital organs of the female vaginate.

Sub-Fam. I. CALOPTERYGINA.

Antecubital veins numerous.

CALOPTERYX Leach.

Wings very broad, densely reticulated, pterostigma absent in the males, that of the female irregular, areolate; basal space with no transverse veins; anal appendages of the male forcipate.

1. C. angustipennis!

Sylphis angustipennis Selys! (☿) Synops. Calopt. 9, 2. Monog. Calopt. 21, 2. Walker, Catal. 590, 2. *Sylphis elegans* Hag.! ♀. Synops. Calopt. 9, 1. Monog. Calopt. 20, 1. Walker Catal. 590, 1.

Brassy-green, shining; labrum and base of the antennæ yellowish; occiput with two acute tubercles; feet very long, with short cilia; abdomen long, slender, sides and venter rufescent (♀); wings narrow, long, hyaline, somewhat flavescent (♀), veins brassy-green; thorax rufescent, a dorsal green stripe, and a lateral, divided, broader blue one. (Female.) Thirty antecubital cross-nervules. No pterostigma.

Length of body, ♂ 67, ♀ 57 millim. Alar expanse 84 millim.

Hab. Georgia (Abbot); ♂. Collection of Dr. Hagen; locality unknown. ♀.

2. C. apicalis!

Calopteryx apicalis Burm.! Handbuch. II, 827, 8. Selys Synops. Calopt.! 9, 3. Monog. Calopt. 23, 3. Walk. Catal. 591, 3.

Brassy-green, shining; labium, antennæ, thoracic sutures and pectus black, or in part flavescent (♀); feet long, black, with long cilia; wings narrow, hyaline, or with the apex narrowly fuscous. (Male.) Twenty antecubitals. Pterostigma absent.

Length of body 42 millim. Alar expanse 62 millim.

Hab. Philadelphia; Massachusetts (Scudder).

3. C. dimidiata!

Calopteryx dimidiata Burm.! Handb. II, 826, 16. Selys! Synops. Calopt. 10, 4. Monog. Calopt. 25, 4. Walk. Catal. 591, 4.—*Calopteryx cognata* Ramb.! Neuropt. 222, 6.—*C. syriaca* Ramb.! Neuropt. 223, 9. (In part. Male.)

Brassy-green or blue, shining; labium, antennæ, thoracic sutures, pectus, venter, and feet black; wings narrow, somewhat flavescent, the apex fuscous; pterostigma of the female snow-white. Male 30 antecubitals; female 20 antecubitals.

Length of body 40—45 millim. Alar expanse 54—56 millim. Pterostigma 1¼ millim.

Hab. Kentucky; Georgia; Pilatka, St. John's River, Florida (Osten Sacken).

4. C. maculata!

Agrion maculata Beauv. 85; tab. vii, fig. 3.—*Calopteryx maculata* Burm.! Handb. II, 829, 17. Selys! Synopt. Calopt. 10, 5 Selys! Monog. Calopt. 27, 5. Walk. Catal. 592, 5.—*Calopteryx holosericeus* Burm.! Handb. II, 828, 13. Ramb. Neuropt. 226, 14.—*Calopteryx papilionacea* Ramb.! Neuropt. 222, 6.—*Calopt. opaca* Say, Jour. Acad. Philad. VIII, 32, 2.

Brassy-green or blue, shining; labium, antennæ, thoracic sutures, pectus, venter and feet black; abdomen with a dorsal yellow stripe upon the 8th to the 10th segment (♀); wings very broad, densely reticulated, black, sometimes with hyaline spots (♂), or clouded with fuscous and fuscous at the apex, with a snow-white pterostigma (female) 19—28 antecubitals.

Length 38—48 millim. Alar expanse 63—65 millim. Pterostigma 2—2¼ millim.

Hab. Chicago (Osten Sacken); Maryland (Uhler); Washington; Trenton Falls (Osten Sacken); Philadelphia; Massachusetts; Dalton, Georgia (Osten Sacken); Carolina; Ohio; Pilatka, Florida (Osten Sacken).

A species common all over the Union.

5. C. virginica!

Calopteryx virginica Drury ed. Westw. I, 118; tab. xlviii, fig. 2. Selys! Synops. Calopt. 11, 6. Selys! Monog. Calopt. 29, 6. Walker Catal. 592, 6.—*Libellula virgo* Drury I, 114; tab. xlviii, fig. 2.—*Calopteryx materna* Say, Jour. Acad. Philad. VIII, 32, 1. ♀.—*Calopt. æquabilis* Say, l. c. VIII, 33, 2.—*Calopt. dimidiata* Ramb. Neuropt. 223, 5.

Brassy-green, shining; labium, antennæ, thoracic sutures, pectus, venter, and feet black; abdomen with the dorsal stripe, and venter with the segments 8—10 yellow; (♀) wings much narrower than in the foregoing species, hyaline, the base somewhat flavescent, the apex blackish-fuscous; pterostigma ♀ snow-white. 26—31 antecubitals. (From the description of De Selys.)

Length of body 50—52 millim. Alar expanse 70—72. Pterostigma 2 millim.

Hab. Virginia; Georgia; Massachusetts; Hudson's Bay.

6. C. splendens!

Calopteryx splendens Selys! Monog. Calopt. 36. 9. (With the complete synonymy.)

Blue (♂), or green (♀) brassy; base of the antennæ yellow; thorax with the second lateral suture yellow; feet black; abdomen with a dorsal yellow stripe upon the segments 8—10 ♀; wings broad, hyaline, a broad blue-black band ♂, or hyaline, with a snow-white pterostigma ♀.

Length of body 45—49 millim. Alar expanse 62—72 millim. Pterostigma 1—2 millim.

Hab. Georgia (Abbot).

I have seen a male from the collection of Abbot, in the Zurich Museum. Is it really from America?

A species common everywhere in Europe and Northern Asia.

Calopteryx virgo Fab. Fauna Groenland. 196, 152, is perhaps erroneously stated. Fabricius says that he only *saw it* once; but according to Schioedte, Berlin. Ent. Zeit. III, 142, it has not hitherto been discovered there.

HETAERINA Hagen.

Wings rather narrow, densely reticulated; pterostigma absent or very small, quadrangular; basal space reticulated; base of the wings, in the male, sanguineous.

* Pterostigma absent.

1. H. septentrionalis!
Hetaerina septentrionalis Selys! Synops. Calopt. 36, 43. Selys, Monog. Calopt. 119, 43.

Blackish-fuscous; head and thorax brassy, sides partly yellow; feet black; superior appendages of the tail semicircular, the apex, exteriorly dentated; the inferior ones long, cylindrical, at the apex thickened; wings hyaline, sanguineous at base, posterior ones with an apical, sanguineous spot. Male. (From the description of De Selys.)
Hab. Georgia (British Museum).

2. H. californica!
Hetaerina californica Hagen! Addit. Synops. Calopt. 6, 49, bis.

Brownish-black; head and thorax coppery; a humeral line and two lateral stripes, yellow; feet black, femora within and tibiæ without, yellow; abdomen brownish-black; superior caudal appendages a little incurved, a quadrangular tubercle upon the internal middle, and another smaller one at the apex; the inferior appendages much shorter, thickened at the base; wings hyaline, almost the basal half sanguineous, apex of the posterior ones dusky.
Length 44 millim. Alar expanse 60 millim.
Hab. Northern California.

3. H. cruentata!
Calopteryx cruentata Ramb.! Neuropt. 228, 19 ♂. Selys! Synops. Calopt. 39, 48. Selys! Monog. 127, 48; tab. xii, fig. 1. Walk. Catal. 625, 21.

Brownish-black; head coppery, epistoma blue (♂), or rufous (♀); dorsum of the thorax orange, with a medial broad black stripe; the sides orange, with a stripe and cuneiform black spot; feet black, tibiæ, exteriorly, yellow; female with the femora interiorly yellow; abdomen brownish-black; superior appendages forcipated, base interiorly, abruptly dilated, inferior appendages short, flat, truncated; wings sanguineous at base, the apex margined with fuscous (♂), or somewhat yellowish (female). 20—29 antecubital cross-nervules.
Length 42—50 millim. Alar expanse 56—68 millim.
Hab. Mexico; Venezuela; Martinique; Surinam; Brazil.

4. H. vulnerata!

Hetaerina vulnerata Hagen! Synops. Calopt. 40, 49. Selys! Monog. Calopt. 130, 49; tab. xii, fig. 2. Walker Catal. 626, 22.

Brownish-black; head brassy, epistoma black; thorax black, brassy, with a yellow humeral line, sides yellow, a broad stripe and a cuneiform mark, brassy black ($\male$); or orange; dorsum with a middle brassy-green stripe, sides with a narrow stripe and mark, brassy-green; feet black, femora inside and tibiæ outside yellow; abdomen brownish-black, superior appendages black, yellow at base, forcipated, at the internal base dilated; inferior ones short, cylindrical, broader at base; wings hyaline, sanguineous at base ($\male$), or anteriorly and at apex yellowish (female). 17—23 antecubital cross-nervules.

Length 42—50 millim. Alar expanse 60—66 millim.

Hab. Mexico; Columbia; Brazil.

** Pterostigma very small, quadrangular.

5. H. americana!

Agrion americana Fab.! Ent. Syst. Suppl. 287, 3—4.—*Calopteryx americana* Burm.! Handb. II, 826, 4. Ramb. Neuropt. 227, 18.—*Hetaerina americana* Selys! Synopt. Calopt. 41, 50. Selys! Monog. Calopt. 131, 50; tab. xii, fig. 3. Walk. Catal. 627, 23.—*Lestes basalis* Say, Journ. Acad. Philad. VIII, 35, 2.

Fuscous, coppery ($\male$), or green-brassy ($\female$); thorax coppery, the sides with three yellow stripes ($\male$) or green-brassy, the sides with four yellow stripes, feet black, the femora inside and the tibiæ outside yellow; abdomen brassy-fuscous, the female has a dorsal interrupted yellow line; superior appendages yellow, with a black apex, forcipated, interiorly with a double tubercle upon the middle; inferior appendages short, truncated, cylindrical; wings hyaline, sanguineous at base ($\male$), or somewhat yellowish ($\female$); the pterostigma is yellow. 20—24 antecubital cross-nervules.

Length 43—46 millim. Alar expanse 54—62 millim.

Hab. Maryland; Massachusetts; Washington; Missouri; Indiana; Mexico; Brazil.

6. H. basalis!

Hetaerina basalis Hagen! Selys, addit. Synops. Calopt. 6, 50, bis.

Very much like *H. americana*, and perhaps a variety of it; it differs, in the male, by having the basal sanguineous spot larger and exteriorly convex; the superior appendages have the middle tubercle triangular; the female has the yellow abdominal line hardly interrupted, the base of the wings yellowish-fuscous.

Length 43—46 millim. Alar expanse 54—62 millim.

Hab. Pecos River, Western Texas; Mexico; Cordova; Atlihuazan; Portrero (Saussure).

7. H. tricolor!

Calopteryx tricolor Burm.! Handb. II, 827, 7. Selys! Synops. Calopt.—
Hetaerina tricolor, 42, 52. Selys! Monog. Calopt. 136, 52; tab. xii, fig. 5. Walk.! Catal. 629, 25.

Brownish-black; thorax with a humeral yellow stripe; sides yellow, with three brownish-black stripes; feet black, tibiæ exteriorly fuscous; abdomen brownish-black; appendages black, the superior ones forcipated, interiorly bi-excised; inferior ones short, cylindrical, the apex truncated; wings hyaline, anterior ones sanguineous at base, posterior ones fuscous at base, all the wings with a fuscous apical margin; pterostigma black ($\male$), or they are hyaline with the base somewhat yellowish, the pterostigma whitish-yellow (female). 20—24 antecubital cross-nervules.

Length 42—50 millim. Alar expanse 60—64 millim.

Hab. Philadelphia; Georgia.

The variety *H. limbata* Selys, from Georgia, is a little smaller, the apex of the wings is more infuscated.

8. H. titia!

Libellula titia Drury, II, 83; tab. xlv, fig. 3.—*Calopteryx titia* Burm.! Handb. II, 826, 3.—*Hetaerina titia* Selys! Synops. Calopt. 43, 53. Selys! Monog. Calopt. 138, 53. Walk. Catal. 630, 26.

Black; head, thorax, feet and abdomen black; superior appendages forcipated, interiorly with a basal tooth and middle dilatation; inferior ones short, cylindrical, obtuse; wings opaque fuscous, upon the middle obliquely hyaline; superior ones sanguineous at base; pterostigma yellow ($\male$), or they are opaque, fuscescent, with the apex of the superiors hyaline, the pterostigma white ($\female$). 19—22 antecubital cross-nervules. (From De Selys' description.)

Length 41—46 millim. Alar expanse 52—60 millim.

Hab. Mexico; Honduras.

9. H. macropus!

Hetaerina macropus Selys! Synops. Calops. 44, 54. Monog. Calopt. 141, 54. Walker, Catal. 631, 27.

Brownish-black; thorax coppery, a humeral yellow stripe, sides black, with three yellow stripes ($\male$); or yellow, dorsum each side with a green-brassy stripe, sides yellow, with two imperfect brassy-green stripes ($\female$); feet long, black; wings hyaline, with a basal fuscous stripe, anterior ones sanguineous at base, posterior ones rosy, with the pterostigma yellow ($\male$), or they are somewhat yellowish, with the pterostigma white ($\female$). 22—24 antecubital cross-nervules.

Length 36—44 millim. Alar expanse 52—54 millim.

Hab. Tampico, Mexico (Saussure); Honduras.

10. H. sempronia!

Hetaerina sempronia Hagen! Synops. Calopt. 45, 56. Selys! Monog. Calopt. 147, 56, tab. xii, fig. 7. Walker, Catal. 632, 29.

Black; head black, labrum and epistoma blue; thorax coppery, a humeral and three lateral lines, yellow; feet black; abdomen black; superior appendages black, forcipated, interiorly a medial dilatation, inferior ones short, with the apex obtuse; wings hyaline, sanguineous at base, posterior ones with an apical fuscous spot; pterostigma black. 27—28 antecubital cross-nervules ($\male$).

Length 46 millim. Alar expanse 58 millim.

Hab. Mexico (Deppe).

Sub-Fam. II. AGRIONINA.

Two antecubital transverse veins; wings petiolated.

Legion I. PSEUDOSTIGMATA.

Pterostigma irregular, areolate.

MEGALOPREPUS Rambur.

Wings broad, rounded, posterior margin densely reticulated, with many incurved branches; areoles pentagonal, the first sector of the triangle forked at apex; quadrangular space oblong.

1. M. caerulatus!
Libellula caerulata Drury, III, 75, tab. 1, fig. 1. *Megaloprepus caerulatus* Ramb.! Neuropt. 290, 1. *Libellula coerulea* Donovan, Nat. Reposit. iv, 110.

Black, beneath pale; thorax with a humeral line, and two inferiorly lateral stripes, pale yellow; feet black, femora inside and tibiæ outside pale yellow; wings broad, hyaline, before the apex a broad blue-black, transverse band, exteriorly, broadly margined with milk-white and emarginated; pterostigma large, oblong, black.

Length 90—115 millim. Alar expanse 115—180 millim.

Hab. Mexico (Saussure); Vera Cruz (Sallé); Guatimala; Choco, New Grenada (Schott); Honduras; Bogota, Columbia.

As yet, this is the most gigantic of the Odonata.

The variety *M. brevistigma* De Selys, from Bogota, differs in being of a smaller size, the pterostigma small and the band of the wings narrower.

PSEUDOSTIGMA De Selys.

Wings narrow, the reticulation of the posterior margin of the wings simple, the areoles tetragonal, regular; postcostal space with two series of areoles; pterostigma irregular; abdomen extremely long.

1. P. accedens!
Pseudostigma accedens Selys!

Black, brassy, beneath yellow; head black, each side in front slightly tinged with yellow; prothorax straight posteriorly, thorax, with the dorsum black, a yellow humeral stripe, broadly divided, sides yellow, with a broad black stripe above; pectus with a fuscous stripe; feet black, femora at base and beneath, and tibiæ extremely yellowish; abdomen black, with a steel blue reflection, the last segment having the apical half yellow; appendages black, the superior ones broad, incurved, interiorly excavated, the apex obliquely truncated; the inferior ones very small, acute; margin of the valves (♀) entire; wings hyaline, apex of the posterior ones entire, pterostigma black, quadrangular, of the posterior wings triangular (♂), apex of the wings with a narrow yellow spot anteriorly, pterostigma absent (♀).

Length 117—124 millim. Alar expanse 126—132 millim.
Hab. Mexico (Saussure); Vera Cruz (Sallé); Columbia.

2. P. aberrans!
Pseudostigma aberrans Selys!

Black, beneath yellow; labrum with a yellow middle spot, front anteriorly yellow, banded with black, and transverse; prothorax broadly emarginate posteriorly; thorax black, a humeral yellow, hardly cleft, line; sides with a black stripe; pectus with a black stripe in the middle; feet black, tibiæ exteriorly yellow; abdomen black, beneath yellow; margin of the valves (♀) dentated; wings hyaline, with a large, oval, apical spot; pterostigma absent (♀).

Length 112 millim. Alar expanse 131 millim.
Hab. Vera Cruz, Mexico (Sallé).

MECISTOGASTER Rambur.

Wings narrow; reticulation of the posterior margin simple; postcostal space having a single series of areoles; pterostigma irregular; abdomen extremely long.

1. M. modestus!
Mecistogastur modestus Selys!

Black, beneath yellowish; labrum yellow, banded with black; front yellow anteriorly; prothorax rounded posteriorly; thorax black, a humeral broad, yellow, obliquely divided stripe; sides with a black, oblique, entire stripe; feet black, femora exteriorly and base of the tibiæ yellowish; wings hyaline, pterostigma oblong, black, in younger individuals it is whitish (♂).

Length 84 millim. Alar expanse 84—91 millim.
Hab. Mexico (Saussure).

2. M. ornatus!
Mecistogaster ornatus Rambur! Neuropt. 288, 12.

Brassy-fuscous, beneath yellowish; head orange in front, base of the antennæ orange; prothorax rounded posteriorly; thorax brassy fuscous, a humeral divided stripe, a lateral stripe and a short mark near the wings, interrupted, yellow; pectus with a middle black stripe; feet fuscous, tibiæ exteriorly yellowish; abdominal appendages forcipated, yellow, at the apex black; wings orange at the apex, margined interiorly with fuscous, the posterior ones whitish beneath the apex.

Length 87—102 millim. Alar expanse 97—116 millim.

Hab. Vera Cruz, Mexico (Sallé); Caracas, Venezuela; Surinam; Lima.

I possess a variety from Venezuela which has the apex of the wings green, beneath black (♂).

3. **M. lucretia!**

Libellula lucretia Drury, II, tab. xlviii, fig. 1. Sulze, Geschichte der Insect. tab. xxiv, fig. 4.—*Agrion lucretia* Burm.! II, 818, 1.—*Agrion amalia* Burm.! Handb. II, 818, 3.—*Agrion tullia* Burm.! II, 818, 2.—*Mecistogaster lucretia* Ramb. Neuropt. 286, 7.—*Mecist. linearis* Ramb.! Neuropt. 282, 1 (♂).—*Mecist. virgatus* Ramb.! Neuropt. 284, 4 (♂ young).—*Mecist. filiformis* Ramb.! Neuropt. 285, 6 (♀).—*Mecist. leucostigma* Ramb.! Neuropt. 286, 8 (♀).

Brassy-black, beneath yellowish; head brassy-black above, a rufous stripe, each side at the ocelli; prothorax with two large rufous spots upon the posterior lobe; thorax, each side, with two approximated yellow lines; sides yellow, with a broad fuscous stripe; pectus yellow, a fuscous stripe upon the middle; feet brownish black, tibiæ exteriorly greenish-yellow; abdomen extremely long brassy-black, the three last segments yellow at sides, the apex of the last one yellow, excised; superior appendages livid, bent into a right angle, the apex subbifid, and interiorly a basal tooth; wings hyaline, posterior ones of the male having the apex dilated *in front*, rounded; pterostigma black, triangular:— in the younger ones pallid;·*females*, pterostigma black, oblong, the apex of the wings subfuscous; the younger ones are yellow, with the apex of the wings milky-white.

Length 110—112 millim. Alar expanse 120—144 millim.

Hab. St. Domingo; Bahia, Para, Rio, San Paul, Brazil.

Legion II. AGRIONINA.

Two antecubital transverse nervules.

LESTES Leach.

The fourth apical sector broken; the postcostal space simple; the quadrangular space trapezoidal, with the exterior inferior angle acute; the pterostigma large, oblong: appendages in the males forcipated.

1. L. grandis!

Lestes grandis Ramb.! Neuropt. 244, 1.

Brassy-green, mouth reddish-yellow; dorsum of the thorax orange, each side with a brassy-green stripe; sides yellow, superiorly with a broad brassy-green stripe, inferiorly with a fuscous one; feet yellowish, femora exteriorly, tibiæ interiorly and tarsi black; abdomen long, slender, brassy-green, a basal yellow lunule upon each side of the segments; superior appendages of the male long, semicircular, the apex a little thicker, incurved, an interior stout basal tooth, one obtuse one upon the middle, and an ante-apical oblique tubercle upon them; inferior appendages short, obtuse, the apex ciliated: valvules of the female yellow, exteriorly broadly black, the apex dentated; wings hyaline; pterostigma large, broader in the middle, fuscous; sixteen postcubital cross-nervules.

Length 59—50 millim. Alar expanse 72—66 millim. Pterostigma 3 millim.

Hab. Mexico (De Selys;) Columbia, Venezuela (Appun).

2. L. rectangularis!

Lestes rectángularis Say, Jour. Acad. Philad. VIII, 34, 1.

Brassy-fuscous, mouth yellow; dorsum of the thorax brassy-brown, a line upon the middle and each side with a broad stripe, narrowed in front yellow; sides pale yellow, superiorly a brassy-brown stripe and posteriorly with two linear black spots; feet yellow, femora exteriorly, tibiæ and tarsi interiorly black; abdomen long, very slender, yellow, the dorsum fuscous, the apex of the segments black, and with an interrupted, yellow, basal lunule; the apical segments entirely blackish-fuscous; appendages black, the superior ones short, forcipated, the base interiorly dilated, armed with two teeth, the apical one larger, the apex narrow, incurved; inferior appendages long, rather slender, approximated, the apex acute, beneath curved; valvules of the female, with the margin entire; wings hyaline, the costa yellow; pterostigma short, the sides a little oblique, black; ten postcubital cross-nervules.

Length 53—41 millim. Alar expanse 49—41 millim. Pterostigma $1\frac{1}{4}$ millim.

Hab. Chicago (Osten Sacken); Indiana; Mass. (Say); Maryland; Pennsylvania; New Jersey (Uhler); New York (Calverly); Savannah, Georgia; Minnesota (Kennicott).

I have seen two females, very much like this (*L. habilis* mihi from Pennsylvania and Georgia); they have the tarsi yellow, and the margin of the valvules dentated. Is it a distinct species?

3. L. alacer!

Lestes alacer Hagen!

Black; mouth yellowish; dorsum of the thorax black, each side, exteriorly, with a yellowish-green stripe, sides livid, with a broad, fuscous, middle fascia; feet yellow, beneath and tarsi black; femora and tibiæ with an external black line; abdomen slender, black, sides yellow; appendages black, the superior ones forcipated, the base interiorly with a tooth, and upon the middle a rounded lamina; the inferior appendages a little shorter, straight, flat, distant, with the apex truncated; wings hyaline; pterostigma black, narrow, margined with yellow in front; nine postcubital cross-nervules. (Male.)

Length 39 millim. Alar expanse 42 millim. Pterostigma $1\frac{1}{2}$ millim.

Hab. Western Texas, Pecos River (Capt. Pope).

4. L. stulta!

Lestes stulta Hagen!

Black, mouth yellow; dorsum of the thorax black, a line upon the middle, and each side exteriorly a narrow stripe, yellow; sides yellow, with a superior, broad black stripe, which is triangularly dilated at the wings; feet yellow, femora exteriorly, tibiæ interiorly, and tarsi black; wings hyaline, costa somewhat yellow; pterostigma long, fuscous, margined on both sides with yellow; eleven postcubital cross-nervules. (The abdomen is wanting.)

Length —? millim. Alar expanse 52 millim? Pterostigma $1\frac{1}{2}$ millim.

Hab. California.

5. L. congener!

Lestes congener Hagen!

Black, mouth yellow; dorsum of the thorax black-brassy, a line upon the middle and a narrow stripe each side yellow; sides yellow, with a superior, broad black-brassy stripe, which is dilated at the wings; beneath yellow, margined with black; feet yellow, femora exteriorly and tibiæ interiorly black; abdomen slender, black-brassy, with a yellow lunule upon the base of the segments; superior appendages black, yellow at the base, forcipated, with a basal tooth interiorly, and a middle lamina, with the margin serrated; inferior appendages short, approximated, the apex obtuse, recurved; wings hyaline; pterostigma oblong, black; ten postcubital cross-nervules. (Male.)

Length 37 millim. Alar expanse 43 millim. Pterostigma $1\frac{1}{2}$ millim.

Hab. New York; Texas (Friedrich).

6. L. simplex!

Lestes simplex Hagen!

Black, mouth pale; thorax black, dorsum each side with a broad yellow stripe, which is cleft at the wings; sides and beneath black, pruinose; feet yellow, femora exteriorly, tibiæ interiorly, and tarsi black; abdomen slender, black, pruinose at the apex, a basal yellow lunule to the segments; appendages black, superior ones forcipated, with an internal basal tooth, the middle of the inner margin somewhat dilated, serrulated; inferior appendages short, approximated, the apex obtuse, curved underneath; wings hyaline; pterostigma oblong, black; twelve or thirteen postcubital cross-nervules. (Male.)

Length 40 millim. Alar expanse 43 millim. Pterostigma $1\frac{1}{3}$ millim.

Hab. Mexico (Deppe).

Similar to *L. congener*, but the thorax is narrower and the appendages are different.

7. L. forficula!

Lestes forficula Ramb.! Neuropt. 247, 5.

Black, mouth pallid; dorsum of the thorax pale blue, each side with a narrow, brassy-green stripe, margined with black; a middle blue line, also margined with black; sides and beneath black, pruinose; feet yellow, femora bilineated above with black, tibiæ black interiorly, the anterior ones exteriorly lineated with black, tarsi black; abdomen brassy black, with the apex pruinose, the middle segments at base and a lunule at apex, pallid; appendages black, the superior ones forcipated, with a basal internal tooth and an obliquely truncated lamina upon the middle, with the apex serrated; the inferior ones long, narrow, straight, the apex rounded, somewhat broader; wings hyaline, the pterostigma short, oblong, black; eleven postcubital cross-nervules. (Male.)

Length 40 millim. Alar expanse 39 millim. Pterostigma $1\frac{1}{4}$ millim.

Hab. Mexico; Cuba (Gundlach); Brazil.

8. L. vidua!

Lestes vidua Hagen!

Brassy-black, mouth yellow; dorsum of the thorax black-brassy, a middle line and a narrow stripe each side, somewhat interrupted at the wings, and subexcised, of a yellow color; sides yellow, with a broad black stripe superiorly, which is broader at the wings, and two spots inferiorly, also black; beneath yellow, each side with a marginal black spot; feet yellow, femora and tibiæ exteriorly lineated with black, tarsi black; dorsum of the abdomen brassy-black, a basal yellow lunule upon the segments; sides yellow, venter black (appendages destroyed); wings hyaline, pterostigma large, oblong, fuscous, margined with yellow at the sides; ten postcubital cross-nervules.

Length 40? millim. Alar expanse 45 millim. Pterostigma $1\frac{1}{2}$ millim.

Hab. New Orleans (Pfeiffer); Vienna Museum.

It is similar to *L. congener* Hag.

9. L. tenuata.

Lestes tenuata Ramb. Neuropt. 245, 2. Selys, Poey Ins. Cuba, 463.

Obscure bluish-green; thorax obscure whitish, with four greenish-blue stripes, two of them dorsal; feet pale, femora trilineated with black, tibiæ beneath and tarsi black; dorsum of the abdomen bluish-green, the sides pale, a yellow basal lunule upon the segments; superior appendages forcipated, inside at the base with a rounded tooth, behind the middle they are denticulated, and exteriorly dentated, the apex somewhat rounded; the inferior ones short, obtuse, the apex rounded, pilose; wings hyaline, pterostigma black. (From the description of Rambur.)

Length 45 millim. Alar expanse 50 millim.

Hab. The island of Martinique. Similar to *L. forficula*.

10. L. eurina.

Lestes eurinus Say! Journ. Acad. Philad. VIII, 36, 3.

Blue, varied with green and violet; mouth yellow; dorsum of the thorax each side with a yellow stripe, which is cleft and dilated at the wings, the sides yellow; abdomen blue, the segments green at apex; venter black; superior appendages forcipated, beneath bidentated, the inferior appendages short, conical; feet black, the femora beneath and tibiæ exteriorly pallid; wings hyaline, pterostigma black. (From the description of Say.)

Length 47 millim.

Hab. Massachusetts (Harris).

11. L. unguiculata!

Lestes unguiculata Hagen!

Green-brassy; mouth yellow; dorsum of the thorax brassy-brown, a line upon the middle and a narrow stripe each side, yellow; sides yellow pruinose, with a broad, superior brassy-brown stripe, and inferiorly with a black, broad vitta; beneath yellow; feet yellow, femora bilineated with black, tibiæ inside, and tarsi black; dorsum of the abdomen green, the apex brown-brassy, à yellow lunule upon the base of the segments, base and apex of the tergum pruinose, the sides yellow, venter black; superior appendages black, yellow at base, forcipated, with a basal internal tooth, and a middle excised lamina, which is dentated upon the margin; the inferior appendages long, narrow, cruciate, incurved at the apex; wings hyaline, pterostigma oblong, fuscous, the sides margined with yellow; nine or ten postcubital cross-nervules.

In the female, the inferior fascia of the thorax is wanting.

Length 40—30 millim. Alar expanse 43—37 millim. Pterostigma $1\frac{1}{4}$ millim.

Hab. Chicago (Osten Sacken); Bergen Hill, New Jersey (Guex); New York; St. Louis (Engelmann); Wisconsin (Robt. Kennicott).

12. L. hamata!

Lestes hamata Hagen!

Brownish-brassy; mouth yellow; dorsum of the thorax brown-brassy, with a middle line, and each side a broad stripe, narrowed at the wings, yellow; sides yellow, pruinose, with a superior, broad, brown-brassy stripe, and a black spot upon the pectus, beneath yellow; feet yellow, femora exteriorly, tibiæ interiorly and tarsi black; abdomen obscure green-brassy, with a basal yellow lunule to the segments; appendages black, the superior ones forcipated, with a basal, internal tooth, and a lamina with the margin straight and its apex dentated; the inferior appendages long, straight, narrow, flat, the apex rounded; wings hyaline, pterostigma oblong, black, the sides margined with yellow; eleven postcubital cross-nervules.

Length 42—38 millim. Alar expanse 45—43 millim. Pterostigma 1½ millim.

Hab. Bergen Hill, New Jersey (Guex); Florida (Osten Sacken); Chicago (*id.*); Wisconsin (Robt. Kennicott); North Red River (*id.*).

13. L. forcipata?

Lestes forcipata Ramb. Neuropt. 246, 4.

Brassy-green; mouth yellow; dorsum of the thorax green-brassy (♂) or with a middle line and a stripe each side, yellow ♀; sides yellow, with a superior, green-brassy stripe, dilated at the wings, or with an inferior black stripe (♂); feet yellow, femora bilineated with black, tibiæ interiorly and tarsi black; abdomen brassy-green, sides yellow, or at the base and apex pruinose (♂); a basal lunule upon the segments yellow; appendages black, the superior ones forcipated, on the inside bidentated, the intermediate lamina with its margin rather straight, serrated; the inferior appendages long, flat, the apex dilated interiorly, somewhat spoon-shaped; wings hyaline; pterostigma black, margined with yellow at the sides; twelve postcubital cross-nervules.

Length 35 millim. Alar expanse 40 millim. Pterostigma 1½ millim.

Hab. Chicago; Washington (Osten Sacken); Wisconsin (Robt. Kennicott). Extremely like *L. nympha*, of Europe, it seems hardly different from that species. Is this the true *L. forcipata* of Rambur?

PARAPHLEBIA Selys.

Postcostal space furnished with two or three areoles; sectors numerous.

1. P. zoe!

Paraphlebia zoe Selys! Monog. Agrion.

Apex of the wings black.

Hab. Mexico (Collection of De Selys Longchamps).

PALAEMNEMA Selys.

The quadrangular space oblong; the second sector of the triangle almost wanting.

1. P. paulina!

Agrion paulina Drury, II; tab. xlvi, fig. 4.—*Euphaea paulina* Ramb. Neuropt. 231, 5. Oliv. Enc. Method. VII, 572, No. 18.

Reddish-blackish; thorax thick; wings hyaline, fuscous at the apex, at the base having the second and third humeral spaces yellowish-rufescent; pterostigma long, narrow. (Rambur.)

Hab. Honduras. (Collection of De Selys Longchamps.)

TRICHOCNEMIS Selys.

Quadrangular space sub-oblong; pterostigma rhomboidal (cf. Poey, Ins. Cuba, 464.)

1. T. tibialis.

Platycnemis tibialis Ramb. Neuropt. 241, 3.

Azure-blue; thorax in front with three stripes, and a lateral line black-greenish; abdomen above greenish-black, a dorsal interrupted line, the posterior margin of the segments, the last segment and the sides yellowish or blue(?); feet armed with long cilia, yellowish, the anterior femora black, the base interiorly yellow, the anterior tibiæ exteriorly black; the posterior femora black exteriorly, lineated with yellow, tarsi black; wings hyaline; pterostigma rufous. (♀. From the description of Rambur.)

Hab. North America. (Collection of De Selys Longchamps.)

2. T. minuta.

Trichocnemis minuta Selys, Poey Ins. Cuba, 464.

Brassy-brown; mouth, front, a transverse occipital stripe, an antehumeral stripe, the sides of the thorax and the base and sides of the segments of the abdomen, pale reddish; wings hyaline;

pterostigma rhomboidal, fuscous, the interior part obscurer. (From the description of De Selys.)

Length near 27 millim. Alar expanse 32 millim.

Hab. Calisco, Cuba (De Selys).

PROTONEURA Selys.

Quadrangular space oblong; no second sector of the triangle (cf. Poey, Ins. Cuba, p. 470).

1. P. capillaris.

Agrion capillare Ramb. Neuropt. 280, 30.—*Protoneura capillaris* Selys, Poey Ins. Cuba, 471.

Extremely slender; thorax steel-blue, above blackish-violet; abdomen hair-like, violet-black, the third segment extremely long, marked with a large, pale greenish-blue spot; wings long, extremely narrow, hyaline; the pterostigma black, subquadrate. ($\male$. From the description of De Selys.)

Length near 20 millim. Alar expanse 35 millim.

Hab. Cuba. (Collection of De Selys Longchamps.)

2. P. antennata.

Agrion antennata Say, Journ. Acad. Philad. VIII, 39, 3.

$\male$. Obscure bluish-green, somewhat metallic; head green before, mouth yellow, vertex and occiput black, the latter with a glaucous band which is clavate at each end; eyes dark greenish, above blackish; antennæ with the two basal joints thicker than the others, equal in length, the second one cylindrical, the third attenuated at base; dorsum of the thorax with a glaucous stripe each side; feet pale, with a broad black line on the femora and one on the tibiæ, excepting the posterior ones; abdomen with a blue band at the base of the segments, the sides green, venter glaucous, with a black line; wings hyaline; pterostigma rhomboidal. (From Say's description.)

Length near 33 millim.

Hab. Indiana.

A species not seen by me. Say says: "Two basal joints of the antennæ subequal," but from the description and from analogy, I conclude that, not the first and second segments, but the second and third, are equal: the first segment is always very short in the *Agrions*.

The length of the second segment in *Agrion antennata* Say, shows that it does not belong to the genus *Agrion* in its stricter sense. I am not quite sure if it is a *Protoneura*.

AGRION Fab.

The *apical sector* straight; the *postcostal space* simple; the *quadrangular space* trapezoidal, with the exterior, inferior angle acute; the pterostigma small, rhomboidal; abdominal appendages of the males short.

(Nehalennia Selys.)

The abdomen long and very slender; the colors brazen.

1. A. irene!
Agrion irene Hagen!

Bright brassy-green; head yellow in front; the third article of the antennæ annulated with pale; the hind margin of the prothorax broad triangular ♂, or biemarginated ♀; dorsum of the thorax bright brassy-green, the sides yellowish, above brassy-green; feet pale, exteriorly lineated with black; the abdomen slender, brassy-green, the sides and a basal yellow lunule upon the 3—6 segments; segment 8 with an apical spot, 9 with a triangular dorsal one, 10 almost altogether blue ♂, or 9 blue at the sides, and 10 blue at the apex ♀, the tenth segment has the margin excised, dentated; appendages extremely short, the superior ones twoparted, obtuse, the interior branch longer; the inferior appendages are longer, blue, triangularly tuberculated; ♀ apex of the 10th segment cleft; with the appendages obtuse, short, yellow; the eighth segment with no ventral spine; wings hyaline; pterostigma short, rhomboidal, luteous; from nine to eleven postcubital cross-nervules.

Length 25—28 millim. Alar expanse 28—30 millim.

Hab. Chicago and Florida (Osten Sacken); Wisconsin and Illinois (Robt. Kennicott); New Jersey (Uhler); Maine (Packard). A most beautiful species.

2. A. macrogaster.
Agrion macrogaster Selys, Poey Ins. Cuba, 465.

Brassy-brown; dorsum of the prothorax testaceous, the hind

lobe black, emarginated upon the middle; dorsum of the thorax, brown-brassy, each side with a testaceous stripe, sides and beneath pale; feet pale, femora exteriorly black; abdomen extremely slender, brassy-brown, with the incisures pale; wings hyaline, pterostigma rhomboidal, fuscous, interiorly obscurer. ($\male$. From the description of De Selys.)

Length near 46 millim. Alar expanse 43 millim.

Hab. Jamaica (De Selys Longchamps).

(**Ischnura** Charp.)

3. **A. iners!**

Agrion iners Hagen!

Brassy-black, varied with green and blue; head black, occiput each side with a green point $\male$, or a bluish one $\female$; prothorax with the posterior lobe short, broader in the middle, rounded, hardly elevated; dorsum of the thorax brassy-brown, each side with a narrow green stripe; sides green, a line beneath black; feet black; femora and tibiæ interiorly and the tarsi in part green; abdomen brassy-black, the first articulations steel blue, 3—5 with a medially interrupted yellow ring upon the base of each, 8 entirely blue, 9—10 sides blue $\male$ and $\female$; appendages short, the superior ones obtuse, with a process interiorly, beneath; the inferior appendages a little longer, cylindrical, subarcuated; the posterior margin of the last segment elevated in the middle, sub-bifid; the female has an acute ventral spine upon the 8th segment; wings hyaline, pterostigma rhomboidal, luteous, the anterior ones of the male black, with the apex whitish; eight postcubital cross-nervules.

$\female$. Var. *aurantiaca.* Head green in front, with bluish occipital points; dorsum of the thorax orange, a broad brassy-brown stripe upon the middle, the sides dirty green; abdomen brassy-black, the sides dirty green; the first segment orange, the second orange, with a brassy-black apical spot; the third to the fifth with a basal yellow ring which is interrupted in the middle; the following segments are brassy-black; feet pale, with an external fuscous line.

Length 31—34 millims. Alar expanse 31—40 millim.

Hab. New York; Maryland (Uhler); Washington (Osten Sacken); Louisiana (Schaum); Mexico (Deppe); Tampico (Saussure); Cuba (Osten Sacken).

The colors of the living insect were made known to me by Baron Osten Sacken.

4. A. tuberculatum.

Agrion tuberculatum Selys, Poey Ins. Cuba, 467.

Black-brassy; a round blue point upon each side of the occiput; posterior lobe of the prothorax produced in the middle; thorax yellowish-green, in front black-brassy, with two blue stripes; eighth segment of the abdomen blue, the tenth, in the males, tuberculated behind; wings hyaline, pterostigma rhomboidal, fuscous; pterostigma of the male black within. (From the description of De Selys Longchamps.)

Length 35 millim. Alar expanse 37 millim.

Hab. Cuba; Campeachy; Cayenne.

5. A. ramburii !

Agrion ramburii Selys, Poey Ins. Cuba, 468.

Brassy-brown, varied with green and blue; head each side with a green occipital point; prothorax with the posterior lobe small, having a flat tubercle upon the middle, in the female broader; dorsum of the thorax brassy-brown, each side with a narrow green vitta; the sides green, with a medial black stripe at the wings; feet pale exteriorly, lineated with black; abdomen brassy-fuscous, the sides green, segments 3—6 with a yellow, medially interrupted, basal band, segments 8—9 blue, with a black stripe each side; appendages short, superior ones thick, triangular, excavated on the inside; inferior ones acute, unguiculated; the last abdominal segment with the posterior margin elevated in the middle and bifid; wings hyaline, pterostigma small, rhomboidal, in the anterior wings of the male black.

♀ Either thorax reddish-yellow, the dorsum of the thorax with a broad brassy stripe, the whole of the abdominal dorsum brassy-fuscous; or pruinose, black, with the apex of the abdominal segments also black.

Length 25—28 millim. Alar expanse 27—30 millim.

Hab. New York; Washington; Dalton, Georgia (Osten Sacken); Philadelphia; Bergen Hill, New Jersey (Guex.); St. Louis. I have not seen the specimens of De Selys; he notes them to be from Martinique; Campeachy; Yucatan and Vera Cruz; are they different? I formerly called my species *Agrion expertum !*

6. A. positum!

Agrion positum Hagen!

Brassy-fuscous, varied with green; head brassy-fuscous, each side with an occipital point green ($\male$), or blue ($\female$); prothorax with the posterior lobe small, rounded and produced in the middle, dorsum of the thorax brassy-brown, each side anteriorly with a stripe and at the wings a point (forming an ! sign) green, sides yellowish-green, with a black line upon the middle; feet yellowish, the femora, and the tibiæ exteriorly black; abdomen brassy-fuscous, sides yellowish-green, the brassy-fuscous color is dilated before the apex of the segments; the incisures black, the first green; segments 3—7 with a basal yellow lunule; the dorsum of the last segment has, sometimes, a blue pruinose, quadrangular spot, the posterior margin of this segment is elevated in the middle, and bifid; appendages short, yellow, the superior ones tuberculose inflated, a small tooth, exteriorly, upon the middle, the inferior ones flat, recurved, with the apex black, serrated; the tenth segment in the female, with the hind margin yellow, entire; no ventral spine; the appendages short, trigonal, approximated, yellow; wings hyaline, pterostigma small, rhomboidal, fuscous, surrounded with pale. 7—9 postcubital cross-nervules.

Length 24—28 millim. Alar expanse 23—34 millim.

Hab. Savannah, Dalton, Georgia; Washington (Osten Sacken).

The colors of the living insect were made known to me by Baron Osten Sacken. The male (from Dalton) is sometimes smaller, having 5 postcubital cross-nervules; but it can hardly be a distinct species. The adult female is black, pruinose, with the apex of the segments black-brassy.

7. A. hastatum!

Agrion hastata Say, Journ. Acad. Philad. VIII, 38, 2. Sélys! Poey Ins. Cuba, 470 (subg. ANOMALAGRION). *Agrion anomalum* Ramb.! Neuropt. 281, 31. *Agrion venerinotatum* Haldeman, Proc. Acad. Philad. 1844, 55.

Brassy-green, varied with orange and yellow; head brassy-green in front, and an occipital point each side orange; prothorax with the posterior lobe somewhat produced in the middle; dorsum of the thorax brassy-green, each side with a narrow yellow stripe, sides yellow, superiorly brassy-green, inferiorly a black stripe at the wings; feet yellow, apex of the femora with a black stripe exteriorly: abdomen yellow, segments 1—2 dorsum brassy-green, 3 and 6 with a very narrow dorsal spot before the apex, 4 and 5 with a basal acute spot and an apical orbicular one, 7 the dorsum entirely, and the eighth with a quadrangular basal spot brassy-green. (The markings in the younger individuals are very variable; the second segment has the dorsal spot incised each side before the apex, 3 with the dorsal spot interrupted, 7 with the basal spot bifid, 8 and the following ones entirely yellow; sometimes 3—6 have a basal stripe, and the apical spot almost obsolete, and 7—10 yellow.) The tenth segment has a long process upon the middle, which is oblique, cylindrical and bifid at the apex; appendages short, yellow, superior ones broader, incurved, broadly bifid, inferior ones a little longer, unguiculated; wings hyaline, pterostigma of the posterior ones rhomboidal black, of the anterior ones very singular, larger, rufous, surrounded with yellow, and not attaining to the costal margin; seven postcubital cross-nervules.

♀ Head orange, having a broad brassy-green, transverse stripe; posterior lobe of the prothorax produced in the middle; dorsum of the thorax orange, with a broad brassy-green stripe; sometimes a black humeral line; sides yellowish; feet pale yellow; abdomen orange, segment 6, a dorsal line dilated at the apex, 7—9 dorsum brassy-fuscous, 9 having a yellow middle fascia; posterior margin of 10 entire; ventral spine of 8 almost absent; appendages short, trigonal, thick, yellow; wings hyaline, pterostigma of each of the wings regular, yellowish.

Var. ♀. Brassy-black, pruinose, thorax and abdomen with the sides yellow; the feet exteriorly lineated with black.

Length 23—27 millim. Alar expanse 23—30 millim.

Hab. Indiana (Say); Maine (Packard); Mass. (Scudder); Maryland (Uhler); Bergen Hill, New Jersey (Guex.); Savannah, Georgia (Osten Sacken); Louisiana (Schaum); Florida (Osten Sacken, Norton); Pennsylvania (Haldeman); Cuba; Merida; Venezuela. A common species.

The form of the pterostigma in the anterior wings of the male is very singular; no other species of Odonata have the pterostigma so separated from the costal margin.

8. A. capreolus!

Agrion capreolus Hagen!

Brassy-black, head in front, and an occipital point each side green; posterior margin of the prothorax, with the middle lobe small, rounded; dorsum of the thorax black, each side of it a green stripe; sides green, with a small black stripe at the wings; feet pale, exteriorly, in part, lineated with black; abdomen very slender, brassy-black, the sides and a basal annulus upon segments 3—6 yellowish-green; apical half of 8, and 9 entirely blue; a stout process upon the margin of the tenth segment, which is two-horned; appendages short, superior ones black, trigonal, obtuse; inferior ones yellowish, longer, two-parted, the external branch broader, trigonal, the internal branch longer, cylindrical, unguiculated, strongly recurved; wings hyaline; pterostigma small, yellow, in the middle fuscous. Six to eight postcubital cross-nervules. Male.

Length 22 millims. Alar expanse 21 millim.

Hab. Porto Rico, Brazil.

Almost the smallest species known.

9. **A. aduncum!**

Agrion aduncum Hagen!

Black, varied with yellow; head black, in front and an occipital spot which is cuneiform, each side, yellow; posterior margin of the prothorax rounded; dorsum of the thorax luteous, with a broad medial, black stripe; sides luteous; feet luteous, exteriorly lineated with black; abdomen very slender, brassy-black, the sides, and a basal ring, which is excised in the middle, yellow, upon segments 3—8; 9—10 blue (♂), or 9 at the sides and 10 entirely luteous (♀); appendages very short, the superior ones longer, biparted, the external branch cylindrical, obtuse, straight; the internal branch slender, curved downwards; the inferior appendages obtuse, emarginated at the apex; ♀ apex of the tenth segment cleft; the appendages obtuse, luteous; eighth segment with an acute ventral spine; wings hyaline; pterostigma small, rhomboidal, luteous, fuscous in the middle. Nine postcubital cross-nervules.

Length 26 millim. Alar expanse 26 millim.

Hab. Cuba.

10. **A. discolor.**

Agrion discolor Burm.! Handb. II, 819, 8.

Uniformly testaceous, or with the dorsum rosy, or brassy-black; thorax two-striped; pterostigma pale. Female. (From Burmeister's description.)

Length 26 millim.

Hab. South Carolina (Zimmerman); unknown to me; is it not a female *Agrion saucium* Burm. ?

A. dorsale Selys, Poey Ins. Cuba is perhaps different.

11. A. credulum!

Agrion credulum Hagen!

Brassy fuscous; head in front and an occipital point each side blue; posterior lobe of the prothorax short, rounded; dorsum of the thorax brassy fuscous, each side with a blue stripe, sides blue, a line in the middle black; feet black, femora within, base of the tibiæ exteriorly, and apex of the tarsi pale; abdomen brassy fuscous, the sides and a basal ring upon segments 3—6 yellow; segment 8 entirely, 9 base only blue; segment 10 elevated in the middle of the margin, sub-bifid; appendages short, apex of the superior ones arcuated, biparted; the internal branch longer, at the apex obliquely truncated, the external branch conical; the inferior appendages a little longer, unguiculated; wings hyaline, pterostigma of the anterior ones black, exteriorly whitish, of the posterior wings luteous. Eight postcubital cross-nervules. Female similarly colored, pterostigma of all the wings luteous. (The specimen is very much mutilated.)

Var. ♀. Head brassy-green, in front and an occipital point each side orange, posterior lobe of the prothorax short, rounded; thorax orange, dorsum with a middle brassy-green stripe; feet yellowish, exteriorly black; abdomen brassy-green, sides, a ring upon the basal segments and the second segment each side at base orange yellow. (The apex of the abdomen is destroyed.)

Length 30 millim. Alar expanse 29 millim.

Hab. Cuba (Poey); St. Thomas. Allied to *Agrion ramburii*.

12. A. defixum!

Agrion defixum Hagen!

Black; head in front and an occipital point each side green; posterior margin of the prothorax short, rounded; dorsum of the thorax black, each side with a green stripe; sides green, a small stripe at the wings black; feet green, exteriorly black; abdomen black, sides, and a basal annulus upon segments 3—6 green, 8—9 blue, at base a little black; 10 with the margin elevated in the middle, sub-bifid; appendages short, superior ones two-branched, external branch conical, straight, internal branch longer, flat; inferior ones unguiculated, longer, oblique, recurved; wings hyaline; pterostigma of the anterior ones black, exteriorly white; of the posterior wings luteous; seven postcubital cross-nervules.

Length 30 millim. Alar expanse 30 millim.

Hab. Northern California.

13. A. denticolle!

Agrion denticolle Burm. Handb. II, 819, 9.

Black; head anteriorly, and an occipital point each side, blue; margin of the prothorax straight, the middle lobe small, narrow, rounded; dorsum of the thorax brassy-black ($\male$), or each side with a blue stripe ($\female$); sides blue, or with an anterior, superior black spot ($\female$); feet pale, femora and tibiæ partly black, or lineated with black ($\female$); abdomen (eight last segments of the male destroyed) brassy-black, the sides and a basal ring upon 3—6 yellowish, 8 blue, 9 with a large dorsal spot, and the base covered with blue; 10 dorsum medially elevated, plicated, yellow; appendages short, yellow; eighth segment with no ventral spine; wings hyaline; pterostigma luteous; anterior pterostigma of the male black; ten postcubital cross-nervules.

Length 27 millim. Alar expanse 30 millim.

Hab. Moretia, Mexico (Saussure).

14. A. demorsum!

Agrion demorsum Hagen!

Brassy-green; head in front, and an occipital point, blue; posterior margin of the prothorax small, rounded; dorsum of the thorax brassy-green, each side of it a blue stripe; sides blue; feet pale, exteriorly black; abdomen brassy-green, the sides and a basal annulus, on segments 3—6, yellowish, segments 8—9 blue; posterior margin of 10 with a narrow, elevated middle process, the apex bifid; appendages short, superior ones fuscous, two-branched, external branch conical, straight, the internal one longer, flat; inferior appendages yellow, broadly bifid, the branches spreading apart, unguiculated, the apex black; the upper branch longer; wings hyaline; pterostigma luteous, anterior ones of the $\male$ black, exteriorly white; 8—9 postcubital cross-nervules. (The abdomen of the female is partly destroyed.)

Length 27 millim. Alar expanse 30 millim.
Hab. Moretia, Mexico (Saussure).

15. A. verticale.
Agrion verticale Say, Journ. Acad. Philad. VIII, 37, 1.

Obscure blue, somewhat pruinose; head green, each side with a blue occipital spot; thorax blue, dorsum with a middle brassy stripe, and the sides with a black line; feet deep green, femora exteriorly black, tibiæ with an exterior black line; abdomen brassy-green, the incisures pale, segments 9—10 blue; 10 with the posterior middle somewhat elevated, elevation excised ($\male$), or the segments pruinose, black at their apex, with pale incisures ($\female$); venter pale green, with a middle black line; wings hyaline, pterostigma rhomboidal, fuscous. (From the description of Say.)

Length 25 millim.
Hab. Indiana (Say). "Rare. August."
Unknown to me; perhaps it is *A. positum?*

16. A. exsulans!
Agrion exsulans Hagen!

Black; head blue in front ($\male$), or yellowish-green ($\female$); occiput each side with a cuneiform blue spot; hind margin of the prothorax short, rounded, with a small tubercle upon the middle, which is larger in the female; dorsum of the thorax black, each side with a blue stripe; sides blue, with a narrow black line upon the middle ($\male$); or green, with a black middle stripe divided by a yellow line; a humeral yellow stripe each side, margined with fuscous, and with the sides green ($\female$); feet pale, exteriorly lineated with black; abdomen brassy-black, the sides and a ring upon the base of segments 2—6 bright blue; segment 10 with the posterior margin elevated and subexcised; appendages black, superior ones rounded bifid, the inferior branch longer; inferior appendages unguiculated, slender, recurved; or ($\female$) dorsum of the abdomen fuscous, sides dirty green, and with the apex of the ninth and the whole of the tenth segment blue; the appendages short; the eighth segment having a long ventral spine; wings hyaline, pterostigma small, rhomboidal, black ($\male$), or luteous ($\female$); nine postcubital cross-nervules.

Length 33—36 millim. Alar expanse 40 millim.

Hab. Philadelphia; Berkeley Springs, Va. (Osten Sacken); Pecos River, Western Texas (Capt. Pope).

The colors in the living insect were communicated to me by Baron Osten Sacken.

17. A. prognatum!

Agrion prognatum Hagen!

Green-brassy, varied with green; head above green-brassy, the mouth and a point upon each side of the occiput bright green; posterior margin of the prothorax very short, with a small tubercle upon the middle; dorsum of the thorax green-brassy, each side with a bright green stripe; sides green, with two short green-brassy stripes at the wings; feet pale, knees exteriorly lineated with black; abdomen slender, green-brassy, the sides, and a basal lunule upon segments 3—6, green; segment 9 entirely, and 10 with the sides bluish-green; the tenth segment has an elevated process upon the middle of the posterior margin, which is long, cylindrical, black, the apex yellow; superior appendages bifid, the exterior branch long, narrow, laminated, incurved; the inferior branch hardly shorter, yellow, curved downwards; the inferior appendages yellow, unguiculated; wings hyaline, pterostigma large, rhomboidal, snow-white, interiorly brownish-black; eight postcubital crossnervules ($\male$).

Length 35 millim. Alar expanse 36 millim.

Hab. Berkeley Springs, Va. (Osten Sacken).

The colors of the living insect were made known to me by Baron Osten Sacken.

18. A. pollutum!

Agrion pollutum Hagen!

Brassy-fuscous; head brassy-fuscous, in front and a cuneiform, occipital spot each side orange; hind margin of the prothorax rounded; dorsum of the thorax brassy-fuscous, each side with a broad orange stripe; sides yellowish, with a black line inferiorly; feet yellowish, knees sublineated with fuscous; abdomen long, slender, brassy-fuscous; sides yellow, lateral margin yellow; segments 2—6 with a basal yellow annulus; 9 entirely and 10 sides blue ($\male$), or the apex of 9 and the whole of 10 blue ($\female$); appendages, superior ones long, with the apex broader, dolabriform;

the inferior ones shorter, unguiculated; apex of the tenth segment in the ♀ cleft; the appendages short; eighth segment with the ventral spine long; wings hyaline, pterostigma rhomboidal, narrow, fuscous; ten postcubital cross-nervules.

Length 34 millim. Alar expanse 34—38 millim.

Hab. Florida (Osten Sacken; Norton).

19. A. signatum!

Agrion signatum Hagen!

Fuscous; head in front and a cuneiform occipital spot each side yellow; posterior margin of the prothorax rounded; dorsum of the thorax each side with a broad yellow stripe; sides yellow, with a middle black line; feet yellow; abdomen long, slender, fuscous, the sides, segments 3—7 with a basal annulus, 9 entirely and 10 at the sides, yellow; superior appendages long, straight, subdolabriform, the apex not broader, at the extremity of the apex subincurved, black; inferior appendages short, black, subincurved; wings hyaline, pterostigma rhomboidal, fuscous, ♂; ten postcubital cross-nervules.

Length 35 millim. Alar expanse 36 millim.

Hab. Georgia (Abbot); Louisiana (Schaum).

20. A. coecum!

Agrion coecum Hagen!

Black; head brassy-black, with a blue occipital spot each side; posterior margin of the prothorax each side sub-excised; dorsum of the thorax brassy-black, each side with a rosy-blue stripe; sides rosy-blue, with a black stripe inferiorly; feet yellowish, exteriorly black; abdomen shorter, slender, black, segments 1—3 rosy-blue, 2 with a forked line, and 3 with the sides and apex black, 8 and 9 blue; appendages black, superior ones long, the base beneath dolabriform, the apex cylindrical; the inferior ones short, approximated cylindrical, recurved; wings hyaline, pterostigma small, rhomboidal, black; female paler, abdomen brassy-fuscous, segments 3—7 with a yellow basal annulus, the sides, and eighth segment almost entirely blue, the ventral spine acute; 10—12 postcubital cross-nervules. Male.

Length 31 millim. Alar expense 36 millim.

Hab. St. Thomas; Cuba. (Osten Sacken, Poey.)

Subgenus Pyrrhosoma Charp.

21. A. saucium!

Agrion saucium Burm.! Handb. II, 819, 10.

Red; head above black ♂, or middle blackish-fuscous ♀; posterior lobe of the prothorax short, the middle sub-depressed; dorsum of the thorax black ♂, or red ♀, sides yellowish-red; feet pale yellow; abdomen red; the seventh segment has the sides at apex black, and the remaining segments are entirely black; ♀ apex of the seventh segment each side with a point, and 8 and 9 are entirely black; appendages short, red, the superior ones depressed, flat, narrow, subsinuated; inferior ones a little longer, unguiculated; the tenth segment has the middle of the posterior margin elevated, excised; appendages of the female short, red, trigonal; the eighth segment with a longer ventral spine; wings hyaline, pterostigma rhomboidal, fuscous; 11—8 postcubital cross-nervules.

Length 26—22 millim. Alar expanse 31—27 millim.

Hab. Washington, Trenton Falls (Osten Sacken); Maryland, Pennsylvania (Uhler); South Carolina (Zimmerman); Illinois (Kennicott); Maine (Packard); Mass. (Scudder).

22. A. salvum!

Agrion salvum Hagen!

Red; head above with a broad brassy-green stripe; the posterior lobe of the prothorax broader, rounded, each side sub-excised; dorsum of the thorax red, upon the middle a broad brassy-green stripe excised each side at the wings; sides yellowish-red, with a superior short stripe brassy-green upon the middle; feet yellowish; abdomen red, venter paler; margin of the tenth segment excised in the middle; appendages short, red; superior ones cylindrical, straight, acute with a tooth inferiorly before the apex; inferior ones a little longer, unguiculated, subrecurved; (♀ apex of the abdomen wanting;) wings hyaline, pterostigma rhomboidal, fuscous; 9—11 postcubital cross-nervules.

Length 28 millim. Alar expanse 31 millim.

Hab. Mexico (Deppe).

23. A. vulneratum!

Agrion vulneratum Hagen!

Brassy-green, varied with red; head brassy-green, in front red; posterior lobe of the prothorax larger, margined with yellow, the sides obliquely truncated; dorsum of the thorax obscure brassy-green, each side with a narrow sulphur-yellow humeral line; sides sulphur-yellow; superiorly, a broad, bifid, brassy-green stripe, and two lines, the second one interrupted, black; feet reddish-yellow, femora exteriorly lineated with black; abdomen long, red, apex of the dorsum infuscated, or (♀) blackish-fuscous; appendages short, red, superior ones broad, triangular, flat, incurved at the apex; inferior ones oblong, broad, the apex truncated; segment 10 with the margin excised in the middle; appendages of the female short, broad, yellow; eighth ventral segment with no spine; wings hyaline, pterostigma rhomboidal, fuscous. 11 postcubital cross-nervules.

Var. ♀ Dorsum of the abdomen fusco-aeneous, with a broadly interrupted yellow ring at the base of the segments.

Length 33 millim. Alar expanse 34 millim.

Hab. Porto Rico (Moritz); Cuba (Poey); Essequibo, Guiana.

24. A. dominicanum.

Agrion dominicanum Selys. Poey, Ins. Cuba, 466.

Red; vertex, occiput, and the thorax above fusco-aeneous, with four pale red stripes; the sides and beneath yellow; feet pale red; wings hyaline, rather broad, pterostigma sub-elongated, fuscous. (From the description of De Selys Longchamps.)

Length 31 millim. Alar expanse 34 millim.

Hab. Hayti.

25. A. rufulum!

Agrion rufulum Hagen!

Rufous; head in front and behind yellowish; hind margin of the prothorax rounded; dorsum of the thorax rufous, sides yellowish; feet yellow; abdomen rufous, the sides and venter yellowish (the apex destroyed); wings hyaline, veins red, pterostigma rhomboidal, sanguineous. ♂. 11 postcubital cross-nervules.

Length about 37 millim. Alar expanse 38 millim.

Hab. North California.

Subgenus **Agrion** Charp.

26. A. annexum!
Agrion annexum Hagen!

Black, brassy; head and thorax villous; head marked with blue-black ($\male$), or reddish-yellow ($\female$); occiput each side with a large spot, which is serrated posteriorly; hind lobe of the prothorax rounded, subexcised on each side; dorsum of the thorax black, brassy, each side with a broad blue stripe ($\male$), or reddish-yellow; sides blue, or reddish-yellow, with an abrupt black, middle line; feet black, femora interiorly, tibiæ exteriorly ($\male$) or base externally ($\female$) pale; abdomen ($\male$) blue, the first segment with a basal spot, segment 2 with an orbicular, pedunculated apical one, 3—5 with the apical half anteriorly hastated, 6—7 almost entirely, and 10 entirely black-brassy; 8 and 9 are blue, with a black point each side on the middle; margin of 10 excised in the middle; appendages short, black, superior ones cylindrical, obtuse, straight; the inferior ones a little longer, trigonal, subunguiculated; ($\female$) reddish-yellow; segment 1 with a basal spot, 2 with a dorsal stripe, dilated before the apex, the rest with the dorsum fusco-aeneous; 3—8 have each side a triangular, larger, reddish-yellow spot; the margin of the tenth segment cleft in the middle; ventral spine of segment 8 long, acute; appendages short, thick, black; wings hyaline, pterostigma rhomboidal, large, fuscous; fourteen postcubital cross-nervules.

Length 35—37 millim. Alar expanse 43—50 millim.
Hab. Sitka (Eschscholz; Berlin Museum).
Allied to *A. cyathigerum* Charp., of Europe.

27. A. durum!
Agrion durum Hagen!

Black-brassy, head and thorax villous; ($\male$) marked with blue, or ($\female$) with yellowish-red; allied to the preceding species, but may be distinguished from it by the occipital spots being narrow, cuneiform, not posteriorly serrated; the prothorax has the posterior lobe rounded, not subexcised; the dorsum of the thorax has a middle line, which is blue or reddish-yellow; the feet pale, femora exteriorly and the tibiæ interiorly black, tarsi pale; abdomen ($\male$), segments 3—6 nigro-aeneous at the apex, longly hastated; superior appendages broad, excavated within, with a pale tubercle beneath; the inferior ones pale, hardly longer, acute; or (♀) dorsal bands of the segments, fusco-aeneous, narrower, dilated before the apex; pterostigma obscure, that of the males black; fourteen postcubital cross-nervules.

Length 37—42 millim. Alar expanse 44—50 millim.

Hab. Maryland (Uhler); Louisiana (Schaum); Florida (Osten Sacken; Norton).

28. A. civile!

Agrion civile Hagen!

Black-brassy, varied with blue (♂), or green (♀); head and thorax villous; head in front blue, occiput each side with an elongated blue spot; posterior margin of the prothorax rounded, entire; dorsum of the thorax nigro-aeneous, each side with a broad blue stripe (♂), or green (♀); sides blue in both sexes; beneath pruinose; feet pale, femora and tibiæ with an imperfect, external black line; abdomen blue (♂), segment 1 with a small basal spot, 2 with an orbicular apical one, 3—5 with an acute apical band, brassy-black; 6—7 brassy-black, blue at base; 8—9 blue; 10 brassy-black, the margin broadly excised; superior appendages black, long, divaricated, bifid, with a pale oval tubercle set between; inferior appendages short, pale, unguiculated; or (♀) blue, a dorsal large, lanceolated spot, dilated before the apex of the segments and not attaining the base upon segments 4—7, nigro-aeneous; margin of the tenth segment cleft; appendages short, thick, lurid; ventral spine of the eighth segment acute; wings hyaline, pterostigma rhomboidal, exteriorly rounded, black (♂), or luteous (♀); eleven postcubital cross-nervules.

Length 32—35 millim. Alar expanse 37 millim.

Hab. New York; Maryland (Uhler); Washington (Osten Sacken); Texas (Friedrich); Pecos River; Matamoras, Mexico.

The colors of the living insect were made known to me by Baron Osten Sacken.

29. A. praevarum!

Agrion praevarum Hagen!

Black-brassy, varied with blue (♂), or green (♀); head and thorax villous; very closely allied to the preceding species; differs in having the posterior margin of the prothorax each side excised;

($♂$) abdominal segment 2 has an orbicular spot, which is subacuminate in front, the sides sometimes have a line brassy-black, 3 has an apical spot, acuminated in front, 4—6 brassy-black, with the base blue; superior appendages bifid, no tubercle inserted between; the abdomen of the female is marked very much like that of *Agrion civile* (the apex is destroyed); dorsum of the thorax with a middle green line.

Length 32 millim. Alar expanse 40 millim.

Hab. Mexico (Deppe); female from Trajos del Oro (Saussure).

30. A. ebrium!
Agrion ebrium Hagen!

Black-brassy, varied with blue; head and thorax villous; very closely allied to *Ag. civile*, differs in having broader occipital spots, the femora and tibiæ exteriorly, and sometimes the whole of the tarsi black; the abdomen has segment 6, upon the apical half, marked with a hastate, black-brassy spot, the superior appendages are bifid, no introduced tubercle, the branches equal, parallel (in *A. civile* divaricated); inferior appendages straight, the apex less acuminated; eleven postcubital cross-nervules. Male.

Length 29—31 millim. Alar expanse 36—40 millim.

Hab. Chicago (Osten Sacken); North America (Zimmerman); New Orleans (Pfeiffer; the specimen is very much mutilated, doubtful).

31. A. doubledayi!
Agrion doubledayi Selys! Revue des Odonates, 209; Poey! Ins. Cuba, 469.

Black-brassy, varied with blue ($♂$), or yellowish-green? ($♀$); head brassy-black, in front blue, the occipital spots sublinear; posterior margin of the prothorax rounded; dorsum of the thorax brassy-black, each side of it is a broad blue stripe, sides blue, a medial linear spot at the wings; feet pale, femora and tibiæ exteriorly lineated with black; abdomen ($♂$) blue, segment 1 with a basal quadrangular spot, segment 2 with an orbicular apical one, 3—5 with an apical ring, 6 with a large hastiform spot, and 7 and 10 entirely brassy-black, 8—9 entirely blue; margin of the tenth segment excised, in the middle somewhat bituberculated; superior appendages black, broad, thick, the apex excised, with a pale tubercle adjacent; the inferior ones pale, acute, oblique; or ($♀$)

dorsum of the abdomen brassy-black, with basal yellowish lunules upon the segments; segment 8 with an acute ventral spine; wings hyaline, pterostigma rhomboidal, small, black, or (♀) fuscous; ten postcubital cross-nervules.

Length 31 millim. Alar expanse 34 millim.

Hab. Florida (Norton); St. John's Bluff, Florida (Doubleday).

32. A. bipunctulatum!

Agrion bipunctulatum Hagen!

Black-brassy, varied with blue; head black, in front blue, occipital spots absent; posterior lobe of the prothorax broader, each side rounded; dorsum of the thorax brassy-black, each side of it a blue stripe; sides blue, with a black middle line; feet pale, femora and tibiæ with an external line, and the tarsi entirely black; abdomen blue; segment 1 has a basal spot, 2 has an apical point each side, 3—6 at the apex, 7 almost entirely brassy-black, 8—10 blue; margin of the last segment subexcised, each side tuberculous, a bifid tubercle upon the middle inferiorly; appendages extremely short, black, superior ones cylindrical, inferior ones a little longer, broader, obtuse, with an apical tooth superiorly; wings hyaline; pterostigma small, rhomboidal, rufous; eleven postcubital cross-nervules.

Length 28 millim. Alar expanse 33 millim.

Hab. Georgia (Abbot).

33. A. violaceum!

Agrion violaceum Hagen!

Violaceous; head with a transverse black stripe superiorly; a large violaceous occipital spot each side; posterior margin of the prothorax rounded, subexcised in the middle; dorsum of the thorax violet, upon the middle a narrow black stripe; sides pale violet, a bifid stripe above at the wings and a line upon the middle, black; feet pale, femora exteriorly, tibiæ interiorly and the tarsi entirely black; abdomen (♂) violet, segments 2 to 6 with an apical spot each side, and 7 almost entirely black; margin of 10 broadly excised; appendages short, superior ones broad, obtuse, inferior ones larger, the apex sub-bifid; or (♀) yellowish-green, segments each side with an apical stripe and point, and 7 almost entirely black;

segment 8 with no ventral spine; wings hyaline, pterostigma rhomboidal fuscous; 11—15 postcubital cross-nervules.

Length 33—36 millim. Alar expanse 40—44 millim.

Hab. Maryland (Uhler); Berkeley Springs, Virginia; Washington (Osten Sacken); Pecos River, W. Texas (Capt. Pope); Massachusetts (Scudder); Connecticut (Norton); New York (Edwards); Illinois (Kennicott); New Jersey, Pennsylvania (Uhler).

34. A. fontium!

Agrion fontium Hagen!

Brassy-black; head black, mouth and an occipital spot each side blue; posterior margin of the prothorax short, sub-rect; dorsum of the thorax black, each side of it a broad blue stripe; sides pale-blue, a stripe superiorly and a line upon the middle black; feet black, femora interiorly and tibiæ exteriorly pale; abdomen slender black, segments 4—7 with an interrupted, pale basal ring, dorsum of 9—10 blue, 10 with a medial black fascia, the hind margin excised; appendages short, black, superior ones reniform, broken, compressed; inferior ones larger, broad, excised; wings hyaline; pterostigma rhomboidal black.

Fourteen postcubital cross-nervules.

Var. Rosaceous; dorsum of the thorax each side with a broad rosy stripe; sides with a rosy point on the superior stripe at the wings; ($♀$) abdominal segments at sides, a dorsal line upon the middle and a basal ring pale; no ventral spine.

Length 36 millim. Alar expanse 42 millim.

Hab. Berkeley Springs, Virginia (Osten Sacken); Georgia (Abbot); the variety from Florida (Osten Sacken).

35. A. apicale!

Agrion apicalis Say, Journ. Acad. Philad. VIII, 40, 4.

Blue; head with a transverse black stripe above; posterior margin of the prothorax subrotund; dorsum of the thorax blue, the sutures black; sides blue, against the prothorax, superiorly, a quadrangular black spot ($♂$); feet pale, femora exteriorly and tibiæ interiorly black; abdomen brassy fuscous, a narrow dorsal line, a basal annulus to the segments and their sides pale; dorsal surface of the three last segments blue ($♂$), or brassy fuscous ($♀$); appendages small, the superior ones transverse, with a middle and internal tooth; inferior ones longer, broad, bifid; margin of the tenth segment excised, tuberculous; appendages of the female short, obtuse; margin of the tenth segment cleft; no ventral spine to the eighth segment; wings hyaline, pterostigma rhomboidal, fuscous; fourteen postcubital cross-nervules.

Length 36 millim. Alar expanse 43 millim.

Hab. United States, "very common" (Say); Washington; Berkeley Springs, Virginia (Osten Sacken).

36. A. funebre!

Agrion funebre Hagen!

Violaceous; head with an arcuated fascia above, and a transverse occipital streak black; margin of the prothorax behind, upon the middle and each side subtruncated; dorsum of the thorax violaceous, a black stripe upon the middle, sides pale violaceous, a stripe superiorly, either divided or excised, and a line upon the middle black; feet pale, femora exteriorly, tibiæ interiorly and tarsi black; abdomen obscure violaceous, segment 2 each side with an angulose line, 3 to 6 apex or a spot each side, or entirely and 7 entirely black, 8 fuscous at base (?), the following ones violaceous; appendages short, superior ones obtuse, rounded at the apex and incurved; inferior ones longer, oblong, the apex bifid, the superior branch incurved; wings hyaline, pterostigma rhomboidal, fuscous. ♂. Fourteen postcubital cross-nervules.

Length 40 millim. Alar expanse 51 millim.

Hab. Mexico (Deppe).

It is allied to the two preceding species.

37. A. extraneum!

Agrion extraneum Hagen!

Very similar to the preceding, differs by having the head black above; the posterior margin of the prothorax rounded; dorsum of the abdomen black; margin of the tenth segment excised, beneath bituberculated; superior appendages broader, emarginated, the apex not incurved; the inferior ones bifid, the superior branch very much recurved, obliquely truncated. ♂.

Length 35 millim. Alar expanse 42 millim.

Hab. Tampico, Mexico (Saussure).

38. A. calidum!

Agrion calidum Hagen!

Very much like the preceding, differs in having the dorsum of the thorax black, each side a broad violaceous stripe; sides pale, a broad stripe above, and an abrupt line upon the middle black; feet almost entirely black; abdomen black, segments 9—10 blue above, margin of segment 10 less excised; superior appendages reniform, the internal tooth longer; inferior ones oblong, broad, the apex excised; wings hyaline sub-infumated, pterostigma larger, black. Fifteen postcubital cross-nervules.

♀ Head luteous (?), a stripe superiorly and a post-occipital streak black; margin of the prothorax behind sub-excised in the middle and each side, the thoracic process on each side laminated, oblong, curved exteriorly; dorsum of the thorax luteous (?), with a black stripe in the middle, sides luteous, with a black humeral line, dilated anteriorly; feet pale, the femora exteriorly, the tibiæ interiorly and the tarsi black; abdomen luteous (?), segment 2 each side, with an ante-apical spot, and 3—7 upon the apex black; dorsum of 10 almost entirely cleft; appendages short, luteous; no ventral spine; wings sub-infumated, pterostigma large, rufous.

Length 37—40 millim. Alar expanse 46—50 millim.

Hab. Tampico, Mexico (Saussure); California.

I saw a male taken at the same place (Tampico), allied to this species, but the epistoma was brassy-green, the sides of the thorax had no middle black line; the appendages destroyed. Is it a distinct species? The male from California is without head and appendages, and is, as yet, doubtful.

39. A. immundum!

Agrion immundum Hagen!

Most like *A. apicale*, but differs in the color, being luteous, perhaps rosaceous; dorsum of the thorax with a middle black stripe; a humeral black line, which is cleft at the wings; abdomen obscure luteous, segment 2 with a spot each side before the apex, the apex of 3—6, and 7 entirely black, the following ones blue (♂) or luteous; segments 2—7 each side with a black streak, the following ones blue (♀); superior appendages obtuse, excised at the apex; the inferior ones broad, sub-bifid at the apex, the superior branch conical, recurved; tenth segment of the female almost entirely cleft; the appendages short, luteous; no ventral spine; wings hyaline, pterostigma rhomboidal, fuscous; fourteen postcubital cross nervules.

Length 36 millim.   Alar expanse 44 millim.

Hab. Tampico, Mexico (Saussure).

40. A. sedulum!

Agrion sedulum Hagen!

Black; head blue above; posterior margin of the prothorax sub-rect; dorsum of the thorax black, each side a blue stripe; sides blue, superiorly with a black fascia, which is biserrated below, and a black line upon the middle; feet pale, femora exteriorly and the tibiæ within black; abdomen black, segments 2 to 7 with a dorsal blue spot at base, the following ones entirely blue; appendages black, short, superior ones cylindrical, straight, obtuse, with an ante-apical tooth beneath; inferior ones longer, bifid, the branches divaricated, recurved beneath; margin of the tenth segment elevated in the middle, excised; wings hyaline, pterostigma rhomboidal, brownish-black. ♂. Thirteen postcubital cross-nervules.

Length 34 millim.   Alar expanse 38 millim.

Hab. Berkeley Springs, Virginia (Osten Sacken); Pecos River, Western Texas (Capt. Pope).

The colors of the living insect were communicated to me by Baron Osten Sacken.

41. A. moestum!

Agrion moestum Hagen!

Fuscous; head blue in front; posterior margin of the prothorax subrect; dorsum of the thorax fuscous, each side with a broad blue stripe(?); sides brassy-fuscous, with an obscure blue middle stripe(?); feet luteous, femora exteriorly and tibiæ interiorly brassy-fuscous; abdomen brassy-fuscous, segments 3—7 with a basal blue lunule; segment 10 margin excised in the middle; appendages extremely short, the superior ones obtuse, incurved at the apex, the inferior ones broad, truncated at the apex, hardly sinuated.

♀ Pale green; head with a post-occipital fuscous streak; posterior margin of the prothorax subrect, each side with a brassy-fuscous point; the process upon the thorax, near each side, laminated, oblong, short, rounded; thorax pale green, a dorsal, fuscous, middle line; feet pale green, the femora sublineated with fuscous; abdomen pale green, segments 3—7 each side, with a lateral fuscous streak; appendages short, pale; the wings hyaline, pterostigma rhomboidal, black ($\male$), or luteous ($\female$). Fifteen postcubital cross-nervules.

Length 43—45 millim. Alar expanse 50—56 millim.

Hab. Pecos River, Western Texas, July (Capt. Pope).

42. A. lugens!

Agrion lugens Hagen!

Luteous.; head above with an arcuated, angulose line, and a postoccipital fascia blackish-brown; posterior margin of the prothorax subrotund, each side with an arcuated black spot; process of the thorax near each side, laminated, small, narrow, curved outwards; thorax luteous, a dorsal middle streak and two narrow stripes each side, fuscous; sides luteous, above with a broadly divided stripe, upon the middle at the wings an abrupt streak, and a line beneath black; feet luteous, femora exteriorly and tibiæ interiorly subfuscous; abdomen thick, luteous, a broad stripe each side, confluent together at the apices of the segments, blackish-brown, the last segment cleft; appendages short, luteous; wings hyaline, pterostigma larger, rhomboidal, fuscous, luteous in the middle; sixteen postcubital cross-nervules. ($\female$.)

Length 50 millim. Alar expanse 67 millim.

Hab. Mexico (Mühlenpford; Berlin Museum).

It belongs to the genus HYPONEURA Selys, which is distinguished by the postcostal space being *multi-areolate*.

43. A. lacrimans!

Agrion lacrimans Hagen!

Luteous; head luteous, above with spots in the middle, and a postoccipital streak black; posterior margin of the prothorax short, broadly bi-emarginated, and with a geminate black spot; laminated process near each side of the thorax broadened at the apex and curved inwards; dorsum of the thorax luteous, a black stripe on the middle; sides luteous, a humeral line dilated anteriorly, and a middle line black; feet luteous, exteriorly and tarsi brownish-black; abdomen luteous, a broad, black stripe each side, confluent together at the apices of the segments (apex destroyed); wings hyaline, pterostigma rhomboidal, luteo-fuscous; sixteen post-cubital cross-nervules. (♀.)

Length about 45 millim. Alar expanse 56 millim.

Hab. Cordova, Mexico (Saussure).

44. A. putridum!

Agrion putridum Hagen!

Fuscous; head fuscous, in front luteous; posterior margin of the prothorax subrect; dorsum of the thorax luteous, a fuscous stripe upon the middle; sides luteous; a stripe superiorly, which is excised at the wings, and a line upon the middle blackish-brown; feet luteous, femora exteriorly and tibiæ interiorly fuscous; abdomen black, segments 3—7 each side with a pale basal lunule; head, thorax, and apex of the abdomen pruinose; margin of the tenth segment excised in the middle; appendages short, superior ones obtuse, an ante-apical tooth beneath, the inferior appendages broad, truncated at the apex. ♀ pale green; head with a post-occipital black streak; posterior margin of the prothorax straight, each side with a black spot; laminated process near each side of the thorax small, straight, rounded; dorsum of the thorax green, a black line upon the middle; sides green, a black line in the middle; feet paler; abdomen green, each side with an interrupted black line; apex of the tenth segment excised; appendages short; wings hyaline, pterostigma rhomboidal, black (♂), or luteous (♀); fourteen postcubital cross-nervules.

Length 40 millim. Alar expanse 48 millim.

Hab. Wisconsin River (Kennicott); Berkeley Springs, Virginia (Osten Sacken); Maryland (Uhler).

45. A. cupreum!

Agrion cupreum Hagen!

Coppery-purple; head cupreous; posterior margin of the prothorax rounded; dorsum of the thorax cupreous, the middle carina black; sides pale, above coppery; feet black, tibiæ pale exteriorly; abdomen black, segment 2 fusco-aeneous, 4—8 with a basal blue annulus, 9—10 entirely blue; margin of 10 excised, bituberculated beneath; appendages black, the superior ones flat, subelongated, triangular, bifid at the apex, the interior branch subincurved; the inferior ones longer, the apex broader, excised. The eighth segment is sometimes all blue ♂. Specimens from Venezuela are smaller, but hardly distinct; their females have the head marked each side with a luteous, occipital point; hind margin of the prothorax slightly sinuated; laminated process near each side of the thorax short, curved inwards; dorsum of the thorax luteous, a cupreous stripe upon the middle; sides yellowish-green, with a brassy stripe above; abdomen yellowish-green, each side with an interrupted, black stripe; wings hyaline, pterostigma rhomboidal, black (♂), or luteous (♀); fifteen postcubital cross-nervules.

Length 40—33 millim. Alar expanse 48—40 millim.

Hab. Cordova, Mexico (Saussure); Venezuela (Appun).

46. A. aspersum!

Agrion aspersum Hagen!

Black, varied with blue; head black, in front and an occipital point each side blue; posterior margin of the prothorax subexcised each side; dorsum of the thorax black, each side with a broad blue stripe; sides blue; feet pale blue, femora exteriorly, tibiæ interiorly and tarsi almost entirely black; abdomen black, the sides blue; segment 1 blue, with a quadrangular, basal, black spot; 2 blue, with an apical, pyriform, black spot; 3 blue, with a large, apical, reversed hastiform, black spot; the apical half of 7, the whole of 8 and 9, and 10 with a large ovate spot each side blue; margin of the tenth segment subexcised; appendages black, superior ones long, straight, cylindrical, the apex subincurved, with a basal process beneath, which is large, laminated; the inferior appendages are short, trigonal, the apex acute, curved inwards; wings hyaline, pterostigma small, rhomboidal, black; twelve postcubital cross-nervules. (♂.)

Length 35—30 millim. Alar expanse 40—36 millim.

Hab. New York; Bergen Hill, New Jersey (Guex); Chicago (Osten Sacken).

47. A. fumipenne!

Agrion fumipenne Burm.! Handb. II, 819, 7.—*Argia obscura* Rambur, Neuropt. 256, 3.

Fusco-aeneous; head in front, and an occipital spot each side blue(?); posterior margin of the prothorax rounded, each side subtruncated; dorsum of the thorax blue(?), a narrow, fusco-aeneous stripe upon the middle; sides blue(?) above fusco-aeneous, a black line in the middle; femora within and tibiæ without pale; abdomen fusco-aeneous; margin of the tenth segment excised, beneath bituberculated; superior appendages short, obtuse, arcuated, inferior ones broader, the apex sub-bifid; or (♀) fuscous, the apex of the segments black, a blue(?) annulus at their base; no ventral spine; wings fuscous, pterostigma rhomboidal, fuscous; sixteen postcubital cross-nervules.

Length 36 millim. Alar expanse 38—45 millim.

Hab. Kentucky; Florida (Osten Sacken).

Kirby, Fauna Bor. Amer. p. 252, describes *Agrion puella* Linn. as having been taken in North America, lat. 65°; perhaps it is another species which is inextricable. The varieties captured, which he describes, are:—

Var. B. Sea-green; dorsum of the thorax black, with a green stripe each side; abdomen black, the base green, inscribed with black; feet black, beneath pale green; the pterostigma black, environed with pale. (Certainly a female.)

Var. C. Dorsum of the thorax black, each side with a whitish stripe; feet black; pterostigma black. (From the description of Kirby.)

Tribe II. AESCHNINA.

Wings unequal; triangles of all the wings of the same form; genital organs of the male having the anterior *hamule* connate; the penis and vesicle conjoined; genital organs of the female vaginated or exposed.

Sub-Fam. III. GOMPHINA.

Eyes distant or sub-distant; head transverse; wings unequal, the posterior ones broader; the triangle short; genital organs of the female exposed.

Division I. Labium entire.

GOMPHUS Leach.

Triangles of all the wings with no transverse veins.

Subgenus Erpetogomphus Selys.

The abdomen blackish, with broad, hastiform, dorsal yellow spots; the feet short; penis with no tooth beneath.

1. G. compositus!

Erpetogomphus compositus Hag.! Monog. Gomph. 400, 16 bis; pl. xx, fig. 2. Selys, Addit. Synops. 10, 21.

Pale yellow; head pale, between the eyes black; thorax pale, dorsum with two broad, approximated stripes, and another external one each side, a little incurved, black; the sides bright yellow, each side with oblique, black lines; the space between the second and third line pale; feet yellow, having a black line exteriorly, the tarsi black; abdomen black, the second segment at sides, and a dorsal, elongated spot, segments 3 to 7 with a large, hastiform spot, the eighth each side of base, and the following ones entirely, pale yellow, appendages yellow; vulvar scale short, divided; wings hyaline, subflavescent at base, pterostigma large, black. Female. Thirteen antecubital cross-nervules. 8—9 postcubital cross-nervules.

Length 46 millim. Alar expanse 62 millim. Pterostigma $3\frac{1}{2}$ millim.

Hab. Pecos River, Western Texas (Capt. Pope).

2. G. designatus!

Erpetogomphus designatus Hag.! Monog. Gomph. 401, 16 ter; pl. xx, fig. 1. Selys, Addit. Synops. 10, 26 bis.

Yellow; head pale yellow; thorax yellow, the dorsum with two subcontiguous stripes, which are broader in front, and another shorter, oblique one each side, fuscous; the sides pale, with three very narrow fuscous lines, the middle one interrupted; feet yellow, femora and tibiæ with an external streak, and the tarsi entirely black; abdomen cylindrical, slender, the dorsum blackish-fuscous, segments 2 to 7 with a large, dorsal, hastiform yellow spot; in the females the sides are interrupted with pale; the males have the four last segments subdilated, yellow, obsoletely varied with fuscous; the superior appendages contiguous, straight, the apical half narrowed, acute, the inferior one narrow, bifid, hardly shorter than the superiors, the apex recurved, obtuse; vulvar lamina with a small triangle each side; wings hyaline, their extreme bases flavescent, pterostigma large, dilated, black; thirteen antecubitals; 8—10 postcubitals; two discoidal areolets.

Length 49—51 millim. Alar expanse 66—68 millim. Pterostigma $3\frac{1}{2}$ millim.

Hab. Pecos River, Western Texas (Capt. Pope).

3. G. boa.

Erpetogomphus boa Selys! Addit. Synops. 11, 21 quart.

Yellow; head yellow; thorax yellow, varied with obscure fuscous; femora yellow, externally with a fuscous fascia, tibiæ fuscous, or yellow, with the outside black, the four anterior tarsi brownish-black; abdomen yellowish; superior appendages inflated at base, an obtuse tooth above; their apex curved inwards, obtuse, villous; the inferior one bifid, shorter; the vulvar lamina excised; wings hyaline; pterostigma pale fuscous. (From the description of De Selys Longchamps.) Male.

Length 47 millim. Alar expanse 69—72 millim.

Hab. Vera Cruz, Mexico.

4. G. cophias!

Erpetogomphus cophias Selys! Monog. Gomph. 72, 17; pl. iv, fig. 6. Selys, Addit. Synops. 11, 21 quint.

Yellow; head yellow, between the ocelli fuscous; thorax yellow, dorsum having an obsolete, humeral, rufous stripe; abdomen yellow, segments 4—9 each side blackish-fuscous; segment 10 with two basal, black spots; femora yellow, with a black fascia externally, tibiæ and tarsi black; superior appendages inflated at base, with a basal tooth beneath; at the apex they are obtuse; the inferior one bifid, shorter; wings hyaline, pterostigma pale fuscous; vulvar lamina short, each side orbicular.

Length 47 millim. Alar expanse 64 millim. Pterostigma 3 millim.

Hab. Mexico; Trojes del Oro (Saussure).

5. G. elaps!

Erpetogomphus elaps Selys! Monog. Gomph. 70, 16; pl. iv, fig. 4. Selys, Addit. Synops. 12, 21 sext.

Yellow; head yellow, between the ocelli fuscous; thorax yellow, dorsum each side with an obsolete, humeral, rufous vestige; femora yellow, externally with a black fascia, tibiæ and tarsi black; abdomen slender, yellowish, before the apex dilated, the second segment each side, lineated with black, and with a trilobed, dorsal, yellow spot; segments 3—6 blackish, with a yellow, basal ring, or yellow with an apical black ring (teneral), segment 7 yellow, or sometimes fuscous behind, segments 8—10 fuscous, obscurely varied with black; superior appendages contiguous, not inflated at base, the apex obtuse, subincurved; the inferior one bifid, one-half shorter than the superior; wings hyaline, pterostigma fuscous or fulvous. Male.

Twelve antecubitals; 8—9 postcubitals; two discoidal areolets.
Length 41 millim. Alar expanse 54 millim. Pterostigma 3 millim.

Hab. Atlihuazan, Mexico (Saussure).

6. G. crotalinus!

Erpetogomphus crotalinus Hag.! Monog. Gomph. 72, 18; pl. iv, fig. 5.
Selys, Synops. 21, 21.—*Ophiogomphus menetriesii* Selys! Synops. 20, 20.

Greenish-yellow; head and thorax greenish-yellow; feet yellow, exteriorly lineated with black, tarsi black; abdomen slender, before the apex dilated, greenish-yellow, with a black stripe each side; superior appendages straight, contiguous, inflated at base, the apex acute; the inferior one bifid, the apex incurved, acute; vulvar lamina excised; wings hyaline, pterostigma yellow, surrounded by black nervures.

Eleven antecubitals; 8—9 postcubitals; two discoidal areolets.
Length 45—49 millim. Alar expanse 66 millim. Pterostigma $3\frac{1}{4}$ millim.

Hab. Mexico; Brazil.

G. menetriesii, from Brazil, very likely, does not differ from this species; but the typical specimen being destroyed, other specimens are to be observed.

Subgenus Ophiogomphus Selys.

7. G. colubrinus!

Ophiogomphus colubrinus Selys! Monog. Gomph. 76, 19; pl. v, fig. 1.
Selys, Synops. 21, 22.

Greenish-yellow; head yellow, in front with four black lines, labium black in the middle; thorax greenish-yellow, a middle stripe, and another each side, lateral, narrow, fuscous; sides, each with three narrow black lines; feet yellow, the posterior femora exteriorly fuscous, tibiæ black with an external yellow line; abdomen cylindrical, before the apex dilated, the dorsum black, segments 3—7 with a basal yellow stripe, the rest with a yellow spot; superior appendages yellow, short, trigonal, subincurved; the inferior one broad, bifid, hardly shorter; wings hyaline, pterostigma pale fuscous. Male.

Fourteen antecubitals; 11—12 postcubitals; two discoidal areolets.

Length 50 millim. Alar expanse 64 millim. Pterostigma 3 millim.

Hab. Hudson's Bay.

This species is very much like *G. serpentinus* Charp., of Europe.

Subgenus Gomphus.

8. G. spinosus!

Gomphus spinosus Selys! Monog. Gomph. 120, 35; pl. vii, fig. 2. Selys, Synops. 40, 51.

Fuscous, spotted with yellow; head yellow, with a black band before the eyes; dorsum of the thorax fuscous, a medial stripe dilated in front, and a subcontiguous streak each side, yellow; sides yellowish; feet black, the anterior femora beneath yellowish; posterior femora extremely long, spinous; abdomen long, yellow, a broad, brownish-black stripe upon each side; superior appendages divaricated, trigonal, the apex acute, recurved, upon the under side on the middle, a blunt tooth; the inferior one broad, forked; the vulvar lamina narrow, bifid; wings hyaline, pterostigma large, yellow; 13—14 antecubitals; eleven postcubitals; two discoidal areolets.

Length 54—61 millim. Alar expanse 76—80 millim. Pterostigma 4 millim.

Hab. Georgia.

9. G. armatus.

Gomphus armatus Selys! Monog. Gomph. 122, 36. Selys, Synops. 40, 52.

Fuscous, spotted with yellow; head yellow, front with a transverse black line inferiorly; thorax fuscous, a middle stripe, dilated in front, and a humeral and antehumeral streak, yellow; sides yellow, with two fuscous stripes; feet black, anterior femora yellowish beneath; posterior femora extremely long, spinous; abdomen long, the apex very much dilated, yellow, a broad brownish-black stripe each side; appendages like those of *G. spinosus*, pale fuscous; wings hyaline; pterostigma large, yellow. Male.

Fifteen antecubitals; ten postcubitals; two discoidal areolets.

Length 54 millim. Alar expanse 76 millim. Pterostigma 4 millim.

Hab. North America (British Museum).

10. G. spoliatus!

Gomphus spoliatus Hag.! Monog. Gomph. 409, 36 bis; pl. xxi, fig. 1. Selys, Addit. Synops. 17, 32 bis.

Yellow, spotted with fuscous; head yellow; thorax yellow, dorsum with two medial, contiguous, anteriorly broadened stripes, and two oblique ones each side, fuscous; sides yellow, with fuscous, oblique lines each side; feet black, the anterior and posterior pairs of femora yellowish beneath; the posterior femora extremely long, spinous; abdomen long, slender, the apex very much dilated, yellow, the second segment each side, with a large angular spot, segments 3—6 each side, with a point and apical triangular spot, black; appendages like those of *G. spinosus,* yellow; wings hyaline, pterostigma large, yellow. Male.

13—14 antecubitals; 8—10 postcubitals; two discoidal areolets.

Length 60 millim. Alar expanse 74 millim. Pterostigma $3\frac{1}{2}$ millim.

Hab. Pecos River, Western Texas (Capt. Pope).

Is this not the teneral stage of *G. armatus?*

11. G. dilatatus!

Gomphus dilatatus Ramb.! Neuropt. 155, 2. Selys! Monogr. Gomph. 123, 37; pl. vii, fig. 3. Selys, Synops. 28, 31.

Black, spotted with yellow; head yellow, with two stripes in front and a third before the eyes, black; dorsum of the thorax black, with two yellow stripes each side; sides yellow, each side with two oblique black streaks; feet black, anterior femora beneath yellowish; the posterior femora longer; abdomen slender, long, the apex strongly dilated, excavated, black, segments 1—7 with a dorsal middle fascia, segments 1—3 each side with a lateral fascia and segment 9 at the sides, yellow; appendages black, superior ones short, cylindrical, incurved, the apex beneath, obliquely truncated, acute; the inferior one broad, bifid; wings hyaline, pterostigma moderate, black; the membranule broader, cinereous; vulvar lamina long, excised, bifurcated; thirteen antecubitals; fourteen postcubitals; two discoidal areolets.

Length 65—72 millim. Alar expanse 84 millim. Pterostigma 3½—4 millim.

Hab. Georgia (Abbot).

12. G. externus!

Gomphus externus Hag.! Monog. Gomph. 411, 37 bis; pl. xxi, fig. 2. Selys, Addit. Synops. 14, 31 bis.

Yellow, spotted with black; head yellow, a narrow black band before the eyes; thorax yellow, dorsum with a straight middle stripe, and two each side, incurved, black; sides yellow, each side with two oblique black stripes; feet black, anterior femora upon the base beneath, yellowish, tibiæ at the base exteriorly, yellow; abdomen long, the apex dilated; yellow, each side with a broad black stripe, which is conjoined upon the dorsum at the apex of the segments; appendages fuscous, superior ones short, trigonal, acute; the inferior one broader, bifurcated; vulvar lamina narrow, the apex bifid; wings hyaline, pterostigma narrow, fuscous; 11—12 antecubitals; 9—10 postcubitals; two discoidal areolets.

Length 52 millim. Alar expanse 66 millim. Pterostigma 3 millim.

Hab. Pecos River, Western Texas (Capt. Pope).

13. G. adelphus.

Gomphus adelphus Selys! Monog. Gomph. 413, 38 bis. Selys, Addit. Synops. 15, 34 ter.

Yellow, spotted with black; head yellow, in front with two confluent black bands; thorax yellow, dorsum each side, with three black stripes, the intermediate ones contiguous; feet black; apex of the abdomen dilated, dorsum black, segments 1—7 with a maculose, median, yellow stripe; appendages black, superior ones incurved at the apex, acute; wings hyaline, pterostigma small, fuscous. Male. (From the description of De Selys Longchamps.)

Length 48 millim. Alar expanse 54 millim. Pterostigma 2 millim.

Hab. New York (Asa Fitch).

14. G. fraternus!

Æschna fraterna Say, Journ. Acad. Philad. VIII, 16, 9.—*Gomphus fraternus* Selys! Monog. Gomph. 125, 138; pl. vii, fig. 4. Selys, Synops. 28, 32.

Yellow, spotted with black; head yellow, thorax yellow, dorsum with a stripe upon the middle, and one each side, laterally, broad, black, divided with yellow; feet black, the anterior and posterior femora partly yellowish; abdomen dilated at the apex, black, a dorsal line broader at the base, yellow, at the apex wanting; a basal, lateral yellow stripe, and the eighth and ninth segments, each side, yellow; appendages black; vulvar lamina narrow, two-parted; wings hyaline, pterostigma yellow; twelve antecubitals; 10—11 postcubitals; two discoidal areolets.

Length 48 millim. Alar expanse 64 millim. Pterostigma 3 millim.

Hab. New York (Schaum); Virginia (Osten Sacken).

15. G. villosipes!

Gomphus villosipes Selys! Synops. 34, 41.—*Gomphus pallidus* Selys! Monog. Gomph. 145, 47; pl. viii, fig. 6. (partly.)

Greenish-yellow, spotted with black; head yellowish, with a black stripe in front; thorax greenish-yellow, dorsum with a stripe upon the middle, and a lateral, broad one, each side, divided with yellow, black; sides with an interrupted, black line; feet black, anterior femora beneath yellowish, tibiæ with an external yellow line; apex of the abdomen a little dilated, dorsum of the abdomen black, with a maculose, yellow stripe upon the middle; segments 8 and 9 black, 10 yellow; appendages yellowish, black at apex, the superior ones divaricated, deplanated, the apex acute and curved inwards; the inferior one broadly forked, the apex recurved; wings hyaline, pterostigma yellow. Male.

Eleven antecubitals; ten postcubitals; three discoidal areolets.

Length 47 millim. Alar expanse 59 millim. Pterostigma $3\frac{1}{2}$ millim.

Hab. North America (Vienna Museum).

16. G. pallidus!

Gomphus pallidus Ramb.! Neuropt. 163, 12. Selys! Monog. Gomph. 145, 47; pl. viii, fig. 6 (Partly). Selys! Synops. 33, 40.

Testaceous; head pale; thorax villous, olivaceous, dorsum each side, with an obsolete rufous line; feet testaceous, femora above and tibiæ beneath blackish-brown; abdomen long, the ninth segment longer than the others; apex hardly dilated, testaceous, each side with a broader subfuscous stripe, which is wanting at the apex; appendages pale; vulvar lamina triangular, the apex bifid; wings hyaline, pterostigma narrow, longer, yellow. Female.

Twelve antecubitals; ten postcubitals; two discoidal areolets.

Length 58 millim. Alar expanse 76 millim. Pterostigma 5 millim.

Hab. Georgia (Abbot).

17. G. pilipes!

Gomphus pilipes Selys! Monog. Gomph. 148, 48; pl. viii, fig. 7. Selys! Addit. Synops. 15, 40 bis.

Testaceous; head pale; thorax villous, olivaceous, dorsum each side, with an obsolete fuscous line; feet testaceous, femora villous, above, and tibiæ beneath, blackish-brown; abdomen long, the ninth segment longer than the others, the apex hardly dilated; testaceous, the middle segments at the apex, and the basal segments each side, with an obsolete fuscous fascia; appendages pale, the superior ones trigonal, the apex acute, curved inwards; the inferior ones broadly bifurcated; vulvar lamina oblong, bifid at the apex; wings hyaline, pterostigma narrow, yellow; twelve antecubitals; eleven postcubitals; 3 discoidal areolets.

Length 53 millim. Alar expanse 68 millim. Pterostigma 4 millim.

Hab. New Orleans; Georgia.

18. G. lividus!

Gomphus lividus Selys! Monog. Gomph. 150, 49; pl. ix, fig. 1. Selys! Synops. 34, 42.—*Gomphus sordidus* Hag.! Selys, Synops. 35, 43.

Olivaceous, spotted with fuscous; head pale yellow; thorax olivaceous, the dorsum with a stripe upon the middle, each side a broad, fuscous one, divided with olive; the sides with two broad, fuscous lines; feet testaceous, tibiæ beneath and the tarsi, black; abdomen equal, the base dilated, fuscous, a dorsal, medial, yellow line, interrupted upon the segments, and absent from the apex; appendages fuscous, the superior ones trigonal, narrower at the apex, acute, somewhat dilated in the middle; the inferior one broadly bifid; wings hyaline, pterostigma small, yellow; twelve antecubitals; twelve postcubitals; two discoidal areolets.

Length 51 millim. Alar expanse 66 millim. Pterostigma 3 millim.

Hab. S. Carolina (Zimmerman); Washington (Osten Sacken).

A male from Washington has the appendages a little different; the specimen, however, is a very freshly excluded one; perhaps it belongs to this same species.

19. G. spicatus!

Gomphus spicatus Hag.! Monog. Gomph. 153, 50, and 415, 50; pl. ix, fig. 2. Selys! Synops. 35, 44.

Fuscous, spotted with luteous; head pale yellow; thorax clothed with fuscous hairs, dorsum with a stripe each side and the sides with two stripes, luteous; femora luteous, above fuscous; tibiæ blackish-fuscous, exteriorly yellowish, tarsi black; abdomen equal, inflated at base, fuscous, the dorsum with an interrupted, yellow line, the base each side with a yellow stripe; appendages fuscous, the superior ones trigonal, acute at the apex, with an external, basal tooth; the inferior one broader, divaricated, broadly bifid; the vulvar lamina triangular, bifid, subdivaricated; wings hyaline, pterostigma yellow; twelve antecubitals; ten postcubitals; two discoidal areolets.

Length 49 millim. Alar expanse 60 millim. Pterostigma 3 millim.

Hab. New York (Schaum); Canada.

20. G. militaris!

Gomphus militaris Hag.! Monog. Gomph. 416, 51 bis; pl. xxi, fig. 3. Selys! Addit. Synops. 16, 44 bis.

Yellow, spotted with blackish-brown; head pale yellow; thorax yellow, dorsum each side with a lateral stripe, which is broad, blackish-fuscous, divided with yellow; the sides with two brownish-black lines; feet yellowish, the femora bilineated with black, the tibiæ within, and the tarsi black; abdomen slender, yellow, dilated at the apex, an interrupted brownish-black line each side, which is absent at the apex; appendages yellow, the superior ones trigonal, the apex curved inwards, acute, with an external obtuser tooth; the inferior appendage broadly bifid; vulvar lamina extremely short, excised; wings hyaline, pterostigma yellow; 12—14 antecubitals; eleven postcubitals; two discoidal areolets.

Length 47—50 millim. Alar expanse 64 millim. Pterostigma 4 millim.

Hab. Pecos River, Western Texas (Capt. Pope).

21. G. intricatus!

Gomphus intricatus Hag.! Monog. Gomph. 418, 51 ter; pl. xxi, fig. 3. Selys! Addit. Synops. 16, 44 ter.

Yellow, spotted with brownish-black; head pale yellow; thorax yellow, dorsum with a medial fascia, divided with yellow, each side an incurved fascia, and a humeral one, brownish-black; femora yellow, with a fuscous stripe above, tibiæ black, exteriorly yellow, tarsi black; abdomen slender, broader at the apex; yellow, each side with an interrupted, fuscous stripe, which is absent at the apex; appendages yellow, the superior ones divaricated, the apex, outwardly, truncated, acute, the inferior appendage broadly bifid; wings hyaline, pterostigma yellow. Male.

Twelve antecubitals; eight postcubitals; two discoidal areolets.

Length 45 millim. Alar expanse 60 millim. Pterostigma 3 millim.

Hab. Pecos River, Western Texas (Capt. Pope).

22. G. minutus!

Gomphus minutus Ramb.! Neuropt. 161, 9. Selys! Monog. Gomph. 155, 51; pl. ix, fig. 3. Selys! Synops. 36, 45.

Yellow, spotted with black; head yellow; thorax yellow, dorsum with a medial fascia, and a broad lateral one each side, black, divided with yellow, the sides with two, almost contiguous, oblique, black stripes; feet yellow, femora exteriorly, the tibiæ interiorly and the tarsi, black; the abdomen somewhat broader at the apex, yellow, each side with a broad black stripe; appendages yellowish, fuscous at the apex, the superior ones trigonal, with a long, basal tooth beneath; the inferior one broadly bifid; vulvar lamina very short, excised; wings hyaline, pterostigma yellow; twelve antecubitals; eleven postcubitals; two discoidal areolets.

Length 49 millim. Alar expanse 60 millim. Pterostigma 3 millim.

Hab. Georgia (Abbot).

23. G. exilis!

Gomphus exilis Selys! Monog. Gomph. 156, 52. Selys! Synops. 36, 46.

Yellow, marked with blackish-fuscous; head yellow; thorax yellow, dorsum with a broad middle stripe and each side of it a broad lateral one, each divided with yellow, fuscous; sides yellow, with a broad, oblique, fuscous fascia; feet yellow, femora exteriorly, tibiæ interiorly, and the tarsi, brownish-black; abdomen with the apex a little dilated, the dorsum blackish-fuscous, with a medial yellow stripe; appendages yellow, superior ones trigonal, dilated and toothed beneath; the inferior one broadly bifid; vulvar lamina oval, short, bifid; wings hyaline, pterostigma yellow; nine antecubitals; eight postcubitals; two discoidal areolets.

Length 42 millim. Alar expanse 50 millim. Pterostigma $2\frac{1}{2}$ millim.

Hab. Maryland (Uhler); Massachusetts (Scudder).

24. G. parvulus.

Gomphus parvulus Selys! Monog. Gomph. 157, 53; pl. xxii, fig. 1. Selys! Synops. 37, 47.

Black; head black, a fascia in front, and two spots, yellow; thorax black, dorsum each side, with a small, yellow line; sides yellow, with two contiguous stripes and a third posteriorly, black; feet black; abdomen equal, black, the dorsum with a basal, maculose, yellow stripe; appendages fuscous, superior ones nearly straight, cylindrical, the apex narrower, acute, beneath with a basal tooth; the inferior one-half shorter, broadly bifid; wings hyaline, pterostigma blackish-fuscous. (Male.)

Thirteen antecubitals; eleven postcubitals; two discoidal areolets.

Length 40 millim. Alar expanse 54 millim. Pterostigma 3 millim.

Hab. Nova Scotia (British Museum).

25. G. plagiatus.

Gomphus plagiatus Selys! Monog. Gomph. 159, 54. Selys! Synops. 38, 48.

Yellow, spotted with black; head yellow; dorsum of the thorax black, each side with a yellow stripe; sides yellow, with two black lines; femora yellow, the basal half exteriorly black, tibiæ and tarsi black; abdomen long, the apex subdilated, luteous; segments 7—9 yellow, with a red apex; appendages yellow, like those of *G. villosipes;* wings hyaline, pterostigma yellow. (From the description of De Selys Longchamps.)

Fourteen antecubitals; eight postcubitals; two discoidal areolets.

Length 54 millim. Alar expanse 64 millim. Pterostigma ? millim.

Hab. North America (British Museum).

26. G. notatus.

Gomphus notatus Ramb.! Neuropt. 162, 10. Selys! Monog. Gomph. 159, 55. Selys! Synops. 38, 49.—*Gomphus elongatus* Selys! Synops. 39, 50 (♀).

Greenish-yellow, spotted with fuscous; head yellowish; dorsum of the thorax fuscous, each side with narrow green stripes; sides greenish-yellow, with two fuscous stripes; feet yellow, femora above, fuscous, tibiæ and tarsi, black; abdomen long, cylindrical, fuscous; vulvar lamina short; wings hyaline, pterostigma long, rufous. (From the description of De Selys Longchamps.)

13—15 antecubitals; eleven postcubitals; two discoidal areolets.

Length 64 millim. Alar expanse 68—78 millim. Pterostigma 5 millim.

Hab. North America (British Museum).

Subgenus Neogomphus Selys.

27. G. specularis!

Neogomphus? *specularis* Hag.! Selys, Addit. Synops. 18, 64 bis.

Yellow, spotted with black; head yellow in front, above black, in the middle yellow; thorax yellow, dorsum each side, with a broad, black stripe; sides yellow; feet black; abdomen equal, black, the dorsum with a narrow yellow stripe, which is almost absent upon the apex, segments 8 and 9 with a yellow spot each side; appendages yellow; vulvar lamina large, bifid, bi-ovate; wings hyaline, pterostigma black. Female.

10—11 antecubitals; 10—11 postcubitals; two discoidal areolets.

Length 45 millim. Alar expanse 58 millim. Pterostigma 3 millim.

Hab. Ft. Tejon, California (John Xantus).

PROGOMPHUS Selys.

Triangles with transverse veins; the superior side longer than the interior one; the feet short.

1. P. obscurus!

Diastatomma obscurum Ramb.! Neuropt. 170, 5.—*Progomphus obscurus* Selys! Monog. Gomph. 201, 70. Selys! Synops. 53, 69.

Fuscous, spotted with yellow; head yellow, fuscous above; dorsum of the thorax fusco-rufous, each side with a yellow stripe; sides fuscous, with three yellow stripes; feet fusco-rufous, femora luteous beneath, tibiæ within and the tarsi black; abdomen ?

; wings hyaline, with a fulvous, narrow, basal spot, pterostigma large, rufo-fuscous. (From the description of De Selys Longchamps.)

15—16 antecubitals; 9—11 postcubitals; two discoidal areolets.
Length 53 ? millim. Alar expanse 70 millim. Pterostigma 5 millim.

Hab. North America (Vienna Museum; collection of De Selys Longchamps).

2. P. zonatus!

Progomphus zonatus Hag.! Monog. Gomph. 203, 71; pl. xi, fig. 3. Selys! Synops. 53, 70.

Black, spotted with yellow; head yellow in front, above black; thorax black, dorsum each side with two stripes, and sides with three broader stripes, yellow; feet black; abdomen long, cylindrical, the base subinflated, black, the dorsum with a basal yellow line, the base of segment 7 yellow; appendages yellow; vulvar lamina very short, emarginated; wings fumose, pterostigma large, black. Female.

17—18 antecubitals; 9—11 postcubitals; two discoidal areolets.
Length 52 millim. Alar expanse 70 millim. Pterostigma 5 millim.

Hab. Mexico (collection of Dr. Hagen).

GOMPHOIDES Selys.

Triangles with transverse veins; the superior side shorter than the others; feet short.

1. G. stigmata!

Æschna stigmata? Say, Journ. Acad. Philad. VIII, 17, 10.—*Progomphus stigmatus* Selys! Monog. Gomph. 205, 72. Selys, Synops. 53, 71.—*Gomphoides stigmata* Hag.! Monog. Gomph. 423, 72; pl. xxi, fig. 5.

Yellow, marked with black; head yellow, above fuscous, the vertex yellow; thorax yellow, dorsum with a stripe in the middle, two each side, and sides with two oblique stripes, black; feet black, femora yellow, bilineated with black at the apex; abdomen slender, inflated at the base, the apex dilated, yellow, segments 2 to 7 each side with a black apical fascia, which meet at the tip; segments 8 and 9 fuscous in the middle; appendages yellow, superior ones cylindrical, incurved at the apex, and with an ante-apical tooth above; the inferior appendage short, orbicular, bifid; vulvar lamina short, excised; wings hyaline, pterostigma large, black; 17—19 antecubitals; 10—12 postcubitals; two discoidal areolets.

Length 65 millim. Alar expanse 84 millim. Pterostigma 5 millim.

Hab. Pecos River, Western Texas (Capt. Pope).

2. G. suasa.

Gomphoides suasa Selys, Addit. Synops. 19, 72 bis.

Fusco-olivaceous; thorax fusco-olivaceous, a dorsal stripe each side, another humeral, and the sides with three bands, yellowish; feet grayish-fuscous, femora paler; abdomen fusco-olivaceous, an interrupted dorsal line, spots at the sides (those of the seventh segment larger) yellow; the eighth and ninth segments not dilated; appendages pale; wings hyaline, pterostigma fuscous. ♀. (From the description of De Selys Longchamps.)

antecubitals;   postcubitals;   discoidal areolets.

Length 58 millim. Alar expanse 86 millim. Pterostigma 5 millim.

Hab. Vera Cruz, Mexico (Sallé).

3. G. perfida!

Gomphoides perfida Hagen.

Black, spotted with luteous; head luteo-fuscous; thorax luteous, dorsum with a middle fascia, and each side a lateral one, broad, black, divided with luteous; sides black, with three oblique, luteous stripes; feet black, base of the femora luteo-fuscous; abdomen slender, the base broader (the apex destroyed); black, the dorsum of the first and second segments, and sides, obsoletely luteous; wings fumose, pterostigma large, black. (Male.)

23—24 antecubitals; fifteen postcubitals; two discoidal areolets.

Length 60 ? millim. Alar expanse 82 millim. Pterostigma 5 millim.

Hab. Tampico, Mexico (Saussure).

4. G. elongata.
Cyclophylla elongata Selys! Monog. Gomph. 224, 84; pl. xii, fig. 5.
Selys! Addit. Synops. 20, 79 ter.

Black, spotted with olive; head olivaceous in front, labrum margined with black, and with a black fascia upon the middle; thorax black, dorsum each side with two narrow stripes, and each side with three stripes, olivaceous; feet black, anterior femora pale beneath; abdomen long, slender, black, the base and apex inflated, segments 3—7 with a basal, hastiform, yellow spot; appendages brownish-black, subcylindrical, forcipated, the apex subexcised, the inferior appendage scarcely apparent; wings hyaline, pterostigma large, rufo-fuscous. ♂. Sixteen antecubitals; ten postcubitals; two discoidal areolets. (From the description of De Selys Longchamps.)

Length 62 millim. Alar expanse 72 millim. Pterostigma 5 millim.

Hab. Mexico (Paris Museum).

5. G. protracta!
Cyclophylla protracta Hagen! Selys, Addit. Synops. 20, 79 ter.

Blackish-fuscous, spotted with yellow; head luteous; thorax blackish-fuscous, dorsum with two stripes, and the sides with three oblique ones, yellow; feet brownish-black, femora luteous; abdomen long, slender, inflated at base, fuscous or luteous, membranously dilated at the apex, dorsum with an interrupted, yellow line, the sides luteous; appendages fuscous, subcylindrical, forcipated, subexcised at the apex, the inferior appendage absent; vulvar lamina very short, excised; wings hyaline, pterostigma large, yellow. Twenty-one antecubitals; ten postcubitals; two discoidal areolets.

Length 62 millim. Alar expanse 79 millim. Pterostigma 5 millim.

Hab. Matamoras, Mexico.

6. G. producta!
Aphylla producta Selys! Monog. Gomph. 230, 83; pl. xii, fig. 6.
Selys! Synops. 60, 81. *Aphylla caraiba* Selys! Poey, Ins. Cuba, 456.

Brownish-black, spotted with yellow; head yellow, banded transversely with fuscous; thorax brownish-black, dorsum each side with two stripes, conjoined at the wings, the external one narrower, and the sides with three oblique ones, the middle one incomplete, yellow or green; feet black, femora rufous, obscurer at the apex; abdomen long, slender, the base inflated, the apex somewhat broader, brownish-black, the base with a yellow, dorsal line; appendages black, subcylindrical, forcipated, obtuse at the apex, the inferior one almost absent; ventral lamina narrow, bifid; wings hyaline, the pterostigma large, yellow. 19—23 antecubitals; 11—15 postcubitals; 2 discoidal areolets.

Length 59—65 millim. Alar expanse 76—84 millim. Pterostigma 5 millim.

Hab. Cuba (Poey); British Guiana (Schomburgk); Bahia, Brazil.

7. G. tenuis!

Aphylla tenuis Hagen! Selys, Addit. Synops. 21, 80 bis.

Luteous; head luteo-fuscous; dorsum of the thorax fuscous, sides luteous; feet black, femora luteous; abdomen long, slender, equal, subinflated at base, luteo-fuscous, the segments obscurer at their apex; appendages fuscous, subcylindrical, forcipated, the apex acuter; the inferior appendage absent; wings hyaline, pterostigma large, luteous. Male. 19—22 antecubitals; 12—13 postcubitals; 2 discoidal areolets.

Length 50 millim. Alar expanse 67 millim. Pterostigma 4 millim.

Hab. Choco, New Grenada (Schott).

The specimen is teneral, the colors hardly perfected, preserved in spirits.

HAGENIUS Selys.

Triangles with transverse veins; the superior side longer than the interior; feet very long.

1. H. brevistylus!

Hagenius brevistylus Selys! Monog. Gomph. 241, 86; pl. xiii, fig. 2. Selys! Synops. 63, 84.

Black, spotted with yellow; head yellow in front, a black fascia before the eyes, above black; thorax black, dorsum each side with a stripe and line, and the sides with two broad oblique stripes, a line between them, yellow; feet very long, black; abdomen long, cylindrical, the dorsum black, with a stripe upon the middle, and each side a ventral one, yellow; appendages short, yellow, the superior ones stout, incurved at apex, bidentated beneath, the inferior appendage quadrangular, broad, incurved at the apex; wings subfumose, pterostigma long, brownish-black. 16—19 antecubitals; 13—14 postcubitals; 2 discoidal areolets.

Length 73—78 millim. Alar expanse 104—114 millim. Pterostigma 6 millim.

Hab. New York (Dr. Asa Fitch); Wisconsin (Kennicott); Columbia.

Division II. Labium bifid.

CORDULEGASTER Leach.

Eyes subcontiguous.

1. C. sayi.

Cordulegaster sayi Selys! Monog. Gomph. 331, 109. Selys! Synops. 85, 106.

Black, spotted with yellow; head yellow, rhinarium black; thorax black, dorsum with two stripes, sides each with two stripes and an intermediate line, yellow; feet black; abdomen long, black, annulated with yellow; appendages of the male black, superior ones trigonal, divaricated, with a basal tooth beneath, the inferior appendage quadrangular; appendages of the female yellow; vulvar lamina elongated, bifid; wings hyaline, pterostigma long, yellow; membranule whitish. 18 antecubitals; 11 postcubitals; 2 discoidal areolets.

Length 60 millim. Alar expanse 84 millim. Pterostigma $4\frac{1}{4}$ millim.

Hab. Georgia (British Museum).

It is similar to C. *annulatus* Charp., of Europe.

2. C. maculatus!

Cordulegaster maculatus Selys! Monog. Gomph. 337, 111. Selys! Synops. 86, 108. *Aeschna obliqua* Say, var. A? Jour. Acad. Philad. VIII. 16, 8.

Brownish-black, hairy, spotted with yellow; head yellow, with a fuscous band in front; thorax brownish-black, dorsum each side with a cuneiform stripe, sides with two oblique stripes, yellow; feet black, femora fuscous, the apex black; abdomen long, brownish-black, segments 2—6 with a dorsal, yellow spot each side; vulvar lamina long, bifid, yellow, fuscous at the apex; wings hyaline, pterostigma yellow, membranule white. Female. 21 antecubitals; 15 postcubitals; 2 discoidal areolets.

Length 75 millim. Alar expanse 93 millim. Pterostigma 4 millim.

Hab. Georgia; Maryland (Uhler); Connecticut (Norton).

3. C. dorsalis!

Cordulegaster dorsalis Hagen! Monog. Gomph. 347, 115. Selys! Addit. Synops. 28, 113 bis.

Fuscous, spotted with yellow; head yellow, with a fuscous band in front; thorax fuscous, dorsum each side with a stripe, sides with two oblique ones, yellow; feet blackish-fuscous, femora luteous; abdomen long, fuscous, segments 2—9 with a dorsal, bifid, yellow spot; vulvar lamina long, bifid, luteous; wings hyaline, the base subfulvous, pterostigma yellow, membranule white. Female. Eighteen antecubitals; twelve postcubitals; two discoidal areolets.

Length 80 millim. Alar expanse 100 millim. Pterostigma 4 millim.

Hab. Sitka, Russian America.

4. C. obliquus!

Æschna obliqua Say, Jour. Acad. Philad. VIII, 15, 8.—*Cordulegaster obliquus* Selys! Monog. Gomph. 349, 116; pl. xviii, fig. 5. Selys! Synops. 89, 113.—*Cordulegaster fasciatus* Ramb.! Neuropt. 178, 1.

Black, spotted with greenish-yellow; head yellow, in front with two black bands, occiput tuberculoid; thorax black, with gray hairs, dorsum with a cuneiform stripe each side, and sides with two oblique stripes, yellow; feet black, base of the femora fuscous; abdomen long, equal, black, dorsum with a greenish-yellow line upon the middle, which is dilated in the middle upon segments 5—8; appendages black, superior ones short, trigonal, acute, with a basal tooth beneath; the inferior one quadrangular, the apex tuberculated each side; vulvar lamina short, bifid, yellow, black at the apex; wings hyaline, pterostigma long, fulvous, membranule whitish. Twenty-six antecubitals; 17—20 postcubitals; two discoidal areolets.

Length 83—88 millim. Alar expanse 112—124 millim. Pterostigma 6 millim.

Hab. Indiana (Say); Georgia (Abbot); Connecticut (Norton).

PETALURA Leach.

Pterostigma extremely long.

1. P. thoreyi!
> *Uropetala thoreyi* Hagen! Monog. Gomph. 373, 122; pl. xix, fig. 3.— *Tachopteryx obscura* Uhler MSS.—*Tachopteryx thoreyi* Selys! Addit. Synops. 25, 116 bis.

Olivaceous, spotted with black; head pale in front, with a black band, and above black; thorax olivaceous, the sides with two obsolete black stripes; feet black; abdomen long, equal, olivaceous, dorsum of the second segment with two spots, the following ones with a spot upon the basal middle, an apical ring, and the last segments almost altogether black; appendages black, superior ones dolabriform, the inferior quadrangular, with a basal tooth above, and the apex each side unguiculated; wings hyaline, pterostigma narrow, very long, fulvous. Male. 18—20 antecubitals; 11—13 postcubitals; three discoidal areolets.

Length 78 millim. Alar expanse 100 millim. Pterostigma 9 millim.

Hab. New York; Maryland (Uhler); Fort Towson, Red River.

Subfamily IV. AESCHNINA.

Eyes contiguous; head globose; wings unequal, the posterior ones broader; triangles long; genital organs of the female vaginated.

ANAX Leach.

Anal angle of the posterior wings rounded in the male; second segment of the abdomen not auriculated; abdomen with a lateral, interrupted carina.

1. A. junius!

Libellula junia Drury, Ins. I, 112; pl. xlvii. fig. 5.—*Aeschna junia* Burm.! Handb. II, 841, 18. Say, Jour. Acad. Philad. VIII, 10, 2. Ramb. Neuropt. 196, 6.—*Anax junius* Selys! Revue Odonat. Europ. 328. Selys! Poey, Ins. Cuba, 458.—*Anax spiniferus* Ramb.! Neuropt. 186, 4; pl. i. fig. 14.

Green, spotted with blue and fuscous; head yellow, above with a black spot, and circular blue band; thorax green; feet black, femora partly rufous; abdomen long, subdepressed, equal, the base very much inflated, narrowed beyond, the first segment and base of the second green, the rest blue, with a dorsal, fuscous fascia, interrupted, and in part angulose; appendages fuscous, superior ones of the male long, straight, towards the apex somewhat broader, with an external spine at the apex, the inferior appendage very short, quadrangular, transverse; wings hyaline, flavescent upon the middle, pterostigma long, yellow, narrow; membranule large, brownish-black, with the base white; seventeen antecubitals; eight postcubitals.

Length 68—74 millim. Alar expanse 104—110 millim. Pterostigma 7 millim.

Hab. New York; Maryland; New Jersey; Kentucky; Georgia; Florida; Louisiana; St. Louis; S. Carolina; Pecos River, Texas; Matamoras, Mexico; San Francisco, California; Cuba; Oahu, Sandwich Islands; Kamtschatka; Petcheli Bay, China.

A common and wide-spread species. Rambur erroneously gives Europe as its *habitat*.

2. A. longipes!

Anax longipes Hagen!

Green, spotted with blue and fuscous; head yellow, above immaculate; thorax green; feet extremely long, black, femora rufous, with the apex black; abdomen long, subdepressed, equal, the base inflated, green; surface fuscous, each side of the segments having an apical, yellow spot, beneath yellowish, apex of the segments fuscous; appendages short, foliaceous, fuscous; wings hyaline, pterostigma yellow; membranule brownish black, white at the base; nineteen antecubitals; nine postcubitals.

Length 80 millim. Alar expanse 105 millim. Pterostigma $5\frac{1}{4}$ millim.

Hab. Georgia (Abbot, Zurich Museum).

3. A. amazili.

Aeschna amazili Burm.! Handb. II, 841, 19, *Anax maculatus* Ramb. Neuropt. 188, 7.

Green, spotted with black; head in front greenish-yellow, the labrum margined with black; front above, with a triangular, black spot, bounded by yellow, each side a triangular blue spot; thorax bright green; feet black, anterior femora luteous beneath; abdomen long, stout, equal, the base inflated, blue? ($\male$) or green ($\female$), segments 3 to 10 with a broad, black, dorsal fascia, narrower upon the middle of the segments; segments 3—7, with two blue or green spots each side, the last segments almost entirely black; appendages black, superior ones of the male long, carinate, villose within, the base narrow, the internal margin dilated, before the apex excised, the apex exteriorly recurved, obliquely truncated, acute; the inferior appendage very short, transverse, quadrangular; appendages of the female shorter, foliaceous; wings hyaline, pterostigma short, blackish-fuscous; membranule brownish-black, the base white. 16—18 antecubitals; 6—8 postcubitals.

Length 70—74 millim. Alar expanse 105 millim. Pterostigma 5 millim.

Hab. Guatemala (Collection of Hagen); Venezuela (Appun); Pernambuco, Brazil (Veilenmann).

AESCHNA Fab.

Anal angle of the posterior wings of the male acute; second segment of the abdomen auriculated.

1. Æ. sitchensis!

Aeschna sitchensis Hagen!

Blackish-fuscous, spotted with blue; head?; thorax fuscous, sides with two oblique, obsolete, yellowish stripes; feet black, tibiæ exteriorly rufous; abdomen long, slender, equal, very much arcuated behind the inflated base; black, spotted with blue; segments 3—10 with two large, apical blue spots, 3 to 7, with two basal blue spots, the second segment with two blue lines each side; appendages black, moderate, a little incurved, foliaceous, the base narrow, within carinated, before the apex inflated, the apex short, acute, incurved; the inferior appendage one-half shorter, elongately-triangular, obtuse; wings hyaline, pterostigma short, black; membranule black. Male. Fifteen antecubitals; nine postcubitals.

Length 58 millim. Alar expanse 78 millim. Pterostigma 4 millim.

Hab. Russian America, Sitka (Collection of Hagen).

It is very much like *Aeschna borealis* Zetterstedt, found in Northern Europe and Siberia.

2. Æ. septentrionalis!

Aeschna septentrionalis Burm! Handb. II, 839, 11.—*Aeschna minor* Ramb? Neuropt. 207, 20.

Blackish-brown, spotted with blue; head yellow in front; front anteriorly with a narrow, transverse line, a spot, large anteriorly, in the shape of a T, superiorly, and the rhinarium, black; labrum margined with black; thorax fuscous, dorsum each side with a point, sides with two, narrow, maculose stripes, yellow; feet black, above rufous; abdomen long, stoutish, narrowed behind the inflated base, black, spotted with blue; sides of the segments, two medial and two apical spots, blue; last segment of the male black, each side blue, an elevated tooth above; appendages brownish-black, moderate, a little incurved, foliaceous, the base narrow, a basal obtuse tubercle beneath; carinated inwards, before the apex inflated, the apex obtuse; the inferior appendage one-half shorter, elongately-triangular, obtuse; appendages of the female moderate, foliaceous, obtuse; wings hyaline, pterostigma fuscous, somewhat broad; membranule gray. 14—16 antecubitals; 11—12 postcubitals.

Length 54—55 millim. Alar expanse 74 millim. Pterostigma 4 millim.

Hab. Labrador; Nova Scotia.

Does *Aeschna minor* Rambur differ from it? the wings with a rufous spot at base. It is very much like *Aeschna sitchensis*, Hagen.

3. Æ. juncea!

Aeschna juncea Linne! Selys, Revue Odonat. Europ. 116, 3.—(With the synonyms.)

Fuscous, spotted with blue and yellow; head yellow, a narrow, transverse line in front, a T spot above, broader anteriorly, and the rhinarium, black; thorax fuscous, dorsum each side with a narrow, short stripe, sometimes almost wanting and the sides with two oblique, broad stripes, yellow; feet black; abdomen long, slender, equal, very much narrowed behind the inflated base; brownish-black, with blue and yellow spots, segments 3—10 with two apical blue spots, 3—8 with two triangular spots upon the middle, yellow, apex of the second segment blue; last segment with the males, having an elevated, obtuse tooth above; appendages brownish-black, superior ones of the male, long, subrect, foliaceous, the base narrower, a carina inwardly, the base narrower, before the apex acuter, subincurved, inflated; the inferior appendage almost one-half shorter, elongately-triangular, obtuse; appendages of the female longer, foliaceous; wings hyaline, pterostigma narrow, fuscous; membranule brownish-cinereous, the base paler. 16 antecubitals; 7—9 postcubitals.

Length 66—75 millim. Alar expanse 92—100 millim. Pterostigma 4—5 millim.

Hab. Russian America; Kenai Island, Norton Sound.—Europe; Asia; Siberia; Kamtschatka; Ural.

4. Æ. multicolor!

Aeschna multicolor Hagen!

Fuscous, spotted with blue; head blue ($\male$) or luteous ($\female$), front with a T spot, each side terminated with yellow, and a band before the eyes, black; thorax fuscous, dorsum each side with a stripe, (interrupted or absent in the female), sides, each side with two oblique ones blue ($\male$) or yellow ($\female$); feet black, femora rufous above, the apex black, anterior femora beneath, luteous; abdomen moderate, slender, cylindrical, narrow behind the inflated base; fuscous, spotted with blue ($\male$) or yellow ($\female$), segments 3—10 with two large, apical spots, segments 3—8 with two triangular spots upon the middle, and a basal, divided spot each side, segment 2 with a medial, interrupted fascia, and a broad apical one, blue or yellow; superior appendages of the male black, long, foliaceous, narrow, the base narrower, inwardly carinated, straight, curved inwardly before the apex, an elevated, triangular lamina above, and a longer tooth placed more inferiorly, the apical tip acute, curved downwards; the inferior appendage, pale fuscous, one half shorter, elongately triangular; appendages of the female moderate, fuscous, foliaceous, broader; wings hyaline, those of the female, towards the apex, subflavescent, pterostigma short, fuscous, or luteous (♀); membranule fuscous, the base white. 16—17 antecubitals; 8—9 postcubitals.

Length 65—67 millim. Alar expanse 90—100 millim. Pterostigma 3—3½ millim.

Hab. Pecos River, Western Texas (Capt. Pope); Upper Missouri; Mexico; Cordova (Saussure).

5. Æ. clepsydra!
Aeschna clepsydra Say. Journ. Acad. Philad. VIII, 12, 4.

Fuscous, spotted with blue; head luteous, an incurved, transverse line in front, a broad T spot above, terminated with blue and yellow, black; thorax fuscous, dorsum each side with a cuneiform, green stripe; each side with two broad, maculose and lacerated stripes, and an intermediate, abbreviated one, bluish-green; feet brownish-black, femora, tibiæ and the outside of the tarsi rufous; abdomen long, slender, equal, very much attenuated behind the inflated base; segments 3—10 with two larger, apical spots, 3—8 with two triangular, medial ones and each side a basal, divided one, segment 2 with a transverse, medial, interrupted fascia, and the apex, blue; the last segment with a small, basal tooth above, black, and blue spots confluent at the apex; appendages fuscous, margined with black, the superior ones long, narrow, straight, narrower at base, interiorly with a carina and clothed with hairs, the apex obtusely truncated, a small, acute, incurved tooth at the apex; before the apex are three teeth, superiorly at the internal margin; the inferior appendage one-third shorter, elongately triangular, acute; wings hyaline, pterostigma moderate, fuscous; membranule fuscous. Male. 16 antecubitals; 11 postcubitals.

Length 68 millim. Alar expanse 94 millim. Pterostigma 4 millim.

Hab. Massachusetts (Say); Boston (Scudder); Baltimore (Uhler).

6. Æ. verticalis!
Aeschna verticalis Hagen!

Fuscous, spotted with green and blue; head green, with a T spot above, and a band before the eyes, black; thorax fuscous, dorsum each side, with a cuneiform, green stripe; each side with three oblique, yellowish-green stripes; feet black, femora and tibiæ above, rufous; abdomen long, slender, equal, very much narrowed behind the inflated base, fuscous, spotted with blue; spots like those of *Æ. clepsydra*, but not confluent on the last segment, with a small, basal tooth upon that segment; appendages similar to those of *Æ. clepsydra*, the tip of the apex acute, hardly incurved, above, before the apex, with an elevated line, no teeth; inferior appendage one half shorter, elongated, triangular, acuter; wings hyaline, pterostigma small, blackish-brown; membranule brownish-cinereous. Male. 17—20 antecubitals; 11—12 postcubitals.

Length 67 millim. Alar expanse 95 millim. Pterostigma 3 millim.

Hab. Washington (Osten Sacken); New York (Calverly).

7. Æ. hudsonica!

Aeschna hudsonica Selys' Collection.

Hab. Nova Scotia.

Similar to *Æ. juncea*, but only known to me by name.

8. Æ. constricta!

Aeschna constricta Say. Journ. Acad. Philad. VIII, 11, 3.

Brownish-black, spotted with green and blue; labrum yellow, head yellowish-green in front, a black T spot above; thorax fuscous, dorsum each side with a stripe, which is broader at the wings, the sides each with two oblique, green stripes; feet black, femora and tibiæ above, rufous; abdomen long, equal, blackish-fuscous, very much narrowed behind the inflated base; segments 3—10 with two, dorsal, apical, quadrangular, blue spots, 3—8 with two, medial, triangular, yellow spots, each side with a basal, divided, blue spot; second segment with a basal, dorsal, line, and each side with a transverse line upon the middle, yellow; the last segment flat above; appendages fuscous, superior ones long, subarcuated, the apex dilated, within carinated, before the apex tuberculous and inwards an acute, recurved tooth, extreme apex with a longer spine, which is acute and placed inferiorly; the inferior appendage one-half shorter, elongately triangular, obtuse; wings hyaline, pterostigma small, fuscous; membranule fuscous, the base white. Male. 17—21 antecubitals; 11—15 postcubitals.

Length 70 millim. Alar expanse 96—100 millim. Pterostigma 3 millim.

Hab. Indiana (Say); Maryland (Uhler); Wisconsin (Kennicott); St. Louis; Pennsylvania; Connecticut (Norton).

9. Æ. armata!

Æschna armata Hagen!

Brownish-black, spotted with blue; head in front obtuse, lurid, above with a T spot and band before the eyes, black; thorax fuscous, dorsum each side, anteriorly, with a yellowish-green spot; sides each with two oblique, yellowish stripes, of which the superior one is arcuated; femora above, in the middle, rufous; abdomen long, equal, narrowed behind the inflated base, black; segments 3—6 with two, blue, apical spots, and two larger, triangular, yellow ones, upon the middle, sides blue? second segment each side, with a line and a narrow, basal triangle, yellow, the last segments almost immaculate, the tenth segment, in the middle, above, with a long, compressed spine, bent backwards; appendages black, the superior ones long, foliaceous, straight, the base inwards narrowed, above carinated, the apex exteriorly obtuse, interiorly acute; before the apex superiorly, with an elevated, oval, dentate lamina; the inferior appendage one-half shorter, triangular, narrow, acute; wings subfumose, posterior ones of the female subflavescent at base, pterostigma very small, black; membranule fusco-cinereous, the base whitish. Twenty antecubitals; twelve postcubitals.

Length 68 millim. Alar expanse 92 millim. Pterostigma 2 millim.

Hab. Trogés del Oro, Mexico (Saussure, Deppe).

I have examined a mutilated male specimen.

10. Æ. mutata!

Æschna mutata Hagen!

Fuscous, spotted with yellowish-green; labrum luteous, black anteriorly; front green, above blue, with a T spot, terminated each side with yellow, and a band before the eyes, black; thorax fuscous, the sides each with two yellowish stripes; feet black, base of the femora rufous; abdomen long, equal, the base inflated, rufous, segments 3—9 with two apical, green? spots, which are margined within with black; segments 3—7 with two triangular, yellow, medial spots; base and sides rufous, paler; appendages fuscous, foliaceous; wings hyaline, the base, anterior margin and middle flavescent; pterostigma longer, narrow, bright orange; membranule black, the base white. Female. Nineteen antecubitals; nine postcubitals.

Length 70 millim. Alar expanse 98 millim. Pterostigma 4 millim.

Hab. North America (Vienna Museum).

11. Æ. janata.

Æschna janata Say, Jour. Acad. Philad. VIII, 13, 6.

Fuscous, spotted with blue and yellow; front yellow, with a black T spot above; thorax fuscous, each side of dorsum with a blue stripe, sides each with two oblique, yellow stripes, which are margined with black; feet yellowish, beneath black; abdomen long, contracted behind the inflated base, fuscous, segments with a yellowish band at base, an interrupted apical one, and a spot in the middle, the last segment but little shorter than the preceding one, carinated at base; appendages subarcuated, near the base somewhat dilated, the apex broader, pediform, obtuse; inferior appendage hardly half as long as the superior ones; wings hyaline, extreme base fuscous, pterostigma fulvous; membranule white. Male. (From the description of Say.)

Length 60? millim.

Hab. Massachusetts.

Similar to *Æ. constricta*, but the last abdominal segment is longer, the apex of the appendages are mutic. It is entirely unknown to me.

12. Æ. florida!

Æschna florida Hagen!

Fuscous, spotted with green; front luteous, above green, immaculate, thorax fuscous, dorsum each side, with a very broad, green stripe; sides green, with an oblique, narrow, fuscous stripe; feet black, base of the femora rufous; abdomen longer than the wings, equal, the base inflated, the last segment shortest, fuscous, with a green? dorsal, interrupted stripe, which is triangularly dilated at the apex of the segments, a lateral green? stripe, and the ninth segment obsoletely bimaculated; appendages shorter than the last segment, very small, black, flat, obtuse; wings subfumose, flavescent anteriorly, pterostigma narrow, fulvous; membranule fusco-cinereous. Female. Twenty antecubitals; twelve postcubitals.

Length 78 millim. Alar expanse 102 millim. Pterostigma 4 millim.

Hab. Mexico (Deppe).

It is most like Æ. *luteipennis* Burm., but distinct by the front, immaculate above, the stripes of the thorax being broader, not well terminated.

13. Æ. dominicana.

Æschna dominicana Selys' Collection.

Hab. St. Domingo. Unknown to me; similar to Æ. *juncea*.

14. Æ. contorta.

Æschna contorta Selys' Collection.

Hab. Nova Scotia. Unknown to me; similar to Æ. *cyanea*.

15. Æ. cyanifrons.

Æschna cyanifrons Selys' Collection.

Hab. Jamaica. Unknown to me; similar to Æ. *confusa*.

16. Æ. grandis!

Æschna grandis Linné. Selys, Revue Odonat. Eur. 131, 10 (with the synonymy).

Fuscous; head luteous, front with a spot above, anteriorly, fuscous; thorax fulvous, the sides each, with two oblique, yellow stripes, which are bounded with fuscous; feet fulvous; abdomen long, equal, behind the base inflated, then slightly narrowed, rufo-fuscous, with lateral, divided, blue spots; appendages fuscous, superior ones straight, foliaceous, carinated within, narrow at the base, at the apex obtuse; the inferior one-half shorter, triangular, obtuse; wings flavescent, pterostigma small, fulvous; membranule cinereous. 20—22 antecubitals; 12 postcubitals.

Length 70 millim. Alar expanse 94 millim. Pterostigma 3½ millim.

Hab. Bergen Hill, New Jersey (Guex); I saw a single male. It is also common in Europe and Asia.

17. Æ. adnexa!

Æschna adnexa Hagen!

Fuscous, spotted with green; labrum pale, fuscous anteriorly; front anteriorly blue, above yellowish-green, with a broader T spot, and an ante-ocular band, black; thorax bright green, dorsum with a divided, middle fascia, and a lateral spot, the sides with two oblique streaks, all badly terminated, fuscous; feet black; abdomen a little narrowed at base, fuscous, the second segment with a medial and apical fascia, the third segment with a dorsal line, which is triangularly dilated upon the middle and apex, and the sides green? (the other segments are destroyed); wings hyaline, pterostigma moderate; brownish-black, membranule black. Male. 19 antecubitals; 10 postcubitals.

Length 60? millim. Alar expanse 87 millim. Pterostigma 4 millim.

Hab. Cuba (Poey).

Is it *Æ. cyanifrons* Selys? I have only examined a single mutilated specimen.

18. Æ. virens!

Aeschna virens Ramb. Neuropt. 193, 3.

Green, spotted with fuscous; labrum black anteriorly; head green, above with a T spot, and a narrow band before the eyes black; thorax bright green, sutures fuscous; feet black, anterior femora beneath yellowish; abdomen long, equal, a little narrowed behind the somewhat inflated base, green, spotted with fuscous, first segment green posteriorly, segments 2 to 8 green, with four fuscous, quadrangular spots, upon segments 2 to 4 they are smaller; segment 3 has the spots linear, basal; apical segments fuscous; appendages black, superior ones straight, foliaceous, obtuse; the inferior appendage one-half shorter, triangular, acute (of the female destroyed), wings hyaline, of the female, subflavescent posteriorly, pterostigma elongated, brownish-black; membranule brownish-gray. 20—24 antecubitals; 12—13 postcubitals.

Length 84 millim. Alar expanse 118 millim. Pterostigma 5—6 millim.

Hab. Cuba (Poey); St. Cruz de Bolivia (Rambur); Venezuela.

I have examined one female from the Island of Cuba; nor am I altogether certain, whether the male described from Venezuela belongs here; it is extremely like it, by its few antecubitals, its long pterostigma, its obscure membranule, and its hyaline wings. I possess two females from Cuba (Poey), which are a little smaller; the bases of all the wings are flavescent; in all the rest they agree entirely with the description of *Æ. virens* Rambur.

19. Æ. ingens!

Aeschna ingens Ramb. Neuropt. 192, 1.

Green, spotted with fuscous; labrum black anteriorly; head green, above with a T spot, and fascia before the eyes, black; dorsum of the thorax fuscous, with a green stripe each side; sides green, with an oblique, narrow, fuscous stripe; feet black, anterior femora pale beneath; abdomen long, gradually narrowing posteriorly, that of ♂ hardly narrowed behind the base, fuscous, marked with green, the first segment green posteriorly, the second green, with a transverse, fuscous fascia at the apex, the following ones fuscous, with a dorsal, interrupted line, a middle fascia, triangularly dilated, an apical fascia, and the sides with a broader, interrupted fascia, green; the last segment fuscous, with two green spots; appendages fuscous; superior ones of the male long, foliaceous, straight, obtuse; the inferior one half as long, triangular, acute, those of the female extremely long, lanceolate, the base broader, before the apex slightly narrowed, subacute; wings hyaline, of the female flavescent at base, pterostigma long, fulvous; membranule gray. 20 antecubitals; 12 postcubitals.

Length 100 millim. Alar expanse 110—120 millim. Pterostigma 5 millim.

Hab. St. John's River, near Lake Harney, Florida. (Osten Sacken; Norton); Cuba; United States (Selys).

20. Æ. heros!

Aeschna heros Fab. Entom. Syst. Suppl. 285.—Ramb.! Neuropt. 194, 4.—
Aeschna multicincta Say, Journ. Acad. Philad. VIII, 9, 1.

Fuscous, marked with yellowish-green; front obscure luteous, above fuscous, each side with a yellowish-green spot; occiput of the female bifid; thorax fuscous, dorsum each side with a stripe, which is angulated at the wings, and the sides with two oblique stripes, green; feet black, base of the femora subrufous; abdomen long, stout, hardly broader at base, fuscous, the base, middle and apex, of the segments, with a subinterrupted, narrow, green fascia; appendages black, subarcuated, the base narrower, a tubercle beneath, the apex carinated, truncated, inner edge villose; inferior appendage one-half the length of the superior, narrow, almost equal, the apex obtusely truncated, sometimes almost bifid; appendages of the female broad, ovate, foliaceous; wings hyaline, subflavescent in the middle, the apex sometimes infuscated, pterostigma long, narrow, fulvous; membranule white; twenty-five antecubitals; sixteen postcubitals.

Length 85—96 millim. Alar expanse 108—120 millim. Pterostigma 5—6 millim.

Hab. Indiana (Say); Massachusetts (Harris); New York (Calverly); N. Jersey (Guex); Maryland (Uhler); Tennessee (Saussure); Waterville; Mobile; Florida, Lake Harney (Osten Sacken); Louisiana (Schaum); Mexico (Rambur).

21. Æ. brevifrons!
Æschna brevifrons Hagen.

Fuscous, varied with blue; head luteous in front, varied with fuscous; front short, broad, above with a T spot in the middle, the root of which is triangularly dilated, black, surrounded with a yellow margin; thorax with the dorsum luteous, a short, fuscous streak each side; the sides blue, obscurely varied with white and black; feet yellow, beneath, knees, and the tarsi, black; abdomen inflated at base, nigro-fuscous, the segments with middle triangular spots and oval apical ones, blue; segment 2 has a transverse, medial, blue line, each side, bounded by black; segment 10 ($\male$) has the apex rounded, blue, a small, elevated tooth at base, and a black spot each side; superior appendages foliaceous, fuscous, narrower at base; the inferior one luteous, broad, triangular, a little shorter than the superiors; appendages of the female short, foliaceous, fuscous; wings hyaline, pterostigma short, fuscous; twelve antecubitals; ten postcubitals.

Length 67 millim. Alar expanse 91 millim. Pterostigma $2\frac{1}{2}$ millim.

Hab. Acapulco, Mexico; Valparaiso.

22. Æ. pentacantha!
Æschna pentacantha Ramb.! Neuropt. 208, 22.

Varied rufous and green; front produced; face yellow, subexcavated, the superior margin bounded by rufous; the front blue above, margined with yellow, the base rufo-fuscous; thorax villose, rufo-fuscous, dorsum each side with an arcuated stripe, sides each with two green ones; feet black, femora partly rufous; abdomen long, sensibly narrowing posteriorly, rufo-fuscous, spotted with green (the markings obsolete); appendages black, superior ones short, narrow, before the apex dilated beneath, obliquely truncated; the inferior one a little shorter, narrow, triangular, obtuse; those of the female very small; wings hyaline, the apex subfumose, pterostigma narrow, yellow; membranule whitish; nineteen antecubitals; nineteen postcubitals.

Length 73 millim. Alar expanse 102 millim. Pterostigma $3\frac{1}{2}$ millim.

Hab. New Orleans (Schaum).

23. Æ. basalis.

Æschna basalis Selys' Collection.

Hab. Canada. Unknown to me.

24. Æ. quadriguttata!

Æschna quadriguttata Burm.! Handb. II, 837, 22.—Selys, Revue Odonat. Eur. 398. *Æschna vinosa* Say, Jour. Acad. Philad. VIII, 13, 5.

Fulvous; head fulvous, above with a fuscous stripe; thorax fulvous, the sides, each with two bright yellow spots, which are encircled with fuscous; feet luteous; abdomen long, equal, much narrowed behind the inflated base, fulvous, spotted with yellow (markings obsolete), segments with a yellow medial fascia, which is triangularly dilated; the apex yellow, with a trifid fuscous spot; appendages fulvous, the superior ones long, foliaceous, obtuse, the base narrower, and beneath with a small tooth; the inferior appendage very short, triangular, broader, obtuse; wings hyaline, with fulvous veins and a basal fulvous spot, the basal space reticulated, pterostigma small, yellow; membranule small, white; 19—20 antecubitals; nineteen postcubitals.

Length 60—65 millim. Alar expanse 85 millim. Pterostigma $3\frac{1}{2}$ millim.

Hab. Pennsylvania; Carolina; Massachusetts; Washington (Osten Sacken); Maryland (Uhler).

25. Æ. furcillata.

Æschna furcillata Say, Jour. Acad. Philad. VIII, 15, 7.—*Gynacantha quadrifida* Ramb.! Neuropt. 209, 1.

Varied green and fuscous; face yellowish, beneath obsoletely spotted, above with a somewhat T-shaped mark, which is dilated at base, black; thorax pubescent, green, dorsum rufo-fuscous, with two green stripes each side, the superior ones being transverse, and short; the sides with a fascia composed of three spots, black; abdomen long, cylindrical, inflated at the base, and then narrowed; varied with black and green, the basal spots larger; superior appendages long, foliaceous, subincurved, with a basal and medial tubercle beneath; the inferior appendage short, bifurcated, the branches diverging; wings hyaline, pterostigma short, broad, quadrangular; membranule sub-obscure. ($\male$. From the descriptions of Rambur and Say.)

Size of *Libellula ferruginea* Ramb.; but longer. Length 55? millim.

Hab. North America (collection of de Selys Longchamps); Massachusetts (Say).

GYNACANTHA Ramb.

Wings, with the anal angle of the posteriors, in the males, acute; second segment of the abdomen auriculated; last segment of the female spinous beneath.

1. Gyn. trifida!

Gynacantha trifida Ramb. Neuropt. 210, 3.—Selys, Poey Ins. Cuba, 459.

Fuscous, spotted with green; head obsoletely green in front, above with a T spot, black; thorax fuscous, dorsum each side with a cuneiform, green stripe; sides green, with two oblique, fuscous lines; feet rufo-fuscous, tarsi black; abdomen long, slender at the base, inflated, then narrowed fuscous, nearly all the segments with spots upon the middle, and two at apex, green; appendages fuscous, superior ones of the male, slender, the base narrow, cultriform, the apex acute, subaduncate, interiorly ciliated; the inferior one very short, triangular, obtuse; those of the female very long, foliaceous, towards the apex broader, obtuse; the last segment produced beneath, with three spines; wings hyaline, the base, in the males, subflavescent, pterostigma moderate, fuscous; nineteen antecubitals; twelve postcubitals.

Length 60—70 millim. Alar expanse 84—90 millim. Pterostigma 3½ millim.

Hab. Cuba (Poey); Jamaica; Brazil.

This species migrates in flocks during the early part of spring. (Poey.)

2. Gyn. septima.

Gynacantha septima Selys, Poey Ins. Cuba, 460.

Similar to the preceding, brownish-olive, the extremity of the front with a transverse, obsolete, fuscous spot; feet pale ferruginous; wings hyaline, or a little infuscated (adult); pterostigma rather short, fuscous; the male with a small, 4-toothed auricle (3-toothed in *Gyn. trifida*); appendages, superior ones long, slender, acute; the inferior one very short. (Male; from the description of De Selys Longchamps.) Of a little smaller size than *Gyn. trifida.*

Hab. Jamaica; Brazil.

Not sufficiently known to me.

Tribe III. LIBELLULINA.

Wings unequal; triangle of the anterior wings dissimilar; anterior genital hamule of the male free; penis and vesicle conjoined; genital organs of the female uncovered.

Sub-family V. CORDULINA.

Eyes with a tubercle in the middle, posteriorly.

MACROMIA Rambur.

Legs very long; tarsal unguiculi bifid, the branches equal.

1. M. taeniolata!

Macromia taeniolata Ramb. Neuropt. 139, 3.—*Macromia vittigera* Ramb. Neuropt. 140, 4.—*Macromia cincta* Ramb. Neuropt. 141, 5.

Obscure brassy-green; mouth luteous; front with a fascia anteriorly yellow, above excavated, brassy-green; thorax brassy-green, dorsum each side, in front, with an abrupt yellow stripe, and the sides with an oblique, medial, yellow one; feet black; abdomen long, slender, brownish-black, segments 2—8 each side with a dorsal, yellow spot; appendages black, the superior ones cylindrical, with a small tooth outside; the apical half a little incurved, the apex acute; the inferior appendage equal, triangular, narrow; wings hyaline, pterostigma small, black; membranule cinereous. Male. The vulvar lamina is bilobed. (Female from the description of Rambur.) Twenty antecubitals; nine postcubitals; one discoidal areolet.

Length 85 millim. Alar expanse 110 millim. Pterostigma 4 millim.

Hab. Philadelphia; Maryland (Uhler).

2. M. cingulata.

Macromia cingulata Ramb. Neuropt. 137, 1.

Varied with black and yellow; mouth yellow; labium in the middle, and margin of the labrum black; front excavated and black superiorly; thorax violet-bluish, each side with three stripes, which are anteriorly abrupt, yellow; abdomen with yellow bands superiorly, which are narrowed; feet black; wings hyaline, a spot at base and the apex broadly flavescent; pterostigma small, rufo-fuscous. (Female from the description of Rambur.) Antecubitals — ? postcubitals — ? two discoidal areolets.

Length near 50 millim. Alar expanse near 85 millim.

Hab. North America.

3. M. annulata!

Macromia annulata Hagen !

Fuscous, varied with yellow; mouth and front yellow, front excavated above and yellow, with a median fuscous line; thorax fuscous, somewhat tinged with brassy-green, dorsum each side with a little abrupted fascia, and the sides each with two oblique stripes, yellow; feet black, base of the anterior femora yellow; abdomen long, slender, fuscous, segment 2 with a transverse fascia, segments 3 to 8 with a large, dorsal, quadrangular spot, yellow; appendages fuscous, yellowish at base; the superior ones cylindrical, with a tooth upon the external middle, the apical half subincurved, the apex obtuse; the inferior appendage yellowish, equal, triangular; the vulvar lamina short, excised; wings hyaline, the extreme base, in the female, flavescent, pterostigma small, black; membranule whitish cinereous; 14—16 antecubitals; 8—9 postcubitals; two discoidal areolets.

Length 68—73 millim. Alar expanse 90—102 millim. Pterostigma 2½ millim.

Hab. Pecos River, Western Texas (Capt. Pope).

4. M. pacifica!

Macromia pacifica Hagen!

Fuscous; thorax fuscous, tinged with brassy-green, dorsum each side with a stripe, and sides each with an oblique stripe, yellow; abdomen fuscous, spotted with yellow in part; feet black; abdominal appendages blackish-fuscous, the superior ones broader at base, a tooth upon the external middle; the basal half narrower, incurved, the apex acute, inferior appendage black, triangular, a little longer; wings hyaline, base of the posterior ones subfumose; pterostigma small, black; membranule whitish-cinereous. Male. Sixteen antecubitals; eleven postcubitals; two discoidal areolets.

Length —? millim. Alar expanse 86 millim. Pterostigma 2¼ millim.

Hab. North America, Pacific R. R. Survey, Lat. 38°.

The specimen is very much mutilated; I saw nothing but fragments, excepting the wings, feet, thorax, and abdomen.

EPITHECA Charp.

The triangles with transverse veins; hind wings of the male with the anal angle rounded; the accessory membranule large.

E. princeps!

Epitheca princeps Hagen!

Fuscous; mouth and front pale, labrum yellow; thorax luteous, dorsum anteriorly obsoletely fuscous, the sides at the feet a little varied with fuscous; feet luteo-fuscous, tibiae black, the anterior ones luteo-fuscous exteriorly; abdomen long, the base inflated, the apex equal, luteous, the dorsum obsoletely marked with fuscous; appendages long, fuscous, superior ones cylindrical at base, narrow, inflated at the apex, subincurved, obtuse; the inferior one luteous, shorter, triangular; vulvar lamina long, bilobed; wings hyaline, base of the anterior ones with a broad streak, a large, triangular basal spot to the posterior ones, a large fenestrated, nodal spot, and the apices of all the wings brownish, pterostigma small, black; membranule large, white, the apex brownish-cinereous.

Var. The spots of the wings smaller, or almost wanting.

Eight antecubitals; 5—6 postcubitals; two discoidal areolets.

Length 63 millim. Alar expanse 88—93 millim. Pterostigma 3 millim.

Hab. Pecos River, Western Texas; Georgia (Abbot); Maryland.

A large specimen (♂) from Georgia, has 72 millims. length; alar expanse 102 millim., the fuscous spots of the wings are broader but it is hardly distinct.

DIDYMOPS Rambur.

Triangles with transverse veins; tarsal nails bifid, the branches equal.

1. D. transversa!

Libellula transversa Say, Journ. Acad. VIII, 19, 3.—*Epophthalmia cinnamonea* Burm. Handb. II, 845, 2.—*Didymops Servillii* Ramb.! Neuropt. 142, 1.

Rufo-fuscous, villous; front with a transverse, yellow fascia, above excavated, each side with a yellow spot; thorax rufo-fuscous, each side with an oblique, whitish stripe; abdomen stout, almost cylindrical, rufo-fuscous, the segments paler at base; appendages short, fuscous; vulvar lamina truncatedly-excised, short; feet rufous, tibiæ yellow exteriorly, tarsi black; wings hyaline, veins rufous, with a short, rufo-fuscous, basal, longitudinal spot, pterostigma small, fulvous; membranule white, the apex cinereous. (Female.)

Appendages of the male lanceolate, subarcuated, the apex exteriorly subdenticulated; the inferior appendage equal to the superiors. (From the description of Say.)

12—13 antecubitals; nine postcubitals; two discoidal areolets.

Length 55 millim. Alar expanse 75—80 millim. Pterostigma 2 millim.

Hab. Carolina (Zimmerman); Washington (Osten Sacken); Massachusetts (Say); Pennsylvania (Ziegler); New York (Asa Fitch).

2. D. obsoleta!

Libellula obsoleta Say, Journ. Acad. Philad. VIII, 28, 17.—*Libellula polysticta* Burm.! Handb. II, 856, 53.

Testaceous, hairy; mouth and front luteous; thorax testaceous, dorsum with a point each side, anteriorly, and the sides with a spot upon the middle, inferiorly, yellow; abdomen long, the base inflated, the apex depressed, broad, testaceous; appendages testaceous, the superior ones long, the base cylindrical, the apex broader outwardly, incurved, subacute; the inferior one a little shorter, triangular; wings hyaline, the second series of antecubital veins banded with yellow, the hind wings with a fulvous spot at base, pterostigma small, yellow; membranule white, the apex black. (Male.)

The female has the basal spot of the wings larger (Say.)

7—8 antecubitals; eight postcubitals; two discoidal areolets, then three following.

Length 43 millim. Alar expanse 62 millim. Pterostigma 2¼ millim.

Hab. New Orleans; Indiana; Massachusetts (Say).

CORDULIA Leach.

Anal angle of the posterior wings of the male, acute (body brassy-green).

1. C. filosa!

Cordulia filosa Hagen!

Obscure brassy green; labium luteous, labrum and front fuscous; front above, and the vertex brassy-green; thorax brassy-green, the sides, each, with two, obsolete, yellow lines; feet black; abdomen long, slender, the base inflated, then becoming more slender, the apex a little broader, the second segment inferiorly, with a lateral, luteous spot; appendages black, the superior ones long, cylindrical, arcuated, before the apex thicker, the apex recurved outwards, the extreme apex unguiculated inside; the inferior appendage half the length of the superior ones, narrow, triangular; wings hyaline, pterostigma small, black; membranule large, fuscous, paler inwardly; anal angle of the posterior wings acute in the male. ($\male$.) Eight antecubitals; six postcubitals; two discoidal areolets.

Length 57 millim. Alar expanse 78 millim. Pterostigma 3 millim.

Hab. Georgia (Abbot).

2. C. linearis!

Cordulia linearis Hagen!

Obscure brassy-green; labium luteous; labrum and front fuscous, the front above, and the vertex brassy-green; thorax small, brassy-green, the sides fuscous, with a subæneous tinge; feet black, base of the anterior femora luteous; abdomen very long, slender, the base compressed, inflated, brownish-black, segments 2—8 with a basal, obsolete, yellow spot each side; appendages black, the superior ones short, the base cylindrical, arcuated, a small tooth externally, the apex dilated, acutely bifid, before the apex is another external tooth; the inferior appendage a little shorter, triangular, narrow; wings hyaline, pterostigma small, black; membranule large, fuscous, the base pale; anal angle of the male acute; nine antecubitals; 8—9 postcubitals; two discoidal areolets.

Length 60 millim. Alar expanse 92 millim. Pterostigma 3 millim.

Hab. St. Louis.

3. C. tenebrosa.

Libellula tenebrosa Say, Journ. Acad. Philad. VIII, 19, 4.

Obscure brassy-green; labium luteous; labrum and front fuscous; front brassy-green above; vertex fuscous; thorax brassy-green, each side with two lines, and a point posteriorly, yellow; abdomen obscure brassy-green, the base inflated, then very slender, behind the middle, fusiform; superior appendages arcuated, a tooth upon the middle superiorly, the apex abruptly incurved, truncated; feet black; wings hyaline, pterostigma black; membranule blackish, the base whitish; interior, anal margin of the posterior wings fulvo-fuscous. (From the description of Say.)

Length 51 millim. or larger.

Hab. Indiana.

4. C. bifurcata.

Cordulia bifurcata Selys' Collection.

Hab. Canada; Nova Scotia. Unknown to me.

5. C. libera.

Cordulia libera Selys' Collection.

Hab. Canada. Unknown to me.

6. C. procera.
Cordulia procera Selys' Collection.
Hab. North America. Unknown to me.

7. C. chalybea.
Cordulia chalybea Selys' Collection.
Hab. Nova Scotia. Unknown to me.

8. C. franklini.
Cordulia franklini Selys' Collection.
Hab. Hudson's Bay. Unknown to me.

9. C. richardsoni.
Cordulia richardsoni Selys' Collection.
Hab. Mackenzie River; Labrador. Unknown to me.

10. C. cingulata.
Cordulia cingulata Selys' Collection.
Hab. Newfoundland. Unknown to me.

11. C. tenebrica.
Cordulia tenebrica Selys' Collection.
Hab. Nova Scotia. Unknown to me.

12. C. saturata.
Cordulia saturata Selys' Collection.
Hab. Nova Scotia. Unknown to me.

13. C. albicincta!
Epophthalmia albicincta Burm.! Handb. II, 847, 8.

Brassy-green, hairy; labium luteous, front inferiorly and at sides, luteous, above and vertex brassy-green; thorax bright green-brassy; feet black; abdomen slender, at the base inflated, then slenderer, the apex equal, brassy-black, the base each side, and the last segment at the apex, luteous; appendages black, the superior ones short, depressed, straight, a basal tooth, and another upon the middle beneath, apex truncated, an internal unguiculus, which is arcuated, produced; inferior appendage triangular, a little shorter; vulvar lamina bilobed; wings hyaline, anterior margin, in the females, subflavescent; pterostigma fulvous; membranule large, fuscous, whitish at the base; anal angle of the males subacute; 7—8 antecubitals; 7—8 postcubitals; two discoidal areolets.

Length 48 millim. Alar expanse 66 millim. Pterostigma 3 millim.

Hab. Labrador. Is it not *C. franklini?*

14. C. septentrionalis!

Cordulia septentrionalis Hagen!

Brassy-green, hairy; labium luteous; front brassy-green above, each side with a yellow spot; vertex brassy-green; thorax brassy-green, dorsum with a spot each side at the wings, and the sides each with two maculose stripes, yellow; feet black, anterior femora yellowish at base; abdomen slender, behind the base inflated, then attenuated, with the apex equal, brassy-black, the base each side, obsoletely luteous; the apex each side luteous, villose; appendages black, superior ones longer, subdepressed, straight, with a larger, basal tooth beneath, and a smaller one upon the external middle, internal, apical hook oblique, longer, the tip recurved; the inferior appendage half the length of the superiors, triangular; vulvar lamina bilobed; wings hyaline, the posterior ones with a small, basal, triangular, brownish-black spot, pterostigma small, fulvous; membranule large, fuscous, the base whitish; anal angle of the males subacute; seven antecubitals; seven postcubitals; two discoidal areolets.

Length 43 millim. Alar expanse 60 millim. Pterostigma $2\frac{1}{2}$ millim.

Hab. Labrador. Is it not *C. richardsoni?*

15. C. lateralis!

Epophthalmia lateralis Burm.! Handb. II, 847, 7. *Libellula cynosura* Say, Jour. Acad. Philad. VIII, 30, 19.

Fuscous; mouth and front luteous, above with an ante-ocular, narrow, black fascia; thorax luteo-fuscous, with gray hair, sides with an obsolete, yellow stripe; feet black, anterior femora almost entirely, and the base of the others luteous; abdomen depressed, a little broadened, the base inflated, compressed; brownish-black, each side with a marginal, maculose, yellow stripe; appendages black, superior ones long, cylindrical, obtuse, sub-arcuated, the base narrow; inferior appendage shorter, triangular; vulvar lamina longly bifid; wings hyaline, posterior ones with a basal streak, and triangular basal spot, which is sometimes larger, blackish-fuscous, pterostigma luteous; membranule large, whitish-gray; anal angle of the males rounded; seven antecubitals; four postcubitals; two discoidal areolets.

Length 35—41 millim. Alar expanse 58 millim. Pterostigma 2 millim.

Hab. Massachusetts (Say); Philadelphia; Ohio; Louisiana; Florida (Osten Sacken).

Does it belong to this genus? Perhaps it is an *Epitheca*.

TETRAGONEURIA Selys.

Reticulation of the wings dense; anal angle of the posterior wings of the male, rounded.

1. T. semiaquea!

Libellula semiaquea Burm.! Handb. II, 849, 61. *Cordulia complanata* Ramb.! Neuropt. 145, 2, (in part.)

Fuscous; mouth and front luteous; thorax luteous, villose; the sides with an obsolete, yellow stripe; feet black, anterior femora luteous; abdomen broad, depressed, short, brownish-black, each side with a marginal, maculose, yellow stripe; appendages black, superior ones long, cylindrical, obtuse, the base narrow; inferior one triangular, a little shorter; vulvar lamina longly bifid; wings hyaline, basal half of the posteriors fuscous, subfenestrated; pterostigma small, luteous; membranule large, whitish; anal angle of the males rounded; six antecubitals; five postcubitals; two discoidal areolets.

Length 32—36 millim. Alar. expanse 52—58 millim. Pterostigma 2 millim.

Hab. Savannah, Georgia; South Carolina.

2. T. balteata!

Tetragoneuria balteata Hagen!

Luteo-fuscous; mouth and front pale yellow; labrum with a basal point, and the front with a band at the eyes, fuscous; the large vertex and the occiput, pale yellow; thorax luteous, villose, the sides yellow, two obsolete stripes each side, and larger spots at the base of the feet, blackish fuscous; feet black, base of the femora luteous; abdomen short, stout, triquetral, the base subinflated, luteous, the incisures and the three apical segments, black; appendages luteous; vulvar lamina short, subemarginate; wings hyaline, with luteous veins, the base with a fulvous spot, that of the anterior wings small, pterostigma yellow; membranule cinereous. (Female.) Six antecubitals; five postcubitals; two discoidal areolets.

Length 37 millim. Alar expanse 68 millim. Pterostigma $2\frac{1}{2}$ millim.

Hab. Pecos River, Western Texas (Capt. Pope).

Does it belong to this genus?

3. T. diffinis.

Tetragoneuria diffinis Selys' Collection.

Hab. Nova Scotia. Unknown to me.

4. T. costalis.

Tetragoneuria costalis Selys' Collection.

Hab. Georgia. Unknown to me.

Sub-Fam. VI. LIBELLULINA.

Eyes entire behind; beginning of the second series of postcubital spaces with no transverse veins.

PANTALA Hagen.

Eyes connected in a long space; posterior lobe of the prothorax small, entire; abdomen cylindrical, stout, the apex sensibly attenuated, basal segments 2—4 with two transverse sutures; feet long, slender; base of the posterior wings triangularly dilated; pterostigma small, trapezoidal; first sector of the triangle of the anterior wings straight; triangles of the anterior wings narrow, long; caudal appendages elongated; genital organs of the male a little prominent, the anterior lamina bifid; internal branch of the hamule unguiculated; no unguiculus to the external one; vulva disclosed, the margin recurved, entire; the following segment carinated beneath, and bituberculated.

1. P. flavescens!

Libellula flavescens Fab.! Ent. Syst. Suppl. 285, 18–19; Selys! Poey, Ins. Cuba, 443.—*Libellula viridula* Beauv. Ins. Afr., et Amer. Neur. 69, pl. iii, fig. 4. Descript. de l'Egypte, Neuropt. pl. l, fig. 4. Rambur! Neuropt. 38, 10.—*Libellula analis* Burm.! Handb. II, 852, 23. *Libellula terminalis* Burm.! Handb. II, 852, 24.—*Libellula sparshallii* Dale. Curtis, Guide. 162, 5. Selys, Monog. Libell. 36. Selys, Revue des Odonat. 322.

Testaceous-yellow; mouth, front and vertex pale; feet black, base of the femora, and the tibia exteriorly, yellowish; thorax with black spots inferiorly; abdomen with a dorsal, maculose, black stripe, which is often almost obsolete; appendages black, yellowish at base; wings hyaline, anal margin of the posterior ones flavescent, apices of all the wings sometimes a little fumose, pterostigma luteous; membranule white; fourteen antecubitals; seven postcubitals; three discoidal areolets.

Length 43—52 millim. Alar expanse 76—91 millim. Pterostigma 3 millim.

Hab. It encircles the whole world; no other species occupies so many countries. *America.* Georgia; St. Louis; Maryland (Uhler, rare and local); Cuba; Martinique; St. Thomas (*Lib. terminalis* Burm.); Venezuela; Surinam; Para, Brazil.

Asia. Banco; Sumatra (*Lib. flavescens* Fab.); Java (*Lib. analis* Burm.); Pondichery; Tranquebar; Bengal; Nicobar Islands; Ceylon; China; Japan; Luzon; Kamtschatka.

Oceanica. Oahu; Borabora; Tahiti; New South Wales.

Africa. Egypt; Senegambia; Sierra Leone; Angola; Owara; Congo (*Lib. viridula* Beauv.); Port Natal; Isle of France.

Europe? England, Horning (Dale); very likely an error.

2. P. hymenæa!

Libellula hymenæa Say, Jour. Acad. Philad. VIII, 19, 1.

Viridescent; mouth, front, and vertex yellowish; feet black, base of the femora, and the tibiæ exteriorly, yellowish; thorax each side, with two oblique, pale lines; abdomen with a maculose, dorsal stripe, which is obsolete anteriorly, and the sutures, black; appendages green; wings hyaline; anal margin of the posterior ones subflavescent, a round, fuscous spot, veined with yellow, before the anal angle; pterostigma yellowish; membrane white; fourteen antecubitals; seven postcubitals; four discoidal areolets (only three at the triangle).

Length 47 millim. Alar expanse 88 millim. Pterostigma 4 millim.

Hab. Indiana (Say); Pecos River, Western Texas (Captain Pope); Matamoras, Mexico.

TRAMEA HAGEN.

Eyes connected in a short space; posterior lobe of the prothorax small, entire; abdomen stout, cylindrical, slightly carinated; attenuated at the apex, segments 3 and 4 with transverse sutures; feet long, slender; base of the posterior wings triangularly dilated; pterostigma small, trapezoidal; first sector of the triangle of the anterior wings, almost straight; triangle long, narrow; caudal appendages very much elongated, slender; genital organs of the male a little prominent, anterior lamina recurved, entire, hamule cylindrical, the external branch elongated, no internal branch; vulvar lamina large, bifid, obtected, the segment following subcarinated beneath.

1. **T. carolina!**
   Libellula carolina Linné, Centur. Insect. 28, 85; Amoen. Acad. VI, 441. Syst. Nat., ed. XII, 904, 17; ed. XIII, V, 2624, 17. Drury, Ins. I, 113, pl. xxxviii, fig. 1. Fab. Syst. Ent. 424, 23; Sp. Ins. I, 524, 30; Mantiss. Ins. I, 338, 33; Entom. Syst. II, 382, 41. Burm.! Handb. II, 852, 26. Say, Jour. Acad. Philad. VIII, 19, 2. Ramb.! Neuropt. 32, 1. Selys, Poey, Ins. Cuba. 440.

Rufo-fuscous; front superiorly, and vertex of the males brassy-purple; feet black, base of the femora rufous; abdomen sometimes pruinose, the three apical segments with a broad, dorsal, black band; superior appendages of the male black, the basal half rufous, as long as the two apical segments; the inferior appendage reaching beyond the denticulated portion of the superiors; hamule not exceeding the genital lobe; vulvar lamina shorter than the segment upon which it lies, excised within; wings hyaline; base of the anterior ones hardly yellow, posterior ones with the basal third fuscous, veined with yellow, the middle of the anal margin having a hyaline spot; pterostigma small, fuscous; membranule white; twelve antecubitals; seven postcubitals; four discoidal areolets.

Length 52 millim. Alar expanse 90 millim. Pterostigma 3 millim.

Hab. Carolina; New Jersey; Georgia; Florida; Cuba; Guadeloupe; St. Thomas; the specimens from the Antilles which I saw were very much mutilated; they may perhaps belong to *T. onusta.*

2. T. chinensis!

Libellula chinensis De Geer, Mém. III, 556; pl. XXVI, fig. 1. Burm. Handb. II, 852, 27. *Libellula virginia* Ramb.! Neuropt. 33, 2.

Rufo-fuscous; front above, and the apex of the vertex, brassypurple; feet black; abdomen having the three apical segments with a dorsal, broad, black band; superior appendages of the male black, as long as the three apical segments; inferior appendage short, acute, reaching beyond the denticulated portion of the superiors; hamule longly exceeding the genital lobe; vulvar lamina shorter than the segment upon which it lies, excised within; wings hyaline, the superior ones yellow at base; basal fourth of the posterior ones fuscous, veined with yellow, not attaining the anterior margin, surrounded with yellow; the anal margin with a large yellowish hyaline spot upon the middle; pterostigma small, fuscous; membranule white; twelve antecubitals; nine postcubitals; four discoidal areolets.

Length 53 millim. Alar expanse 104 millim. Pterostigma 3 millim.

Hab. China (De Geer); Madras (Burm.); Carolina (Vienna Museum); Virginia (Rambur).

3. T. onusta!

Tramea onusta Hagen.

Very much like *T. carolina*, but smaller; differs, in having front and vertex hardly obscurer; the superior appendages of the male a little longer; the inferior appendage just reaching to the denticulated portion of the superiors, the hamule long, exceeding the genital lobe; the vulvar lamina of the same length as the segment upon which it lies; base of the posterior wings less dilated, the basal, fuscous spot smaller, not attaining to the anterior margin of the wing, divided in front, and irregular exteriorly, the anal margin with a large, hyaline spot; the pterostigma longer; twelve antecubitals; nine postcubitals; four discoidal areolets.

Length 43—47 millim. Alar expanse 78—90 millim. Pterostigma 3 millim.

Hab. Pecos River, Western Texas (Capt. Pope); Matamoras, Mexico.

I possess males with the fuscous spot of the wings almost like that of *T. carolina*, but they are not a different species.

I have a female from North America? very much mutilated, without head or abdomen, of the size of *T. onusta*, but the wings are narrower, the basal spot of the wings small and entire. Perhaps it is a different species.

4. T. lacerata!

Tramea lacerata Hagen!

Brownish-black; labrum black ($\male$), or margined with black ($\female$); face lurid, front superiorly shining violet, vertex shining violet ($\male$), or yellow in front ($\female$); thorax with a violet tinge; base of the abdomen sometimes pruinose, the seventh segment above with a quadrangular, yellowish-green spot ($\male$), or with double lines upon segments 2 to 5, replaced upon segments 6 and 7 by a large, quadrangular, posteriorly narrowed spot, yellowish-green; feet black; superior appendages very long, slender; hamule short, not reaching as far as the genital lobe; vulvar lamina half the length of the segment upon which it lies, excised within and at the apex; anterior wings with two fuscous, basal spots, posterior wings with a broad, basal, fuscous band, which is ragged exteriorly, and very deeply emarginated interiorly; pterostigma long, brownish-black; membranule snow-white; ten antecubitals; nine postcubitals; four discoidal areolets.

Length 44—49 millim. Alar expanse 84—94 millim. Pterostigma 4 millim.

Hab. Pecos River, Western Texas (Capt. Pope); Matamoras, Mexico; Maryland (Uhler).

5. T. abdominalis!

Libellula abdominalis Ramb.! Neuropt. 37, 8.—*Libellula basalis* Selys! Poey, Ins. Cuba, 441.

Rufo-fuscous, front and vertex rufo-fuscous; feet black; three apical segments of the abdomen with a black, dorsal fascia; superior appendages of the male fuscous, rufous at base, as long as the two apical segments; the inferior appendage extending a little farther than the denticulated portion of the superiors; hamule exceeding the genital lobe; vulvar lamina as long as the segment upon which it is placed, excised; posterior wings with a narrow fuscous band, veined with yellow, not attaining the anterior margin; the anal margin with a very small hyaline spot; pterostigma short, brownish-black; membranule white; twelve antecubitals; ten postcubitals; four discoidal areolets.

Length 46 millim. Alar expanse 86 millim. Pterostigma $2\frac{1}{4}$ millim.

Hab. Mexico; Guadeloupe; Cuba (Poey).

6. T. insularis!

Tramea insularis Hagen!

Rufo-fuscous; middle of the labrum, front above, and the apex of the vertex, brassy-purple; feet black, base of the femora rufous; the two anteapical segments of the abdomen above with a black band; superior appendages of the male long, rufo-fuscous, the base rufous, as long as the three apical segments of the abdomen; inferior appendage short, reaching a little beyond the denticulated portion of the superiors; hamule shorter than the genital lobe; vulvar lamina of the length of the segment upon which it lies, excised, rounded at the apex; wings partly veined with rufous, the posterior ones with a narrow, fuscous band at base, which is veined with yellow, and does not attain to the anterior margin; the anal margin with an oblong, hyaline spot; pterostigma short, fulvous; membranule white; twelve antecubitals; nine postcubitals; four discoidal areolets.

Length 45 millim. Alar expanse 80 millim. Pterostigma 3 millim.

Hab. Cuba (Poey).

7. T. simplex!

Libellula simplex Ramb. Neuropt. 121, 128. Selys, Poey Ins. Cuba, 452.

Rufo-fuscous; front and vertex brassy-purple; thorax pruinose above (adult male), the sides obscurely marked with black; feet nigro-fuscous, base of the femora rufescent; three apical segments of the abdomen above with a black band; superior appendages of the male hardly as long as the two apical segments of the abdomen, black, the base hardly rufous; the inferior appendage extending beyond the denticulated portion of the superiors; hamule shorter than the genital lobe; vulvar lamina extremely short, excised; wings with rufous veins, the posterior ones with a narrow, fuscous, anal band, veined with yellow, not attaining to the front margin, the anal margin with an oblong, hyaline spot; pterostigma short, nigro-fuscous; membranule white; 8—10 antecubitals; 7—8 postcubitals; two discoidal areolets.

Length 38 millim. Alar expanse 70 millim. Pterostigma 2 millim.

Hab. Cuba (Poey); Tampico, Mexico (Saussure).

The specimen described by Rambur is smaller, and may be distinct. *Lib. marcella* Selys l. c. from Brazil, is of the same size as the specimens described by me; perhaps the same species.

CELITHEMIS Hagen.

Eyes connected in a short space; posterior lobe of the prothorax broad, excised in the middle; abdomen shorter than the wings, slender, compressed, trigonal, the base a little thicker, segments 2 and 3 with transverse sutures; feet long, slender; base of the posterior wings a little dilated; pterostigma oblong, long; the first sector of the triangle sinuated; triangle broad; caudal appendages short; genital organs of the male hardly prominent; hamule two-parted; vulva disclosed, the segment following it carinated beneath, bituberculated.

1. C. eponina!

Libellula eponina Drury, Ins. II, 86; pl. xlvii, fig. 2. Fab. Ent. Syst. II, 382, 39. Coquebert, Icon. 27, pl. vii, fig. 1. Burm. Handb. II, 853, 30. Ramb. Neuropt. 45, 20. Selys! Poey Ins. Cuba, 442. Oliv. Enc. Méth. VII, 572, 19. Say, Jour. Acad. Philad. VIII, 24, 11.— *Libellula camilla* Ramb.! Neuropt. 46, 21.—*Libellula lucilla* Ramb.! Neuropt. 46, 22.

Reddish-yellow; labium pale; thorax yellow, with a medial, fuscous stripe anteriorly; the sides with two lines, and a third, intermediate, abrupt one, brassy-black; feet black, base of the femora yellowish; abdomen yellow, dorsum each side with a broad, longitudinal, black stripe, beneath pale; superior appendages of the male short, yellow; inferior one triangular, acute, a little shorter than the superiors; vulva uncovered, the margin recurved, excised in the middle; wings yellowish, veined with yellow; anterior ones with a basal spot, two bands and the apex, posterior ones with a basal double spot, two bands, the internal one mostly divided, and the apex, fusco-rufous; pterostigma fulvous or yellow; membranule white; ten antecubitals; nine postcubitals; five discoidal areolets, or an irregular number.

Length 40 millim. Alar expanse 74 millim. Pterostigma 4 millim.

Hab. Boston; Maryland (Uhler); New Jersey; Pennsylvania; Kentucky; Carolina; Indiana; Georgia; St. Louis; New Orleans; Pensacola; Cuba.

2. C. superba!

Celithemis superba Hagen!

Black; mouth and front black, front obsoletely yellow above; thorax black, dorsum scabrous, each side obsoletely marbled with yellow; feet black, exteriorly lineated with yellow; abdomen black, the middle segments each side with an oblique, obsolete, yellow line; appendages black; vulvar lamina erect, triangular, excavated, acute; wings hyaline, a broad, fenestrated, middle band, the apical margin narrowly, dentated posteriorly, fuscous; antecubital veins of the second space marked with fuscous, triangles with a fuscous spot, which is smaller upon the anterior wings, and the posterior wings with a basal, fuscous spot at the hind margin; pterostigma large, fuscous, the exterior half white, surrounded with fuscous; membranule white; ten antecubitals; six postcubitals; 3—4 discoidal areolets, at the triangle 4 or 5.

Length 34—37 millim. Alar expanse 62—66 millim. Pterostigma 4½ millim.

Hab. Oaxaca, Mexico (Collection of Sommer); a male from Tampico (Saussure).

The fuscous bands and spots are broader in the male. A peculiar and most beautiful species; it differs from *C. eponina*, in having the posterior lobe of the prothorax small, rounded, the triangle narrow, the base of the hind wings not dilated.

PLATHEMIS Hagen.

Eyes connected in a short space; posterior lobe of the prothorax small, entire; the abdomen short, broad, depressed; the legs stout, short; pterostigma long, oblong; the first sector of the triangle sinuated; the triangle narrow, long; caudal appendages short; genital organs of the male rather prominent; the first abdominal segment, beneath, with a large, prominent fork; vulva disclosed, the segment following it excavated in the middle, bituberculated; the eighth segment in the female dilated at the sides.

1. P. trimaculata!

Libellula trimaculata De Geer, Mém. III, 556, 2; pl. xxvi, fig. 23. Fab. Ent. Syst. II, 374, 5. Burm.! Handb. II, 861, 78. Ramb.! Neuropt. 52, 28.—*Libellula lydia* Drury, Ins. I, 112; pl. xlvii, fig. 4. Say Jour. Acad. Philad. VIII, 20, 5. (Male.)

Rufescent; thorax each side with two oblique, yellowish stripes; abdomen of the male pruinose, female with lateral oblique, yellow spots, margined with fuscous; feet black, base of the femora rufescent; wings hyaline, a basal, longitudinal stripe, which is margined inferiorly with lacteous on the posterior wings, and a very broad band upon the middle ($\male$), or with the basal stripe, a spot upon the middle anteriorly, and the apex ($\female$), fuscous; pterostigma fuscous; membranule white; twelve antecubitals; nine postcubitals; four discoidal areolets.

Length 40 millim. Alar expanse 70 millim. Pterostigma 5 millim.

Hab. It is found from Maine to Florida, and from Texas to Minnesota; also in North California. A common species.

2. P. subornata!

Plathemis subornata Hagen!

Brownish-black, thorax with a stripe each side above, and the sides with two very oblique yellow stripes; feet black; abdomen with a broad, maculose stripe each side, on the dorsum and broader ones on the venter, yellow (in the male it is wanting towards the apex); wings hyaline, a basal, fenestrated streak, and two angulose bands, the one nodal, the other pterostigmatical, fuscous; pterostigma narrow, fuscous; membranule white. The adult male has the bands of the wings joined together with fulvous; twelve antecubitals; nine postcubitals; four discoidal areolets.

Length 42 millim. Alar expanse 70 millim. Pterostigma 5 millim.

Hab. Pecos River, Western Texas (Capt. Pope).

"An adult male, in my collection (from the same locality), has the thoracic stripes wanting, and with merely yellowish spots at the origin of the anterior legs; the labium has a large, square, blue-black, middle band, and the labrum is entirely black, the upper part of the front is blackish. A similar, mutilated male, is in the Smithsonian Collection, labelled 'San Diego trip.'"— Uhler.

LIBELLULA Linné.

Eyes connected in a short space; posterior lobe of the prothorax small, entire; abdomen stout, rotundo-triquetral, sensibly narrowing posteriorly; feet long, stout; pterostigma oblong, large; the first sector of the triangle sinuated; triangle narrow, long; appendages short; genital organs of the male hardly prominent; vulva disclosed, the segment following it carinated in the middle and bituberculated.

1. L. quadrimaculata!

Libellula quadrimaculata Linné! Syst. Nat. ed. XII, 901, 1. Fab. Burm. Ramb. Selys, Revue des Odonat. 7, 2 (with synonymy).—*Libellula quadripunctata* Fab.! Entom. Syst. II, 375, 5.—*Libellula ternaria* Say, ♂ Jour. Acad. Philad. VIII, 21, 7.

Reddish-yellow, villose; front pale, above terminated with black; sides of the thorax yellowish, lineated with black; feet black; abdomen attenuated at the apex, fuscous behind, the sides yellow; superior appendages of the male black, very long; wings at base anteriorly, yellow, a costal spot and sometimes an apical one, the posterior wings with a triangular spot at base, reddish-black, veined with yellow; pterostigma brownish-black; membranule white; sixteen antecubitals; fourteen postcubitals; four discoidal areolets.

Length 48 millim. Alar expanse 80 millim. Pterostigma 4 millim.

Hab. Lake Michigan, Wisconsin. It migrates in immense flocks (Dr. Hoy); Canada; Massachusetts (Scudder); Europe; Asia; Siberia; Kamtschatka.

Common everywhere that it occurs. The male *L. ternaria* Say, from Massachusetts, certainly belongs to this species. The female of that species belongs to the following.

2. L. semifasciata!

Libellula semifasciata Burm.! Handb. II, 862, 80.—*Lib. maculata* Ramb.! Neuropt. 55, 31.—*Libellula ternaria* Say (♀), Journ. Acad. Philad. VIII, 21, 7.

Reddish-yellow, villose; front lurid, above terminated with black; sides of the thorax obliquely twice marked with yellow; feet black, femora yellowish rufous; apex of the abdomen attenuated, the dorsum with apical, triangular, fuscous spots, and lateral brighter yellow ones; superior appendages of the male short, blackish fuscous; base of the wings yellowish, a basal, longitudinal stripe, which is sometimes double upon the posteriors, an abrupt band upon the middle and a pterostigmatical band, sometimes also the apex fuscous; pterostigma large, rufo-fuscous; membranule white; fourteen antecubitals; ten postcubitals; four, or sometimes three discoidal areolets.

Length 37—45 millim. Alar expanse 66—77 millim. Pterostigma 5 millim.

Hab. New Jersey, Massachusetts, Maryland (Uhler); New York, Savannah, Georgia; Carolina, Florida (Osten Sacken).

3. L. nodisticta!

Libellula nodisticta Hagen!

Fulvous, clothed with white hair; front pale, brassy-fuscous above, terminated with black; dorsum of the thorax incanous, each side fuscous, sides pale with four sulphur spots; feet black, base of the femora fuscous; apex of the abdomen attenuated, fulvous, with a broad dorsal, black stripe; appendages short, black; wings hyaline, a basal fascia and a nodal point, black; pterostigma narrow, black; membranule white. Male.

Thirteen antecubitals; nine postcubitals; four discoidal areolets.

Length 47 millim. Alar expanse 77 millim. Pterostigma 4 millim.

Hab. Mexico (Saussure). It is allied to *Lib. quadrimaculata.*

4. L. saturata!

Libellula saturata Uhler, Proceed. Acad. Philad. 1857, 88, 4.

Reddish-yellow, villose; feet rufous; abdomen stout, the apex narrowed; wings hyaline, the anterior margin and basal half yellowish-rufous; a basal streak, especially to the posteriors, fusco-rufous; of the female hyaline, with the anterior margin flavescent; pterostigma small, fulvous; membranule black; twenty-one antecubitals; fifteen postcubitals; five discoidal areolets.

Length 52 millim. Alar expanse 90 millim. Pterostigma 5 millim.

Hab. California, "San Diego trip," Mexico (Collection of Hagen); Cordova; Tampico (Saussure).

5. L. luctuosa!

Libellula luctuosa Burm.! Handb. II, 861, 76.—*Libellula basalis* Say, Journ. Acad. Philad. VIII, 23, 10.

Brownish-black; front dark metallic blue (adult male); thorax with a dorsal yellow stripe, sides brown, marked with fuscous, or brownish-black, pruinose above (adult male); feet black, or with the femora rufo-fuscous (♀); abdomen brownish-black, dorsum and venter each side, with a broad yellow stripe, or brownish-black, pruinose above (adult male); appendages short, black; wings hyaline, the basal half blackish-fuscous, the apex sometimes clouded with fuscous, the middle band in the males broadly margined with milky-white; pterostigma black; membranule gray.

Var. Base of the anterior wings shortly or slightly blackish-fuscous, a basal streak blackish-fuscous. ♀.

15—19 antecubitals; 12—17 postcubitals; four discoidal areolets.

Length 38—45 millim. Alar expanse 73—84 millim. Pterostigma 4½ millim.

Hab. Pennsylvania; New Jersey; New York; Maryland (Uhler); Chicago; Washington (Osten Sacken).

6. L. odiosa!

Libellula odiosa Hagen!

Entirely brassy-black, or, excepting the front, medial thoracic vitta, and each side of the abdomen, which are yellow; base of the femora rufous (♀ teneral); wings hyaline, the basal half fuscous, the immediate base paler; female with the apex of the wings subinfuscated; pterostigma black; membranule gray; eighteen antecubitals; fourteen postcubitals; five or four discoidal areolets.

Length 47 millim. Alar expanse 85 millim. Pterostigma 5 millim.

Hab. Pecos River, Western Texas (Capt. Pope).

Similar to *Lib. luctuosa*, but the body is more robust, the spot at the base of the wings is clearer, or fenestrated. The wings of the female are also a little narrower.

7. L. julia!

Libellula julia Uhler! Proc. Acad. Philad. 1857, 88, 5.

Fuscous, villose; front lurid; thorax gray above, each side nigro-fuscous, the sides brown; feet black, base of the femora rufous; apex of the abdomen attenuated, apex of the dorsum fuscous, the sides with yellowish spots; appendages short, yellowish-rufous; wings hyaline, a small line at base, and a triangular spot behind the line at base, upon the posteriors, fuscous; pterostigma narrow, fuscous; membranule white. (Male.)

Fifteen antecubitals; twelve postcubitals; three discoidal areolets.

Length 42 millim. Alar expanse 72 millim. Pterostigma 3 millim.

Hab. Fort Steilacoom, Puget Sound, Washington Territory; Wisconsin (Dr. Hoy). This is the North American analogue of the European *Lib. fulva*, and belongs to the same group; the colors are defaced by alcohol.

8. L. pulchella!

Libellula pulchella Drury, Ins. I, 115; pl. xlviii, fig. 5. Ramb.! Neuropt. 54, 30. Duncan, Introduct. 292, pl. xxix, fig. 2.—*Libellula versicolor* Fab.! Ent. Syst. II, 380, 29 ♂; Syst. Ent. 423, 17; Sp. Ins. I, 523, 22; Mant. Ins. I, 337, 23.—*Libellula bifasciata* Fab.! Syst. Ent. 421, 3 ♀; Sp. Ins. I, 520, 3; Mant. Ins. I, 336, 3; Ent. Syst. II, 374, 4. Burm.! Handb. II, 862, 81; Blanch. Hist. Ins. 58, 9. Say, Journ. Acad. Philad. VIII, 20, 6.—*Libellula confusa* Uhler! Proc. Acad. Philad. 1857, 87, 3 (teneral).

Fuscous, villose; dorsum of the thorax grayish-fuscous, sides with two oblique yellow marks; abdomen stout, the apex attenuated, fuscous, each side with a yellow stripe, or pruinose (♂ adult); feet black, or with the base of the femora rufous (♀);

wings hyaline, a broad, basal, longitudinal stripe, an abrupt, medial band, and the apex, rufo-fuscous; the males with two alternate spots, and a spot at the anal angle of the posterior wings, milky-white; pterostigma large, black; membranule white; sixteen antecubitals; thirteen postcubitals; four discoidal areolets.

Length 48—52 millim. Alar expanse 86—90 millim. Pterostigma 6 millim.

Hab. New York; New Jersey; Philadelphia; Boston; Baltimore (Uhler); Texas; Mississippi (Edwards).

9. L. forensis!

Libellula forensis Hagen!

Rufo-fuscous, villose; front lurid, above brassy-black; dorsum of the thorax pruinose, the sides fuscous, each side binotated with yellow; feet black; abdomen stout, the apex attenuated, rufous, the base pruinose, the apex fuscous, sides spotted with yellow, venter fuscous, spotted with yellow; wings hyaline, a broad basal stripe, and a broad nodal band, rufo-fuscous; two alternating spots, and the anal part of the posteriors milky-white; pterostigma moderate, black; membranule white. Male.

Fourteen antecubitals; twelve postcubitals; four discoidal areolets.

Length 47 millim. Alar expanse 78 millim. Pterostigma 4 millim.

Hab. California (Berlin Museum).

10. L. deplanata!

Libellula deplanata Ramb.! Neuropt. 75, 61.—*Libellula exusta* Say, Jour. Acad. Philad. VIII, 29, 18.

Rufo-fuscous, villose; front luteous, vertex fuscous; the thorax rufous in front, with two yellow stripes, margined exteriorly with fuscous; feet fuscous; the abdomen short, triquetral, rufous, a dorsal stripe and the margins and sutures blackish-fuscous; wings hyaline, anterior ones with two lines at the base, posterior ones with a triangular spot at base, divided with yellow, rufo-fuscous; pterostigma small, fulvous; membranule whitish; twelve antecubitals; nine postcubitals; three discoidal areolets.

Length 32 millim. Alar expanse 56 millim. Pterostigma 3 millim.

Hab. Georgia; Massachusetts (Say). I am not quite sure whether it belongs to this genus.

L. exusta Say, differs in having twelve to thirteen postcubital cross-nervules; it may be a different species.

* * * * * * * *

(The females have the sides of the eighth abdominal segment dilated.) Species 11—17.

11. L. auripennis!

Libellula auripennis Burm.! Handb. II, 861, 77.—*Libellula costalis* Ramb.! Neuropt. 59, 36.

Reddish-yellow; thorax red, or with a middle, dorsal yellow stripe (teneral); feet reddish; abdomen long, slender, triquetral, reddish-yellow, a dorsal stripe, lost anteriorly, black; wings subfumose, veined with yellow; the anterior margin flavescent; the apex sometimes infuscated; pterostigma large, yellow or red; membranule black; 15—18 antecubitals; 11—15 postcubitals; four discoidal areolets.

Length 48—56 millim. Alar expanse 76—85 millim. Pterostigma 6 millim.

Hab. New Jersey (Guex); Maryland (Uhler); New York; Ohio; Savannah, Georgia; New Orleans, Louisiana; Florida (Osten Sacken).

12. L. incesta!

Libellula incesta Hagen!

Black, pruinose; labium luteous, front superiorly, brassy-black; sides of the thorax paler, pruinose, terminated inferiorly with black; feet black, base of the femora fuscous; abdomen long, slender, triquetral, black, pruinose; wings hyaline, veined with black, the apex hardly infuscated; pterostigma long, black; membranule cinereous. (Male.)

Fifteen antecubitals; twelve postcubitals; three discoidal areolets.

Length 54 millim. Alar expanse 84 millim. Pterostigma 6 millim.

Hab. Carolina (Zimmerman).

13. L. lydia!

Libellula lydia Drury, Ins. II, 85; pl. xlvii, fig. 1. Ramb.! Neuropt. 55, 32; Oliv. Enc. Méth. VII, 570, 8.—*Libellula leda* Say, Journ. Acad. Philad. VIII, 22, 8, var. A.

Reddish-yellow; front whitish; vertex, and labium in the middle, black; dorsum of the thorax rufous, the median sulcus yellow; the sides greenish-white, beneath terminated with black; abdomen long, narrow, triquetral, yellow, the base greenish-white, a dorsal stripe, and another each side at base, shorter, and the sutures, black; appendages black; feet black, base of the femora yellowish; wings hyaline, a short basal line, a nodal point, and the apex, blackish-fuscous; pterostigma large, black; membranule cinereous.

Adult Male. Thorax above, pruinose.

17—20 antecubitals; 15—17 postcubitals; four discoidal areolets.

Length 58—61 millim. Alar expanse 100 millim. Pterostigma 7 millim.

Hab. New Orleans, Louisiana; Georgia; Virginia.

14. L. axillena!

Libellula axillena Westwood. Duncan, Introduct. 292, pl. xxix, fig. 1.—
Libellula lydia Ramb.! Neuropt. 55, 32 (in part).—*Libellula leda* Say, Jour. Acad. Philad. VIII, 22, 8.

Similar to *Lib. lydia*, but differs from it by the male having the front and labrum black, carbonareous, front metallic-blue above; of the female, the labium and rhinarium black, the front reddish-yellow, above metallic-blue; tip of the vertex yellowish; feet black, the base of the femora hardly rufous; the dorsal stripe of the abdomen reaching to the thorax; a stripe upon the anterior margin of the wings, between the nodus and pterostigma, blackish-fuscous.

Length 50—60 millim. Alar expanse 80—92 millim. Pterostigma 6—7 millim.

Hab. Georgia; New Orleans, Louisiana; Florida (Osten Sacken).

Is it a variety of *L. lydia?*

15. L. flavida!

Libellula flavida Ramb.! Neuropt. 58, 35.

Reddish-yellow; mouth, front and tip of the vertex, pale yellow; thorax rufous anteriorly, the median sulcus yellowish; the sides yellowish-white, with an oblique fuscous stripe; abdomen long, triquetral, yellow; a dorsal stripe, another at base, each side, and the sutures, brownish-black; the inferior appendage pale; feet black, anterior femora yellowish beneath; wings hyaline, the anterior margin flavescent, the base hardly rufescent, the apex subinfuscated; pterostigma large, bicolored, yellow, exteriorly fuscous; membranule gray.

Adult Male. Thorax and abdomen brownish-black, wings hardly flavescent anteriorly.

Fifteen antecubitals; eleven postcubitals; four discoidal areolets. Length 48—52 millim. Alar expanse 84—88 millim. Pterostigma 6 millim.

Hab. Pecos River, Western Texas (Capt. Pope).

16. L. quadrupla!

Libellula quadrupla Say, Jour. Acad. Philad. VIII, 23, 9.—*Libellula bistigma* Uhler! Proc. Acad. Philad. 1857, 87, 1. Adult male.

Reddish-yellow; mouth and front yellowish, vertex fuscous; thorax anteriorly rufous, the median sulcus yellowish; sides pale yellow, with an interrupted, oblique, fuscous stripe; feet black, base of the femora luteous; abdomen triquetral, luteous, with a broad dorsal stripe, anteriorly absent, brownish-black; wings hyaline, the anterior margin, especially at the apex, flavescent, the base with a brownish-black streak; the apex sometimes infuscated; pterostigma large, broader in the middle, bicolored, yellow, exteriorly black; membranule black.

Adult Male. Thorax and abdomen nigro-fuscous, altogether pruinose, mouth, front, and the vertex black, wings sometimes hyaline anteriorly.

13—15 antecubitals; 9—11 postcubitals; three discoidal areolets.

Length 40—46 millim. Alar expanse 70—76 millim. Pterostigma 5 millim.

Hab. Baltimore (Uhler); Massachusetts; New Jersey; Maryland.

May this not be *Lib. cyanea* Fab.? (compare South American Neuroptera.)

17. L. plumbea!

Libellula plumbea Uhler! Proc. Acad. Philad. 1857, 87, 2.

Rufo-fuscous; mouth and front brassy-black, margined with yellow ($\male$), or luteo-fuscous ($\female$); vertex fuscous; thorax in front fuscous, pruinose ($\male$), or rufous, with the median sulcus yellowish ($\female$), sides yellowish-white, with an interrupted, oblique, fuscous stripe; abdomen triquetral, fuscous, pruinose, beneath yellowish (♂), or rufous, a dorsal, brownish-black stripe, absent anteriorly (♀); feet black, femora partly rufescent; wings hyaline, the anterior margin entirely flavescent, a basal, not well terminated, fuscous streak, and the apex (in the female) also fuscous; pterostigma large, rufous; membranule whitish; sixteen antecubitals; twelve postcubitals; three discoidal areolets.

Length 46 millim. Alar expanse 74 millim. Pterostigma 6 millim.

Hab. Baltimore, Maryland; New Jersey (Uhler); Carolina.

* * * * * * * *

18. L. funerea!

Libellula funerea Hagen!

Male Adult. Black; mouth and front brassy-black; feet black, the four posterior tibiæ yellow exteriorly; abdomen slender, triquetral, black; the appendages yellow; wings blackish-fuscous; the apex, and base of the anterior ones hyaline; pterostigma large, black, membranule black. *Teneral male and the female* approaching a yellow color, the mouth and front yellowish; thorax yellow, the dorsum each side, infuscated; feet lurid; abdomen yellowish, the dorsum and sides subinfuscated; the wings somewhat yellowish, the apex hyaline, the apical margin infuscated; pterostigma pale; twelve antecubitals; ten postcubitals; three discoidal areolets.

Length 50 millim. Alar expanse 70 millim. Pterostigma 5 millim.

Hab. Mexico.

19. L. umbrata!

Libellula umbrata Linné, Syst. Nat. 903, 13; Fab. Syst. Ent. 422, 14; Sp. Ins. I, 522, 18; Mant. Ins. I, 337, 18; Ent. Syst. II, 378, 21; Burm. Handb. II, 856, 48. Ramb.! Neuropt. 73, 58. Selys! Poey, Ins. Cuba, 448.—*Libellula unifasciata* De Geer, Mém. III, 557, 3; pl. xxvi, fig. 4.—*Libellula fallax* Burm.! Handb. II, 855, 45 (teneral).—*Libellula subfaciata* Burm.! Handb. II, 855, 46 (male teneral).—*Libellula tripartita* Burm.! Handb. II, 856, 47 (male adult).—*Libellula ruralis* Burm.! Handb. II, 856, 49 (female).—*Libellula flavicans* Ramb.! Neuropt. 87, 79 (female).

Male teneral, and Female. Olivaceous, mouth and front flavescent; dorsum of the thorax obsoletely varied with fuscous; feet fuscous, femora partly yellowish; abdomen olivaceous, a dorsal stripe, almost absent anteriorly, and the apex of segments 4—10, brownish-black; appendages yellowish; wings hyaline, the apex subfuscous, base of the posterior ones ochraceous; pterostigma large, fulvous; membranule fuscous.

Male Adult. Mouth and front steel-blue; body nigro-fuscous, with a violet tinge, pruinose; wings with a broad, blackish-fuscous band, between the nodus and pterostigma; pterostigma brownish-black, the base of the posterior ones rufo-fuscous; the apex of each, often hyaline; 11—13 antecubitals; 9—12 postcubitals; three discoidal areolets.

Length 38—47 millim. Alar expanse 56—72 millim. Pterostigma 4—5 millim.

Hab. Georgia (Abbot), a single male in Hagen's collection; Matamoras, Mexico, a single male in Hagen's collection; Cuba (Poey); Martinique; St. Thomas; Barbadoes; Porto Cabello, Venezuela; Surinam, Essequibo, Guiana; Bahia, Rio, Brazil; Buenos Ayres. An extremely common species in tropical South America.

20. L. angustipennis!

Libellula angustipennis Ramb. Neuropt. 63, 42; Selys, Poey Ins. Cuba, p. 446.

Yellowish-red; front pale, steel-blue above; thorax fuscous, dorsum with three lines, the sides with two stripes and two lines, yellow; abdomen triquetral, toward the apex narrower, fuscous, dorsum with three yellow streaks; the female has the eighth segment dilated at the sides; feet blackish-fuscous, the anterior femora yellowish beneath; wings hyaline, narrow, the apex subinfuscated; pterostigma long, fuscous; membranule cinereous; fifteen antecubitals; ten postcubitals; two discoidal areolets.

Length 40 millim. Alar expanse 68 millim. Pterostigma 4 millim.

Hab. Cuba (Poey). Does it belong to this genus?

21. L. vibex!

Libellula vibex Hagen!

Brownish-black; labium yellow, with a triangular spot in the middle; front yellowish, chalybeous above; thorax black, dorsum with a yellow stripe in the middle; sides with two stripes, and two lines, yellow; feet black, anterior femora yellowish beneath; abdomen triquetral, black, slender, almost equal, the base with a short, dorsal stripe, and the sides obsoletely yellow; wings hyaline, narrow; pterostigma long, black; membranule blackish-gray. (Male.)

Fifteen antecubitals; ten postcubitals; two discoidal areolets.

Length 40 millim. Alar expanse 69 millim. Pterostigma 4 millim.

Hab. Cordova (Saussure).

It is most like *Libellula angustipennis*, but the posterior lobe of the prothorax is shorter, not rounded, and the external hamule is narrower, divided.

Subgenus Orthemis HAGEN.

The first sector of the triangle straight; the abdomen broad, depressed; female having the sides of the eighth segment dilated; pterostigma large.

22. O. discolor!

Libellula discolor Burm.! Handb. II, 856, 51.—*Libellula macrostigma* Rambur! Neuropt. 57, 54. Selys! Poey, Ins. Cuba, 447.—*Libellula ferruginea* Fab. Syst. Entom. 423, 19. Sp. Ins. I, 523, 25. (Not of Entom. Systemat.)

Rufous or blue, pruinose (*adult male*), labium yellowish, fuscous in the middle; thorax with the dorsal sulcus yellow, each side with four yellow lines; feet rufous, the femora in part paler; abdomen rufous, a dorsal stripe, and each side at base yellowish; wings hyaline, the apex sometimes infuscated; pterostigma large, fuscous; membranule black.

Var. Thorax and abdomen with no yellow stripes.

16—19 antecubitals; 13—15 postcubitals; three discoidal areolets.

Length 48—55 millim. Alar expanse 70—95 millim. Pterostigma 7 millim.

Hab. Western Texas; Matamoras, Tampico, Mexico; Cuba; Martinique; San Domingo; Guadaloupe; St. Thomas; Porto Rico; St. Croix; Jamaica; Porto Cabello, Venezuela; Surinam, Guiana; Chili; Equador; Guayaquil; Rio, Minas Geraes, Bahia, Pernambuco, Brazil. A most common species.

LEPTHEMIS HAGEN.

Eyes very slightly connected; posterior lobe of the prothorax large, bilobed; abdomen long, almost longer than the wings, narrow, slender, equal, triquetral, the base vesicle-like, compressed; feet long, stout; the first sector of the triangle sinuated; the triangle narrow, short; appendages short; male genital organs hardly prominent; the vulva obtected, the segment following it carinated in the middle, bituberculated; the sides of the eighth segment of the female entire.

1. Lep. vesiculosa!

Libellula vesiculosa Fab. Syst. Ent. 421, 7; Sp. Ins. I, 521, 9; Mant. Ins. I, 336, 9; Entom. Syst. II, 377, 12. Burm.! Handb. II, 857, 54. Ramb.! Neuropt. 50, 26. Selys! Poey, Ins. Cuba, 443. *Libellula acuta* Say, Jour. Acad. Philad. VIII, 24, 12.

Yellowish-green; head and thorax uniform in color; feet black; femora yellowish-green, lineated above and below with black; abdomen yellowish-green, the base immaculate, lineated and margined with black, segments 3 to 6 with quadrangular, apical, blackish-fuscous spots; appendages yellowish; wings narrow, hyaline, base of the posterior ones subochraceous; pterostigma long, yellowish; membranule black; sixteen antecubitals; twelve postcubitals; three discoidal areolets.

Length 53—63 millim. Alar expanse 74—90 millim. Pterostigma 5 millim.

Hab. Matamoras, Mexico; Cuba; St. Domingo; St. Thomas; Guiana; Bahia, Rio, Pernambuco, Brazil.

2. Lep. hæmatogastra!

Libellula hæmatogastra Burm.! Handb. II, 837, 55.

Red; labium yellowish, with a middle, black stripe; front brassy-fuscous ($\male$); feet black, the femora red within; abdomen red, or with the sutures and the apex of the segments fuscous ($\female$); appendages red; wings hyaline, the base of the posterior ones with a fuscous spot; pterostigma red; vulvar lamina triangular, recurved; 14—15 antecubitals; twelve postcubitals; three discoidal areolets.

Length 45—50 millim. Alar expanse 70—74 millim. Pterostigma $3\frac{1}{2}$—4 millim.

Hab. Georgia (Abbot; Zurich Museum); Surinam; Pernambuco, Brazil.

3. Lep. verbenata!

Lepthemis verbenata Hagen!

Luteous; mouth fuscous, sides of the labium pale; dorsum of the thorax luteous, each side fuscous; feet black, the femora partly luteous; abdomen luteous, the sutures and margins, the apex of segments 4 to 7, and 8—9 entirely fuscous; appendages luteous; vulvar lamina triangular, recurved; wings hyaline, the posterior ones with a basal, fulvous spot, which is veined with fuscous; pterostigma luteous; membranule black.

Male Adult. Entirely blackish-fuscous, appendages luteous; spot of the base of the posterior wings, blackish-fuscous.

12—14 antecubitals; 10—12 postcubitals; three discoidal areolets.

Length 43—48 millim. Alar expanse 66—74 millim. Pterostigma 4 millim.

Hab. Cuba (Poey); Porto Cabello, Venezuela; Surinam; Brazil.

DYTHEMIS Hagen.

Eyes connected in a short space; posterior lobe of the prothorax small, entire; abdomen a little shorter than the wings, slender, triquetral, the base a little inflated, compressed, the apex a little broadened; feet long, slender; the first sector of the triangle a little sinuated; the triangle moderate, narrow; appendages short; genital organs a little prominent; vulva disclosed, the lamina emarginated, the segment following it carinated, bituberculated; sides of the eighth segment of the female entire.

1. D. rufinervis!

Libellula rufinervis Burm.! Handb. II, 815, 15.—*Libellula conjuncta* Ramb.! Neuropt. 91, 84. Selys! Poey, Ins. Cuba, 444.

Reddish-yellow; mouth and front yellowish-red; dorsum of the thorax rufo-fuscous, or each side with an obsolete yellow line (♀); sides yellowish, four-striped with black; feet black, or with the femora partly luteous (♀); abdomen slender, reddish-yellow, the incisures, a basal and lateral stripe, and a dorsal streak each side upon segments 8 and 9, black; appendages rufous; wings hyaline, with red veins, the base yellowish, base of the posterior wings with two fuscous streaks; pterostigma rufo-fuscous; membranule black; fifteen antecubitals; 8—10 postcubitals; three discoidal areolets.

Length 39 millim. Alar expanse 65 millim. Pterostigma 3 millim.

Hab. St. Domingo, Port au Prince; Cuba (Poey).

2. D. velox!
Dythemis velox Hagen!

Brownish-black; labium and front yellowish-green; thorax fuscous, subaeneous, the dorsum with a middle line, a lateral one each side, and a transverse one before the wings, yellow; sides yellow, with four fuscous stripes; feet black, anterior femora yellow beneath; abdomen slender, the apex thicker, brownish-black, dorsum of segments 1—7 each side with a greenish-yellow spot, that of the seventh segment larger, those of the basal segments double, the third segment each side yellowish-green; appendages black; wings hyaline, the extreme base rufo-fuscous, the apex fuscous; the pterostigma black; membranule black; 14—16 antecubitals; 9—10 postcubitals; three discoidal areolets.

Length 44 millim. Alar expanse 70 millim. Pterostigma 4 millim.

Hab. Pecos River, Western Texas (Capt. Pope).

3. D. fugax!
Dythemis fugax Hagen!

Brownish-black; mouth and front luteous; thorax fuscous, or the dorsum having each side a broader stripe, and transverse streak before the wings, yellowish-green; sides yellowish-green, with four black stripes; feet black; abdomen slender, the apex stouter, nigro-fuscous, dorsum of the second segment with a trilobed spot, segments 3 to 6 with a double spot each side, and the seventh with a larger spot each side, greenish-white; segments 1—7 with a greenish-white spot each side, laterally; appendages black; wings hyaline, the extreme apex sometimes infuscated, the base with a large, fulvous spot, fenestrated with fuscous, and including two basal, brassy-fuscous streaks, upon all the wings; pterostigma black; membranule whitish-gray; 13—15 antecubitals; 8—9 postcubitals; three discoidal areolets.

Length 45 millim. Alar expanse 76 millim. Pterostigma 4 millim.

Hab. Pecos River, Western Texas (Capt. Pope).

4. D. mendax!

Dythemis mendax Hagen!

Blackish-fuscous; mouth and front pale yellow; thorax fuscous, dorsum each side with a fascia, which is broader at the wings, angulose, greenish-white; sides greenish-white, with two oblique, approximate, fuscous stripes; feet black; the anterior femora pale beneath, abdomen slender, a little longer than the wings, the base compressed, more inflated, the apex stouter; brownish-black, segments 1—7 with a double spot each side upon the dorsum, greenish-white, upon segments 4—6 it is almost linear, upon segment 7 posteriorly, a large dilated spot, the sides and venter spotted with greenish-white; appendages black; wings hyaline, the posterior ones fulvous at the extreme base; pterostigma small, black; membranule black; twelve antecubitals; eight postcubitals; two discoidal areolets.

Length 55—60 millim. Alar expanse 76—86 millim. Pterostigma 3 to $3\frac{1}{2}$ millim.

Hab. Pecos River, Western Texas (Capt. Pope).

I saw a female from Tampico (Saussure) which had the head chalybeous above: is it different?

5. D. praecox!

Dythemis praecox Hagen!

Fuscous; mouth pale, the front fusco-aeneous above; dorsum of the thorax fuscous, a green stripe each side, which is broader at the wings, angulose; the sides fuscous, three stripes, the middle one interrupted, green; feet black, the femora luteous in part; abdomen slender, a little longer than the wings, the base compressed, more inflated, the apex thicker; fuscous, dorsum each side upon segments 1—7, with a double, yellowish spot; upon segments 4—6 the spots almost linear; upon segment seven a larger, broader spot posteriorly; appendages black; wings fusco-fumose, fulvous at base; pterostigma small, black; membranule black. Female.

Twelve antecubitals; seven postcubitals; two discoidal areolets.

Length 48 millim. Alar expanse 70 millim. Pterostigma $2\frac{1}{2}$ millim.

Hab. Mexico (Collection of Hagen).

6. D. frontalis!

Libellula frontalis Burm.! Handb. II, 857, 56; Selys! Poey, Ins. Cuba, 453.

Black, pruinose; front white, above greenish-chalybeous; thorax pruinose, the dorsum with a yellowish spot each side, which is not very clear; feet black, anterior femora pale inside; abdomen slender, a little shorter than the wings, black, segments 7 to 9 dilatedly ovate; appendages black; wings hyaline; pterostigma black; membranule black; fifteen antecubitals; postcubitals — ? three discoidal areolets.

Length 44 millim. Alar expanse 73 millim. Pterostigma $2\frac{1}{4}$ millim.

Hab. St. Domingo; Cuba (Collection of De Selys Longchamps).

7. D. pleurosticta !

Libellula pleurosticta Burm.! Handb. II, 849, 3.—*Libellula celaeno* Selys! Poey, Ins. Cuba, 454.

Brownish-black; front whitish, chalybeous above; thorax nigro-fuscous, dorsum with a stripe each side, which is larger at the wings, angulose, and an intermediate line, greenish-white; sides black, each with three larger spots and two smaller ones, greenish-white; feet blackish-brown; abdomen of the length of the wings, slender, almost equal, black, segments 1—8 (or 9 ♀) marked upon the dorsum with a double, linear, greenish-white spot; appendages black; wings hyaline, a basal small streak, almost absent in the males, fuscous; base of the posterior wings a little fulvous; pterostigma black; membranule cinereous; fourteen antecubitals; 8—10 postcubitals; two discoidal areolets.

Length 43 millim. Alar expanse 59—64 millim. Pterostigma 2 millim.

Hab. Cuba; St. Domingo; St. Thomas; Brazil.

8. D. didyma!

Libellula didyma Selys. Poey, Ins. Cuba, 453.—*Libellula phryne* Ramb. Neuropt. 121, 27.

Brownish-black; mouth and front yellowish, front chalybeous above; thorax nigro-fuscous, dorsum each side, with an oblique line, the intermediate sulcus, and a transverse line at the wings, greenish-yellow; sides greenish-yellow, with three brassy-brown stripes; feet black, the anterior femora interiorly partly pale; the abdomen a little shorter than the wings, slender, broader before the apex, black, segments 1—6 with a linear, yellowish spot each side, the base of the seventh with a larger, twin-spot, greenish-yellow; appendages black; hamules not prominent; wings hyaline, the extreme base fulvous; pterostigma oblong, blackish-brown; membranule black.

The female varies by having the abdominal spots larger.

9—11 antecubitals; seven postcubitals; two discoidal areolets.

Length 33—35 millim. Alar expanse 57 millim. Pterostigma 2½ millim.

Hab. Cuba (Poey); Matamoras, Mexico; Tampico (Saussure).

The Mexican specimens are larger, and the stripes and spots are larger; perhaps they constitute a distinct species.

9. D. dicrota!

Dythemis dicrota Hagen!

Brownish-black; mouth and front yellowish, front chalybeous above; thorax black, dorsum each side with an oblique line, the intermediate sulcus and a transverse line at the wings, yellowish-green; sides greenish-yellow with two brassy-fuscous stripes; feet black, the anterior femora beneath partly yellowish; abdomen a little shorter than the wings, slender, broader before the apex, black, segments 1—6 with a linear spot each side, the seventh segment with a larger, basal yellowish twin-spot; appendages black; hamules prominent, large, recurved; wings hyaline, the extreme base fulvous; pterostigma oblong, fuscous, membranule black; ten antecubitals; seven postcubitals; two discoidal areolets.

Length 33—36 millim. Alar expanse 53—57 millim. Pterostigma 3 millim.

Hab. Cuba (Poey).

10. D. pertinax!

Dythemis pertinax Hagen!

Nigro-fuscous; mouth and front pale yellow; middle of the labium black; front above and vertex chalybeous; thorax blackish-fuscous, the dorsum each side with a stripe, which is broader at the wings, angulose, green; the sides nigro-fuscous, with two oblique, green stripes; feet black, anterior femora at the base beneath rufous; abdomen slender, a little longer than the wings, the base compressed, more inflated, the apex a little stouter;

black, the base each side with a maculose, green stripe, dorsum of the seventh segment each side, with a lanceolate, long, green spot; appendages black; wings hyaline, the anterior margin at base subflavescent; pterostigma small, black; membranule black. Male.

Fifteen antecubitals; ten postcubitals; two discoidal areolets.

Length 54 millim. Alar expanse 86 millim. Pterostigma 2 millim.

Hab. Mexico (Vienna Museum).

Similar to *Libellula nubecula* Rambur, but certainly distinct.

11. D. aequalis!

Dythemis aequalis Hagen!

Fuscous; mouth and front whitish-yellow; the vertex, and the front above, chalybeous; thorax brassy-fuscous, the dorsum each side with an oblique streak, middle sulcus, and a transverse line at the wings, yellow; the sides brassy-fuscous, with three broad, irregular, yellow stripes; feet black, the extreme base fuscous; abdomen shorter than the wings, slender, broader before the apex, triquetral, brassy-fuscous, the base each side with a maculose stripe, and the seventh segment each side with a large, cuneiform, yellow spot; appendages black; anterior genital lamina each side with a large, prominent auricle; the hamule not prominent; vulvar lamina large, oval; wings hyaline; pterostigma oblong, black; membranule black.

Adult Male. Thorax and base of abdomen pruinose.

Female. Abdomen each side, with a broad, interrupted, yellow stripe.

Eight antecubitals; six postcubitals; two discoidal areolets.

Length 28 millim. Alar expanse 46 millim. Pterostigma 2 millim.

Hab. Cuba (Poey); Matamoras, Mexico.

12. D. naeva!

Dythemis naeva Hagen!

Brownish-black; mouth and front black, with two yellow spots each side; front superiorly and the vertex, chalybeous; thorax black, subpruinose, a little clothed with cinereous hair; sides each with oblique stripes, which are obsolete above, yellow; feet black; abdomen shorter than the wings, slender, triquetral, hardly thicker before the apex, black, subpruinose, segments 2—7 each side with a larger yellowish spot, which is obsolete in the female; appendages black; anterior lamina entire; hamules prominent, black, furcated, the external branch large, truncated; vulvar lamina large, erect, triangular, excavated; wings hyaline; pterostigma oblong, fuscous; membranule black; 7—10 antecubitals; 6—7 postcubitals; two discoidal areolets.

Length 30 millim. Alar expanse 48 millim. Pterostigma $2\frac{1}{3}$ millim.

Hab. Cuba (Poey).

13. D. debilis!

Dythemis debilis Hagen!

Nigro-fuscous; mouth and front yellowish-white; vertex, and the front above, chalybeous; thorax nigro-fuscous, clothed with cinereous hair, pruinose; the sides brassy-fuscous, obsoletely spotted with yellow; feet black, anterior femora pale beneath; abdomen shorter than the wings, slender, somewhat broader before the apex, triquetral, black, the base pruinose, the seventh segment each side with a lateral spot, which is long, triangular, segments 5—6 each side with a lateral line, yellowish; appendages black; anterior genital lamina each side with an impressed, flat, pyriform lobe; hamule not prominent; wings hyaline; pterostigma oblong, fuscous; membranule blackish-gray. Adult male.

Six antecubitals; four postcubitals; two discoidal areolets.

Length 24 millim. Alar expanse 37 millim. Pterostigma 2 millim.

Hab. Cuba (Poey).

ERYTHEMIS Hagen.

Eyes connected in a short space; posterior lobe of the prothorax large, broad, bilobed; abdomen a little shorter than the wings, broad, depressed, the apex sensibly narrower; feet long, rather strong; first sector of the triangle a little sinuated; triangle moderate, narrow; caudal appendages short; genital organs hardly prominent; vulva disclosed or obtected, the segment following it a little carinated, bituberculated; sides of the eighth abdominal segment of the female not dilated.

1. E. furcata!
Erythemis furcata Hagen!

Ferruginous; front luteous; feet black, femora rufo-fuscous; superior appendages of the male recurved, thicker at the apex; the inferior appendage short, quadrangular, the apex forked; anterior genital lamina prominent, forked; vulva disclosed, the apex of the lamina excised; wings hyaline, base of the hind ones narrowly orange; pterostigma oblong, luteous; membranule black; nine antecubitals; eight postcubitals; three discoidal areolets.

Length 40 millim. Alar expanse 70 millim. Pterostigma 4 millim.

Hab. Cuba (Osten Sacken); Bahia, Brazil; Tampico, Mexico (Saussure).

2. E. bicolor!
Libellula bicolor Erich.! Schomburgk, Voyag. Guiana III.

♂. Mouth, front and vertex brassy-black; thorax blue-black, subpruinose; abdomen ferruginous, the base black; appendages ferruginous; feet black; wings hyaline, base of the posterior ones narrowly fuscous; pterostigma luteous; membranule black.

♀. Luteo-testaceous; incisures of the abdomen black; feet black, anterior femora luteous beneath; vulvar lamina produced, erect, acute, triangular; wings subfumose, the apex a little infuscated, the base of the posterior ones yellowish; 12—14 antecubitals; 9—10 postcubitals; three discoidal areolets.

Length 40 millim. Alar expanse 63 millim. Pterostigma 3 millim.

Hab. Choco, New Grenada (Schott); Surinam, Guiana; Brazil. Is it different from *Libellula peruviana* Rambur?

3. E. longipes!
Erythemis longipes Hagen!

Rufous; mouth rufo-fuscous, front chalybeous above; thorax villose, rufo-fuscous; feet brownish-black, slender, very long; abdomen longer, depressed, rufo-fuscous, the sides yellow; superior appendages of the male rufo-fuscous, long, cylindrical, the apex thicker, beneath upon the middle a little inflated; the inferior appendage triangular, acute; vulvar lamina broad, excised in the middle; wings hyaline with red veins, the base of the posterior wings flavescent; pterostigma oblong, yellow; membranule black; 8—9 antecubitals; 6—7 postcubitals; two discoidal areolets.

Length 38 millim. Alar expanse 66 millim. Pterostigma 3 millim.

Hab. Cuba (Poey); Minas Geraes, Rio Janeiro, Brazil.

MESOTHEMIS Hagen.

Eyes connected in a short space; posterior lobe of the prothorax large, broad, bilobed; abdomen a little shorter than the wings, narrow, triquetral, the base compressed, somewhat broadened before the apex; feet long, rather strong; the first sector of the triangle sinuated; the triangle moderate, narrow; appendages short; genital organs not prominent; vulva obtected; sides of the eighth segment of the female not dilated.

1. M. simplicicollis!

Libellula simplicicollis Say, Journ. Acad. Philad. VIII, 28, 16. *Libellula caerulans* Ramb.! Neuropt. 64, 44 ($\male$). Selys! Poey, Ins. Cuba, 448. *Libellula maculiventris* Ramb.! Neuropt. 87, 78 ($\female$).

Yellowish-green; mouth and front yellowish, a narrow black band before the eyes; thorax yellowish-green, the sides inferiorly varied with black; abdomen compressed at base, vesiculose, triquetral, a little broader before the apex, yellowish-green, the sutures and margins black, the segments 4—10 with a quadrangular, dorsal spot behind, black; the last segments sometimes altogether black; venter obscure; appendages yellow; feet black, the anterior femora yellowish beneath; the vulvar lamina erect, triangular, excavated; wings hyaline; pterostigma oblong, yellow; membranule black.

Adult Male. Thorax and abdomen blue-pruinose.

11—12 antecubitals; 9—12 postcubitals; three discoidal areolets.

Length 41—45 millim. Alar expanse 60—70 millim. Pterostigma 3½—4 millim.

Hab. Indiana; Illinois; Massachusetts; Philadelphia; New York; New Jersey; Savannah; Florida; New Orleans; Pecos River, Texas (Capt. Pope); Matamoras, Huastee (Saussure), Mexico; Cuba.

A common species.

2. M. collocata!

Mesothemis collocata Hagen!

Yellowish-green; mouth and front yellowish, a narrow black band before the eyes; thorax yellowish-green, dorsum with a black spot each side, the sides with three oblique lines, the middle one interrupted, a spot behind, and some streaks at the feet, black; feet black, anterior femora yellowish beneath; abdomen compressed at base, vesiculose, triquetral, the apex almost equal, yellowish-green, the sutures and margins all banded with black; appendages black; wings hyaline; pterostigma oblong, yellow; membranule black. Teneral male.

11—12 antecubitals; nine postcubitals; three discoidal areolets.

Length 43 millim. Alar expanse 67 millim. Pterostigma 3 millim.

Hab. Pecos River, Western Texas (Capt. Pope).

3. M. corrupta!

Mesothemis corrupta Hagen!

Luteous; mouth, front and vertex yellowish; head robust; thorax luteo-fuscous, clothed with white hairs; dorsum with a white stripe each side; sides each with two oblique white stripes, and at the feet a sulphureous spot, which is bounded inferiorly with fuscous; feet black, yellow above, tarsi black; abdomen stoutish, the base a little more robust, luteous (with the teneral ones, whitish-yellow); each side an arcuated fuscous stripe, dorsum with an interrupted stripe, two points upon the apical segments, and a larger spot upon the middle of segments 8 and 9, fuscous; an interrupted, whitish, ventral stripe; appendages yellow; vulvar lamina flat, the apex emarginated; wings hyaline, with yellow veins; pterostigma oblong, yellow, fuscous in the middle; membranule white; seven antecubitals; 6—7 postcubitals; three discoidal areolets.

Length 37—43 millim. Alar expanse 58—64 millim. Pterostigma 3 millim.

Hab. Pecos River, Western Texas (Capt. Pope); Illinois (Kennicott); Matamoras, Mexico; Ajan, Sea of Ochotsk.

The adult male from Matamoras is obscurer, the pterostigmata are uni-colored, luteo-fuscous.

4. M. illota!

Mesothemis illota Hagen!

Luteous; mouth yellowish, front rufous above; thorax luteous, with luteous hair, the sides each with two white spots at the feet, which are margined beneath with fuscous; feet luteous; abdomen rufous, appendages rufous; wings hyaline, veined with luteous, the base, and anterior margin as far as the nodus, flavescent; the anterior wings with one rufo-fuscous, basal streak, the posterior ones with a double one; pterostigma luteo-fuscous; membranule whitish. Male.

Nine antecubitals; seven postcubitals; three discoidal areolets.

Length 37 millim. Alar expanse 56 millim. Pterostigma 2½ millim.

Hab. North California; Mexico.

I saw a female from Ajan (Sea of Ochotsk), which was a little larger; the alar expanse was 62 millim. :—the anterior margin of the wings all flavescent, no basal streaks, the thorax upon each of the sides with two oblique white stripes; the feet blackish-fuscous; is it the same species?

Libellula gilva Hagen, from Columbia, is very similar to *M. illota:*—I am in doubt whether it is different.

5. M. attala.

Libellula attala Selys. Poey, Ins. Cuba, p. 445.

Blackish-smoky; base of the abdomen inflated, the dorsum with obsolete rufous spots each side; feet blackish; wings hyaline, veined with black, anterior ones with a small, basal spot, upon the posterior wings the spot is larger and produced almost to the origin of the triangle, fuscous; pterostigma moderate, brownish-olive. (From the description of De Selys Longchamps.)

Fifteen antecubitals; nine postcubitals; three discoidal areolets.

Length 42 millim. Alar expanse 70 millim. Pterostigma 3 millim.

Hab. Cuba.

This is *Libellula annulata* Rambur, 78, 65, in part.

6. M. mithra.

Libellula mithra Selys. Poey, Ins. Cuba, p. 446. *Libellula annulata* Ramb. Neuropt. 78, 65 (in part).

Very much like the preceding species, but the posterior wings are narrower, and the basal spot smaller. (From the description of De Selys Longchamps.)

Length 40 millim. Alar expanse 66 millim.

Hab. Island of Martinique.

7. M. longipennis!

Libellula longipennis Burm. Handb. II, 850, 12. *Libellula socia* Ramb.! Neuropt. 96, 94. *Libellula truncatula* Ramb. Neuropt. 95, 92?

Fuscous; mouth and front yellowish-white; vertex, and front superiorly, chalybeous; thorax fuscous, clothed with luteous-hairs, dorsum each side with a streak, and a transverse line at the wings, yellow; sides yellow, with three oblique, fuscous lines; abdomen triquetral, short, sensibly attenuated; of the female, broader at the apex, yellowish, dorsum with three broad, fuscous stripes, confluent towards the apex; the last segment extremely short; appendages black; abdomen of the adult male (more rarely of the female), pruinose; feet black; wings hyaline, veins black, the base flavescent; of the adult male often dusky towards the apex; posterior wings of the male, with a double fuscous streak at base; wings of the female hardly flavescent, with no basal streaks; pterostigma fulvous; membranule black; six antecubitals; six postcubitals; three discoidal areolets.

Length 35—44 millim. Alar expanse 59—70 millim. Pterostigma 3—4 millim.

Hab. Maryland; New York; Illinois; Savannah, Dalton, Georgia; Florida; New Orleans, Louisiana; Pecos River, Western Texas (Capt. Pope); North California; Matamoras, Mexico. A common species.

Specimens from Western Texas have the thorax and abdomen almost entirely brassy-black; but they are not different from the others.

A male from California has the thorax and abdomen very pruinose, the extreme base of the wings only is flavescent, and the fuscous streaks are almost absent.

DIPLAX Charp.

Eyes connected in a short space; posterior lobe of the prothorax large, broad, bilobed; abdomen a little shorter than the wings, slender triquetral, the base compressed; feet long, slender; the first sector of the triangle sinuated; triangle moderate, broad; caudal appendages short; the genital organs not prominent; vulva obtected; the sides of the eighth segment in the female not dilated.

1. D. assimilata!

Libellula assimilata Uhler! Proc. Acad. Philad. 1857, 88, 6.

Yellowish; mouth and front pale yellow, a narrow black band before the eyes; dorsum of the thorax luteous, sides yellow; abdomen slender, the base compressed, inflated, yellowish, dorsum of the first and second segments black at base, segments 4—9 each side with a marginal, black stripe; appendages yellowish, the inferior one triangular, truncated at the apex and a little excised; vulvar lamina short, narrow, almost quadrangular, inflated, bifid, recurved at the apex; feet black, the femora partly yellowish; wings hyaline, the base flavescent, the basal half with the males and sometimes with the females, flavescent; pterostigma short, yellow, obscure in the middle, membranule white; 7—9 antecubitals; 6—8 postcubitals; three discoidal areolets.

Length 33—37 millim. Alar expanse 56—60 millim. Pterostigma 2½ millim.

Hab. Fort Union, Nebraska (Dr. Suckley); Illinois and Wisconsin (Kennicott); St. Louis; Washington; Chicago (Osten Sacken); Pennsylvania; Maryland (Uhler).

It is very much like *Diplax flaveola* Linn. of Europe.

2. D. madida!

Diplax madida Hagen!

Flavescent; dorsum of the thorax luteous; the sides yellow, with two of the sutures black; abdomen yellowish, the two basal segments black at base; segments 3—5 each side with the lateral margin and a lateral stripe, black; feet black, the anterior femora yellow beneath; wings fumose, the anterior margin, and the base of the posteriors, flavescent; pterostigma long, narrow, yellow; membranule white. Female.

Six antecubitals; six postcubitals; three discoidal areolets.

Length — ? Alar expanse 58 millim. Pterostigma 3 millim.

Hab. Upper Missouri.

Described from a single, mutilated specimen; the head, and apex of the abdomen is destroyed.

3. D. costifera!

Libellula costifera Uhler! Mss.

Yellowish; thorax densely covered with long whitish hairs; second segment of the abdomen with a dorsal, triangular, fuscous spot, the following segments having the lateral margin black; the vulvar lamina short, truncated, excavated, a little erected; feet yellow; wings hyaline, the anterior margin and immediate base, flavescent; pterostigma broadened, yellow; membranule white. (Teneral female). Adult female:—sides of the thorax whitish-yellow, with a black vestige upon the posterior suture; the abdomen is a little pruinose beneath, the eighth and ninth segments have an ill-defined, longitudinal, black spot upon the middle; the femora have a black line exteriorly, and the tarsi are black. The genital hamule of the male is bifid, the branches widely separated; the posterior branch elongately-triangular, at tip a little decurved, the anterior branch shorter, very slender, strongly recurved, acute at the apex, the extreme point black; genital lobe oblong, slightly rounded at tip, hairy; denticles of the superior appendage subequal; inferior appendage but little shorter than the superiors, triangular, rounded at the sides, emarginate at tip, and with a minute denticle each side; 7—8 antecubitals; 5—6 postcubitals; three discoidal areolets.

Length 35—39 millim. Alar expanse 58—60 millim. Pterostigma 3 millim.

Hab. Massachusetts (Scudder); New York (Edwards).

4. D. vicina!

Diplax vicina Hagen!

Yellowish-red; front rufescent above, with a small, black band before the eyes; thorax and abdomen yellowish-red or altogether yellowish (teneral); abdomen compressed at base, very much inflated beneath; hamules longly bifid, the branches equal; vulvar lamina truncated, erect, excavated; feet yellowish-red; wings hyaline, veins luteous, the extreme base flavescent; pterostigma oblong, luteous, broader in the middle; membranule whitish gray; 6—7 antecubitals; six postcubitals; three discoidal areolets.

Length 31—36 millim. Alar expanse 46—52 millim. Pterostigma $2\frac{1}{2}$ millim.

Hab. Bergen Hill, New Jersey; Pennsylvania; Washington (Osten Sacken).

Similar to D costifera, but the base of the abdomen is more inflated, the pterostigma shorter and broader, the anterior margin of the wings clear hyaline. Is it distinct? May it not be a variety?

5. D. semicincta!

Libellula semicincta Say. Jour. Acad. Philad. VIII, 27, 15.

Rufous; front yellowish-red, with a broader black stripe before the eyes; dorsum of the thorax rufous, the sides inferiorly with two obsolete, luteous spots, which are margined in part with black; feet black, the anterior femora luteous beneath; abdomen short, triquetral, the base a little inflated, rufo-fuscous, the lateral margin and venter black; the superior appendages rufous, cylindrical, the apex black, before the apex beneath with a larger tooth; the inferior appendage hardly shorter, black, triangular, the apex a little excised; genital hamule short, bifid, the external branch stout, conical, the internal one equal, unguiculated; the genital lobe of the length of the hamule, the apex rounded, broader; wings hyaline, fuscescent from the base to the nodus (not extending so far upon the anterior wings); pterostigma quadrangular, fulvous, surrounded with black nerves; membranule white. Male.

Seven antecubitals; six postcubitals; three discoidal areolets.

Length 30 millim. Alar expanse 46 millim. Pterostigma 2 millim.

Hab. Indiana; Massachusetts (Say); Pennsylvania; Maryland (Uhler).

6. D. rubicundula!

Libellula rubicundula Say. Jour. Acad. Philad. VIII, 26, 14. *Libellula ambigua* Ramb. Neuropt. 106, 105; Selys, Revue Odonat. 325.

Yellowish-subrufescent; front yellowish, with a black band before the eyes; thorax rufous, the sides sometimes luteous; feet black, anterior femora luteous beneath; abdomen rather long, slender, sanguineous (adult male), or yellowish rufous, the sides with a maculose, black stripe; appendages rufescent; superior ones of the male longer, the apex acute, recurved, beneath upon the middle with a stouter tooth; inferior appendage shorter, rufescent, triangular, the apex a little excised; the genital hamule rather long, very bifid, the external branch triangular, the internal one a little longer, narrow, subincurved; the genital lobe short, triangular, the apex narrow; vulvar lamina small, triangular, the base inflated, longly bifid; wings hyaline, the extreme base yellowish; pterostigma quadrangular, fuscous, terminated at each end with pale; membranule white; 7—8 antecubitals; 7—8 postcubitals; three discoidal areolets.

Length 32—37 millim. Alar expanse 50—58 millim. Pterostigma 2 millim.

Hab. Indiana; Massachusetts (Say); Maryland (Uhler); Bergen Hill, New Jersey (Guex); Chicago; Washington; New York; Philadelphia (Osten Sacken).

A common species. The variety described by Say l. c. p. 27, "wings with the basal half ferruginous"—is unknown to me.

I possess a male from Chicago most like this species, except that the form of the hamules is different; being shorter, the apex only bifid, the external branch broad, truncated; the internal branch small, unguiculated :—is it a distinct species?

7. D. albifrons!

Libellula albifrons Charp.! Libell. Europ. 14; tab. ix, fig. 3.—*Libellula ambigua* Selys, Revue Odonat. 325.

Yellowish-subrufescent; front narrow, yellow, no band before the eyes; dorsum of the thorax luteo-fuscous, the sides paler, varied with fuscous at the feet; feet luteous, the anterior femora exteriorly, and the tarsi partly, fuscous; abdomen long, slender, sanguineous (adult male), or luteous; segments 1 and 2 at base, and segments 4—9 each side at the apex, with a triangular, black spot; appendages luteo-rufous, superior ones of the male long, the apex acute, recurved, beneath in the middle with a stout tooth; inferior appendage shorter, triangular, the apex a little excised; hamules long, the apex bifid, the external branch small, stout, truncated; the internal branch longer, narrow, unguiculated; genital lobe shorter, triangular; vulvar lamina broad, short, rounded, the apex a little incised on the middle; wings hyaline, extreme base a little flavescent; pterostigma quadrangular, fuscous, terminated at each end with pale; membranule whitish-cinereous; eight antecubitals; 6—8 postcubitals; three discoidal areolets.

Length 33—36 millim. Alar expanse 54—58 millim. Pterostigma 2 millim.

Hab. Georgia (Abbot); St. Louis (Engelmann).

I possess the male described and figured by Charpentier; the locality as reported by him ("Switzerland") is erroneous.

8. D. berenice!

Libellula berenice Drury, Ins. I, 114; tab. xlviii, fig. 3. Oliv. Enc. Meth.; Say, Jour. Acad. Philad. VIII, 25, 13; Rambur, Neuropt. 88, 80.— *Libellula histrio* Burm.! Handb. II, 849, 7. ♀.

Black; mouth black, the labium yellow each side; front black beneath, with a yellow spot each side, above and the vertex chalybeous; eyes black posteriorly, spotted with yellow; thorax black, subpruinose; the sides of the same color, or (teneral) with some yellow spots towards the legs; feet black; abdomen slender, triquetral, the base hardly inflated, altogether black, subpruinose (adult male), or with segments 3—7 having a yellow spot each side (male and female, less adult); or black, and segments 3—7 with a large, phalerated, fulvous spot, divided by a medial black line; the last segment partly fulvous (teneral female); appendages black; the vulvar lamina long, erect, triangular, excavated; wings hyaline, base of the posterior ones, in the female, subrufous; pterostigma long, yellow; membranule black.

Var. ♀ (*L. histrio* Burm.). Labium yellow, the middle narrowly black; labrum yellow, margined with black; front yellow, with a transverse black stripe, and a small T-shaped chalybeous spot above; vertex chalybeous, with a bright yellow spot above; prothorax black, spotted with yellow; thorax bright yellow, the middle sulcus and a double stripe, which is joined together at each end, black; sides yellow, with five partly interrupted, oblique, black streaks; the more adult female has the black markings broader and more confluent; feet black, extreme base of the femora yellow; abdomen black, segments 1—7 with a large, dorsal, phalerated spot, incisures black; the tenth segment and appendages fulvous; wings hyaline, the extreme base flavescent, all the wings with a large medial, fuscescent cloud; pterostigma yellow; membranule black; nine antecubitals; 7—9 postcubitals; three discoidal arcolets.

Length 32—34 millim. Alar expanse 50 millim. Pterostigma 3 millim.

Hab. Bergen Hill, New Jersey (Guex); New York; Maryland (Uhler); Virginia. A common species. I possess a male and female of the variety, taken in copula.

9. D. scotica!

Libellula scotica Donovan; Selys! Revue des Odonat. 48, 22 (with the synonyms).

Fusco-olivaceous; labium yellow, with a middle black band; labrum yellow, margined with black; front yellow, a band anteriorly, obsolete or absent with the female, and another before the eyes, black; dorsum of the thorax olivaceous, the middle sulcus broadly, triangularly black; dorsum of the male sometimes fuscous, the middle black, with two yellowish spots each side; sides yellow, with a broad, oblique black band; beneath black, with three cordiform, yellow spots; feet black; abdomen short, triquetral, black, each side with a yellow, maculose stripe; dorsum of the abdomen entirely fulvous in the females; appendages black; vulvar lamina triangular, erect, excavated; wings hyaline, posterior ones of the females flavescent at the extreme base; pterostigma quadrangular, black; membranule whitish.

Adult Male. Mouth, and the front almost entirely, black; thorax and abdomen black, with the yellowish marks absent, or almost absent. Seven antecubitals; 5—7 postcubitals; three discoidal areolets.

Length 33 millim. Alar expanse 52 millim. Pterostigma 2 millim.

Hab. North Red River (Robt. Kennicott); almost everywhere in Europe; Asia; Wilui River, Irkoutsk, Siberia.

The American specimens are hardly distinct; but the color is a little different; the black labial stripe is narrow anteriorly, triangular; the dorsum of the thorax is of an olive fuscous color, transversely interrupted, so as to appear 4-spotted; dorsal middle of the abdomen, in the female, somewhat black.

10. D. intacta!

Diplax intacta Hagen!

Fuscous; mouth and front white; labium in the middle (♀) black, and in adult male, all black; front with a black band before the eyes; vertex black, with a pale spot above, or all black (adult); thorax nigro-fuscous, dorsum each side with an obsolete fulvous stripe, sides fuscous, obsoletely varied with black; the adult male has the thorax brassy-black; feet black; abdomen short, somewhat broader before the apex, fuscous, with dorsal, phalerate, fulvous spots; upon the base and segments 6—7 they are larger; or black, with a dorsal yellowish spot upon the seventh segment (adult male); appendages black; the inferior one half the length of the superiors, quadrangular, broadly bifid; wings hyaline, posterior ones at base, with a triangular black spot; base of the wings, in the females, flavescent; pterostigma short, quadrangular, black; membranule blackish-gray; 7—8 antecubitals; 7—9 postcubitals; three discoidal areolets.

Length 32 millim. Alar expanse 52 millim. Pterostigma 2 millim.

Hab. Wisconsin (Dr. Hoy); Chicago (Osten Sacken); Ohio (Schaum); Massachusetts (Scudder).

11. D. hudsonica.

Libellula hudsonica Selys, Revue des Odonat. 53.

Similar to *Diplax dubia* Vander Linden (perhaps its variety ?); it differs in being smaller, the basal spot of the posterior wings is small, the reticulation of the wings is less narrow; the vertex is yellow above; the labrum is hardly margined with black; the teeth upon the inferior surface of the superior appendages of the male are almost equal. (From the description of De Selys Longchamps.)

Length 27 millim. Alar expanse 46 millim.

Hab. New Brunswick; Hudson's Bay.

12. D. dubia!

L. dubia Selys! Revue des Odonat. 50, 21.

Black; front white, labium black, labrum white, margined with black; the vertex and a band before the eyes, black; thorax obscure brassy-green, with brown villosity; dorsum with a subinterrupted, fulvous stripe each side; sides spotted with fulvous; feet black; abdomen slender, triquetral, the dorsum spotted with yellow, base spotted, and segments 6 and 7 with larger spots; wings hyaline, or fumose, sometimes with the base flavescent, anterior ones with two basal points, and the posterior ones with a point and triangular spot at base, black; pterostigma quadrangular, nigrofuscous; membranule cinereous; eight antecubitals; seven postcubitals; three discoidal areolets.

Length 37 millim. Alar expanse 58 millim. Pterostigma 2 millim.

Hab. Europe.

13. D. ochracea!

Libellula ochracea Burm.! Handb. III, 854, 38.—*Libellula fervida* Erichs.!
Voyag. Schomburgk II, 584.—*Libellula justiniana* Selys. Poey, Ins.
Cuba, 450.

Rufous, or yellowish; mouth yellow, front rufous above; thorax rufous or yellow, dorsum pointed with fuscous; sides inferiorly bright yellow; feet black, base of the femora partly yellowish; abdomen a little thickened, short, triquetral, rufous or yellowish, a dorsal stripe and each side a lateral one, submaculose, nigro-fuscous; the apical segment and appendages yellowish; genital hamule bifid, the external branch stout, truncated; the internal branch small, unguiculated; genital lobe equal, obliquely truncated behind; vulvar lamina triangular, erect, excavated; wings hyaline, the base flavescent, or rufescent; pterostigma rather long, oblong, yellowish; membranule blackish-gray.

Adult Male. Almost entirely rufous;—female with the apex of the wings sometimes a little infuscated. I saw a very adult male from Surinam, which was almost entirely black, the front chalybeous above, the base of the wings brownish-black, and the abdomen partly pruinose. 10—11 antecubitals; 7—8 postcubitals; three discoidal areolets, then two.

Length 30—35 millim. Alar expanse 50—56 millim. Pterostigma 3 millim.

Hab. Choco, New Grenada (Schott); Cuba (Poey); Surinam, British Guiana; Bahia, Brazil; Porto Cabello, Venezuela; Tampico, Mexico (Saussure).

It is a common species in meridional America.

14. D. justiniana.

Libellula justiniana Selys. Poey, Ins. Cuba, 450.—*Libellula minuscula*
Ramb. Neuropt. 115, 118, in part.

Fuscous; front above, and the vertex chalybeous (adult male), or yellowish (teneral male and female); thorax yellow, dorsum each side fuscous, or altogether blackish-fuscous (adult male); feet black, femora yellowish in part; abdomen short, slender, triquetral, yellowish, each side spotted with black, or black, pruinose (adult male); appendages brownish-black; genital lobe broader at the apex, oval; vulvar lamina broad, oval, excavated, suberect; wings hyaline, base of the anterior ones a little flavescent, base of the posteriors broadly rufo-fuscous, or flavescent (♀); pterostigma oblong, yellow; membranule nigro-cinereous; 8—10 antecubitals; 6—7 postcubitals; three discoidal areolets, then two.

Length 25—31 millim. Alar expanse 38—47 millim. Pterostigma 2—2½ millim.

Hab. Cuba (Poey).

15. D. elisa!
Diplax elisa Hagen!

Fuscous, head yellowish in front, the labium with a medial, fuscous stripe; front with a narrow black band before the eyes; thorax fuscous, the middle sulcus obscurer; the sides fuscous or yellow, moderately punctated with black; feet black, base of the femora partly yellowish; abdomen a little thickened, triquetral, black, segments 1—7 with a dorsal, larger, phalerate, yellow spot; appendages yellowish; genital lobe narrow, small, triangular; vulvar lamina broad, oval, the apex excised; wings hyaline, the anterior margin and base flavescent, an apical and ante-apical fuscous spot; anterior wing at base with a small spot, and the posterior ones with a large fuscous spot, which is lacerated, divided, veined with yellow, and a broad yellow band; antecubital veins margined with fuscous in part; pterostigma oblong, large, yellow; membranules white; eight antecubitals; 7—8 postcubitals; three discoidal areolets.

Length 33 millim. Alar expanse 60 millim. Pterostigma 3 millim.

Hab. Bergen Hill, New Jersey (Guex); Chicago; New York (Osten Sacken).

16. D. ornata!
Diplax ornata Ramb. Neuropt. 96, 93.

Yellow varied with black; head yellow in front, labium with a black stripe in the middle; front with a narrow black band before the eyes; thorax yellow, dorsum with a broad, medial, black stripe; sides yellow, with three oblique, black, somewhat brassy stripes; abdomen triquetral, black, segment 1—7 with a dorsal, large, phalerate, yellow spot; superior appendages yellow, the inferior one fuscous; genital lobe narrow, linear; vulvar lamina short, truncated, each side with an inflated tubercle; feet black, the anterior femora yellowish at base; wings hyaline, the posterior ones with a large, basal, fulvous spot, and two lacerated, fuscous stripes, the anterior one narrow, bipartite; the female sometimes has the base of the anterior wings flavescent, and some of the antecubital nervules marked with fuscous. I have also seen females with the fulvous spot and the fuscous stripes on the posterior wings very small; pterostigma oblong, yellow; membranule white, cinereous inwardly.

Adult Male. Almost entirely black, subpruinose.

6—9 antecubitals; 5—7 postcubitals; three discoidal areolets, then two.

Length 30—32 millim. Alar expanse 55 millim. Pterostigma 2½ millim.

Hab. Philadelphia; Florida (Norton).

17. D. amanda!

Libellula pulchella Burm.! Handb. II, 849, 2.

Bright yellow; mouth and front yellow, before the eyes a narrow fuscous band; thorax yellow, dorsum with a broad black stripe; sides yellow, sutures fuscous at the wings; abdomen triquetral, yellow, the segments black posteriorly, the three last black; appendages yellow; feet black; femora partly yellow; genital lobe narrow linear; vulvar lamina rounded, excised in the middle; base of the wings broadly flavescent, the posterior ones with a double stripe, veined with yellow, the anterior one narrower, bipartite, fuscous; pterostigma short, yellow; membranule white; eight antecubitals; five postcubitals; two discoidal areolets.

Length 25—27 millim. Alar expanse 44—47 millim. Pterostigma 1¾ millim.

Hab. Savannah, Georgia.

18. D. minuscula!

Libellula minuscula Ramb.! Neuropt. 115, 118.

Yellow, varied with black; front yellow, above chalybeous; thorax black, pruinose (adult male), or yellow, dorsum each side, with a fuscous stripe; the sides yellow, the sutures narrowly fuscous; feet black, anterior femora yellowish at base; abdomen short, triquetral, yellow, the dorsum with three maculose, black stripes, and the apex black; appendages pale yellow; vulvar lamina triangular, erect, excavated; wings hyaline, the extreme base of the posterior ones fulvous; pterostigma oblong, yellow; membranule cinereous; eight antecubitals; five postcubitals; two discoidal areolets.

Length 21—26 millim. Alar expanse 34—46 millim. Pterostigma 1½—2 millim.

Hab. Kentucky; Georgia; Florida; Brazil.

19. D. credula!

Diplax credula Hagen!

Fuscous; mouth luteous, front rufo-fuscous above; dorsum of the thorax fuscous, a luteous stripe upon the middle; sides luteous; feet brownish-black, base of the femora luteous; abdomen rather long, triquetral, the base compressed, inflated, nigro-fuscous, subpruinose, with the base fuscous (male), or luteous, with the dorsal middle fuscous, and the incisures nigro-fuscous (female); vulvar lamina triangular, excavated; wings hyaline, the extreme base of the posterior ones fulvescent; pterostigma larger, yellow; membranule black; twelve antecubitals; ten postcubitals; three discoidal areolets.

Length 38 millim. Alar expanse 62 millim. Pterostigma 4 millim.

Hab. Island of St. Thomas; Minas Geraes, Brazil.

20. D. abjecta!

Libellula abjecta Ramb.! Neuropt. 83, 73.

Brownish-black; mouth fuscous, front chalybeous above; thorax nigro-fuscous; feet black; abdomen slender, triquetral, the base hardly inflated, nigro-fuscous, pruinose; appendages fuscous; vulvar lamina triangular, erect, excavated; wings hyaline, the extreme base of the posterior ones fuscous; pterostigma large, yellow; membranule black; eleven antecubitals; seven postcubitals; three discoidal areolets.

Length 38 millim. Alar expanse 58 millim. Pterostigma 3½ millim.

Hab. Cuba; Venezuela; Brazil.

In specimens from Cuba, the basal spot of the posterior wings is wanting, or almost wanting, but they are not different. *D. abjecta* is similar to the preceding species, but the posterior lobe of the prothorax is small: does it belong to this genus? It may be an *Erythemis*?

21. D. imbuta.

Libellula imbuta Say, Journ. Acad. Philad. VIII, 32.

♂. Abdomen red, the segments black at apex; thorax green; vertex chalybeous.

♀. Abdomen greenish, segments black at the apex.

Hab. Island of Sanipuxten, coast of Maryland. (From the description of Say.) It is entirely unknown to me.

PERITHEMIS Hagen.

Eyes connected in a short space; posterior lobe of the prothorax large, broad, bilobed; abdomen much shorter than the wings, broad, depressed, narrower at base; legs moderate, slender; the first sector of the triangle hardly sinuated; triangle moderate, broad; caudal appendages short; genital organs not prominent; vulva obtected; sides of the eighth segment of the female not dilated.

1. P. domitia!

Libellula domitia Drury, Ins. II, 83; pl. xlv, fig. 4. Burm. Handb. II, 855, 40. Ramb.! Neuropt. 124, 132.

Var. 1. *Libellula tenuicincta* Say, Jour. Acad. Philad. VIII, 31, 21 (♂). *Libellula tenera* Say, Jour. Acad. Philad. VIII, 31, 20 (♀). *Libellula chlora* Ramb.! Neuropt. 125, 133. *Libellula metella* Selys, Poey Ins. Cuba, 451.

Var. 2. *Libellula iris* Hagen.

Flavescent, villose; the sides of the thorax similarly colored: dorsum of the abdomen, with an interrupted, brownish-black line each side; feet flavescent; wings flavescent (♂), or the basal half flavescent, with two fuscous, transverse stripes, the internal one of which is often almost absent (♀); pterostigma rufo-fuscous; membranule cinereous.

Var. 1. Sides of the thorax fuscous, two interrupted yellow lines each side; all the wings of the male, with a basal, fuscous point.

Var. 2. Sides of the thorax of the same color with the remainder of the body; the wings hyaline, subflavescent, the anterior margin yellow; posterior wings of the female, with a fuscous nebula at the apex; seven antecubitals; five postcubitals; two discoidal areolets.

Length 23 millim. Alar expanse 36 millim. Pterostigma 2 millim.

Hab. Maryland; New Jersey; Bay of Campeachy; Cuba; Venezuela; Bahia, St. Leopold, Brazil.

Var. 1. Indiana, Pennsylvania, Massachusetts, New York, Louisiana; Matamoras, Mexico; Atlihauzan (Saussure).

Var. 2. Mexico, Alvarado; Brazil.

I saw in the collection of Schneider, *Uracis fastigiata* Burm., from Mexico; the *habitat* is perhaps erroneous; it is a meridional species.

NANNOPHYA Ramb.

Eyes connected in a short space; posterior lobe of the prothorax entire; abdomen shorter than the wings, slender, triquetral; the appendages short; genital organs not prominent; reticulation of the wings large and simple; the triangle large, broad; the first sector of the triangle sinuated.

1. N. bella!

Nannophya bella Uhler! Proc. Acad. Philad. 1857, 87, 1.

♀. Black; mouth black, front and epistoma white, the former with a large quadrangular, black spot, labrum black; vertex chalybeous; thorax black, dorsum each side with an interrupted, yellow line; sides with two oblique stripes and a triangular patch behind, interrupted, yellow; abdomen black, the base, a band at the base of segments 3 and 4, a spot at the base of 5—7, that upon 7 almost obsolete, minute, and the dorsum of the last segment, yellow, segments 8—9 entirely black; feet black; appendages yellow; vulvar lamina large, reaching to the tip of the last segment, triangular, excavated; wings hyaline, fulvous at base; pterostigma small, black; 6—7 antecubitals; 5—6 postcubitals; one discoidal areolet, then two.

Length 18 millim. Alar expanse 32 millim. Pterostigma $1\frac{1}{4}$ millim.

♂. Black, pruinose; mouth black, front white, with a quadrangular black spot inferiorly; vertex chalybeous; thorax and abdomen black, very pruinose; feet black (apex of the abdomen destroyed); wings hyaline; pterostigma small, black, terminated with a white nervule at each end; membranule white; seven antecubitals; five postcubitals; one discoidal areolet, then two.

Length 18? millim. Alar expanse 30 millim. Pterostigma 1 millim.

Hab. North America (Vienna Museum); Baltimore and New Jersey (Uhler); Maine (Packard); Connecticut (Norton).

2. N. maculosa!

Nannophya maculosa Hagen!

Fuscous; mouth black, nasus white, front chalybeous, each side with a white spot; thorax fuscous, each of the sides with obsolete, yellow spots; feet black; abdomen brownish-black, segments each side with a triangular, yellow spot, the three apical segments brownish-black; appendages white; wings hyaline, base of the posteriors fulvo-fuscous; pterostigma small, yellow; membranule white. (Male.) Eight antecubital veins; five postcubitals; one discoidal areolet; two at the triangle.

Length 20 millim. Alar expanse 31 millim. Pterostigma $1\frac{1}{2}$ millim.

Hab. Georgia (Abbot).

Section II. NEUROPTERA. Erich.

Fam. VII. SIALINA.

Body short, thick; prothorax large; antennæ long, setiform; wings large, reticulated, posterior ones with the anal space plicated; tarsi 5-articulate. The larva with a mandibulated mouth.

SIALIS Latreille.

Prothorax quadrangular, almost equal to the head; no ocelli; antennæ filiform; the wings irregularly reticulated, the veins stout; the fourth article of the tarsi dilated, bilobed.

The larva is aquatic; with lateral branchiæ.

1. S. infumata!

Sialis infumatus Newm.! Entom. Mag. V, 500; Walk. Catal. 195, 2.

Black, head not narrowed posteriorly, a little narrower than the prothorax, the occiput with flat streaks and spots, which are ferruginous and somewhat shining; antennæ rather slender; anterior angles of the prothorax rounded, the sides with impressed points; feet black; wings black, the veins thick and blacker.

Length to tip of wings 12—15 millim. Alar expanse 22—26 millim.

Hab. Arctic America (Richardson); Nova Scotia (Redman); St. Martin's Falls, Albany River, Hudson's Bay (Barnston); Trenton Falls, New York; Washington, in May (Osten Sacken); Baltimore, Maryland; Pennsylvania (Uhler).

A variety has the head spotted beneath with yellow; or the prothorax spotted with black: is it a different species?

2. S. americana!

Semblis americanus Ramb.! Neuropt. 447, 1.—*Sialis ferrugineus* Walk.! Catal. 195, 3.

Ferruginous; head narrower behind, occiput with streaks and spots, which are flat, somewhat shining, and surrounded with black; prothorax a little narrower, the anterior angles square, the sides with yellowish, impressed punctures; antennæ black; feet fuscous, femora ferruginous; wings pale ferruginous, the veins darker ferruginous.

Length to tip of wings 12—14 millim. Alar expanse 24—26 millim.

Hab. Georgia (Abbot); Pennsylvania.

3. S. bifasciata!

Sialis bifasciata Hagen!

Ferruginous; head not narrowed posteriorly, orange-colored, two broad black stripes, the occiput with flat streaks and spots, which are somewhat shining, orange; antennæ stout, black, pilose; anterior angles of the thorax obtuse, orange, each side with a broad, fuscous stripe and flat points, somewhat shining, orange; feet fuscous, femora yellowish, with the base fuscous; wings pale fuscous, somewhat shining, anterior ones obscurer upon the costal margin, the veins pale fuscous.

Length to tip of wings 10—12 millim. Alar expanse 17—20 millim.

Hab. Cuba (Poey).

CHAULIODES Latreille.

Prothorax quadrangular, almost equal to the head; three approximate ocelli; antennæ pectinated or serrated; wings veiny, the transverse veins slender; articles of the tarsi cylindrical; caudal appendages of the male conical, simple.

The larva is unknown; perhaps it is aquatic.

1. Ch. pectinicornis!

Hemerobius pectinicornis Linné, Amoen. Acad. VI, 412. Linné, Centur. Ins. 1763, 29, 87. Linné, Syst. Nat. ed. XII, 911, 1; ed. XIII, vol. V, 2638, 1. Fab. Syst. Ent. 309, 1. De Geer, Mém. III, 562, 2; tab. xxvii, fig. 3. Drury, Ins. I, 105; tab. xlvi, fig. 3.—*Semblis pectinicornis* Fab. Sp. Ins. I, 386, 1. Mant. Ins. I, 244, 1. Entom. Syst. II, 72, 1.—*Chauliodes pectinicornis* Latr. Gen. Crust. III, 198. Burm.! Handb. II, 950, 2. Cuv. Icon. Regn. Anim. Masson. tab. cv, fig. 2. Ramb.! Neuropt. 444, 1. Walk.! Catal. 198, 1.—*Hermes indecisus* Walker! Catal. 204, 7. (Female.)

Luteo-cinereous; antennæ fuscous, pectinated; occiput with yellowish flat streaks and spots; prothorax with a middle stripe behind, and another flexuous one each side, yellowish; feet luteous, tarsi fuscous; the anterior wings subcinereous, obscurely clouded with fuscous, veins with white interrupted spots; the wings sometimes have rather clearly-defined fuscous transverse streaks. Male and female.

Length of body 37—55 millim. Alar expanse 58—90 millim.

Hab. Philadelphia, Pennsylvania; Wilmington, Delaware; Massachusetts; Trenton Falls, New York; Berkeley Springs, Virginia (Osten Sacken); Maryland (Uhler); Columbia (collection of Saussure)—is not this an error?

2. Ch. rastricornis!

Chauliodes rastricornis Ramb.! Neuropt. 444, 2. Walk.! Catal. 198, 2.

Luteo-cinereous; antennæ fuscous, denticulated; occiput with flat black streaks and spots; prothorax posteriorly, with a flexuous stripe each side, obsolete upon the middle, impressed; feet luteous, tarsi fuscous; anterior wings subcinereous, obscurely clouded with fuscous, veins interruptedly white. Female.

Length of body 35—46 millim. Alar expanse 64—80 millim.

Hab. Savannah; South Carolina (Zimmerman).

3. Ch. californicus!

Chauliodes californicus Walker! Catal. 199, 4.—*Hermes dubitatus* Walker! Catal. 204, 6. Female.

Brownish-black; mouth rufous; antennæ serrate? (almost altogether mutilated); occiput with rufous, somewhat shining, flat streaks and spots; prothorax each side posteriorly with a flexuous, obsolete, rufous stripe, elevated and more obsolete in the middle; feet black; anterior wings cinereous, the longitudinal veins transversely lineated with fuscous; a basal, brownish-black streak, and sometimes apical ones upon the costal margin of all the wings.

Length to tip of wings 45—60 millim. Alar expanse 70—100 millim.

Hab. California (Hartweg).

4. Ch. virginiensis.

Chauliodes virginiensis Westw. ed. Drury, I, 105; tab. xlvi, fig. 3.—*Hemerobius virginiensis* Drury, Ill. II, App.—*Hemerobius pectinicornis* Palisot Beauv. Ins. Afr. et Amer. Neuropt. tab. i, fig. 2; Walk. Catal. 200, 6.

Head and thorax black, pointed with fulvous; wings broad, hyaline, the veins pointed with black. (From the description of Walker.)

Alar expanse 72 millim.

Hab. Virginia.

Unknown to me;·is it a distinct species? I cannot examine the authority reported by Mr. Westwood: I saw the identical specimen figured by Palisot Beauv., in the collection of De Selys Longchamps; it differs a little from *Ch. pectinicornis* Linn.; but I neglected to make a more complete description of it.

5. Ch. serricornis!

Chauliodes serricornis Say, Long's Exped. II, Append. 307.

Fuscous; head rufous, the disk fuscous, the occiput with flat rufous streaks; antennæ black, serrate; prothorax each side with an impressed, rufous spot; feet luteo-fuscous, the tarsi obscurer;

wings nigro-fuscous, the longitudinal veins obscure, marked with black; anterior wings with a broad, white band, pointed with fuscous, not attaining the posterior margin, an apical marginal spot, and some of the transverse veins with white spots; posterior wings with a broad, arcuated band, not attaining the posterior margin, and a larger anal spot, also an apical small spot, and sometimes the transverse veins spotted, white.

Length to tip of wings 40 millim. Alar expanse 66 millim.

Hab. Arkansas (Nuttall); Pennsylvania; Missouri; Lake of the Woods (Bigsby); Red River of Lake Winnipeg, always rare (Say); New York (collection of Hagen); Maryland (Uhler); Mexico (Muehlenpfordt).

The Mexican specimen has a narrower band, and none to the posterior wings.

6. **Ch. maculatus!**

Neuromus maculatus Ramb.! Neuropt. 442, 3, tab. x, fig. 2; Walker! Catal. 202, 1.—*Chauliodes serricornis* Burm.! Handb. II, 949, 1.

Black; occiput with flat, ferruginous streaks and spots; antennæ black, serrate; thorax fuscous, impressed each side; feet nigro-fuscous; wings black, a transverse interrupted, middle line, dilated at the anterior margin, but not attaining the posterior margin, and some apical spots, white.

Length to tip of wings 30—36 millim. Alar expanse 45—55 millim.

Hab. Philadelphia; Savannah; Massachusetts (Scudder); Maryland (Uhler).

I saw a male from Massachusetts, communicated to me by Mr. Uhler under the name of *Ch. unifasciatus*, which differs a little; the occipital streaks are black; a band on the anterior wings broader, white, not attaining the margin, and with one apical point. Is it a distinct species?

7. **Ch. angusticollis!**

Chauliodes angusticollis Hagen!

Fusco-testaceous; antennæ of the male nodulose, erectly-villose, of the female moniliform; occiput with flat, fulvous streaks and spots; prothorax narrow, a middle stripe posteriorly, and each side a lateral one, fulvous; feet fuscous; wings gray, confertly marked with brownish-black points; appendages of the male stout, oblique, obtuse. (♂ and ♀).

Length to tip of wings 35—42 millim. Alar expanse 60—70 millim.

Hab. Dalton, Georgia; Berkeley Springs, Virginia (Osten Sacken); Northern Illinois (Robt. Kennicott).

CORYDALIS LATREILLE.

Prothorax quadrangular, much narrower than the head; three large, approximate ocelli; antennæ filiform; mandibles of the male often extremely long, incurved; wings numerously veined; the transverse veins stout; appendages of the male forcipated; tarsi cylindrical.

The larva is aquatic, furnished with abdominal branchiæ.

1. **C. cornuta!**

Raphidia cornuta Linné, Syst. Nat. ed. XII, 916, 3.—*Hemerobius cornutus* Linné, Syst. Nat. ed. X, 551, 14; De Geer, Mém. III, 559, 1; tab. xxvii, fig. 1; Fab. Sp. Ins. I, 392, 1; Mant. Ins. I, 246, 1; Entom. Syst. II, 81, 1; Linné, Syst. Nat. ed. XIII. V, 2639,20.—*Corydalis cornuta* Latr. Gen. Crust. et Ins. III, 199, 1; Palisot Beauv. Ins. Neuropt. tab. i, fig. 1; Oliv. Enc. Meth. VII, 59; Burm.! Handb. II, 950, 1; Cuvier, Icon. Regn. Anim. ed. Masson. tab. civ.—*Corydalus cornutus* Haldem. Journ. Acad. Boston, 1848, 158; tab. i—iii.

Luteo-fuscous; mandibles of the male elongated; head large, broad, the sides convex; the occiput with impressed, yellow spots and streaks, which are surrounded with fuscous; beneath, each side, with an oblique yellow stripe; prothorax much narrower than the head, a little longer than broad, behind in the middle, with a hastiform streak, and each side with irregular, elevated, flat points, yellow; feet lurid, the knees, and the apex and incisures of the tarsi fuscous; the males have four appendages, the superior ones forcipated, infracted at the apex, dolabrate; wings subcinereo-hyaline, the veins fuscous, middle of the transverse ones, on the anterior row of costal spaces, pale, the areoles each with two white dots; those of the disk with white points.

Length to tip of wings 75 millim. Alar expanse 100—135 millim.

Hab. Canada; Pennsylvania; New York; Madrid; Carolina; Northern Illinois (Kennicott); Maryland (Uhler).

2. C. lutea!

Corydalis lutea Hagen!

Luteous; mandibles impressed at base superiorly, transversely sulcated, of the male a little elongated; head large, broad, ferruginous, the sides convex; the occiput with obsolete, luteous spots; prothorax much narrower than the head, longer than broad, each side of the middle obsoletely impressed, luteous spots behind and at the sides; feet lurid, base of the tibiæ, base and apex of the first and second articles of the tarsi, and the other articles entirely nigro-fuscous; male with four appendages, the superior ones cylindrical, long, oblique, truncated at the apex; the inferior ones recurved at the apex, clavate; wings luteo-hyaline, veins luteous, partly fuscous, with a few white points. ($\male$ and $\female$.)

Length of body 70—85 millim. Alar expanse 110—140 millim.
Hab. Mexico (Sallé); Cordova (Saussure).

3. C. cognata!

Corydalis cognata Hagen!

Luteous-yellow; male with elongated mandibles; head large, broad, the sides convex; the occiput behind with two punctate ochraceous streaks and a few obsolete points; prothorax almost quadrangular, a little narrower than the head, behind with a hastiform streak upon the middle, and lateral, elevated ochraceous points; feet lurid, apex of the tarsi obscurer, nails fuscous; wings yellowish-hyaline, the transverse veins fuscous; upon the base and apex of the costal space, a fuscous mark; costal areoles with a single white point, the other areoles with a series of white points, at the radius clouded with fuscous.

Length to tip of wings 60 millim. Alar expanse 100 millim.
Hab. Pecos River, Western Texas (Capt. Pope's Expedition).

4. C. soror!

Corydalis soror Hagen!

Luteous; mandibles of the male not elongated; head broad, depressed, the sides flat, with an alate, bidentate process; a fuscous stripe each side; antennæ short, slender, black, the two basal articles yellowish; prothorax narrower than the head, longer than broad, each side with a fuscous, trifoveolated stripe; feet lurid, the knees and apex of the tarsi obscurer; appendages of the male four, the superior ones forcipated, clavate at the apex, the inferior appendages extremely short, cylindrical; wings luteo-subhyaline, an obsolete band upon the middle of the anterior ones, and some spots nearer the apex, fuscous; veins fuscous, luteous upon the middle of the costal space. (♂ and ♀.)

Length to tip of wings 60—75 millim. Alar expanse 85—130 millim.

Hab. Mexico (Koppe); Cordova (Saussure).

5. C. hieroglyphica!

Neuromus hieroglyphicus Ramb.! Neuropt. 442, 2. *Hermes hieroglyphicus* Walk.! Catal. 206, 12.

Pale yellow; mandibles of the male not elongated; antennæ black, with the base yellow; head with the sides convex; prothorax cylindrical; occiput with two spots, prothorax with four, and the mesothorax with two spots, black; appendages of the male, the superior ones longer, with the apex recurved; the inferior ones stout, with the apex clavated; feet yellow, base and apex of the tibiæ, and apex of the tarsi black; wings yellowish-hyaline, the transverse veins in part black; the anterior wings spotted with black posteriorly.

Length to tip of wings 40—63 millim. Alar expanse 64—90 millim.

Hab. Mexico (Ehrenberg); Venezuela; Brazil.

It varies very much in size and marking; sometimes it is almost unicolored, pale yellow.

RAPHIDIA Linné.

Prothorax cylindrical, long, much narrower than the head; antennæ short, filiform; wings with a pterostigma; anal space of the posterior wings very small, inflexed; the third article of the tarsi dilated, bilobed; the fourth article extremely short, cylindrical; vagina of the female long, ensiform.

Larva living under bark.

† Three ocelli.

1. Raph. adnixa!
Raphidia adnixa Hagen!

Rufous; head brownish-black, scabrous, long, sensibly narrowed behind, the occiput with a flat streak; antennæ rufous, the apex fuscous; prothorax long, narrow, rufous; feet rufous; abdomen rufous, the ventral segments having the posterior margin black; wings hyaline, veins fuscous; pterostigma long, narrow, trapezoid, occupying two areolets, yellow; subpterostigmatical areole almost one-half longer within, truncated; outer equal, broken; a series of five areoles beneath the pterostigma. ($\male$ and $\female$.)

Length to tip of wings 16 millim. Alar expanse 23 millim.

Hab. California; Oregon (Willcox, Berlin Museum).

A female from Oregon has the dorsal base of the prothorax blackish-brown, with a trifid rufous spot; the colors of the male are not perfected.

2. Raph. oblita!
Raphidia oblita Hagen!

Fusco-aeneous; head scabrous, shorter, posteriorly suddenly compressed, occiput with a flat streak; antennæ with the basal article nigro-fuscous, second yellowish, the rest — ? prothorax short, rufo-fuscous, upon the dorsal middle posteriorly, a large, ovate, nigro-fuscous spot; feet rufo-fuscous; abdomen brassy-black, the ventral segments having the posterior margin yellow; wings hyaline, veins fulvous; pterostigma long (shorter than in *Raph. adnixa*), narrow, trapezoidal, occupying two areolets, yellow; subpterostigmatical areole almost one-half longer within, truncated, outwards equal, truncated; a series of five areolets beneath the pterostigma.

Length to tip of wings 14 millim. Alar expanse 21 millim.

Hab. California.

3. Raph. media!
Raphidia media Burm. Handb. II, 964, 3. Schneider! Monogr. 76, 4.
   (With the synonymy.)

Brownish-black; head obovate, the sides rounded, mouth yellow; neck short; vertex punctured, with a flat rufous streak; base of the antennæ yellow; prothorax black; feet testaceous, base of the anterior femora, and the whole of the posterior ones black; abdomen black; wings yellowish-hyaline, especially at base; veins fuscous; pterostigma trapezoidal, luteo-fuscous, occupying three areolets, with an internal hyaline spot; subpterostigmatical areolet exteriorly almost equal, interiorly one-half longer; five areolets beneath the pterostigma.

Length to tip of wings 19 millim. Alar expanse 27 millim.

Hab. North America (Knoch, Berlin Museum. One female). It is a common species in Europe.

† † Ocelli wanting. (*Inocellia* Schneider.)

4. Raph. inflata!

Raphidia inflata Hagen!

Fusco-aeneous; head quadrangular, the disk impressed, opaque; base of the mandibles, two broad approximate streaks, and three occipital spots each side, fulvous; prothorax short, conical, two arcuated, transverse rugæ; feet lurid, femora above, and the apex of the tibiæ fuscous; abdomen black, middle beneath yellow; posterior margin of the dorsal segments pointed with yellow; vagina black; wings hyaline, veins black; pterostigma short, almost oblong, the exterior side a little oblique, occupying one areolet, black; subpterostigmatical areolet equal within, longer without; a series of three areolets beneath the pterostigma.

Length to tip of wings 18 millim. Alar expanse 24 millim.

Hab. California.

Fam. VIII. HEMEROBINA.

Body usually cylindrical, narrow; wings large, numerously veined, the posterior ones with no anal space; tarsi with five articles; ocelli commonly absent.

Larva with a haustellate mouth.

ALEURONIA Fitch.

Covered with whitish powder; eyes reniform; antennæ moniliform; wings ciliated, longitudinal veins few, transverse ones almost absent.

1. A. westwoodii.

Aleuronia westwoodii Asa Fitch, Report I, 98.

Covered with whitish powder; black, head depressed anteriorly, antennæ with 28 articles, shorter than the body, moniliform, black, not powdered; abdomen yellowish; feet pale; wings broad, the apex rounded, the anterior ones with six longitudinal veins, two of them forked; posterior ones with five longitudinal veins, the second and third joined together by a transverse vein; wings ciliated at the apex and posteriorly. (From the description of Dr. Fitch.)

Length to tip of wings 2½ millim.

Hab. United States, in June and July.

CONIOPTERYX Haliday.

Powdered with whitish, eyes globose, antennæ moniliform; wings not ciliated, longitudinal veins few, some transverse veins; posterior wings of the male small.

C. vicina!

Coniopteryx vicina Hagen!

Covered with grayish powder; black, head rounded, antennæ –? feet lurid; wings broader at the apex, rounded, eight longitudinal veins, three and four forked, all joined together by a single transverse vein.

Length to tip of wings 4 millim. Alar expanse 6 millim.

Hab. Washington (Osten Sacken). The only specimen seen is mutilated.

SISYRA Burm.

Antennæ moniliform; subcosta and radius of the wings joined together at the apex; costal space of the base of the anterior wings with no recurrent vein; transverse veins almost absent.

Larva aquatic.

S. vicaria.

Hemerobius vicarius Walk. Catal. 297, 65.

Ferruginous, antennæ pale, abdomen obscurer, feet testaceous; wings fuscous, the anterior ones obscurer. (From the description of Walker.)

Length to tip of wings 5? millim. Alar expanse 9 millim.

Hab. Georgia (Abbot).

MEGALOMUS Rambur.

Antennæ moniliform; wings with the subcosta and radius joined together at the apex, the costal space of the anterior wings strongly dilated, with a forked, recurrent vein; transverse veins in a gradative series; the last article of the maxillary palpi subulate.

M. pictus!
Megalomus pictus Hagen!

Fuscous, hairy, face fusco-aeneous, palpi luteous; occiput fuscous, varied with black; antennæ luteous, the first article entirely, and the apex of the second, brownish-black; dorsum of the pro- and mesothorax blackish-fuscous; feet and abdomen luteous; wings broad, the apex obtuse, luteo-hyaline; the anterior wings with three gradate series of veins, the second series of which is fuscous; veins luteous, all pointed with fuscous, some larger points at the anterior and posterior margins, at the radius and at the external series of gradate veins; posterior wings yellow-hyaline, clouded with cinereous at the anterior margin and before the apex.

Length to tip of wings 8 millim. Alar expanse 15 millim.
Hab. Mexico (Deppe).

MICROMUS Rambur.

Antennæ moniliform; wings with the subcosta and radius joined together at the apex; costal space of the anterior wings narrowed at base, no recurrent vein, transverse series gradate; last article of the maxillary palpi not subulate.

* Wings excised at the apex.

1. M. flavicornis!
Hemerobius flavicornis Walk. Catal. 278, 4.

Luteous, ciliated; head and thorax luteous, pointed with fuscous, antennæ yellow; abdomen piceous, with two cylindrical appendages (male?); feet pale, with long pile, freckled with numerous fuscous points; apex of the wings excised, hamate, pilose, hyaline, a little clouded with fuscous; pterostigma yellow, fuscous at each side, apical margin of the anterior wings fuscescent; veins white, thickly pointed with brown; transverse veins of the costal space forked; six sectors; the discoidal series of veins six-gradate, the four intermediate ones joined together; posterior wings with a fuscous point at the posterior margin.

Length to tip of wings 11 millim. Alar expanse 20 millim.
Hab. Washington (Osten Sacken); Georgia (Abbot).

2. M. hamatus.
Hemerobius hamatus Walk. Catal. 278, 5.

Testaceous; antennæ yellowish, feet pale; wings subhyaline, sprinkled with fuscous, the apex excised, subhamate. (From the description of Walker.) It is similar to the preceding, but the costal space is narrower.

Length to tip of wings 11 millim. Alar expanse 20 millim.
Hab. North America.

** Apex of the wings rounded.

3. M. areolaris!
Micromus areolaris Hagen!

Yellowish; head rufous, antennæ black, thorax fuscous; feet yellow; apex of the wings ovate, yellow-hyaline, veins sparingly pilose, partly yellow, fuscous upon the disk and posterior margin, areoles of the last-named areas streaked with fuscous; two series of areolets, four-gradate, infracted; pterostigma yellow, each side fuscous; posterior wings yellow-hyaline; (reticulation irregular.)

Length to tip of wings 6 millim. Alar expanse 11 millim.
Hab. Florida, in March (Osten Sacken.)

4. M. insipidus!
Micromus insipidus Hagen!

Luteous; sparely pilose, head and thorax varied with fuscous, antennæ pale; abdomen luteous; feet pale, anterior tibiæ with two fuscous bands; wings hyaline, anterior ones obsoletely striated with fuscous; veins pale, with fuscous interruptions; four sectors; two series, 6 and 4 gradate, infracted.

Length to tip of wings 9 millim. Alar expanse 18 millim.
Hab. New York; Philadelphia.

5. M. sobrius!
Micromus sobrius Hagen!

Pale; sparely pilose; antennæ whitish-yellow, the apex obscurer;

head and thorax pale luteous; feet pale, white; wings whitish-hyaline, the anterior ones marmorated with fuscous; veins white, sparely interrupted with fuscous; gradate veins 6 and 4 brownish-black.

Length to tip of wings 9 millim. Alar expanse 17 millim.

Hab. Chicago (Osten Sacken).

HEMEROBIUS Linné.

Antennæ moniliform, wings with the subcosta and radius joined together at the apex; costal space of the anterior wings broader at base, with a recurrent, forked vein; transverse series gradate, broken; maxillary palpi with the last article subulate.

† One sector.

1. H. longicollis.

Hemerobius longicollis Walk. Catal. 281, 12.

Piceous, hairy; head ferruginous, antennæ luteous, a little longer than the body; prothorax much longer than broad, narrower anteriorly; tricarinated; feet testaceous; wings subcinereous, the anterior ones obsoletely clouded with fuscous; pterostigma lurid; transverse costal veins few, radius widely distant from the subcosta; one trifurcated sector; first gradate series interrupted, second almost absent; posterior wings short, pale. (From the description of Walker.)

Length to tip of wings 9 millim. Alar expanse 16 millim.

Hab. Georgia (Abbot). An irregular species; it seems to be allied to *Micromus areolaris*.

† † Two sectors.

2. H. amiculus.

Hemerobius amiculus Asa Fitch, Report I, 95.

Fuscous; antennæ yellowish, feet whitish; wings hyaline, irregularly clouded and spotted with fuscous; margin of the anterior wings pointed with black; veins fuscous pointed with black; gradate series banded with fuscous; posterior wings pale. (From the description of Dr. Fitch.)

Length to tip of wings 7? millim. Alar expanse 12 millim.

Hab. New York; Illinois; May to October (Asa Fitch). On peach trees and wild shrubs.

3. H. occidentalis.

Hemerobius occidentalis Asa Fitch, Report I, 95.

Blackish; antennæ shorter than the body, black; feet pale; wings hyaline, the areoles with two obscure parallel lines; margin obscure; veins stout, black, transverse veins almost as in the preceding species. (From the description of Dr. Fitch.)

Length to tip of wings 5? millim. Alar expanse 8 millim.

Hab. Henderson River, Illinois; October (Asa Fitch). (Washington, June. The antennæ of this specimen, ♂?, are longer than the body, and their basal third only, black, the remainder pale. Osten Sacken.)

Schioedte Berlin, Ent. Zeit. III, p. 143, reports *Hemerobius obscurus* Zett. Ins. Lapp. 1063, 12, from Greenland; I have not seen the specimens, nor is that species known to me.

4. H. delicatulus.

Hemerobius delicatulus Fitch, Report I, 96.

Obscure yellow; antennæ longer than the body, fuscous; feet pale; wings hyaline, veins fuscous, pointed obscurely; single gradate series banded with fuscous. (From the description of Dr. Fitch.)

Length to tip of wings 6? millim. Alar expanse 10 millim.

Hab. Illinois; October (Asa Fitch).

† † † Three sectors.

5. H. alternatus.

Hemerobius alternatus Fitch, Report I, 93.

White or yellowish; varied with fuscous, with fulvous pile; head in front and thorax each side with a blackish-fuscous stripe; abdomen whitish, each side with a longitudinal white stripe, which is margined above with a series of brown points, and below by a brown line; wings hyaline, iridescent, veins interrupted black and white; gradate series black, stout, marked with fuliginous; posterior wings pale, sparingly marked with black. (From the description of Dr. Fitch.)

Length to tip of wings 11? millim. Alar expanse 20 millim.

Hab. New York; June (Asa Fitch). Upon pine and hemlock bushes.

6. H. stigmaterus.

Hemerobius stigmaterus Fitch, Report I, 93.

Luteous; head and antennæ luteous, feet pale; thorax and abdomen fuscous; wings hyaline, anterior ones with black veins, which are banded with white; areoles fumose, with hyaline points; pterostigma fulvous; two gradate series, black. (From the description of Dr. Fitch.)

Var. Apex of the abdomen yellowish, or with a pale lateral streak.

Length to tip of wings 8—10 millim. Alar expanse 15—18 millim.

Hab. North America, Northern and Western States; common from March to October (Asa Fitch).

7. H. castaneae.

Hemerobius castaneae Fitch, Report I, 94.

Whitish; head with a spot beneath each eye, thorax each side with a stripe, and the abdomen with lateral spots, fuscous; wings hyaline, the margin a little dusky; veins whitish, interruptedly black, two gradate series black; a basal larger spot, another smaller, and the bases of the series of discoidal veins black.

The color of the veins often varies; they are sometimes either black, fuscous, or with fulvous interruptions; sometimes deep black, and the discoidal spots are confluent into a vitta. (From the description of Dr. Fitch.)

Length to tip of wings 10 millim. Alar expanse 18 millim.

Hab. Northern and Northwestern States, everywhere common, from April to October (Asa Fitch). Upon chestnut, walnut, and other trees.

8. H. tutatrix!

Hemerobius tutatrix Fitch, Report I, 94.

Yellow; head each side with an external fascia beneath the eyes; thorax each side with three spots, which sometimes are confluent, forming a stripe, fuscous; antennæ a little annulated with fuscous; feet yellowish; wings hyaline, veins whitish, interrupted with fuscous, V-shaped clouds of a fuscous color upon the areoles, having the angle on the fuscous interruptions, and the open side towards the apex of the wing; two series of transverse nervures, 7 and 6 gradate, black; a black point at base.

Length to tip of wings 9 millim. Alar expanse 16 millim.

Hab. New York, September (Asa Fitch), upon apple trees; Washington, June (Osten Sacken); California.

9. H. conjunctus.

Hemerobius conjunctus Fitch, Report I, 94.

Wings hyaline, the margin infuscated; veins white, interrupted with black, and banded; gradate veins, the two internal ones excepted, banded with fuscous, a black point at the base of the discoidal veins; posterior wings immaculate. The spots of the wings are almost as in *H. alternatus*, but the margin is immaculate. (From the description of Dr. Fitch.)

Length to tip of wings 8 millim. Alar expanse 14 millim.

Hab. New York, May (Asa Fitch), upon pine bushes.

10. H. pinidumus.

Hemerobius pinidumus Fitch, Report, I, 95.

Yellowish; sides of the thorax fuscous; wings hyaline, a little fumose, the margin with fuscous points; veins white, interrupted with fuscous; gradate series black, clouded with fuscous; three or four of the gradate veins forming a maculose band across the disk; similar to *H. tutatrix*, differing in the basal reticulation. (From the description of Dr. Fitch.)

Length to tip of wings 7 millim. Alar expanse 12 millim.

Hab. New York, May to July; common (Asa Fitch) upon pine bushes.

11. H. hyalinatus.

Hemerobius hyalinatus Fitch, Report, I, 95.

Similar to the preceding, perhaps a variety of it; wings more hyaline, veins finely interrupted with fuscous; gradate veins uncolored, not banded with fuscous; reticulation a little different. (From the description of Asa Fitch.)

Length to tip of wings 7 millim. Alar expanse 12 millim.

Hab. New York, May to July (Asa Fitch); upon pine bushes.

12. H. subanticus.

Hemerobius subanticus Walk. Catal. 282, 13.

Ferruginous; head testaceous in front; antennæ paler; feet testaceous; wings sublurid, narrow, veins testaceous, dotted with fuscous, two interrupted, fuscous gradate series, which are clouded with fuscous; sectors of the radius 1 and 2 bifurcated, 3 unifurcated. (From the description of Walker.)

Length to tip of wings 6 millim. Alar expanse 11 millim.

Hab. St. John's Bluff, East Florida (Doubleday).

13. H. posticus.

Hemerobius posticus Walk. Catal. 283, 15.

Ferruginous; head paler; antennæ testaceous, longer than the body; wings subhyaline, the anterior ones clouded with fuscous, especially at the apex and posterior margin; veins pale testaceous, interrupted with fuscous; two complete series of gradate veinlets, which are fuscous, and clouded with fuscous; three bifurcate sectors; posterior wings with two complete series of gradate veinlets, the internal one of which is fuscous, and clouded with fuscous. (From the description of Walker.)

Length to tip of wings 9 millim. Alar expanse 14—16 millim.

Hab. Georgia (Abbot).

14. H. citrinus!

Hemerobius citrinus Hagen!

Yellow; occiput each side, and the sides of the prothorax, fuscous; feet yellow; wings yellow-hyaline, veins yellow, pointed with fuscous; gradate veins (6 and 5) yellow.

Length to tip of wings 10 millim. Alar expanse 18 millim.

Hab. North America (Knoch; Berlin Museum).

15. H. simulans.

Hemerobius simulans Walk. Catal. 285, 22.

Piceous; head ferruginous; antennæ piceous, ferruginous at base; prothorax short, broad; feet testaceous; wings cinereous, the anterior ones clouded with fuscous, veins black; two gradate series almost contiguous, banded with fuscous; sector 1 unifurcated, sector 2 bifurcated, sector 3 trifurcated. (From the description of Walker.)

Length to tip of wings 8 millim. Alar expanse 14 millim.

Hab. St. Martin's Falls, Albany River, Hudson's Bay (Barnston).

16. H. marginatus?

Hemerobius marginatus Walk. Catal. 286, 23.

Pale ochreous; wings white, with the transverse veins, and some clouds at the internal margin, fuscous; sectors 1 and 2 unifurcated, 3 quadrifurcated. (From the description of Walker.) I believe it to be different from the European insect of this name.

Length to tip of wings 10 millim. Alar expanse 19 millim.

Hab. Nova Scotia (Redman).

17. H. humuli?

Hemerobius humuli Walk. Catal. 286, 24.

Pale ochreous; antennæ annulated with fuscous and white; feet pale; wings hyaline, sparingly pointed with fuscous; sectors 1 and 2 unifurcated, 3 trifurcated. (From the description of Walker.) I believe it to be different from the European species of this name.

Length to tip of wings 8 millim. Alar expanse 14 millim.

Hab. Georgia (Abbot).

18. H. crispus?

Hemerobius crispus Walk. Catal. 288, 31.

Testaceous; sides of the thorax and the abdomen obscurer; wings opaline, narrow, the anterior ones spotted with fuscous, transverse veins fuscous; posterior wings immaculate; sectors 1 and 2 unifurcated, 3 trifurcated. (From the description of Walker.) I believe it to be different from the European species of this name.

Length to tip of wings 7 millim. Alar expanse 12 millim.

Hab. North America; Nova Scotia (Redman).

19. H. obliteratus.

Hemerobius obliteratus Walk. Catal. 289, 35.

Testaceous; antennæ longer than the body, fuscous, annulated with whitish, the apex fuscous; the basal article testaceous; feet pale testaceous; wings subhyaline, the anterior ones hardly clouded with fuscous; veins testaceous, interrupted with fuscous; gradate series two, broken, banded with fuscous; sectors 1 and 2 unifurcated, 3 trifurcated. (From the description of Walker.)

Length to tip of wings 7 millim. Alar expanse 12 millim.

Hab. Georgia (Abbot).

20. H. neglectus!

Hemerobius neglectus Hagen!

Yellow; head and sides of the prothorax fuscous; antennæ and feet pale yellow; wings luteo-fuscous, the anterior ones densely streaked with whitish-hyaline; veins luteous, pointed with black and fuscous; 6 and 5 of the gradate veins luteous.

Length to tip of wings 11 millim. Alar expanse 20 millim.

Hab. Mexico (Ehrenberg; Berlin Museum).

† † † † Four sectors.

21. H. longifrons.

Hemerobius longifrons Walk. Catal. 291, 40.

Testaceous, marked with fuscous; antennæ longer than the body, fuscous annulated with pale; abdomen piceous; feet pale testaceous; wings cinereous, anterior ones with three oblique, interrupted fasciæ, and marginal spots, black; veins pale testaceous, interrupted with black; gradate series two, broken; sector 3 unifurcated. (From the description of Walker.)

Length to tip of wings 10 millim. Alar expanse 18 millim.

Hab. St. Martin's Falls, Albany River, Hudson's Bay (Barnston).

POLYSTOECHOTES Burm.

Antennæ short, moniliform; subcosta and radius of the wings confluent at the apex; costal space of the anterior wings broader at base, with a recurrent vein, forked; a gradate series of several transverse veins; last article of the maxillary palpi truncated.

Larva perhaps aquatic.

1. P. punctatus!

Semblis punctata Fab.! Entom. Syst. II, 73, 4.—*Hemerobius nebulosus* Fab. Entom. Syst. Suppl. 202, 1—2.—*Hemerobius irroratus* Say, Long's Exped. II, 306, 1; Asa Fitch, Report, I, 92.—*Polystoechotes sticticus* Burm. Hand. II, 982, 1; Walk. Catal. 231, 1.—*Osmylus validus* Walk.! Catal. 233, 3.

Piceous, hairy; mouth testaceous; antennæ piceous, with the base testaceous; head and thorax clothed with gray hair; feet hairy, testaceous, the anterior ones annulated with fuscous, apex of the tarsal articles fuscous; abdomen piceous, beneath fuscous;

wings cinereous, subhyaline, the anterior ones marked with fuscous upon the margin; veins white, with fuscous interruptions; posterior wings immaculate; sector 1 seventeen-branched.

Length to tip of wings 28—38 millim. Alar expanse 52—76 millim.

Hab. North West Territory; Lake Erie, common (Say); North Red River (Kennicott); New York, July, rare (Asa Fitch); Philadelphia, Pennsylvania, Washington (Osten Sacken); California; Texas; Fort Steilacoom, Puget Sound (Dr. Suckley); Maryland (Uhler). I saw the specimen described by Fabricius in Bank's Museum.

2. P. vittatus.

Hemerobius vittatus Say, Long's Exped. II, 307, 2; Asa Fitch, Report, I, 92.

Pale yellow; head with a quadrangular black spot between the eyes; antennæ yellowish-red, the base and apex black; thorax greenish-white, the sides with a black vitta; wings hyaline, pointed with black; costal veins white, with black interruptions; pterostigma small, whitish; posterior wings almost immaculate, at the middle of the anterior margin a large orbicular spot, and another apical, smaller; feet black, base of the femora, an apical ring upon the posterior ones, and an apical ring upon the posterior tibiæ, pale; abdomen black, a small, dorsal, pale spot upon the segments. (From the description of Say.)

Length to tip of wings 30 millim. Alar expanse 55 millim.

Hab. Pennsylvania, New Jersey (Titian Peale, Say).

MANTISPA Illiger.

Antennæ short; prothorax elongated, cylindrical; anterior feet stout, raptatorial; wings narrow, subcosta and costa confluent at the middle of the anterior margin.

1. M. brunnea!

Mantispa brunnea Say, Long's Exped. II, 309; Amer. Entom. II, tab. xxv; Erichson, Germar's Zeitschrift, I, 161, 2; Westwood. Trans. Ent. Soc. Lond. ser. 2, I, 253, 2; Walk.! Catal. 214, 2.—*Mantispa varia* Erich.! Germar's Zeitschr. I, 161, 3; Westw. Trans. Ent. Soc. ser. 2, I, 253, 3; Walker! Catal. 214, 3; Hagen! Stettin. Ent. Zeit. XX, 406.

Color very variable; fuscous, varied with black and yellow;

head fuscous, a transverse streak at the base of the antennæ, and another, occipital, sometimes absent, black; antennæ fuscous, base and extreme apex yellowish; prothorax varying in robustness, anteriorly broadest, upon the middle transversely rugose, narrower between the anterior and posterior tubercles, fuscous; with a broad, transverse, yellow band behind the black anterior margin; or with a triangular yellow spot at base, before a black band; or with the middle also yellow; mesothorax fuscous, or fuscous margined with yellow; abdomen fuscous or yellow, base above and beneath black; anterior feet entirely rufo-fuscous, or with the femora black, tibiæ black inside, outside sometimes with a longitudinal black stripe; intermediate feet yellowish-red, with the femora obscure, or yellowish, the femora black, with the apex yellowish; tibiæ behind the base, banded with fuscous; tarsi sometimes (perhaps the other sex) with two broad lamelliform, yellowish lobes, which are rounded at the apex; (I have not seen this to be the case but in two specimens; types of *M. brunnea* Erichson, and of Uhler;) posterior feet the same color as the intermediate ones, with no lobes; wings fuscous; the posterior half hyaline.

Length to tip of wings 18—34 millim. Alar expanse 30—34 millim.

Hab. North West Territory (Say); N. Illinois (Kennicott); Philadelphia (Say); Georgia (Abbot); St. John's Bluff, E. Florida; Fort Steilacoom, Puget Sound; Mexico (Deppe); Central America.

I have seen many specimens; I believe the species of Say and Erichson not to be different; Mr. Say describes both sexes, but does not appear to have observed the remarkable lobes of the tarsi.

(The tarsal lobes are not characteristic of sex, but are found present in both males and females; the membranous character of these lobes, and their great delicacy seems to render them liable to disappear, by shrinking or accident; this probably accounts for their absence in most of the specimens observed by Dr. Hagen; in a specimen which I examined the one middle tarsus had the lobes beautifully apparent, while on the opposite tarsus only a vestige was present; on another tarsus only a white membrane was apparent; when well conditioned, the lobes are obvious upon both the middle and posterior tarsi. The male has robust, cylindrical, hairy anal appendages, superiorly, which will abundantly distinguish the sex. Uhler.)

2. M. interrupta!

Mantispa interrupta Say, Amer. Entomol. II, tab. **xxv**; Erichs. Germ. Zeits. I, 171, 21; Westw. Trans. Ent. Soc. ser. 2, I, 255, 21; Walk. Catal. 219, 21.

Yellowish; antennæ black, yellow at base; head yellow in front, with a black line upon the middle; posteriorly black, exteriorly yellow; a streak upon the middle, and a spot each side, yellow; prothorax long, slender, tuberculous, yellowish-fuscous; the apical and basal margin, and a longitudinal dorsal line, black; mesothorax fuscous, varied with yellow; abdomen fuscous (mutilated); feet yellowish, the anterior femora exteriorly and interiorly striated with fuscous, tibiæ and tarsi black; posterior femora interiorly at base with a fuscous line, intermediate tibiæ with a fuscous ring; wings hyaline, veins black, subcosta fuscous; pterostigma long, brownish-black.

Length to tip of wings 23 millim. Alar expanse 36 millim.

Hab. Philadelphia (Say, Uhler); Virginia (Uhler).

This species is very rare; I have seen only one specimen; the words of Mr. Say, "On the submargin is an irregular, quadrate, dark, fuscous spot, confluent with the carpus," do not agree with my specimen.

(The species varies in sometimes wanting the quadrate brown spot of the wings; the tarsal lobes are apparent in this species, in common with the preceding: I have seen a specimen in which the apical spot of the wings is absent. The abdomen is generally yellowish, with dorsal, triangular, black spots. Uhler.)

3. M. viridis.

Mantispa viridis Walk. Catal. 227, 47.

Green or yellow, with a reddish stripe each side, along the whole length of the body; face varied with rufous; antennæ reddish; prothorax long, slender, broader anteriorly; wings hyaline, veins pale, dotted with black. (From the description of Walker.)

Length to tip of wings 13 ? millim. Alar expanse 18 millim.

Hab. East Florida.

Walker, Catal. 215, 7, reports *M. prolixa*, from Georgia; I saw the specimen, but *M. prolixa* Erichson, is a different species. The locality of Mr. Walker's species is doubtful.

4. M. moesta!

Mantispa moesta Hagen!

Brownish-black; palpi fuscous; face fuscous, transversely rugose; front depressed, rufous, a spot between the antennæ, a black band posteriorly; antennæ fuscous; prothorax dilated anteriorly, luteous, margined with black; posteriorly narrower, cylindrical, transversely sulcated; abdomen black, apex of segments 1 and 2 margined with yellow; 3 and 4 polished at base, with very numerous red points; anterior feet black, first article of the tarsi exteriorly varied with yellow; posterior femora fuscous, with the apex yellow, tibiæ yellow, with an external fuscous spot; wings fuscous, shining; twelve discoidal areoles; a gradate vein upon areoles 6 and 7. (Female.)

Length to tip of wings 27 millim. Alar expanse 47 millim.

Hab. Tennessee (Saussure).

MELEOMA Fitch.

A genus not seen by me, allied to *Chrysopa*, but the bases of the antennæ are distant, and there is an intermediate frontal horn. (Asa Fitch.)

1. M. signoretii.

Meleoma signoretii Fitch, Report I, 82.

Yellowish-green, pale, sparingly pilose; between the antennæ a cylindrical horn, which is longer than the basal joint of the antennæ, deflexed anteriorly into a lamina, upon the middle of which is a black tooth; face each side with a fuscous spot, antennæ pale fuscous, the two basal articles green, the first elongated, thicker; base of the prothorax elevated; feet whitish, tarsi yellowish, with the apex black; apex of the wings a little angulated, hyaline, pterostigma a little opaque; veins whitish, gradate veins, and transverse ones of the interior side of the radius, black. (From the description of Dr. Fitch.)

Length to tip of wings 15? millim. Alar expanse 27 millim.

Hab. Mt. Antonio, Rupert, Vermont, July (Asa Fitch).

2. M. longicornis.

Osmylus longicornis Walk. Catal. 235, 8.

Testaceous, somewhat marked with fuscous; antennæ longer

than the wings, straw-colored, slender, a little pubescent; feet straw-colored; wings hyaline, long, narrow; the anterior ones with whitish veins, which are interrupted with fuscous; veins of the posterior wings whitish; fuscous points between the radius and subcosta. (From the description of Walker.)

Length to tip of wings 22 millim. Alar expanse 40 millim.

Hab. Georgia (Abbot).

Does it belong to this genus? I saw the specimen, and noted "that it belonged to *Chrysopa*."

CHRYSOPA Leach.

Antennæ setiform, long; subcosta and radius of the wings not conjoined at the apex; the costal space of the anterior wings narrow at base, no recurrent vein; transverse veins in gradate, continuous series; the last article of the maxillary palpi compressed at the apex, narrowed.

† Second article of the antennæ with a black ring.

1. Ch. oculata!

Chrysopa oculata Say, Journ. Acad. Philad. VIII, 45; Walk. Catal. 260, 56.—*Chrysopa euryptera* Burm. Handb. II, 980, 7; Schneider, Mon. Chrys. 129, 39, tab. xlv.—*Chrysopa omikron* Fitch, Report I, 85.

Greenish-yellow; antennæ yellowish, the apex obscure, the second article annulated with black, the first joint with a red, dorsal spot or annulus; head yellow, bases of the antennæ surrounded with black rings, above upon the middle interrupted with sanguineous; sides of the cheeks with a black streak; occiput with four black points, which are sometimes confluent into two lines; the anterior spots often conjoined with the rings around the antennæ, each side behind the eyes with a black point; prothorax each side with three black points, forming two intermediate series, and two more laterally, also black; wings hyaline, transverse veins of the anterior ones almost entirely, or in part black.

Length to tip of wings 16—18 millim. Alar expanse 26—30 millim.

Hab. St. Martin's Falls, Albany River, Hudson's Bay (Barnston); United States (Say), extremely common; common in June (Asa Fitch); I have seen many specimens; Washington (Osten

Sacken); New York; Savannah, Dalton, Georgia; Pennsylvania; Virginia (Osten Sacken); Illinois (Kennicott); Maryland (Uhler); New Orleans (Pfeiffer); Tennessee (Saussure).

2. Ch. illepida!

Chrysopa illepida Fitch, Report I, 84.

Very much like the preceding species, but the four occipital spots are conjoined in two lines; the anterior wings with the transverse veins only of the costa, at their base and apex, the base of the second sector, and the gradate veins, black.

Same size as the preceding species.

Hab. New York; Illinois, June (Asa Fitch); perhaps a variety of the preceding.

3. Ch. albicornis.

Chrysopa albicornis Fitch, Report I, 84.

Very much like *Ch. oculata*, the four occipital black points conjoined in two lines; the basal article of the antennæ annulated with sanguineous, the transverse veinlets of all the wings entirely, or in part black. (From the description of Dr. Fitch.)

Same size as the preceding.

Hab. Mississippi, April (Asa Fitch); perhaps a variety.

4. Ch. chlorophana!

Chrysopa chlorophana Burm. Handb. II, 979, 1; Schneid.! Monog. Chrys. 127, 32, tab. xliv.—*Chrysopa xanthocephala* Fitch, Report I, 85.

Very much like *Ch. illepida*, head having the same picturation, but differs in the wings being a little viridescent, the apex more rounded, the pterostigma obscurer, and the ciliæ of the veins longer.

Same size as preceding.

Hab. New York; Lake Michigan, June (Asa Fitch).

Its appearance is different; but it is difficult to be separated by distinct marks. Further experience will decide whether the species of Dr. Fitch can be justly separated from it.

5. Ch. fulvibucca.

Chrysopa fulvibucca Fitch, Report I, 86.

Very much like *Ch. oculata*, but differs in wanting the external black streaks of the cheeks; points of the prothorax variable. (From the description of Dr. Fitch.)

Same size as preceding.

Hab. New York, July and August. Perhaps a variety.

6. Ch. transmarina!

Chrysopa transmarina Hagen!—*Ch. chlorophana* Walker! Catal. 259, 55.

Similar to *Ch. chlorophana*, but differs by wanting the two occipital middle points; two well-defined spots at the eyes anteriorly and two posteriorly; wings densely and longly ciliated, the transverse veins entirely green, the costal ones hardly black at base.

Length to tip of wings 13 millim. Alar expanse 23 millim.

Hab. La Chine, near Montreal (Barnston); C. St. John, Newfoundland; Nova Scotia (Redman).

7. Ch. mississippiensis.

Chrysopa mississippiensis Fitch, Report I, 86.

Picturation of the head very much like that of the preceding species, but it differs in size; the wings are rounded at the apex, all the transverse veins or a part of them black. (From the description of Dr. Fitch.)

Alar expanse 33 millim.

Hab. Jackson, Mississippi, in April (Asa Fitch).

8. Ch. chi.

Chrysopa chi Fitch, Report I, 87.

Antennæ pale, the apex obscurer; at the base of the antennæ an *x*-shaped spot, two lateral spots each side, and an intermediate point black; occiput with four black points in a transverse series; prothorax and mesothorax with four black points, and a point at the base of the anterior wings; abdomen black, the apex pale; transverse veins black, those of the costal middle green; posterior wings with the transverse veins black, base of the first sector black, the second sector black, green upon the middle. (From the description of Dr. Fitch.)

Length to tip of wings 19? millim. Alar expanse 34 miilim.

Hab. New York, June (Asa Fitch).

9. Ch. ypsilon!

Chrysopa ypsilon Fitch, Report I, 87.

Greenish-yellow, pale; antennæ pale, the apex obscurer, the basal article beneath with an apical black point, the second article with a black ring; between the antennæ is a black Y; a series of semilunar streaks at the base of the antennæ, a quadrangular spot before and a streak upon the sides of the cheeks, black; occiput with four black points in a transverse series; prothorax with four quadrangular black spots, mesothorax with two, and a spot at the bases of the anterior wings, black; abdomen obscure green, the segments with two dorsal, medial, fuscous points; wings hyaline, transverse veins black, green on the middle.

Length to tip of wings 16 millim. Alar expanse 29 millim.

Hab. New York, May, June (Asa Fitch); Washington (Osten Sacken).

At first sight it resembles the preceding; is it different?

10. Ch. latipennis !

Chrysopa latipennis Schneid. Monog. Chrys. 118, 34, tab. xl; Walk. Catal. 259, 54.—*Chrysopa bipunctata* Fitch, Report I, 87.

Yellowish-green; apex of the antennæ obscurer, the second article with a black ring; face at the base of the antennæ with a semilunar, short streak, a streak at the sides of the cheeks, and a point anteriorly, black; occiput with two black points; thorax and abdomen green, one-colored; wings broader, the apex rounded, transverse veins of the costal space black at their bases, black all over in the posterior wings.

Length to tip of wings 19 millim. Alar expanse 34 millim.

Hab. Pennsylvania (Zimmerman); St. Martin's Falls, Albany River, Hudson's Bay (Barnston); New York, June (Asa Fitch).

> † † Second article of the antennæ of the same color as the rest.
>
> * Antennæ partly black.

11. Ch. nigricornis !

Chrysopa nigricornis Burm. Handb. II, 980, 6; Schneid.! Monog. Chrysop. 126, 37, tab. xliii; Walk. Catal. 259, 50.—*Chrysopa colon* Fitch, Report I, 88.

Pale yellow; antennæ yellowish, black at base, the first article whitish; face with a black streak at sides upon the cheeks; prothorax each side anteriorly with a black point; body pale yellow; wings hyaline, transverse costal veins, gradate veins entirely and the second sector at base, black.

Length to tip of wings 18 millim. Alar expanse 38 millim.

Hab. Carolina (Zimmerman); New York, June (Asa Fitch); collection of Hagen.

12. Ch. ampla!

Chrysopa ampla Walk. Catal. 268, 72.

Luteous; antennæ longer than the wings, the basal article large, inflated, articles 3—8 within, lineated with black; prothorax broad, narrow in front; mesothorax spotted with fuscous above; wings hyaline, veins white, stigma small, fuscous; anterior wings with fuscous veins at base, two basal, costal ones, the last one of the cubitus, the second one of the first sector, and some of those of the costa at their apex, blackish-fuscous.

Length to tip of wings 27 millim. Alar expanse 48 millim.

Hab. Georgia (Abbot); Mexico.

Another specimen from Mexico is only 21 millim. long, but it is hardly different.

13. Ch. lineaticornis!

Chrysopa lineaticornis Fitch, Report I, 91.—*Chrysopa puncticornis* Fitch, Report I, 92.

Pale green; antennæ longer than the wings, black at base, the basal article pale, inflated, above lineated with black; head spotted with fuscous anteriorly; prothorax exteriorly margined with fuscous; wings hyaline, all the transverse veins black.

Length to tip of wings 17 millim. Alar expanse 31 millim.

Hab. New York, July (Asa Fitch); North America (Vienna Museum).

Chrysopa puncticornis is, very probably, nothing more than a variety.

14. Ch. cubana!

Chrysopa cubana Hagen!

Bright green; antennæ of the length of the wings, black, the basal article bright green, above with a broad, black streak; wings hyaline, transverse veins all black.

Length to tip of wings 12 millim. Alar expanse 20 millim.

Hab. Cuba, in March (Osten Sacken); Alleghany Mountains, Virginia (Osten Sacken).

15. Ch. lateralis.

Hemerobius lateralis Guér. Iconogr. Règn. Anim. Ins. p. 388. Schneid. Monog. Chrys. 162, 6.—*Chrysopa lateralis* Walk. Catal. 274, 86.

Bright green; antennæ longer than the body, blackish-fuscous, the basal article rufous; head anteriorly at the margins of the eyes, and sides of the prothorax with a line, rufous; veins of the wings green; feet green, tarsi fulvous. (From the description of Guérin.)

Length to tip of wings 17 millim. Alar expanse 30 millim.

Hab. Vera Cruz (Saulcy).

16. Ch. conformis !

Chrysopa conformis Walk. Catal. 269, 74.

Testaceous; antennæ longer than the wings, blackish at base; feet pale; abdomen testaceous; wings hyaline, pterostigma testaceous, veins green, some of them black. (From the description of Walker.)

Length to tip of wings 17 millim. Alar expanse 30 millim.

Hab. Jamaica (Gosse); Cuba; St. Thomas; Mexico (Deppe).

Perhaps a specimen from Jamaica (Cuming; Vienna Museum); belongs here; but the antennæ are destroyed; the basal article i testaceous; the prothorax is margined anteriorly with rufous. Does it possibly belong to *Chrysopa transversa*?

17. Ch. pavida !

Chrysopa pavida Hagen !

Pale, whitish-yellow; occiput truncated behind; antennæ long, black; the basal article large, yellow, above with a longitudinal rufous spot; the second and third articles yellowish; prothorax flat, quadrangular, anteriorly obliquely truncated, the sides narrowly red; wings large, hyaline, pterostigma yellow; veins yellowish; anterior wings with the middle of the costal veins or the whole of them, black; the apex of the second sector, the gradate veins (10 and 11) almost entirely, apices of the rest of the transverse veins, and the marginal forks entirely, black; hind wings with the apex of the second sector, and vein of the posterior margin, black.

Length to tip of wings 22 millim. Alar expanse 41 millim.

Hab. Cordova, Mexico (Saussure, Deppe); South Carolina (Zimmerman).

May this not be *Hemerobius lateralis* Guér. Icon. Règn. Anim. p. 388?

18. Ch. explorata!

Chrysopa explorata Hagen!

Yellowish; face with a large, quadrangular spot, occiput with a Y-shaped streak and spot, red; antennæ yellowish, fuscous at base; the first article yellow, with the apex above, red; prothorax broad, obliquely truncated in front; anterior margin black; wings hyaline, narrow, pterostigma yellow, interiorly with a red spot; transverse veins of the anterior wings almost all blackish-fuscous; gradate veins 5 and 5.

Length to tip of wings 13 millim. Alar expanse 23 millim.

Hab. Cordova, Mexico (Saussure).

** Antennæ immaculate; veins varied with black.

19. Ch. insularis.

Chrysopa insularis Walk. Catal. 269, 73.

Testaceous, beneath paler; antennæ testaceous, much longer than the wings; head testaceous, mouth rufous, a vertical rufous streak; prothorax long, conical; segments of the abdomen fuscous posteriorly; wings hyaline, veins green, some of them black; pterostigma small, fuscous; anterior wings with a discoidal fuscous spot, internal gradate veins black. (From the description of Walker.)

Length to tip of wings 20 millim. Alar expanse 36 millim.

Hab. Jamaica (Gosse).

20. Ch. transversa.

Chrysopa transversa Walk. Catal. 255, 46.

Yellow; antennæ shorter than the wings, yellow, pubescent, the base paler; head yellow; face with a spot at the base of the antennæ, and the lateral margin, rufous; palpi partly black; prothorax broad, short, narrower anteriorly, the lateral margins rufous; feet pale green; wings hyaline, veins green, transverse ones almost all black; pterostigma pale green; areoles rather few. (From the description of Walker.)

Length to tip of wings — ? millim. Alar expanse 22 millim.

Hab. Jamaica (Gosse).

21. Ch. collaris.

Chrysopa collaris Schneid. Monog. Chrys. 80, 9, tab. xv. Walk. Catal. 245, 19.

Yellowish-green; a red streak each side, upon the cheeks, at the eyes, another upon the lateral margin of the clypeus and labrum; a red point each side upon the occiput near the eyes; prothorax a little broader than long, sides bright ferruginous; antennæ shorter than the wings, paler at base; anterior wings with the gradate veins and all the subcubital ones, base and apex of the costal ones, base of the second sector, the first sector, and some cubital ones partly, black; posterior wings with the costal veins black. (From the description of Schneider.)

Length to tip of wings 16 millim. Alar expanse 29 millim.
Hab. Island of St. Thomas.

Perhaps it is not distinct from *Ch. transversa*.

22. Ch. thoracica!

Chrysopa thoracica Walk.! Catal. 243, 15.

Green, striped with yellow, robust; antennæ (absent from my specimen) stout, much shorter than the wings, testaceous, yellow at base; face pale; a transverse rufous streak each side at the antennæ; palpi dusky; prothorax broad, short, a dorsal, longitudinal, yellow stripe upon the middle; abdomen with a similarly placed yellow stripe; feet pale green; wings narrow hyaline, veins of the costa, transverse ones of the second sector and gradate ones, black; pterostigma pale green.

Length to tip of wings 16 millim. Alar expanse 29 millim.
Hab. Havana (collection of Hagen); St. Domingo (Pierret).

23. Ch. quadripunctata!

Chrysopa quadripunctata Burm.! Handb. II, 980, 5. Schneid.! Monog. Chrys. 84, 12, tab. xviii. Walk. Catal. 246, 22.—*Chrysopa sichelii* Fitch, Report I, 89.

Pale yellowish-green; thorax and abdomen with a middle orange stripe; head pale, with a yellow spot above; sides of the face, a little between the antennæ, and each side posteriorly, at the eyes, orange; antennæ whitish, palpi whitish, with the apex fuscous; prothorax pale yellow, each side with three orange points; mesothorax with an orange point each side anteriorly; feet pale; wings hyaline, transverse veins almost all black.

Length to tip of wings 18 millim. Alar expanse 32 millim.

Hab. Carolina (Zimmerman); Pennsylvania; New York, August (Asa Fitch).

The other locality cited by Mr. Walker does not belong to this species.

24 Ch. virginica.

Chrysopa virginica Fitch, Report I, 91.

Yellowish-green, immaculate; prothorax each side anteriorly with a black point; wings hyaline, veins green, transverse veins of the second sector fuscous at base, first gradate vein of the external series black, clouded with fuscous; pterostigma with a fuscous point, which is larger in the posterior wings; basal areole quadrangular. (Is it irregular?) (From the description of Dr. Fitch.)

Length to tip of wings 19 millim. Alar expanse 35 millim.

Hab. Cartersville, Virginia (Asa Fitch).

25. Ch. sulphurea.

Chrysopa sulphurea Fitch, Report I, 89.

Yellowish-sulphureous; a subocular orange point; prothorax each side anteriorly, and the basal segments of the abdomen each side, with an orange point; antennæ and feet whitish; apex of the wings rounded, of the posterior ones slightly angulated, veins whitish, transverse veins with the base and apex of almost all of them, and the gradate veins, black. (From the description of Dr. Fitch.)

26. Ch. rufilabris!

Chrysopa rufilabris Burm. Handb. II, 979, 2. Schneid. Monog. Chrys. 78, 8, tab. xiv. Walk. Catal. 245, 18.—*Chrysopa novaeboracensis* Fitch, Report I, 90.

Pale green, with a yellowish stripe in the middle; antennæ whitish, the apex obscurer; face with a lateral streak and the mouth red; palpi luteous, the apex and exteriorly fuscous; occiput each side with a rufous point; prothorax often each side with a black point; feet pale; wings hyaline, the apex angulated, transverse veins almost all black, green in the middle.

Length to tip of wings 15 millim. Alar expanse 27 millim.

Hab. Pennsylvania; New York, common in June and July (Asa Fitch); Savannah, Georgia; Mexico.

27. Ch. interrupta!

Chrysopa interrupta Schneid. Monog. Chrys. 76, 16, tab. xli. Walk. Catal. 242, 12.—*Chrysopa tabida* Fitch, Report I, 92.

Pale green, almost white, immaculate; wings narrow, gradate and subcubital veins black, transverse almost all black, with white middles.

Length to tip of wings 14 millim. Alar expanse 26 millim.

Hab. Pennsylvania; New York, August (Asa Fitch).

28. Ch. emuncta.

Chrysopa emuncta Fitch, Report I, 88.

Pale yellow; head each side with a transverse, small, subocular line, and an intermediate one black; prothorax anteriorly with a black point each side; apex of the wings rounded, bases of the transverse costal veins, and the base and apex of the second sector black; palpi exteriorly black. (From the description of Dr. Fitch.)

Length to tip of wings 19 millim. Alar expanse 34 millim.

Hab. New York, August (Asa Fitch).

29. Ch. attenuata!

Chrysopa attenuata Walk. Catal. 242, 14.

Yellow, very slender; sides of the head anteriorly rufous; palpi varied with rufous; antennæ yellowish; prothorax narrow, the sides anteriorly rufescent; feet pale; wings hyaline, veins green, transverse costal veins, the second sector and gradate veins obscurer.

Length to tip of wings 11 millim. Alar expanse 20 millim.

Hab. St. John's Bluff, East Florida (Doubleday); Berkeley Springs, Virginia (Osten Sacken).

30. Ch. repleta.

Chrysopa repleta Walk. Catal. 244, 17.

Testaceous; apex of the antennæ a little obscurer; prothorax long, narrow in front; segments of the abdomen each side with a fuscous spot; feet pale; wings hyaline; all the transverse veins of the anterior wings, and some of those of the posterior wings, partly tinged with fuscous. (From the description of Walker.)

Length to tip of wings 12 millim. Alar expanse 22 millim.

Hab. Georgia (Abbot).

* * * Antennæ immaculate; veins of the wings green.

31. Ch. harrisii.

Chrysopa harrisii Fitch, Report I, 90.—*Chrysopa perla* Harris, Ins. New England, 215.

Very much like *Ch. novaeboracensis*, but a little broader; the veins all green. (From the description of Dr. Fitch.)

Length to tip of wings 15 millim. Alar expanse 28 millim.

Hab. New York, in July and August (Asa Fitch).

32. Ch. externa!

Chrysopa externa Hagen!

Greenish-yellow; thorax and abdomen with a middle, yellow vitta; the mouth anteriorly and the sides sanguineous; antennæ fulvous, yellowish at base; wings narrow, acuminate, fimbriated with green; all the veins green; the divisory-veinlet of the third cubital areole not reaching the first transverse veinlet of the first radial sector.

Length to tip of wings 14 millim. Alar expanse 26 millim.

Hab. Washington (Osten Sacken); Mexico; California.

May not this be *Ch. harrisii?* the wings, however, are narrower. The species has the divisory veinlet not reaching the first transverse veinlet, or rather not clearly exceeding it; and it is very much like *Ch. vulgaris*, of Europe; but differs by the wings being narrower, and more acuminate. *Ch. acuta*, of the Berlin Museum, is perhaps this species (from Brazil, Surinam, Mexico); but it differs in having fewer gradate veins.

33. Ch. robertsonii.

Chrysopa robertsonii Fitch, Report I, 88.

Pale green, with a pale dorsal stripe; head sulphureous, a short, black line each side at the eyes; antennæ yellowish, the basal article whitish; wings rounded at the apex, pterostigma green, veins all green. (From the description of Dr. Fitch.)

Length to tip of wings 15 millim. Alar expanse 26 millim.

Hab. Tullehassie, Creek Indian Territory (Robertson).

34. Ch. plorabunda.

Chrysopa plorabunda Fitch, Report I, 88.

Pale green, with a yellow dorsal stripe; head yellow, with a small black line at the eyes; antennæ whitish, with the apex yellowish; feet green-white, tarsi yellowish; apex of the wings rounded, the posterior ones with the apex a little acuminate.

A variety has a reddish point each side of the head. (From the description of Dr. Fitch.)

Length to tip of wings 14 millim. Alar expanse 25 millim.

Hab. New York, Illinois, September and October, common (Asa Fitch).

35. Ch. pseudographa.

Chrysopa pseudographa Fitch, Report I, 89.

Very much like the preceding, stramineous; head yellow, face each side with a small black line; antennæ, feet, and veins of the wings whitish; apex of the wings rounded; abdomen with a narrow, dorsal, white line, and the segments each side with an apical, yellowish spot.

Var. Apex of the segments with a yellowish fascia. (From the description of Dr. Fitch.)

Length to tip of wings 14 millim. Alar expanse 25 millim.

Hab. Northern Illinois, October (Asa Fitch).

36. Ch. flava!

Hemerobius flavus Scopol. Ent. Carn. 270, 707.—*Chrysopa vittata* Wesm.! Bullet. Acad. Brux. VIII, 211, 7 (partly); Schneid.! Monog. Chrys. 65, 1, tab. vii.—*Chrysopa alba* Brauer! Monog. No. 5; Burm.! Handb. II, 981, 13.—*Chrysopa subfalcata* Steph.! Illustr. VI, 105, 13.

Entirely whitish-green; basal article of the antennæ thick, elongated; wings acuminate, the costal margin of the anterior ones broadly emarginated; veins white, a few of the transverse veins at base a little blackish.

Length to tip of wings 26 millim. Alar expanse 46 millim.

Hab. Philadelphia (collection of Hagen); Europe; Asia.

37. Ch. innovata!

Chrysopa innovata Hagen!

Pale yellow; maxillary palpi with an external black streak upon the articles; face with a black streak and spot on both sides; antennæ pale yellow (partly destroyed), the first articles, long, narrow, cylindrical, hardly thicker than the following ones; front tuberculous between the antennæ; vertex citron-colored; prothorax subelongate, narrower anteriorly, each side anteriorly with a black point; feet pale yellow, nails black; abdomen yellow; wings long, the apex elliptical; veins and their fimbriæ pale yellow; base of the costal veins, the first and second sector, some of the cubital at the apex and sometimes at the base, and the gradate veins (12 and 10) all black.

Length to tip of wings 23 millim. Alar expanse 41 millim.

Hab. Mexico (Deppe; Berlin Museum).

ACANTHACLISIS Rambur.

Antennæ short, stout, the apex thickened; labial palpi longer than the maxillary; body stout, abdomen long, the apex forcipated in the males; feet stout; spurs infracted; base of the nails dilated; wings long, narrow, densely veined; the male having a tubercle at base of posterior wings.

1. **A. americana.**

Myrmeleon americanum Drury, Ins. I, 111, 4; tab. xlvi, fig. 4. Burm. Handb. II, 996, 17. Walk. Catal. 317, 31.—*Acanthaclisis americana* Ramb. Neuropt. 380, 4.

Gray, clothed with gray hairs; head with a black stripe in the middle, face gray; antennæ black; thorax yellow-gray, with a stripe in the middle and a lateral one each side black, clothed with long gray pile; abdomen fuscous, the sides obscurer; apex of the abdomen of the male with short, straight, forcipated cerci; feet black, with gray hair; wings grayish-hyaline, densely pointed with fuscous; costal space fuscescent in the middle, biareolate. (From the figure and description of Drury.)

"Grayish-fuscous, front and two dorsal stripes rosy-gray; feet annulated with flesh-color; veins of the wings hyaline, alternately rosy and fuscous, wings with fuscous and pearly spots." (Burm.)

Length to tip of wings 71 millim. Alar expanse 126 millim.

Hab. New York (Drury) ♂; South Carolina (Zimmerman) ♀.

I have never seen it; the specimen of Burmeister is larger, the wings spread 96 millim. Is it different?

2. **A. fallax!**

Myrmeleon fallax Ramb.! Neuropt. 385, 1. Walk. Catal. 329, 45.—*Myrmeleon impostor* Walk.! Catal. 324, 41.—*Myrmeleon senilis* Klug! Berlin Museum.

Lurid, with gray villosity, beneath yellowish; face, palpi, and base of the antennæ beneath yellowish; antennæ lurid, annulated with fuscous; vertex varied with fulvous and fuscous, a middle longitudinal line, and each side with a transverse streak, fulvous; occiput with two approximated fuscous lines; prothorax lurid, each side with three longitudinal fuscous stripes, the intermediate ones being less clear; the middle ones approximated, with a whitish line, which is thicker anteriorly, separating them; thorax lurid, streaked with fuscous, and with a dorsal whitish, middle line; feet pale, apex of the femora exteriorly fuscous, tibiæ, especially the anterior ones, annulated with fuscous; nails black; abdomen lurid, above with three fuscous streaks; thorax and feet with long and dense gray villosity; appendages of the male cylindrical, short, almost straight, above with black pile; wings long, narrow, the apex acuminated, the apex of the posterior ones a little emarginated, hyaline, with pearly spots; veins alternated with white and fuscous spots; radius punctated; the space between the median nervure and the subcosta sometimes spotted with fuscous; pterostigma small, white; transverse veins often bifid at the apex of the costal space.

Length to tip of wings 70 millim. Alar expanse 120 millim.
Hab. Mexico (Coffin); Cuba; Columbia; Guiana; Brazil.
It may perhaps constitute a new subgenus.

3. **A. congener!**

Acanthaclisis congener Hagen!

Black, clothed with gray hair; face, palpi, and base of the antennæ beneath, yellowish-white; antennæ black, the apex with narrow whitish rings; vertex black with two transverse stripes, the posterior one interrupted in the middle, and two points posterior to the bands, yellow, the surface with white hair; prothorax each side with a maculose stripe, which is double anteriorly, fulvous; posterior margin fulvous, black in the middle; mesothorax spotted with yellow; abdomen black, with gray pile, the posterior margins of the apical segments narrowly fulvous; feet fuscous, with gray hair, tibiæ yellowish, annulated with fuscous, tarsi black; wings hyaline, a little acuminate, veins yellow, with fuscous interruptions, pterostigma small, black, margined with yellow; subcosta and median nervule distinctly punctate; the costal space with one series of areoles. (Female.)

Length to tip of wings 43 millim. Alar expanse 72 millim.
Hab. Pecos River, Western Texas, July (Capt. Pope).

MYRMELEON Linné.

Antennæ short, robust, the apex thickened; body elongated, slender; feet long, slender; spurs straight or a little incurved; base of the nails not dilated; wings long, narrow, densely veined.

† Apex of the wings with a broad fuscous band.

1. M. gratus!

Formicaleo grata Say, Journ. Acad. Philad. VIII, 45, 2.—*Myrmeleon gratus* Walk.! Catal. 392, 157.—*Myrmeleon roseipennis* Burm.! Handb. II, 995, 13; Ramb.! Neuropt. 408, 38, tab. xii, fig. 2.

Black; margin of the labium, a transverse stripe upon the face and the occiput yellow; antennæ long, the apex hardly thickened; labial palpi short, black, the last article longer, fusiform; prothorax black, a middle line, broader at base and apex, white; abdomen fuscous; feet slender, long, rufo-fuscous, base of the femora pale; posterior tibiæ pale, with the apex fuscous; spurs long, straight, as long as the two basal articles of the tarsi; tarsi pale, with the apex fuscous; wings large, hyaline, the apex rosy, interior to which is a large, trifarious, fuscous spot; anterior wings with a spot at the middle of the posterior margin, and a series of points at the submedian nervure, fuscous; median and submedian nervures yellow, interrupted with fuscous.

Length to tip of wings 52 millim. Alar expanse 94 millim.

Hab. Indiana; St. Louis; Philadelphia; Mississippi (Edwards).

† † Wings with ocellate fuscous spots.

2. M. obsoletus!

Formicaleo obsoleta Say, Jour. Acad. Philad. VIII, 44, 1.—*Myrmeleon ocellatus* Burm.! Handb. II, 995, 12; Walk. Catal. 401, 172.—*Myrmeleon nigrocinctus* Ramb.! Neuropt. 398, 20; Walk.! Catal. 361, 101.

Luteous; face with a transverse, broad, fuscous fascia; antennæ long, the apex clavate, luteous, the base and apex black; labial palpi short, luteous, the last article longer, fusiform; prothorax elongated, narrower anteriorly, luteous, a little granulated with black; meso- and metathorax with a broad, dorsal, fuscous stripe; at each side a broad black stripe; abdomen black, a luteous, dorsal band upon the middle of each segment; feet elongated, very slender, black; base of the anterior femora, and apex of the tibiæ brown;

posterior femora with a luteous band before the apex, tibiæ luteous, with the base and apex black, tarsi luteous, obscurer at the apex; spurs as long as the two basal articles of the tarsi, luteous; wings hyaline, beautifully spotted with fuscous; the anterior ones with an ocellate spot at the middle of the posterior margin, a double spot at the pterostigma, an apical interrupted series, and some points at the median nervure, fuscous; posterior wings with a larger, orbicular spot before the pterostigma, and some apical spots, also fuscous.

Length to tip of wings 34 millim. Alar expanse 62 millim.

Hab. United States, not rare (Say); New York; St. Louis; Carolina (Cabanis); Alabama (Gosse); Maryland (Uhler).

Very much like *M. pantherinus* Fab. (*ocellatus* Borkhausen), from Europe, but a different and most beautiful species. (Gosse (Letters from Alabama) figures this species on p. 248—Uhler.)

† † † Wings not spotted, but hyaline or sprinkled with fuscous.

* Costal space with a double series of areoles.

‡ No spurs.

3. M. abdominalis!

Myrmeleon abdominalis Say, Godman's West. Quart. Report, II, 163.—*Myrmeleon irroratus* Burm.! Handb. II, 995, 11.—*Myrmeleon conspersus* Ramb.! Neuropt. 387, 3; Walk.! Catal. 329, 47.—*M. talpinus* Klug. Berlin Museum.

Fuscous; face pale, with a broad, brownish-black band upon the middle, which is emarginated anteriorly; vertex black, a transverse, pale line above at the base of the antennæ; antennæ long, stout, not clavate, black; palpi equal, luteo-fuscous; thorax fuscous, obscurely and interruptedly lineated with pale; prothorax short; abdomen long, slender, longer than the wings, the apex forcipated, fuscous, hirsute; two longitudinal, dorsal lines, which are sometimes partly confluent, pale; feet pale, densely sprinkled with black, apex of the tibiæ, and apex of the tarsal articulations black; tibiæ armed with long, black spines, no spurs; wings short, broader before the apex, a little fumose, subhyaline, veins fuscous, interrupted with white, the anterior wings closely sprinkled with fuscous, especially at the median and submedian nerves; abdomen of the female shorter than the wings; fuscous, the segments with middle and apical yellow points.

Length to tip of wings 32 ♂; 26 ♀ millim. Alar expanse 50 millim.

Hab. Arkansas, Rocky Mountains; South Carolina (Zimmerman); Savannah, Georgia; Florida (Norton); New Jersey (Uhler).

Does *M. abdominalis* Say, perhaps belong to the following species?

‡ Spurs present.

4. M. longicauda !

Myrmeleon longicaudus Burm.! Handb. II, 994, 8; Ramb.! Neuropt. 386, 2, tab. xii, fig. 3; Walk.! Catal. 329, 46.

Luteo-fuscous; face luteous, fuscous at the base of the antennæ; vertex obscurely varied with fuscous; antennæ long, thick, clavate, fuscous; palpi equal, luteous; thorax fuscous, obscurely varied with pale; prothorax short; abdomen long, slender, hairy, longer than the wings, the apex forcipated, fuscous; the basal half above obsoletely luteous; feet pale, sprinkled with black; apex of the tibiæ, the whole of the third and fourth articulations of the tarsi and the apex of the last article, black; tibiæ with black spines; spurs as long as the two basal articles of the tarsi; wings narrow, hyaline, veins fuscous; the median and submedian nervure interrupted with white; pterostigma whitish; anterior wings rarely sprinkled with fuscous, with three obsolete, fuscous points at the submedian nervure. I have not seen the female.

Length to tip of wings 40 millim. Alar expanse 48 millim.

Hab. Savannah, Georgia.

5. M. contaminatus.

Myrmeleon contaminatus Burm. Handb. II, 995, 11. Note.

"Most like *M. irroratus*, but entirely black-gray, the hind wings also are densely sprinkled with black." Unknown to me. (From the description of Burm.)

Hab. South Carolina (Zimmerman).

6. M. salvus !

Myrmeleon salvus Hagen !

Luteo-fuscous; face luteous, above black; vertex fuscous, obsoletely variegated; antennæ long, clavate, fuscous, slightly annulated with luteous; palpi luteous, equal; thorax fuscous, varied with pale; prothorax short; abdomen of the male long, slender, the apex forcipated, hairy, longer than the wings, luteous, with two dorsal pale lines; feet yellowish, sprinkled with black, apex of the tarsal articulations, and the fourth entirely black; tibiæ with black spines; spurs as long as the two basal articles of the tarsi; wings narrow, hyaline, veins fuscous, pterostigma white; subcosta, median and submedian nerves white, a little sprinkled with fuscous; posterior margin of the wings a little sprinkled with fuscous, the costal space upon the basal half uniareolated.

Length to tip of wings 32 millim. Alar expanse 46 millim.

Hab. Washington (Osten Sacken); South Carolina (Zimmerman).

M. nebulosus Ramb.! Neuropt. 387, 4; Walk. Catal. 330, 48, is perhaps the female of *M. salvus;* I possess two specimens from Pennsylvania, the one the size of our typical male, the other larger. (Expanding 62 millim.)

7. M. nebulosus.

Myrmeleon nebulosum Oliv. Enc. Method. VIII, 127, 35; Walk. Catal. 409, 212.

Black, marked with yellow; abdomen black, the base of the segments pale; feet yellow; wings hyaline, reticulated with fuscous, with obscure points and spots. (From the description of Olivier.)

Hab. New York.

Unknown to me; does it belong to this section?

8. M. versutus.

Myrmeleon versutus Walk.! Catal. 331, 51.

Black, very slender; front of the head shining, at the eyes and around the base of the antennæ, yellow; vertex with two, interrupted on the middle, yellow bands; face each side with an angular, yellow stripe; palpi yellow, black at the apex; antennæ subfiliform, much longer than the thorax, black; prothorax short, yellow, bivittated with black; a yellow point anteriorly upon the vittæ; meso- and metathorax lineated and pointed with yellow; abdomen very long, slender, the apex forcipated, testaceous, the base striped with piceous, the apex black; feet testaceous; wings hyaline, short, narrow, finely dotted with fuscous; pterostigma whitish; the apex only of the costal space biareolated. (From the description of Walker.)

Length to tip of wings 30 millim. Alar expanse 46 millim.
Hab. Mexico (Coffin).

9. M. ferox.

Myrmeleon ferox Walk. Catal. 332, 52.

Black, very slender; base of the antennæ encircled with yellow; vertex luteous, with an interrupted black band; face pale yellow; palpi testaceous; antennæ black, almost filiform, longer than the thorax; prothorax narrow, with a dorsal line and two points each side, yellow; beneath yellow; meso- and metathorax margined and pointed with yellow; abdomen much longer than the wings, the apex forcipated, segments each side behind with a testaceous point; feet testaceous, tibiæ and tarsi black at apex; wings cinereous, pterostigma whitish; a brown mark adjoining it on the front wings; veins fuscous, sometimes interrupted with white; anterior wings with three fuscous points at the submedian nerve, and an oblique, apical fuscous streak; posterior wings immaculate; the apex only of the costal space biareolated. (From the description of Walker.) Male.

Length to tip of wings 42 millim. Alar expanse 60 millim.
Hab. California (Hartweg).

10. M. exitialis.

Myrmeleon exitialis Walk. Catal. 376, 133.

Black; mouth luteous, each side with a yellow point; vertex each side with a yellow line and point; antennæ clavate, shorter than the thorax; prothorax short, narrower anteriorly, with six luteous spots, the four anterior ones being placed in a transverse series; meso- and metathorax partly margined with yellow; abdomen shorter than the wings, the segments margined posteriorly with yellow; feet black, femora partly yellow; tibiæ bifasciate with yellow, tarsi yellow at base; wings subcinereous, long, narrow, subacuminate; pterostigma pale yellow, marked each side by a fuscous point, which is obsolete in the posterior wings; veins black, interrupted with yellow; anterior wings with a series of points at the median and submedian nerves, and the veins partly banded with fuscous; only the extreme apex of the costal space biareolated. (From the description of Walker.)

Length to tip of wings 30 millim. Alar expanse 73 millim.
Hab. California (Hartweg).
Female? Does it belong to this section?

11. M. inscriptus!

Myrmeleon inscriptus Hagen!

Black; face yellow, black above; vertex black, with an interrupted line each side, and two points behind, yellow; antennæ black, a little annulated with yellow (apex destroyed); palpi fuscous, articulated with pale; prothorax short, black, a middle line, a lateral one each side and a point anteriorly, yellow; meso- and metathorax black, pointed with yellow; abdomen short, black; feet black, clothed with white hair, base exteriorly of the posterior tibiæ yellow; spurs luteous, of the length of the first tarsal articulation; wings narrow, long, acuminate, subcinereous; anterior ones with the veins fuscous, slightly banded with fuscous, rarely interrupted with white; pterostigma small, white, exteriorly fuscous; at the posterior margin is a fuscous, flexuous, bi-incurved line, reaching the apex; at the median nervure are some hyaline nebulæ, whitish; posterior wings hyaline, veins fuscous, sometimes interrupted with white; the whole of the costal space of the anterior wings biareolated.

Length to tip of wings 34 millim. Alar expanse 60 millim.
Hab. Pecos River, Western Texas (Capt. Pope).

12. M. pumilis!

Myrmeleon pumilis Burm.! Handb. II, 995, 10; Walk. Catal. 401, 173.

Black; face luteous, black above; vertex black, in front with a pale band, clothed with white hairs, transverse; basal article of the antennæ whitish (destroyed in my specimen), "pale, annulated with black, club abrupt, black, Burm.," palpi pale, annulated with fuscous; prothorax narrow, with a triangular, white spot each side anteriorly; meso- and metathorax with some pale points; abdomen black, segments with a pale band upon the middle; feet pale, with white and black spines, femora black above, the apex white, tibiæ white, with a broad basal and apical black ring; articles of the tarsi black at the apex; spurs as long as the two basal articles of the tarsi; wings hyaline, broad; veins white, interrupted with fuscous; anterior wings sprinkled with rare, but sufficiently distinct fuscous points; pterostigma small, white; only the apex of the costal space biareolated.

Length to tip of wings 20 millim. Alar expanse 35 millim.

Hab. South Carolina (Zimmerman).

* * Costal space with one series of areoles.

‡ No spurs.

13. M. pygmaeus!

Myrmeleon pygmaeus Hagen!

Fuscous, spotted with yellow; face black, with yellow spots; palpi yellow, the last article black; occiput yellow, spotted with black; antennæ short, black, annulated with yellow, the club large, almost orbicular, luteous, varied with fuscous; prothorax short, fuscous, varied with yellow; abdomen short, the dorsum pointed with fuscous, with black hair, and white villosity, venter luteous; feet short, pale, spotted with black; apex of all the tarsal articles black; wings short, the apex very much dilated, the reticulation peculiar, simple, hyaline, pterostigma snow-white, brown interiorly; veins fuscous, the longitudinal ones interrupted with white.

Length to tip of wings 15 millim. Alar expanse 26 millim.

Hab. Mexico (Deppe).

A very singular species; as yet, the smallest of this genus.

‡ ‡ Spurs of the anterior feet as long as the first tarsal joint.

14. M. immaculatus!

Myrmeleon immaculatus De Geer, Mém. III, 365, tab. xxvii, fig. 8; Burm.! Handb. II, 994, 5; Walk. Catal. 401, 174.

Brownish-black; face black, shining, yellowish anteriorly; vertex opaque, with shining black streaks, in front with a transverse, interrupted stripe, the middle with two interrupted, approximated ones, and each side a small one posteriorly; antennæ lurid, clavate, the second article black; palpi lurid; thorax fusco-piceous, obsoletely varied with lurid; abdomen fuscous; feet yellowish, densely sprinkled with black; base and apex of the tibiæ with a black ring; tarsi black, the basal article yellowish, with its apex black; anterior feet obscurer; wings narrow, long, acute, hyaline, a little cinereous; veins with white and black interruptions, pterostigma white, black within.

Length to tip of wings 38—44 millim. Alar expanse 70—80 millim.

Hab. Savannah; Washington (Osten Sacken); Alleghany Mountains, Virginia (Osten Sacken).

Dr. Burmeister's specimen is pale, being a recently excluded one; a specimen from Virginia expands 70 millim.; but it is hardly different; the apices of the abdominal segments are pale; but in Burmeister's specimen and another (from Washington), the colors are not distinct.

15. M. tectus.

Myrmeleon tectus Walk. Catal. 378, 135.

Black-gray, robust; head shining, black; mouth luteous, the eyes half encircled with yellow; antennae black, subclavate, the base annulated with yellow, shorter than the thorax; palpi luteous; prothorax short; meso- and metathorax margined with testaceous; feet black; tibiæ with testaceous bands, those of the posterior ones broader; femora and tarsi testaceous at base; (abdomen mutilated); wings hyaline, narrow subacuminate, pterostigma white, the anterior ones marked with fuscous; veins black, interrupted with yellow. (From the description of Walker.)

Length to tip of wings 42? millim. Alar expanse 74 millim.

Hab. St. John's Bluff, East Florida (Doubleday).

Do the spurs correspond with this section?

16. M. crudelis.

Myrmeleon crudelis Walk. Catal. 388, 152.

Piceous, slender; head anteriorly and beneath testaceous, front black; vertex ferruginous, antennæ ferruginous, clavate, the apex piceous, shorter than the thorax; prothorax long, testaceous, with three piceous vittæ; meso- and metathorax margined with testaceous; abdomen shorter than the wings; feet testaceous; wings hyaline, narrow, subacute; pterostigma obsolete, whitish; veins whitish; subcostal and submedian veins interrupted with fuscous. (From the description of Walker.)

Length to tip of wings 30 millim. Alar expanse 54 millim.

Hab. St. John's Bluff, East Florida (Doubleday).

Do the spurs correspond with this section?

17. M. rusticus!

Myrmeleon rusticus Hagen!

Piceous, robust; front nigro-piceous, shining; mouth and beneath yellowish; eyes narrowly encircled with yellow; palpi luteous, the last article of the labial ones thickened, fusiform, nigro-piceous; antennæ clavate, obscurely annulated with yellow; vertex obscure ferruginous, each side with a yellow point; occiput fuscous, opaque, with two middle, interrupted stripes and a lateral, flat shining spot each side; prothorax short, fuscous, the anterior margin, and three obsolete stripes, yellowish; meso- and metathorax margined with yellow; abdomen luteo-fuscous, the posterior margin of the segments, and sometimes a dorsal middle line, yellowish; feet yellowish, femora and tibiæ with a stripe beneath and an apical ring, fuscous; apex of the tarsi fuscous; wings narrow, hyaline, pterostigma a little whitish; veins yellowish-white, the median and submedian nerves distinctly interrupted with fuscous.

Length to tip of wings 30—33 millim. Alar expanse 50—60 millim.

Hab. Pecos River, Western Texas, August 4 (Capt. Pope); Matamoras; Florida (Norton). Is this *M. crudelis*?

18. M. insertus!

Myrmeleon insertus Hagen!

Piceous, slender; face black, shining, each side and the mouth yellow; palpi yellowish, the last article fuscous; antennæ piceous, a little annulated with yellow, clavate; vertex opaque piceous, with a transverse, interrupted yellow band upon the middle; occiput opaque, with two streaks upon the middle, interrupted, and flat, shining spots upon the sides, fuscous; prothorax luteous, obsoletely trivittate with piceous; meso- and metathorax hoary, narrowly margined with yellow; abdomen piceous, margin of the segments posteriorly luteous; femora fuscous, the base and an apical ring yellow; tibiæ yellow, within and an apical ring brownish-black; tarsi with brownish-black rings; wings long, narrow, acuminate, pterostigma obsoletely white; veins white, the median one distinctly, and the others obsoletely interrupted with fuscous.

Length to tip of wings 33 millim. Alar expanse 58 millim.

Hab. Cuba (Poey); Port au Prince, St. Domingo.

Chanvallon reports that *Myrmeleons* are frequently found in the island of Martinique; but does not describe any species. Compare Voyage à la Martinique, p. 185.

19. M. leachii.

Formicaleo leachii Guilding, Trans. Linn. Soc. Lond. XVI, 49, 1; Walk. Catal. 373, 127.

Fuscescent, spotted with yellowish; eyes coppery; feet short, pale, tarsi simple, nails moderate; wings hyaline, subfalcate, immaculate, veins ciliated. (From the description of Walker.)

Hab. Jamaica. Unknown to me. Does it belong to this section?

‡ ‡ ‡ Spurs of the anterior feet as long as the two basal articles of the tarsi.

20. M. peregrinus!

Myrmeleon peregrinus Hagen!

Yellow, variegated with blackish-fuscous; head yellow, face with a black spot between the antennæ; palpi yellow, the last article fuscous; antennæ clavate, black, annulated with yellow; vertex yellow, with two transverse black stripes, the posterior one interrupted in the middle, arcuated; prothorax short, yellow, above with four black lines, beneath each side with a black stripe; meso- and metathorax yellow, varied with black; abdomen yellow, the dorsum with three black lines, venter fuscous; feet yellow, densely sprinkled with black, the posterior femora sometimes black in the middle; apex of the tibiæ and tarsi annulated with black; wings long, broad, hyaline, pterostigma yellow, interiorly fuscous; veins yellow, hardly distinctly interrupted with fuscous, at the median and submedian nerves pointed with fuscous; the smaller forks and the transverse veins at the posterior margin of the anterior wings distinctly marked with fuscous.

Length to tip of wings 40 millim. Alar expanse 74 millim.

Hab. California; Pecos River, Western Texas, July (Capt. Pope). Specimens from Matamoras are smaller (expanding 54 millim.), but they are hardly different.

21. M. juvencus!

Myrmeleon juvencus Hagen!

Yellow, varied with black; head and palpi yellow, a spot between the antennæ, and two points upon the vertex, black; antennæ yellow, clavate, annulated with black; prothorax short; thorax all yellow; above and beneath bilineated with black; prothorax with the anterior part yellow; abdomen clothed with white hairs, yellowish, dorsum trilineated with black; feet yellow, the whole of the fourth article of the tarsi, and the apex of the last one, black; wings broad, yellowish-hyaline, pterostigma obsoletely whitish; veins yellow, thickly sprinkled with fuscous, especially so at the median and submedian nerves; base and apex of the transverse veins of the costal space, and forks at the posterior margin, fuscous; posterior wings only at the median nerve, sprinkled with fuscous.

Length to tip of wings 30 millim. Alar expanse 54 millim.

Hab. Pecos River, Western Texas, July (Capt. Pope); North America (Collection of Hagen).

22. M. blandus!

Myrmeleon blandus Hagen!

Yellow, varied with black; head yellow; last article of the palpi fuscous; a spot between the antennæ, trifid, black; vertex yellow, black anteriorly, above with two transverse black lines, the hind one interrupted; antennæ black, annulated with yellow; prothorax short, yellow, with two black stripes upon the middle, which are anteriorly, exteriorly incised, beneath each side with a black stripe; meso- and metathorax yellow, lineated with black; abdomen yellow, clothed with white hair, above narrowly trilineated with black; beneath black; feet yellow, all the articles of the tarsi annulated with black at the apex; wings hyaline, broad, pterostigma obsoletely yellow; veins yellow, interrupted with black, especially at the subcosta; transverse ones almost black.

Length to tip of wings 22 millim. Alar expanse 40 millim.

Hab. Pecos River, Western Texas (Capt. Pope).

23. M. bistictus!

Myrmeleon bistictus Hagen!

Testaceous, varied with piceous; face testaceous, last article of the palpi fuscous; a fuscous spot between the antennæ; antennæ clavate, black, annulated with testaceous; vertex opaque, testaceous, with some transverse piceous marks; prothorax short, testaceous, with two stripes in the middle, and a lateral one each side, piceous; meso- and metathorax piceous, varied with testaceous; abdomen (mutilated) piceous, the segments with two longitudinal, testaceous, medial spots; femora piceous, annulated with yellow before the apex; tibiæ yellow, biannulated with fuscous; tarsi black, the anterior ones with the base of the last article yellow; wings long, narrow, acuminate, pterostígma obsoletely white, the anterior ones fuscous within; veins fuscous, interrupted with white; the anterior wings with an oblique apical line, and another at the middle of the posterior margin, fuscous, narrow.

Length to tip of wings 34 millim. Alar expanse 60 millim.
Hab. Cuba (Poey).

‡ ‡ ‡ ‡ Spurs of the anterior feet as long as the three basal articles of the tarsi.

24. M. macer!

Myrmeleon macer Hagen!

Luteous, varied with piceous, slender; face black, mouth and palpi luteous; vertex opaque, luteous, a 4-spotted transverse line, and occipital points, black; antennæ slender, subclavate, longer than the thorax, luteous, annulated with fuscous; prothorax narrow, luteo-fuscous, anteriorly trimaculate with pale; meso- and metathorax obscurely luteo-fuscous; abdomen luteo-fuscous, the segments 2 to 4 yellowish upon the middle; feet long, whitish, slender, knees at the femora, and the base and apex of the tibiæ, annulated with black; tarsi with articles 3 and 4 entirely, and the apex of the last article, black; spurs long, whitish; wings broad, hyaline; pterostigma obsoletely whitish; veins white, with fuscous interruptions, especially at the median nerve; transverse veins almost all fuscous.

Length to tip of wings 34 millim. Alar expanse 60 millim.
Hab. Mexico (Vienna Museum).

25. M. ingeniosus!

Myrmeleon ingeniosus Walk.! Catal. 337, 63.

Fuscous; face yellow, black above; mouth and palpi luteous; apical article of the labial palpi pointed with black in the middle; vertex fuscous, occiput with two transverse, maculose, yellow stripes; antennæ slender, subclavate, longer than the thorax, black, annulated with yellow; prothorax narrow, fuscous, each side with an obsolete line, and the anterior margin, luteous; mesothorax pointed with luteous; feet short, yellowish, sprinkled with black; third and fourth joints of the tarsi entirely, and the apex of the last joint, black; spurs long, luteous; abdomen fuscous, dorsum of the intermediate segments with a geminate, luteous spot; wings narrow, hyaline, partly milky, pterostigma whitish-yellow; veins pale, densely interrupted with fuscous; anterior wings with two oblique, fuscous streaks, the one at the middle of the posterior margin, the other before the apex.

Length to tip of wings 34 millim. Alar expanse 64 millim.

Hab. South Carolina (Zimmerman); Columbia; Brazil.

The specimens from meridional America are a little different; the occiput is obscurer, less spotted, the prothorax is broader anteriorly: but it is hardly a peculiar species.

EUPTILON Westwood.

This genus is very doubtful; it is only based upon a figure of Drury. It is a *Myrmeleon* with pectinated antennæ.

1. **Eu. ornatum.**
Hemerobius ornatus Drury, I, 110, 2, tab. xlvi, fig. 2.—*Euptilon ornatum* Drury, ed. Westwood, ib.—*Chauliodes ornatus* Ramb. Neur. 445, 3.—*Myrmeleon ornatus* Walk. Catal. 410, 217.

Green; antennæ pectinated; prothorax anteriorly with a black point; abdomen with yellow rings, and a middle black line; wings hyaline, the anterior ones with two oblique fuscous lines, at the apex and at the middle of the posterior margin.

Length to tip of wings 44 millim. Alar expanse 77 millim.

Hab. Dinwiddie, Virginia (Drury).

I am inclined to believe that antennæ have been affixed to this species artificially, or that the wings have been glued to the body of another kind of insect, by error. The green color is foreign to the genera of *Myrmeleons*.

ASCALAPHUS Fab.

Antennæ very long, slender, capitate; body short; feet short, stout, tibiæ with spurs; wings large, less densely veined than *Myrmeleon*.

* Eyes sulcated.

1. A. hyalinus!

Ascalaphus hyalinus Latr. Humboldt Recueil, II, 118, tab. xl, fig. 7.—*Ascalaphus macleayanus* Guild. Trans. Linn. Soc. Lond. XIV, 140, tab. vii, fig. 11; Walk. Catal. 436, 51.—*Ascalaphus senex* Burm.! Handb. II, 1001, 7.—*Ascalaphus 4-maculatus* Say, Long's Exped. II, 305.

Fusco-ferruginous; front fuscous, above gray, vertex with fuscous villosity; antennæ fuscous, the base with fuscous hair, the apex luteous, incisures black, club oblong, black, beneath striated with luteous; eyes lurid posteriorly; thorax fuscous upon the dorsum, varied with ferruginous; pectus clothed with white hair; feet fusco-luteous, tibiæ with a narrow, black basal annulus, apex of the tarsal articles black; abdomen fusco-cinereous, the dorsum with oblique black streaks each side; wings equal, the apex subobtuse, base of the anterior ones subemarginated, the base of the posterior ones with fuscous villosity; hyaline, veins luteous, partly fuscous; pterostigma small, nigro-fuscous.

Alar expanse 55 millim. Length of the antennæ 25 millim.

Hab. Savannah; Pennsylvania (Say); Matamoras, Mexico; Cuba; Island of St. Vincent; Pecos River, Western Texas (Capt. Pope).

2. A. avunculus!

Ascalaphus avunculus Hagen!

Very closely allied to the preceding; it differs in having the vertex clothed with gray villosity; the eyes above, posteriorly yellow, with a transverse brownish-black band, beneath brownish-black; club of the antennæ yellow beneath; in the males, the antennæ much longer; feet fuscous, tibiæ and tarsi black; the head less thick.

Alar expanse 50 millim. Length of the antennæ 23; ♂ 33 millim.

Hab. Cuba (Poey).

3. A. quadripunctatus!

Ascalaphus quadripunctatus Burm.! Handb. II, 1001, 9.—*Ascalaphus trimaculatus* Lefeb.!

Fuscous; front fuscous, gray above, vertex with fuscous villosity; antennæ luteo-fuscous, the incisures black; base with fuscous pile, club oblong, black; thorax with the dorsum fuscous, beneath with white pile; feet brown-black, the tibiæ exteriorly spotted with luteous; abdomen brownish-cinereous, the base with white villosity, each side with an oblique black streak; wings hyaline, veins black, the costa luteous; pterostigma yellow; the hind wings with three apical, fuscous clouds.

Alar expanse 60 millim. Length of the antennæ 27 millim.

Hab. New York; Baltimore.

4. A. limbatus!

Ascalaphus limbatus Burm.! Handb. II, 1001, 8; Walk. Catal. 436, 53.

Allied to *A. avunculus*, but differs by having shorter antennæ, the club smaller; the apex of the posterior wings, and the posterior margin of the wings clouded with fuscous.

Alar expanse 50 millim. Length of the antennæ 22 millim.

Hab. North America? Jamaica (Gosse).

Ascalaphus surinamensis Walk. Catal. 439, 57, is this species; but the description and synonymy does not belong to it.

5. A. subiratus.

Ascalaphus subiratus Walk. Catal. 439, 58.

Black, with black hair; antennæ fulvous, the incisures black, the club black, testaceous beneath; thorax striped with testaceous; feet piceous; abdomen short; wings hyaline, apex of the anterior ones subfuscescent, base of the posterior ones blackish-fuscous, with four oblique abbreviated fuscous bands posteriorly. (From the description of Walker.)

Alar expanse 58 millim.

Hab. Honduras, Guatemala.

* * Eyes entire.

6. A. albistigma!

Ascalaphus albistigma Walk.! Catal. 452, 80.

Ferruginous, with fuscous hairs; face luteous; antennæ luteous, the club fuscous, yellow beneath; thorax fulvous, anteriorly fuscous; the sides fuscous, spotted with yellow, an obscure cinereous stripe above; feet yellow, tarsi black; abdomen long, fuscous; wings hyaline, the apex fuscescent, pterostigma large, white; anterior wings with the whole costal margin, and the apex of the posterior wings fuscous.

Alar expanse 81 millim. Length of the antennæ 18 millim.

Hab. Honduras; Columbia (Appun).

7. A. microcerus.

Byas microcerus Ramb. Neuropt. 362.

Hab. West Indies.

May it not be *A. costatus* Burm. Handb. II, 1000, 1.? (Compare South American Neuroptera.)

FAM. IX. PANORPINA.

Body cylindrical or conical; head exserted; antennæ shorter than the wings; mouth rostrated; lateral palpi bi-articulated; prothorax small; wings either almost absent or narrow, equal, longer than the body, narrowed at base; the posterior wings with no anal space; tarsi of five articles.

BOREUS Latr.

Ocelli absent; wings of the males imperfect, of the females hardly present.

1. B. nivoriundus!

Boreus nivoriundus Fitch! Winter Ins. Amer. Journ. Agricult. 1847, V, 277, 1; Trans. Ent. Soc. ser. 2, I, 96, 1; Walk.! Catal. 456, 2.

Fusco-aeneous; mouth, wings, feet, and genital organs fulvous; apex of the tarsi fuscous.

Length 4 millim.

Hab. New York, April (Asa Fitch).

2. B. brumalis!

Boreus brumalis Fitch! Winter Ins. Amer. Journ. Agricult. 1847, V, 278, 2; Trans. Ent. Soc. ser. 2, I, 96, 2; Walk.! Catal. 456, 3.

Entirely brassy-black.

Length 3 millim.

Hab. New York, April (Asa Fitch); Washington (Osten Sacken).

PÁNORPA Linné.

Three ocelli; wings narrow; genital organs of the male elongated, forcipated, the last segment inflated; two tarsal unguiculi serrated; antennæ setaceous.

1. P. lugubris!

Panorpa lugubris Swederus, Act. Holm. Nov. VIII, 279, 31.   Linné, Syst. Nat. ed. XIII. vol. V, 2647, 10.   Klug! Act. Berol. 1836, 106, 6. Westw.! Trans. Ent. Soc. Lond. IV, 188, 11.   Walk.! Catal. 462, 11.—*Panorpa scorpio* Fab. Entom. Syst. II, 97, 3.   Oliv. Enc.' Méthod. VIII, 715, 5.   Leach. Zool. Misc. II, 99, tab. xciv, fig. 3—4.   Burm.! Handb. II, 927, 1.   Ramb.! Neuropt. 331, 8.—*Bittacus scorpio* Latr. Gen. Crust. et Ins. III, 189.

Black, abdomen ferruginous; the apex black; wings black, with three transverse, abbreviated, middle white streaks.

Alar expanse 27 millim.

Hab. South Carolina; Georgia; Florida (Glover).

2. P. rufescens!

Panorpa rufescens Ramb. Neuropt. 330, 6.—*Panorpa germanica* var. Walk. Catal. 459, 2?

Head, rostrum and thorax yellowish-rufous; antennæ black, the extreme base rufous; feet rufo-flavous, apex of the tarsi fuscous, unguiculi tridentate; abdomen fuscous, the venter rufo-flavous; abdominal segment 5 of the male cylindrical, truncated at the apex, above obliquely emarginated, with a long process, which is compressed, somewhat elevated; segments 6 and 7 equal, conical, apex of segment 6 more inflated; segment 8 oval, appendages long, linear; forceps short, trigonal, the apex unguiculated, slender; wings somewhat yellowish, the apex, a pterostigmatical, narrow, maculose band, which is subinterrupted in the middle, and some basal spots, brownish-black.

Alar expanse 24 millim.

Hab. Sharon Springs; Trenton Falls, New York; Washington (Osten Sacken); Maryland (Uhler); La Chine near Montreal? (Barnston).

3. P. rufa!

Panorpa rufa Gray! Griffith, Anim. Kingdom, Ins. tab. cv, fig. 2. Westwood! Trans. Ent. Soc. Lond. IV, 188, 10. Walk.! Catal. 461, 10.— *Panorpa fasciata* Klug! Act. Berol. 1836, 105, 2 (partly).

Head rufous, black around the ocelli; rostrum and thorax fusco-rufous; antennæ brownish-black, the extreme base fusco-rufous; feet rufous, apex of the tarsi fuscous; unguiculi 5-toothed, the teeth short; abdomen rufous; segment 5 of the male conical, with the apex truncated; segments 6 and 7 equal, the base narrow, cylindrical, subincurved, the apex conical, segment 6 more inflated; segment 8 narrow, elongate-oval, appendages linear, short; forceps trigonal, short, the apex slender, unguiculated; wings yellow, their apex subacute; apex, a subpterostigmatical band, which is forked behind, a medial costal spot, a basal oblique band, and two basal spots fuscous.

Alar expanse 27 millim.
Hab. Georgia.

4. P. americana!

Panorpa americana Swederus, Act. Holm. Nov. VIII, 279, 32. Linné, Syst. Nat. ed. xiii, vol. V, 2647, 9. Westwood, Trans. Ent. Soc. Lond. IV, 189, 15. Walk. Catal. 463, 15.—*Panorpa fasciata* Fab. Ent. Syst. II, 98, 4. Klug! Act. Berol. 1836, 105, 2 (in part). Ramb. Neuropt. 331, 7?

Testaceous; head rufous, black around the ocelli; rostrum rufous; antennæ black, with the extreme base rufous; feet testaceous, apex of the tarsi fuscous, unguiculi 4-toothed (♀); abdomen of the male upon the fifth segment with an erect, short horn (from the description of Westw.); wings yellow, broader at the apex; the apex, a pterostigmatical broad, straight band, a point upon the costa of the anterior wings, a basal oblique band, and a basal point upon the anterior wings, brownish-black.

Alar expanse 25 millim.
Hab. Georgia; Kentucky.

5. P. venosa!

Panorpa venosa Westw.! Trans. Ent. Soc. Lond. IV, 190, 16; Walk.! Catal. 463, 16. *Panorpa fasciata* Klug! Act. Berol. 1836, 105, 2 (in part). *Panorpa americana* Say! Collection of Hagen.

Head rufous, black around the ocelli; antennæ black, the extreme base rufous; feet luteo-rufous, the apex of the tarsi fuscous;

unguiculi 4-toothed, teeth long, distant; abdomen fuscous, with the apex rufous; segment 5 of the abdomen of the male cylindrical, the apex truncated, subemarginated above, with a long, very much elevated, triangular process; segments 6 and 7 equal, obconical, apex of the sixth segment more inflated; segment 8 orbicular, with long, linear appendages; forceps short, unguiculate; wings subhyaline, the apex, a pterostigmatical band, which is interruptedly forked behind, a costal, medial spot, which is sometimes almost absent from the hind wings, a basal band, which is sometimes interrupted, and a basal spot, blackish-brown. (Male and female.)

Alar expanse 23—27 millim.

Hab. Philadelphia (Say); Georgia (Abbot); Southern Illinois (Kennicott).

6. P. debilis!

Panorpa debilis Westw.! Trans. Ent. Soc. Lond. IV, 191, 18. Walk.! Catal. 464, 18.

Luteo-fuscous; head rufous, black around the ocelli; antennæ black, the extreme base rufous; feet luteous, apex of the tarsi hardly obscurer; unguiculi 4-toothed, teeth long, distant; abdomen fuscous, the apex luteous; segment 5 of the male cylindrical, the apex truncated, emarginated above, with a short, very erect, obtuse, triangular, rather short process; segment 6 long, obconical, the base narrow, arcuated; segment 7 shorter, obconical, the base a little narrower; segment 8 elliptical, the apex broad, appendages linear, long; forceps short, unguiculated; wings hyaline, subflavescent at base, an apical, fenestrated band, an arcuated, pterostigmatical one, subinterrupted in the middle, a middle point, a basal interrupted band, and a basal point, fuscous; transverse veins sometimes a little marked with fuscous. (Male.)

Alar expanse 22—23 millim.

Hab. Philadelphia; Trenton Falls, New York; Savannah, Georgia.

7. P. nebulosa!

Panorpa nebulosa Westw.! Trans. Ent. Soc. Lond. IV, 188, 12. Walk.! Catal. 462, 12.

Luteo-fulvous; head luteo-rufous, around the ocelli black; antennæ black, the base luteous; feet luteous; unguiculi tridentate;

abdomen fuscous, the apex luteous; segment 5 of the male abdomen conical, truncated at the apex; segments 6 and 7 equal, obconical; segment 8 oval, appendages long, linear; forceps short, unguiculated; wings hyaline, pterostigma subflavous, with a large, fuscous spot interiorly; a fuscous point on some of the areoles, which are sometimes larger on the basal areoles.

Alar expanse 22—26 millim.

Hab. Trenton Falls; Washington (Osten Sacken); Massachusetts (Scudder).

8. P. punctata.

Panorpa punctata Klug! Act. Bérol. 1836, 105, 3, fig. 9. Westw. Trans. Ent. Soc. Lond. IV, 188, 12. Walker, Catal. 462, 13.

Testaceous; antennæ black; thorax with spots, and the abdomen at base fuscous; wings subflavescent, narrow, the areoles all pointed with fuscous. (From the description of Klug.)

Alar expanse 23 millim.

Hab. Mexico (Koppe). It is similar to the preceding species.

9. P. confusa.

Panorpa confusa Westw.! Trans. Ent. Soc. Lond. IV, 190, 17. Walk. Catal. 463, 17.

Fulvous; head black around the ocelli; antennæ black; segment 5 of the abdomen of the male armed with a long, acute spine, above; segment 6 not emarginated at the base; wings tinged with luteous, the costa and base deeper luteous; veins blackish; a small basal point, a slender, interrupted, middle band, a slender, irregular, pterostigmatical one, upon the middle geniculated, band, and the apex slenderly, nigricant; the transverse veins, especially towards the apex of the wings, tinged with black; hind wings less variegated; apex of the tarsal articulations black. (From the description of Westw.)

Alar expanse 24 millim.

Hab. Massachusetts (Harris).

10. P. subfurcata.

Panorpa subfurcata Westw.! Trans. Ent. Soc. Lond. IV, 191, 19. Walk. Catal. 464, 19.

Obscure fulvous; head rufescent, black around the ocelli; antennæ black, the two basal articles rufescent; dorsum of the thorax obscure luteous; feet luteous, apex of the tarsal articles obscure; abdomen luteo-fulvous, the dorsal base obscure; segment 5 with a short dorsal horn; segment 6 not emarginated at the base superiorly; wings pale, with two basal spots, a transverse band before the middle, a transverse, costal medial spot, an oblique pterostigmatical, irregular band, hardly angulated in the middle, but dilated at the costa; the apex, somewhat broadly, upon which are some white points, and a spot at the anal angle, black; basal spots of the posterior wings obsolete. (From the description of Westwood.)

Alar expanse 24—28 millim.

Hab. Nova Scotia; St. Martin's Falls, Albany River, Hudson's Bay (Barnston, Redman).

11. P. maculosa!

Panorpa maculosa Hagen!

Testaceous; head fulvous, rufo-fuscous around the ocelli; antennæ black, the two basal articles fulvous; dorsum of the thorax fulvous, spotted with black; feet luteous, the apex fuscous; unguiculi 4-toothed, teeth long; abdomen testaceous, the apex luteous; segment 5 conical, the apex truncated; segments 6 and 7 equal, conical, the sixth stouter, the base above sub-emarginated; segment 8 elongated, oval, appendages linear, long; forceps short, unguiculated; wings hyaline, veins fuscous, apical transverse veins partly marked with fuscous; two basal spots, a spot upon the middle, and some apical spots, fuscous, pterostigma luteous, each side with a fuscous spot.

Alar expanse 24 millim.

Hab. Pennsylvania (Uhler).

12. P. terminata!

Panorpa terminata Klug! Act. Berol. 1836, 106, 4, fig. 10. Westwood Trans. Ent. Soc. Lond. IV, 189, 14. Walk. Catal. 463, 14.

Fusco-testaceous; middle of the head brownish-black, rostrum rufous; prothorax entirely, and the sides of the mesothorax blackish-brown; antennæ black, the two basal articles rufous; feet luteous, unguiculi tridentate; wings hyaline, the apex fuscous. (Female.)

Alar expanse 23 millim.

Hab. Mexico (Deppe).

BITTACUS Latreille.

Ocelli three; wings narrow; antennæ setaceous, very slender; abdomen rather long, cylindrical, feet longer than the wings, the apex of the tibiæ calcarated; tarsi with a single, long, simple nail.

1. B. mexicanus.

Bittacus mexicanus Klug! Act. Berol. 1836, 99, 6. Walk. Catal. 466, 6.

Testaceous; head with a middle spot, and apices of the femora and tibiæ with a vestige, fuscous; antennæ almost unclothed; wings subflavescent, veins and transverse marks obscurer; appendages of the male long, narrow, incurved. (From the description of Klug.)

Alar expanse 46 millim.

Hab. Mexico (Deppe).

2. B. pilicornis!

Bittacus pilicornis Westw. Trans. Ent. Soc. Lond. IV, 196, 4. Walk. Catal. 468, 15.

Pale fusco-luteous, shining; head fuscous between the ocelli; antennæ luteo-fuscous, with long and dense pile; wings sublutescent, transverse veins obsoletely banded with fuscous; superior appendages of the male broad, triangular, flat.

Alar expanse 40 millim.

Hab. Trenton Falls (Osten Sacken); La Chine near Montreal (Barnston).

3. B. strigosus!

Bittacus strigosus Hagen!

Pale testaceous, shining; head black around the ocelli; palpi black; antennæ pale, sparingly and shortly pilose; apex of the femora and tibiæ blackish-fuscous; wings hyaline, with some basal, fuscous points, transverse veins broadly banded with fuscous; pterostigma a little clouded; superior appendages of the male broad, oblong, the superior margin broadly excised, pilose.

Alar expanse 40 millim.

Hab. Chicago; Washington; St. Louis (Osten Sacken).

4. B. punctiger.

Bittacus punctiger Westw.! Trans. Ent. Soc. Lond. IV, 195, 2. Walk. Catal. 468, 13.

Testaceo-fulvous; femora sparingly clothed with black, bristly hair, tibiæ with a slender, apical black ring; wings yellowish-hyaline, with numerous, rather obscure points, especially at the base of the longitudinal veins, and at the transverse veins; veins pale. (From the description of Westwood.)

Alar expanse 42 millim.

Hab. Georgia.

5. B. stigmaterus!

Bittacus stigmaterus Say, Godman's West. Quart. Report, II, 164.—*Bittacus pallidipennis* Westw.! Trans. Ent. Soc. Lond. IV, 195, 3. Walk. Catal. 468, 14.

Fulvo-luteous; ocelli somewhat surrounded with fuscous; palpi black; anterior femora and apex of the tibiæ sub-fuscous; wings luteo-fusco-hyaline, the pterostigma a little obscurer; veins luteous; superior appendages of the male oblong, long, the apical margin subemarginated above.

Alar expanse 37—46 millim.

Hab. Missouri, near Fort Osage (Say); Maryland (Uhler); Dalton, Georgia (Osten Sacken).

The female from Maryland is smaller, and agrees better with the descriptions and size of *B. stigmaterus*, and *pallidipennis*. The male from Georgia is larger (46 millim.), the wings are also broader, but it is hardly different.

6. B. occidentis.

Bittacus occidentis Walk.! Catal. 469, 16.

Testaceous; apex of the rostrum, the palpi, and the antennæ black; dorsal middle of the thorax fuscous; posterior femora fulvous, with the apex black, the anterior femora black, with the base fulvous; anterior tibiæ piceous; wings subiurid, pterostigma fuscous; veins black. (From the description of Walker.)

Alar expanse 46 millim.

Hab. Erie, Pennsylvania.

It is very much like the preceding species. Is it distinct from it?

7. B. apicalis!

Bittacus apicalis Uhler! MSS.

Luteous, shining; ocelli somewhat obscured with black; apex of the tarsal articles brownish-black; wings hyaline, the apex nigro-fuscous; abdomen fuscous; the superior appendages of the male short, oblong, the apex broader, obliquely truncated.

Alar expanse 36 millim.

Hab. Southern Illinois (Kennicott).

(The pterostigma of the female is dusky, and there is a dusky mark each side upon the upper part of the face; the antennæ are honey-yellow, obscurer towards the apex, and covered with blackish pile. Uhler.)

MEROPE Newman.

Ocelli absent; eyes large, reniform, connate at the vertex; antennæ short, thick, the apex narrowed; wings broad, transverse veins very numerous; subcosta and radius joined together at the apex; feet shorter than the wings, slender, apex of the tarsi with two unguiculi, which are entire, and a plantula between them; abdomen of the male with a very large forceps.

1. M. tuber!

Merope tuber Newm.! Entom. Mag. V, 180. Westw.! Trans. Ent. Soc. Lond. IV, 194, tab. xiv. fig. 2. Walk.! Catal. 196, 1.

Luteous; apex of the rostrum fuscous; antennæ luteous, fuscous in the middle; prothorax luteo-fuscous; feet luteous, the anterior ones a little thicker, luteo-fuscous; apex of the tibiæ with two spurs; wings cinereous, veins luteous, radius and longitudinal ones posteriorly, black; anterior wings on the posterior margin at the base, with a small, rounded, fuscous lamina; abdomen luteous; appendages of the male very long, flat, almost as long as the body, luteous; the basal article almost straight, the base a little curved; the apical article shorter, cylindrical, the apex dilated, emarginated, subbifid.

Alar expanse 30 millim.

Hab. Berkeley Springs, Virginia (Osten Sacken); Pennsylvania.

An extremely rare insect; it is not to be met with in any of the European collections, excepting the type (a female) in the British

Museum, and a male and female in my own collection; it is not extant in the American collections (teste Osten Sacken), excepting a unique female in that of Dr. Asa Fitch. The genus and species is very singular and abnormal; perhaps the most remarkable of all hitherto known Neuroptera. It certainly belongs to the *Panorpina*.

Fam. X. PHRYGANINA.

Body compressed; head exserted; antennæ long, setiform; mouth connate, imperfect; labial palpi triarticulate; prothorax small; wings longer than the body, transverse veins rather few; posterior wings with the anal space large, plicated (rarely absent); tarsi with 5 articulations. *Larva* aquatic; living in a tube-like case.

I. Maxillary palpi differing in the sexes.

Sub-Family PHRYGANIDES.

Spurs arranged 2, 4, 4; maxillary palpi in the males 4-jointed, in the females 5-jointed; three ocelli.

NEURONIA Leach.

Antennæ shorter than the wings; wings rather broad, the apex ovate, naked or almost naked.

1. N. irrorata!

Phryganea irrorata Fab.! Sp. Ins. I, 389, 9; Mantis. Ins. I, 245, 10; Entom. Syst. II, 77, 11.—*Neuronia concatenata* Walk.! Catal. 8, 4.

Rufous, shining; antennæ blackish-piceous, the basal article rufous within; head and thorax clothed with white hair; feet luteous, with black spines; abdomen testaceous; anterior wings whitish-hyaline, densely, transversely irrorated with fuscous; posterior wings hyaline, the apex spotted with fuscous, the anterior margin with a medial, larger, fuscous spot. (Female.)

Length to tip of wings 18 millim. Alar expanse 32 millim.

Hab. St. John's Bluff, East Florida; N. Red River (Kennicott).

The insect does not altogether agree with the description of Fabricius; the type in the collection of Banks is to be examined again.

2. N. pardalis.

Neuronia pardalis Walk.! Catal. 7, 3.

Black, clothed with luteous hair, beneath luteous; anterior femora ferruginous; anterior wings confertly pointed with luteous (which are confluent in the males); posterior wings anteriorly pointed with luteous, and with a broad luteous, subapical band. (From the description of Walker.)

Length to tip of wings 27 millim. Alar expanse 50 millim.
Hab. Nova Scotia (Redman).

3. N. ocelligera.

Neuronia ocelligera Walk.! Catal. 8, 6.

Black, with pale hair; tibiæ piceous; wings testaceous, the anterior ones reticulated and guttated with black, posterior wings having the margin spotted with black. Male. (From the description of Walker.)

Length to tip of wings 16 millim. Alar expanse 28 millim.
Hab. Nova Scotia (Redman).

It is very much like *N. reticulata* of Europe; is it different?

4. N. signata.

Phryganea signata Fab. Sp. Ins. I, 389, 7; Mant. Ins. I, 245, 8; Entom. Syst. II, 76, 8.

Small; head fuscous; wings grayish-fuscous, shining, spotted with yellow, the posterior margin striated with yellow. (From the description of Fabricius.)

Length to tip of wings ——?
Hab. North America (collection of Banks); does it belong to this genus?

5. N. semifasciata!

Phryganea semifasciata Say, Western Quart. Report. II, 161, 4; American Entomology, II, pl. 44 (upper figures). — *Neuronia fusca* Walk.! Catal. 9, 7.

Fulvous; antennæ annulated with fuscous, the apex fulvous; head fuscous; dorsum of the mesothorax each side, black; head and thorax partly ciliated with black; feet with brown spines; wings fulvous, the veins obscurer, the anterior ones transversely flecked with brownish-black, a small basal spot, and an abrupt, medial streak at the posterior margin, brownish-black, the disk with two yellowish points; posterior wings with the apical margin hardly irrorated with fuscous, having a short, fuscous subapical band.

Male. Having the dorsal lamina elongated, the sides involuted, the apex with two long spines; superior appendages longer than the lamina; ventral lamina 4-toothed.

Female. Ventral lamina shining, the base brownish-black, very much narrower at the apex, recurved, bifid.

Length to tip of wings 23—28 millim. Alar expanse 44—52 millim.

Hab. St. Martin's Falls, Albany River, Hudson's Bay (Barnston); Nova Scotia (Redman); St. John, Newfoundland; Ohio; Pennsylvania; New Jersey; Massachusetts; Kentucky (Say); Washington (Osten Sacken); New York (Collection of Hagen). Everywhere north of the Southern States (Uhler).

A variety has the band absent from the posterior wings (Nova Scotia).

6. **N. postica!**

Neuronia postica Walk.! Catal. 9, 9.

Fulvous; antennæ annulated with fuscous, the apex fulvous; head and thorax fuscous, with fuscous hair; feet with fulvous spines; wings fulvous, veins of the same color; the anterior ones transversely irrorated with fuscous, a small basal spot and an abrupt streak upon the middle of the posterior margin, fuscous; disk with two whitish points; hind wings with an angulated, subapical, fuscous band.

Male. Having the dorsal lamina elongated, the apex narrower, incised; superior appendages with a longer lamina; the ventral lamina bidentate.

Female. Ventral lamina shining, middle of the base brownish-black, each side ciliated with fulvous, the apex narrow, recurved, entire; each side with a rather long anal palpus.

Length to tip of wings 28 millim. Alar expanse 52 millim.

Hab. Georgia (Abbot); Pennsylvania (Collection of Hagen); Washington; Massachusetts (Osten Sacken); N. Red River (Kennicott).

A variety has the band absent from the posterior wings.

Do not some of the localities cited for *N. semifasciata* Say, belong to *N. postica*?

7. N. ocellifera!

Neuronia ocellifera Walk.! Catal. 8, 5.

Fulvous; antennæ shorter, fuscous; thorax ciliated with fuscous-gray; wings short, fulvous, veins same color; anterior wings a little transversely irrorated with fuscous, a medial spot upon the posterior margin fuscous; disk with two whitish points; posterior wings with an angulated band, which is subapical, fuscous; feet with gray spines.

Male. Dorsal lamina long, acute, ensiform, bifid; superior appendages shorter than the lamina; ventral lamina bidentate.

Female. Ventral lamina shining, middle of the base fuscous; the apex narrower, recurved, bi-impressed, ciliated.

Length to tip of wings 20 millim. Alar expanse 40—42 millim.

Hab. Northern Illinois; N. Red River (Kennicott); Ohio (Schaum).

8. N. notata.

Phryganea notata Fab. Sp. Ins. I, 390, 12; Mant. Ins. I, 246, 15; Entom. Syst. II, 78, 18.

Fuscous; antennæ and feet testaceous; anterior wings yellowish-gray, unicolored, with a marginal fuscous spot; posterior wings white, hyaline, shining. (From the description of Fabricius.)

Length to tip of wings —? millim.

Hab. North America (Collection of Banks).

Is this *N. semifasciata?* The type, if I am not mistaken, yet exists.

PHRYGANEA Linné.

Antennæ robust, as long as the wings; anterior wings pilose.

1. Ph. cinerea.

Phryganea cinerea Walk.! Catal. 4, 2.

Testaceous, striped above with cinereous; apex of the anterior tibiæ, and the tips of the articles of the anterior tarsi, black; anterior wings fuscous, densely guttated with cinereous, posterior wings fusco-cinereous. (From the description of Walker.)

Length to tip of wings 26—28 millim. Alar expanse 48—54 millim.

Hab. St. Martin's Falls, Albany River, Hudson's Bay (Barnston). It is very much like *P. striata* Linn. (*Beckwithii* Steph.), but differs obviously by the anal appendages of the male; a description of those parts is wanting to me.

2. Ph. vestita!
Neuronia vestita Walk.! Catal. 10, 10.

Ferruginous; antennæ fuscous, thorax bivittated above with fuscous, and clothed with fuscous hair; feet luteous, anterior femora, apex of the tibiæ and apex of the tarsal articles, fuscous; apex of the intermediate tibiæ fuscous; anterior wings narrow, rufo-fuscous closely irrorated with fuscous, the disk paler; posterior wings cinereous, the apex margined with fuscous. Female.

Length to tip of wings 21 millim. Alar expanse 38 millim.
Hab. Georgia (Abbot).

3. Ph. commixta.
Neuronia commixta Walk.! Catal. 10, 11.

Black, clothed with pale hair; beneath, antennæ and feet ferruginous; anterior wings fuscous, with a large discoidal sub-hyaline spot, and apical whitish points, veins fuscous, posterior wings sub-cinereous, the apex and posterior margin fuscous. (From the description of Walker.)

Length to tip of wings 14 millim. Alar expanse 26 millim.
Hab. Georgia (Abbot).
Allied to *Ph. minor*, Curtis, of Europe.

Sub-Fam. LIMNOPHILIDES.

Maxillary palpi of the males three, of the females five-jointed; ocelli three; anterior wings rather narrow, the apex obliquely truncated or rounded.

LIMNOPHILUS Leach.

Spurs arranged 1, 3, 4; apex of the anterior wings truncated.

Sub-Genus Colpotaulius Kolenati.

Posterior wings with the middle of the hind margin emarginated.

1. L. perpusillus!

Limnephilus perpusillus Walk.! Catal. 35, 54.

Testaceous, with testaceous hair; antennæ fulvous; anterior wings narrow, the apex a little acuminate, subtestaceous, posteriorly and the apex obscurely guttated; veins fulvous; posterior wings whitish. (From the description of Walker.)

Length to tip of wings 7 millim. Alar expanse 13 millim.

Hab. St. Martin's Falls, Albany River, Hudson's Bay (Barnston).

It is very closely allied to *Colpotaulius incisus* Stephens.

Sub-Genus Limnophilus LEACH.

Anterior wings narrow, the apex broader, obliquely truncated.

2. L. rhombicus!

L. rhombica Linn. Walk.! Catal. 22, 13. (With the synonymy.)—*Phryganea rhombica* Otho Fab. Fauna Groen. 196, 153. Berlin. Ent. Zeit. III, 143.

Ochreous, with luteous hair, antennæ luteous; thorax luteo-fuscous; feet luteous, tibiæ with yellow, tarsi with black spines; anterior wings ochreous, rufous posteriorly, with a large, discoidal, oblique, rhombical spot, and another, not well defined, about the anastomosis, subhyaline; posterior wings hyaline, the apex subflavescent.

Male. Posterior wings underneath with a subapical fuscous fringe; superior appendages oblong, the apex and beneath a little emarginated, with black teeth.

Length to tip of wings 23 millim. Alar expanse 44 millim.

Hab. St. Martin's Falls, Albany River, Hudson's Bay (Barnston); Greenland (Fab.); Europe; Asia.

The larva described by Otho Fab. l. c. p. 197, belongs to *Colymbetes dolabratus*.

3. L. interrogationis.

Phryganea interrogationis Zetterst. Ins. Lapp. 1063, 12.—*Grammotaulius interrogationis* Kol. Trichopt. 40, 3. Walk. Catal. 19, 6; Berlin. Ent. Zeit. III, 143.

Grayish, shining; antennæ testaceous; head and thorax hairy, each side black; feet testaceous, posterior femora with a lateral line, which is grayish; wings rather narrow, anterior ones brownish, with numerous, confluent fuscous points; a discoidal longitudinal line and a middle spot, hyaline; posterior wings subhyaline, the apex with a small, fuscous line. (From the description of Zetterstedt.)

Length to tip of wings 20 millim. Alar expanse 34—40 millim.

Hab. Greenland; Lapland; Europe.

It is not sufficiently known to me.

4. L. combinatus.

Limnephilus combinatus Walk.! Catal. 28, 34.

Ferruginous, clothed with pale hair; abdomen and feet testaceous; anterior wings fuscous, the anterior margin testaceous, a large rhombical, discoidal spot and some points, testaceous; the apex testaceous, sprinkled with fuscous; posterior wings hyaline. Male. (From the description of Walker.)

Length to tip of wings 18 millim. Alar expanse 34 millim.

Hab. St. John, Newfoundland.

It is allied to *L. rhombicus*.

5. L. divergens.

Limnephilus divergens Walk.! Catal. 30, 39.

Testaceous, clothed with pale hair; antennæ ferruginous; the anterior wings closely dotted with ferruginous tubercles, the apex sub-fuscous; a broader tubercle at the base of the third apical areole; posterior wings whitish. (From the description of Walker.)

Length to tip of wings 18 millim. Alar expanse 34 millim.

Hab. North America.

6. L. dossuarius.

Phryganea dossuaria Say, American Entom. III, pl. 44. Lowest figure.

Pale ochreous; antennæ fuscous; abdomen obscure, apex of the segments pale; anterior wings whitish-yellow, veins black; some transverse, sometimes dilated lines, a pterostigmatical, quadrangular spot, and an anal one, black; posterior wings with two costal spots, and the margin obscure. (From the description of Say.)

Length to tip of wings 11 millim. Alar expanse 22 millim.

Hab. Salem, Massachusetts (Say).

Not seen by me; is it a *Limnophilus?*

7. L. interruptus.

Phryganea interrupta Say, American Entom. III, pl. 44, right middle figure.

Clothed with grayish hair; palpi and antennæ black; tibiæ obscure, tarsi obscure, the joints pale at their bases; anterior wings gray, obscurer upon the disk, a longitudinal, medially interrupted line, extending from the humerus to near the apex, and an abbreviated line nearer the costal margin, towards the apex, black; the posterior area hoary with white pubescence, immaculate; posterior wings ochreous, the apex broadly black. (From the description of Say.)

Length to tip of wings 21 millim. Alar expanse 40 millim.
Hab. New Jersey (Say).
I have not seen it; does it belong to *Limnophilus?*

8. L. radiatus.

Phryganea radiata Say, Long's Exped. II, 308, 2.

Pale yellowish-fuscous; antennæ fuscous; vertex and prothorax pilose; mesothorax each side and two dorsal stripes hairy; anterior wings subhyaline, beyond the middle a large fuscous circle from which a dilated line proceeds to the tip, another to the inferior angle, a third to the carpal spot, and a fourth towards the base, interrupted in its middle, the interior margin, particularly at the base, fuscous; surface of the wings with scattered hairs, those of the nervures more distinct and blackish. (From the description of Say.)

Length to tip of wings 19 millim. Alar expanse 36 millim.
I have not seen it; does it belong to *Limnophilus?*

9. L. sericeus.

Phryganea sericea Say, Long's Exped. II, p. 309, 3.

Blackish, sericeous; antennæ fuscous, annulated with yellow; head with a cinereous gloss, sparingly pilose; thorax with a cinereous gloss; posterior feet pale ochreous, sericeous, with black setæ; anterior wings varied with fuscous and pruinose, a transverse, quadrate, black spot on the middle of the posterior margin; membrane densely pilose; veins with black hairs; posterior wings immaculate. (From the description of Say.)

Length to tip of wings 12 millim. Alar expanse 23 millim.
Hab. Northwest Territory (Say).
I have not seen it; does it belong to *Limnophilus?*

10. L. externus!

Limnophilus externus Hagen!

Luteous; head and thorax obscure above, with luteous hair; antennæ (base) luteous; feet ochreous, with black spines; apex of the abdomen obscurer; anterior wings shining, narrow, hardly luteo-pilose, luteous, densely guttated with fuscous, the marks often confluent; a rhombical spot upon the middle, which is oblique, narrow, hyaline; the anterior margin immaculate; at the anastomosis are a few spots; veins luteous, the fourth apical areole narrow at base, shorter than the rest; posterior wings luteo-hyaline.

Female. The four anal appendages almost equal, short, acute; the valvule short, incised.

Length to tip of wings 20 millim. Alar expanse 38 millim.

Hab. N. Red River (Kennicott).

11. L. gravidus!

Limnophilus gravidus Hagen!

Rufo-fuscous; antennæ (at base) with luteous hair; head and disk of the thorax rufous, with luteous hair, each side with black hair; abdomen luteous beneath; feet luteous, with black spines, base of the four anterior tibiæ, as well as their middle and apex, and the apex of the posterior tibiæ, black, apex of the tarsal articles black; wings long, broad at the apex, a little rounded, sparingly clothed with white hair; surface grayish-hyaline, closely pointed with fuscous, points often confluent; an oblique, discoidal streak, and a semicircle at the apex of the anastomosis, pale hyaline; veins pale, sparingly interrupted with fuscous; posterior wings luteo-hyaline, their apex obsoletely spotted with fuscous, and an obscurer spot at the pterostigma. Female.

Hab. North California.

12. L. vastus!

Limnophilus vastus Hagen!

Nigro-fuscous; base of antennæ fuscous; head and thorax with black hair; mesothorax black, a grayish spot upon the middle, and each side behind marked with a black point; feet luteous, with black spines; four anterior tibiæ at base, middle and apex, apex of the posterior tibiæ, and apices of the tarsal articles, black; wings long, broader at the apex, elliptical, grayish-hyaline, almost nude, all over closely covered with fuscous dots, the anterior margin with fewer dots; veins fuscous, sparingly interrupted with pale; posterior wings grayish-hyaline, obscurer at the apex. Female.

Length to tip of wings 21 millim. Alar expanse 40 millim.

Hab. Isle Kenai, Russian America.

13. L. perjurus!

Limnophilus perjurus Hagen!

Luteo-fuscous, with luteous hair; feet luteous, with black spines; wings narrow, the apex obliquely truncated, luteo-ochreous, almost shining, with luteous veins; apical veins a little clouded; posterior wings luteo-hyaline. Female.

Length to tip of wings 16 millim. Alar expanse 30 millim.

Hab. Isle Kenai, Russian America.

Allied to *Chaetotaulius striatus* Kolenati.

14. L. hyalinus!

Limnophilus hyalinus Hagen!

Pale ochreous, with yellow hair; antennæ ochreous; feet pale, with black spines; anterior wings pale ochreo-hyaline, somewhat glossy, veins ochreous; the fourth apical cellule acute at base; posterior wings pale yellowish-hyaline.

Male. Superior appendages ovate, prominent; the inferior ones obtuso-acute.

Length to tip of wings 12 millim. Alar expanse 22 millim.

Hab. N. Red River (Kennicott).

Sub-Genus Goniotaulius Kol.

15. L. indicans.

Limnephilus indicans Walk.! Catal. 23, 18.

Ferruginous; antennæ paler; palpi and feet testaceous; anterior wings testaceous, margined with whitish, with a short discoidal vitta, contracted in the middle, white, drawn out into five rays towards the apex; posterior wings whitish. (From the description of Walker.)

Length to tip of wings 18 millim. Alar expanse 38 millim.

Hab. Georgia (Abbot).

It is allied to *L. elegans* Curtis.

16. L. despectus.

Limnephilus despectus Walk.! Catal. 31, 42.

Grayish-ferruginous, with pale pile, and longer hair, which is black;. antennæ subfuscous, the bases of the articles testaceous; maxillary palpi fuscous, labial palpi testaceous; abdomen and feet testaceous; mesothorax above with a double whitish streak; anterior wings fuscous, freckled with whitish; thyridium and first subapical areole with a whitish spot; costa and disk towards the apex still more whitish; posterior wings whitish. (From the description of Walker.)

Length to tip of wings 11 millim. Alar expanse 21 millim.

Hab. Nova Scotia (Redman).

Allied to *L. griseus* Linn.

17. L. nebulosus.

Limnephilus nebulosus Kirby. Faun. Bor. Amer. 253, 349; Walk. Catal. 50, 126.

Black, with white hair; antennæ (at base) black; mesothorax testaceous; superior wings testaceous, spotted and irrorated with whitish, the costal area immaculate; posterior wings whitish, with testaceous veins; feet testaceous. (From the description of Kirby.)

Length of body 15 millim.

Hab. North America, latitude 65°.

18. L. multifarius.

Limnephilus multifarius Walk.! Catal. 32, 43.—*Phryganea variegata* Barnston, Mss.—*Limnephilus perforatus* Walk. Catal. 33, 46. (In part.)

Black, with pale hair, and longer pile, which is black; antennæ fuscous, annulated with testaceous; feet testaceous; anterior wings fuscous, freckled with whitish; thyridium and base of the apical areoles spotted with white; posterior wings cinereous. (From the description of Walker.)

Length to tip of wings 11 millim. Alar expanse 21 millim.

Hab. St. Martin's Falls, Albany River, Hudson's Bay (Barnston); *L. perforatus* Walk. (from St. Martin's Falls), certainly is the same species; a very much mutilated specimen from Arctic America (Mackenzie and Slave Rivers, Richardson) is different, but indeterminable; possibly the true *L. nebulosus* of Kirby. *L. despectus* and *L. multifarius* are very closely allied; are they distinct?

19. L. femoralis.

Limnephilus femoralis Kirby, Faun. Bor. Amer. 253, 350; Walk. Catal. 50, 127.

Black; feet testaceous, femora black; anterior wings dilute testaceous, spotted and freckled with white; posterior wings white, with the veins testaceous. (From the description of Kirby.)

Length of body 14 millim.

Hab. North America, latitude 65° (Richardson).

I have never seen it; very closely allied to *L. nebulosus* Kirby.

20. L. submonilifer.

Limnephilus submonilifer Walk.! Catal. 33, 48.

Black, with pale hair, and longer, black pile; bases of the antennal articles testaceous; abdomen ferruginous beneath; feet testaceous; anterior wings fuscous, a discoidal, whitish spot, and spots, which are almost obsolete, hyaline; a line anteriorly, and two posteriorly, black and dotted with whitish; posterior wings subcinereous. Female. (From the description of Walker.)

Length to tip of wings 13 millim. Alar expanse 25 millim.

Hab. North America.

It is very closely allied to *L. obscurus* Ramb. Is it different?

21. L. extractus.

Limnophilus extractus Walk.! Catal. 34, 49.

Obscure testaceous, with pale hair; apex of the antennæ fuscous; palpi and feet pale testaceous; mesothorax bivittated with fuscous; abdomen fuscous above; wings dirty whitish, anterior ones with the posterior margin testaceous; veins pale testaceous. Young male. (From the description of Walker.)

Length to tip of wings 12 millim. Alar expanse 23 millim.

Hab. St. Martin's Falls, Albany River, Hudson's Bay (Barnston).

May this not be *L. hyalinus?*

22. L. indivisus.

Limnephilus indivisus Walk.! Catal. 34, 51.

Pale testaceous; antennæ a little obscure; anterior wings subtestaceous, sub-tuberculated, veins testaceous, pterostigma subfuscous; posterior wings hyaline. (From the description of Walker.)

Length to tip of wings 15 millim. Alar expanse 28 millim.
Hab. Nova Scotia (Redman).
It is allied to *L. impurus*, Rambur.

23. L. subguttatus.
Limnephilus subguttatus Walk.! Catal. 34, 52.

Testaceous, with pale hair; base of the anterior wings, margin behind, and the apex subguttated with whitish, a fuscous spot at the pterostigma which is broadly surrounded with hyaline; posterior wings subbyaline. (From the description of Walker.)
Length to tip of wings 12 millim. Alar expanse 23 millim.
Hab. St. Martin's Falls, Albany River, Hudson's Bay (Barnston).
It is allied to *L. rufus* Rambur.

24. L. subpunctulatus!
Phryganea subpunctulata Zetterst. Ins. Lapp. 1065, 20.—*Limnephilus stipatus* Walk.! Catal. 29, 37.

Black, tinged with gray; covered with luteous hair; antennæ fuscous, annulated with luteous; thorax black-gray, above with a double, luteous, hairy stripe; abdomen annulated beneath with luteous; feet yellowish, with black spines; wings whitish-hyaline, somewhat clothed with snow-white hair, partly veined with fuscous, marked with large, confluent, fuscous guttæ, the anterior margin, disk, and thyridium, almost immaculate; posterior wings whitish-hyaline.
Female. Four anal appendages short, acute, yellowish, valvule broader, emarginated.
Length to tip of wings 13 millim. Alar expanse 25 millim.
Hab. St. Martin's Falls, Albany River, Hudson's Bay (Barnston); Arctic America, Mackenzie and Slave Rivers (Richardson); Europe, Umea, Lapland.

25. L. trimaculatus!
Phryganea trimaculata Zetterst.! Ins. Lapp. 1065, 18; Kolen. Trichopt. 53, 7; Walk. Catal. 26, 27.—*Limnophilus partitus* Walk.! Catal. 32, 45.

Black, with black and white hair; antennæ fuscous, annulated with brown, the basal article black; feet testaceous, with black spines, femora black; anterior wings fuscous, veined with fuscous, a rhombical, medial spot, and some larger spots about the anastomosis, whitish-hyaline, somewhat clothed with snow-white hair; posterior wings cinereo-hyaline.

Var. Wings pale. (Young.)

Length to tip of wings 10 millim. Alar expanse 19 millim.

Hab. St. Martin's Falls, Albany River, Hudson's Bay (Barnston); Europe, Lapland (Zetterstedt); Iceland (Staudinger).

26. L. pudicus!

Limnophilus pudicus Hagen!

Fusco-cinereous, with fuscous hair; antennæ fuscous, subannulated with pale, the basal article blackish-fuscous; abdomen testaceous beneath; feet testaceous, with black spines, anterior ones a little obscure; anterior tibiæ spotted with black, apices of the tarsal articles blackish; wings brownish-hyaline, partly with fuscous veins, the posterior margin and apex obsoletely guttated with fuscous; pterostigma fuscous, with a discoidal subhyaline spot; posterior wings grayish-hyaline.

Length to tip of wings 14 millim. Alar expanse 25 millim.

Hab. New York; Washington (Osten Sacken).

Allied to *L. costalis*, Stephens.

27. L. griseus!

Phryganea grisea Linn.—*Limnephilus griseus* Walk.! Catal. 27, 28. (With the synonyms); Berlin. Ent. Zeit. III, p. 143.

Rufo-cinereous; antennæ fuscous, annulated with pale; thorax paler in the middle; abdomen blackish-gray, each side with a luteous stripe; feet testaceous; anterior wings narrow, cinereous, spotted with fuscous and black, the apex and posterior margin with spots which are often confluent; a rhombical spot upon the middle, and spots about the anastomosis, which are milky-hyaline; veins fuscous; posterior wings grayish-hyaline, the apex obscurer.

Var. Points and spots partly or altogether confluent, or almost absent.

Length to tip of wings 13 millim. Alar expanse 22 millim.

Hab. Greenland (Kolenati); Europe; Asia, common everywhere.

28. L. plaga.

Limnephilus plaga Walk.! Catal. 35, 53.

Testaceous, with pale hair, and longer black pile; anterior wings pale testaceous, a large, subquadrate, fuscous spot behind the middle; the apex subreticulated with fuscous, and with two patches of fuscous. (From the description of Walker.)

Length to tip of wings 13 millim. Alar expanse 21 millim.

Hab. Nova Scotia (Redman).

Allied to *L. trimaculata*;—a most beautiful species.

Goniotaulius sitchensis Kolenati, Wiener Ent. Monatschr. 1859, p. 17, from North America is spoken of, but only by name; it is unknown to me.

Sub-Genus Desmotaulius Kolenati.

29. L. bimaculatus.

Limnephilus bimaculatus Walk.! Catal. 30, 40.

Testaceous, with pale hair, and longer, black pile; antennæ ferruginous; thorax bivittated with piceous; anterior wings obsoletely irrorated with pale, especially at the base; posterior wings whitish. (From the description of Walker.)

Length to tip of wings 19 millim. Alar expanse 34 millim.

Hab. St. Martin's Falls, Albany River, Hudson's Bay (Barnston).

It is allied to *L. fumigatus* Germar, but the wings are shorter.

30. L. planifrons!

Desmotaulius planifrons Kol. Trich. 56, 1; Walk. Catal. 36, 56.

Fuscous, with luteous hairs; antennæ brown, annulated with luteous; head with two tubercles posteriorly, prothorax, and a double stripe upon the metathorax, luteous; feet luteous, with black spines; anterior wings broader, luteo-fuscous, with fuscous hair, obsoletely marked with luteous; at the posterior margin the veins elevated fuscous; posterior wings luteo-hyaline.

Length to tip of wings 14 millim. Alar expanse 25 millim.

Hab. Greenland; Labrador (Collection of Hagen).

ANABOLIA Stephens.

Spurs 1, 3, 4; apex of the anterior wings elliptical.

1. A. sordida!
Anabolia sordida Hagen!

Rufo-fuscous, with black hair; antennæ fuscous; head and thorax at disk rufous; feet rufo-fuscous, with black spines, the tibiæ obscurer exteriorly; anterior wings soiled-luteous, densely pointed with fuscous, almost naked, finely rugulose, thyridium pale; elevated veins smooth, fuscous, the apex partly interrupted with luteous; posterior wings fusco-hyaline.

Male. Superior anal appendages long, laminated, the apex a little oblique; the inferior appendages acute, a little shorter, oblique.

Length to tip of wings 18 millim. Alar expanse 35 millim.

Hab. N. Red River; Northern Illinois (Kennicott).

2. A. punctatissima.
Hallesus punctatissimus Walk.! Catal. 17, 16.

Testaceous, broad; antennæ stout; anterior wings broad, finely rugulose, closely freckled with whitish, the anterior margin almost whitish; a spot upon the middle, and the thyridium whitish; posterior wings whitish. (From the description of Walker.)

Length to tip of wings 13 millim. Alar expanse 25 millim.

Hab. Nova Scotia (Redman).

3. A. consocia.
Limnephilus consocius Walk.! Catal. 33, 47.

Ferruginous, with pale hair; base of the antennæ black; thorax with a broad black stripe; abdomen black above; feet testaceous; anterior wings testaceous, closely irrorated with whitish, the spots often confluent; veins fuscous; posterior wings subhyaline. (From the description of Walker.)

Length to tip of wings 14 millim. Alar expanse 26 millim.

Hab. North America.

It is allied to *Stathmophorus striatus* Kolenati.

4. A. modesta!

Anabolia modesta Hagen!

Nigro-piceous, with black hair; antennæ black, narrowly annulated with luteous; feet luteous, with black spines, femora piceous; anterior wings obtuse at the apex, fuscous, almost naked, subrugulose, sparingly irrorated with luteous, veins fuscous; posterior wings fusco-hyaline.

Male. Superior anal appendages laminated, the apex incurved.
Length to tip of wings 14 millim. Alar expanse 26 millim.
Hab. Labrador (Christopher).

HALLESUS Stephens.

Spurs arranged 1, 3, 3.

1. H. scabripennis!

Limnephila scabripennis Ramb.! Neuropt. 488, 30; Walk. Catal. 47, 105.
— *Neuronia antica* Walk.! Catal. 9, 8.

Ferruginous, with luteous hair; antennæ ferruginous, obsoletely annulated; abdomen luteous beneath; feet luteous, with black spines; apex of the anterior wings broad, elliptical, lurid, subtuberculated, with numerous fuscous points, some of which are confluent; with a short, discoidal, incurved, fuscous band, veins lurid; posterior wings luteo-hyaline.

Length to tip of wings 20 millim. Alar expanse 36 millim.
Hab. Georgia (Abbot).

2. H. amicus!

Hallesus amicus Hagen!

Luteous, with luteous hair; antennæ luteous; head, thorax, and dorsum of the abdomen fuscous; feet yellowish, with black spines; anterior wings with the apex obtuse, pale luteous, subnude, subtuberculated, with an apical band and another posteriorly, at the elevated veins, fuscous, both longitudinal; veins luteous, the fourth and fifth apical ones, and behind the elevated one, fuscous; posterior wings luteo-hyaline. Male and female.

Male. Superior appendages small, luteous, ovate; the larger hooks fuscous, distant between the superior appendages.

Length to tip of wings 17 millim. Alar expanse 32 millim.

Hab. New Orleans.

May it not be *H. indistinctus* Walker?

3. H. hostis!

Hallesus hostis Hagen!

Luteo-rufous, with luteous hair; antennæ stout, luteous; thorax each side above, rufo-fuscous; feet luteous, with black spines; apex of the wings broader; pale luteo-hyaline, hardly with luteous hairs, subrugulous, base, at the anal angle, and the third apical vein fuscous; a large, oblique, paler spot upon the middle, veins luteous; posterior wings luteo-hyaline. Male and female.

Male. Posterior appendages short, luteous, ovate, adpressed; the intermediate ones longer, straight, conical, fuscous.

Length to tip of wings 20 millim. Alar expanse 36 millim.

Hab. N. Red River; Northern Illinois (Kennicott).

4. H. guttifer!

Halesus guttifer Walk.! Catal. 16, 15.

Testaceous; antennæ ferruginous; anterior wings tuberculous, with an obsolete, subfuscous spot in the apical areolets, another at the thyridium, and a black dot in the third apical areolet; posterior wings whitish; feet and palpi testaceous.

Male. The fuscous spots of the anterior wings are sometimes obsolete.

Length to tip of wings 20 millim. Alar expanse 36—42 millim.

Hab. St. Martin's Falls, Albany River, Hudson's Bay (Barnston); Georgia (Abbot); New Orleans.

It is very much like *Enoicyla subfasciata* Say, but the spurs will easily distinguish it.

5. H. indistinctus.

Limnephilus indistinctus Walk.! Catal. 37, 60.

Testaceous; antennæ pale ferruginous; head and thorax ferruginous; anterior wings pale testaceous; with a broad fuscous vitta at the posterior margin, and a fuscous line between the fourth and fifth subapical areolets; thyridium whitish. (From the description of Walker.)

Length to tip of wings 16 millim. Alar expanse 29 millim.

Hab. St. John, Newfoundland.

Is it *H. amicus*?

6. H. mutatus!

Hallesus mutatus Hagen!

Fuscous, with fuscous hair; antennæ brown, annulated with luteous; feet yellowish, with black spines, base of tibiæ, as well as the middle and apex, marked with fuscous; wings fuscous, finely tuberculated, closely guttated with pale; a semicircular stripe at the anastomosis apically, and a discoidal irregular spot, pale hyaline; veins fuscous; posterior wings brownish-hyaline. Female.

Length to tip of wings 15 millim. Alar expanse 29 millim.
Hab. Labrador.

The specimen is mutilated.

Hallesus maculipennis Kolenati, from North America, Wien. Ent. Zeit. 1859, p. 18, is noticed only by name;—it is unknown to me.

7. H. solidus!

Hallesus solidus Hagen!

Luteo-testaceous; antennæ brownish-black, the basal article and head luteo-fuscous; feet luteous, with black spines; wings luteo-testaceous, the dorsal portion densely covered with black hair, subhyaline, subscabrous, veins sparingly interrupted with fuscous; with a maculose streak behind, and a marginal one, brownish-black; posterior wings luteo-hyaline. Female.

Length to tip of wings 16 millim. Alar expanse 30 millim.
Hab. Mexico (Deppe).

ENOICYLA Rambur.

Spurs arranged 1, 2, 2.

Sub-Genus (new).

1. E. areolata.

Limnephilus areolatus Walk.! Catal. 35, 55.

Black-gray, with black hair; femora obscure ferruginous; anterior wings whitish, with black veins, many of the areoles with fuscous bands, the apical ones with broader bands; margins ciliated. (From the description of Walker.)

Length to tip of wings 7 millim. Alar expanse 13 millim.
Hab. St. Martin's Falls, Albany River, Hudson's-Bay (Barnston).

It is a most beautiful species.

2. E. intercisa!

Limnephilus intercisus Walk.! Catal. 30, 41.

Fuscous, with white hair; antennæ fuscous, annulated with luteous; feet luteous, with black spines, spurs short; anterior wings long, narrow, fuscous, subtuberculous, with white hair; with a discoidal, oblique, spot, the thyridium and a point at the margin of each apical areole, whitish-hyaline; veins lurid; posterior wings grayish-hyaline. Male.

Var. Black, antennæ and feet ferruginous; thorax striped with hoary; anterior wings fuscous, irrorate with whitish, with some oblong darker brown and whitish discoidal spots, and with small white spots at the apex; posterior wings somewhat gray. (From the description of Walker.)

Length to tip of wings 18 millim. Alar expanse 34 millim.

Hab. St. Martin's Falls, Albany River, Hudson's Bay (Barnston).

3. E. praeterita!

Limnephilus praeteritus Walk.! Catal. 32, 44.

Black, with pale hair; antennæ stout, black; feet blackish-brown, with fuscous spines, spurs rather short, fuscous; anterior wings short, the apex elliptical; surface subtuberculated, with a few longer, fuscous hairs, gray-hyaline, sparingly sprinkled with fuscous; fuscous guttæ at the anal angle, at the posterior margin and at the pterostigma, which are confluent; veins black; the margins with short ciliæ; posterior wings cinereo-hyaline.

Length to tip of wings 13 millim. Alar expanse 23 millim.

Hab. Arctic America, Mackenzie and Slave Rivers (Richardson).

4. E. difficilis.

Limnephilus difficilis Walk.! Catal. 34, 50.

Testaceous, with pale hair; antennæ fuscous, the two basal articles altogether and the base of the following ones testaceous; anterior wings subtestaceous, closely, but indistinctly irrorated with hyaline, spots often confluent; veins ferruginous; posterior wings hyaline. (From the description of Walker.)

Length to tip of wings 15 millim. Alar expanse 28 millim.

Hab. Nova Scotia (Redman).

Sub-Genus (new).

5. E. subfasciata!

Phryganea subfasciata Say. Long's Exped. II, 308, 1; American Entom. III, pl. 44 left hand figure. Walk. Catal. 11, 14.

Yellow, with luteous hair; antennæ black, annulated with luteous, the basal article rufous beneath; head and thorax orange above; feet yellow, with black spines, spurs fuscous; anterior wings broad, subrugulose, ochreous, the apex margined with fuscous, the disk with a fuscous circle, which is interrupted anteriorly and posteriorly; thyridium whitish; veins ochreous; posterior wings luteo-hyaline. Female.

Length to tip of wings 22 millim. Alar expanse 40 millim.

Hab. Philadelphia, Pennsylvania; Northwest Territory (Say).

Var. Wings immaculate. (Say.)

6. E. designata!

Limnephilus designatus Walk.! Catal. 24, 19.

Fuscous, with luteous hair; antennæ lurid; thorax above, bivittated with lurid; abdomen luteous beneath; feet yellow, with black spines, spurs long, luteous; anterior wings luteous, almost shining, with a longitudinal stripe, which is broader towards the apex, and margined with fuscous; veins luteous; posterior wings luteo-hyaline. Male.

Length to tip of wings 18 millim. Alar expanse 34 millim.

Hab. St. Martin's Falls, Albany River, Hudson's Bay (Barnston); Arctic America, Slave and Mackenzie Rivers, Great Bear Lake (Richardson); Nova Scotia (Redman).

7. E. lepida!

Enoicyla lepida Hagen!

Luteo-rufous, with luteous hair; antennæ fuscous, annulated with luteous, the basal article luteous; head and thorax above, rufous; feet yellowish, with black spines; spurs yellowish; anterior wings broader, rugulose, subnude, luteous, with a fuscous point in the base of the third areole; veins luteous; posterior wings luteo-hyaline. Male.

Length to tip of wings 15 millim. Alar expanse 28 millim.

Hab. Pennsylvania.

APATANIA Kolenati.

Spurs arranged 1, 2, 4.

1. A. nigra.
Potamaria nigra Walk.! Catal. 83, 4.

Black, with black pile; beneath, a little clothed with luteous hair; antennæ rather short; breast grayish; apices of the abdominal segments, base of the tarsi, and tibiæ ferruginous; wings blackish, clothed with black pile. (From the description of Walker.)

Length to tip of wings 9 millim. Alar expanse 16 millim.

Hab. St. Martin's Falls, Albany River, Hudson's Bay (Barnston).

2. A. pallida!
Apatania pallida Hagen!

Black, with luteous pile; antennæ black; feet pale, with black spines, femora fuscous; anterior wings luteo-hyaline, and the veins same color, with luteous pile and cilia; posterior wings hyaline. Male.

Length to tip of wings 8 millim. Alar expanse 15 millim.

Hab. St. Lawrence River, Canada (Osten Sacken).

Sub-Family SERICOSTOMIDES.

Ocelli absent; palpi pilose.

SERICOSTOMA Latreille.

Spurs arranged 2, 2, 4; maxillary palpi of the males 4-jointed, covering the face like a mask.

1. S. americanum.
Sericostoma americanum Walk.! Catal. 85, 8.

Black, clothed with black hair; antennæ twice the length of the body; feet piceous; wings blackish-fuscous, pilose; the anterior wings much longer than the posterior ones. (From the description of Walker.)

Length to tip of wings 19 millim. Alar expanse 34 millim.

Hab. Georgia (Abbot).

2. S. crassicorne.

Hydropsyche crassicornis Walk.! Catal. 113, 35.

Ferruginous, with lurid hair; antennæ stout, longer than the body, articles paler at their bases; palpi and feet testaceous; wings cinereous, with fulvous pile; anterior wings with a hyaline spot at the base of the apical areolets; veins fuscous. (From the description of Walker.)

Length to tip of wings 11 millim. Alar expanse 20 millim.
Hab. Georgia (Abbot).

NOTIDOBIA Stephens.

Spurs arranged 2, 2, 4; maxillary palpi of the males masking the face, recurved.

1. N. borealis!

Notidobia borealis Hagen!

Brownish-black, with luteous hair; antennæ bright yellow, the basal article and the palpi black, hairy; feet pale, whitish; wings fusco-hyaline, the anterior wings densely covered with luteous hair, and ciliated with luteous. Male.

Length to tip of wings 7 millim. Alar expanse 13 millim.
Hab. Washington; St. Lawrence River, Canada (Osten Sacken).

2. N. pyraloides!

Notidobia pyraloides Walk.! Catal. 90, 2.

Fulvous, with fulvous hair; antennæ twice the length of the body, testaceous, with the base fuscous, and the apices of the basal articles testaceous; the first article stout, testaceous; feet testaceous; wings fuscous, with fuscous pile and ciliæ; veins fuscous.

Length to tip of wings 14 millim. Alar expanse 25 millim.
Hab. Georgia (Abbot); North America; Pennsylvania.

3. N. lutea!

Notidobia lutea Hagen!

Yellow, with luteous hair; antennæ subannulated with brown; palpi yellow, interiorly with black hair; feet yellowish; wings yellowish hyaline, sparingly clothed with luteous hairs and ciliated with luteous; posterior wings hyaline. Male and female.

Length to tip of wings 6½ millim.   Alar expanse 11 millim.
Hab. St. Domingo.

BRACHYCENTRUS Curtis.

Spurs arranged 2, 3, 3.

1. B. fuliginosus.
Brachycentrus fuliginosus Walk.! Catal. 88, 7.

Black, with hoary hair; antennæ long, ferruginous, apices of the abdominal segments, and the legs testaceous; palpi testaceous, with the apex blackish; the anterior wings grayish-fuscous, veins ferruginous; posterior wings cinereous. (From the description of Walker.)

Length to tip of wings 14 millim.   Alar expanse 26 millim.

Hab. St. Martin's Falls, Albany River, Hudson's Bay (Barnston).

2. B. incanus!
Brachycentrus incanus Hagen!

Black; sparingly clothed with hoary hair; antennæ black, feet pale, femora black; anterior wings long, grayish-hyaline, with some luteous spots, and sparse luteous pile; veins gray; posterior wings grayish-hyaline.   Female.

Length to tip of wings 13 millim.   Alar expanse 24 millim.

Hab. Washington, April (Osten Sacken).

It is similar to *B. subnubilus* Curtis.

SILO Curtis.

Spurs arranged 2, 4, 4.

1. S. californicus!
Silo californicus Hagen!

Fuscous; antennæ stout, brownish-black; head and thorax black, with yellow pile; feet fuscous; anterior wings fuscous, with fuscous pile, veins blackish fuscous; some yellow, hairy streaks between the longitudinal veins; posterior wings fuscous.   Female.

Length to tip of wings 17 millim.   Alar expanse 32 millim.

Hab. North California.

2. S. griseus!
Silo griseus Hagen!

Brownish-gray, with fuscous hair; antennæ brownish-gray, the apex subannulated with lurid; head, and thorax above, rufescent; feet pale, the posterior ones and the spurs fuscous; anterior wings narrow, brownish-gray, hairy, with long cilia; posterior wings cinereous. Male.

Length to tip of wings 6 millim. Alar expanse 11 millim.
Hab. Trenton Falls (Osten Sacken).

MORMONIA Stephens.

Spurs arranged 2, 4, 4; antennæ with the basal joint long, thick, very hirsute.

1. M. togata!
Mormonia togata Hagen!

Brownish-gray; with luteous hair; antennæ pilose, pale yellow, annulated with fuscous, the basal article long, brownish-gray, hairy; palpi and feet pale; abdomen fuscous; anterior wings narrow, fuscous, with luteous hair, veins fuscous, with fuscous pile; posterior wings cinereous. Female.

Length to tip of wings 9 millim. Alar expanse 16 millim.
Hab. Washington; St. Lawrence River, Canada (Osten Sacken).

DASYSTOMA Rambur.

Spurs arranged 2, 2, 2.

1. D. numerosum.
Phryganea numerosa Say, Western Quart. Rep. 1823, II, p. 160, 2.

Black, with cinereous hair; antennæ as long as the body, pale fuscous, the basal article black, hairy; palpi pale fuscous; head short, black, densely covered with cinereous hair; thorax black, with cinereous hair; feet pale fuscous; abdomen black, the apices of the segments pale rufous, lateral line rufous; wings whitish-brown, immaculate, veins fuscous. (From the description of Say.)

Length to tip of wings 12 millim. Alar expanse 23 millim.

"This species appears in vast numbers early in May, from the
"7th to the 9th of that month, on the Ohio River. Having a
"white appearance when flying, they might be compared to flakes
"of snow in a moderate fall of that meteor." (Say.)

May it not belong to *Brachycentrus?* Can it be *B. fuliginosus?*

2. D. laterale.

Phryganea lateralis Say, Western Quart. Rep. 1823, II, p. 161, 3.

Black, above with cinereous hair, beneath with plumbeous hair; antennæ and mouth pale; feet whitish; abdomen black, with a lateral pale stripe, and the apices of the segments pale; appendages white; wings whitish, the anterior ones spotted with fuscous, a common spot on the middle of the inner margin, and several near the tip somewhat arranged into a band, the costal one of which is larger; posterior wings white, immaculate. (From the description of Say.)

Length to tip of wings 10 millim. Alar expanse 18 millim.

Hab. "Shippingsport, Kentucky, Ohio River; they appeared
"in very great numbers at the banks of the Ohio on the 21st of
"May; judging from the small space of about half a mile on the
"Indiana side of the river, where I had the opportunity to see
"them, their number could have been but little inferior to that of
"*P. numerosa*, which occurred a few days before, but of which a
"specimen was now rarely to be seen." (Say.)

May it not belong to *Brachycentrus?*

HYDROPTILA Dalman.

Spurs of the male arranged 0, 3, 4; female 0, 2, 4.

1. H. tenebrosa.

Hydroptila tenebrosa Walk. Catal. 134, 11.

Blackish; antennæ fuscous, the basal article larger, ovate; feet testaceous; wings blackish-gray, ciliated, with black veins. (From the description of Walker.)

Length to tip of wings 4 millim. Alar expanse 6 millim.

Hab. St. Martin's Falls, Albany River, Hudson's Bay (Barnston).

2. H. albicornis!

Hydroptila albicornis Hagen!

Gray; antennæ stout, snow-white, with the middle and apex fuscous; palpi whitish; head with snow-white hair, the vertex with fuscous hair; thorax fuscous; feet whitish, the posterior ones ciliated with white; anterior wings grayish-fuscous, ciliated with gray, the margin and disk pointed with snow-white; posterior wings gray, clothed and ciliated with gray hair. Female.

Length to tip of wings $3\frac{1}{2}$ millim. Alar expanse 6 millim.

Hab. St. Lawrence River, Canada (Osten Sacken).

3. H. tarsalis!

Hydroptila tarsalis Hagen!

Gray; antennæ somewhat robust, rather long, fuscous, with gray hair; palpi black, the apex snow-white; head black, the vertex white; thorax fuscous; feet whitish, anterior tibiæ, spurs, and tarsi fuscous, the latter annulated with white; posterior feet with gray cilia; anterior wings fuscous, the anterior margin black, ciliated with gray, and pointed with snow white; posterior wings with gray hairs and cilia. Male.

Length to tip of wings 3 millim. Alar expanse $5\frac{1}{4}$ millim.

Hab. St. Lawrence River, Canada (Osten Sacken).

Is this the other sex of the preceding species?

I. Maxillary palpi of both sexes with five articles.

Sub-Fam. LEPTOCERIDES.

Ocelli wanting; antennæ setaceous, long, or extremely long; maxillary palpi elongated, hirsute, with the last article mobile.

MOLANNA Curtis.

Spurs arranged 2, 4, 4.

1. M. inconspicua.

Leptocerus inconspicuus Walk.! Catal. 71, 63.

Ferruginous, with pale hairs: base of the antennæ testaceous; palpi and feet testaceous; abdomen blackish; wings gray, with testaceous hair and pale veins. (From the description of Walker.)

Length to tip of wings 12 millim. Alar expanse 23 millim.
Hab. Georgia (Abbot). It is allied to *M. angustata*.

2. M. cinerea!

Molanna cinerea Hagen!

Ferruginous, sparingly clothed with gray hair; antennæ stout, ferruginous; palpi ferruginous; anterior feet ferruginous, the four posterior ones gray, the tarsi with black spines; wings narrow, gray, clothed with gray hair, the apex obsoletely marmorated with fuscous; posterior wings gray.

Length to tip of wings 12 millim. Alar expanse 23 millim.
Hab. St. Lawrence River, Canada (Osten Sacken). Can this be *M. inconspicua?*

3. M. rufa!

Molanna rufa Hagen!

Rufo-fuscous, with fuscous hair; antennæ and palpi rufous; feet testaceous, the anterior ones and femora rufous; abdomen fuscous; wings fuscous, with rufous hair; posterior wings fuscous; veins fuscous.

Length to tip of wings 10 millim. Alar expanse 18 millim.
Hab. Trenton Falls (Osten Sacken).

LEPTOCERUS Leach.

Spurs arranged 2, 2, 2; antennæ of the males extremely long.

1. L. albostictus!

Leptocerus albostictus Hagen!

Luteous; antennæ black, the basal half narrowly annulated with white, the basal article rufous; palpi fuscous; head with snow-white hair; abdomen fuscous; feet whitish, anterior tibiæ and tarsi spotted with fuscous; anterior wings luteous, all over very finely pointed with white, and with an anal snow-white spot; veins luteous; cilia fuscous; posterior wings gray. Male.

Length to tip of wings 11 millim. Alar expanse 21 millim.
Hab. North America. (Collection of Hagen.)

2. L. lugens!

Leptocerus lugens Hagen!

Fuscous; antennæ black, the basal half annulated with snow-white; palpi fuscous; head with snow-white hair; feet snow-white, base of the femora fuscous, the four anterior tarsi spotted with fuscous; anterior wings rufo-fuscous, with fuscous hair, and luteous hair intermixed, a whitish-yellow spot at the anal angle; veins fuscous; cilia paler; posterior wings gray. Male and female.

Length to tip of wings 11 millim. Alar expanse 21 millim.

Hab. St. Lawrence River, Canada (Osten Sacken).

3. L. dilutus!
Leptocerus dilutus Hagen!

Grayish-fuscous; antennæ fuscous, the basal half broadly annulated with snow-white; palpi fuscous, with snow-white hair; head with snow-white hair; feet snow-white, bases of the femora a little obscured; abdomen fuscous; anterior wings gray, with luteous hair, sometimes obsoletely varied with fuscous; veins gray; cilia fuscous; with an anal yellowish spot; posterior wings gray. Male and female.

Length to tip of wings 7—10 millim. Alar expanse 13—19 millim.

Hab. Chicago (Osten Sacken).

4. L. niger!
Phryganea nigra Linné.—*Mystacides nigra* Pict.! Phryg. 169, 10, pl. xii, fig. 5.—*Leptocerus niger* Walk.! Catal. 58, 6. (With the synonymy).

Black, shining, with black hair; antennæ black, the basal half annulated with snow-white, the basal article rufous; head black, shining; palpi very densely black-hirsute; abdomen black; feet luteous, intermediate ones snow-white, tarsi spotted with fuscous; anterior wings steel-blue black, posterior wings blackish. Male.

Length to tip of wings 7½ millim. Alar expanse 14 millim.

Hab. Washington (Osten Sacken); it is found everywhere in Europe.

5. L. sepulchralis.
Leptocerus sepulchralis Walk.! Catal. 70, 57.

Black, with black hair; antennæ black, the base annulated with white; apex of the abdomen ferruginous; feet testaceous; wings blackish. (From the description of Walker.)

Length to tip of wings 8 millim. Alar expanse 13 millim.

Hab. St. Martin's Falls, Albany River, Hudson's Bay (Barnston). Very closely allied to *L. ater*, Pictet; is it distinct?

6. L. variegatus!

Leptocerus variegatus Hagen!

Luteo-fuscous, with snow-white hair; antennæ luteo-fuscous, the basal half annulated with snow-white, the basal article luteo-fuscous; palpi fuscous, with gray hair; head fuscous, sparingly clothed with white hair; feet gray, tarsi snow-white, spotted with fuscous; anterior wings grayish-fuscous, with brown and gray hairs, spotted with gray, especially at the apex, margin and anal angle; veins stout, fuscous; posterior wings cinereous. Male.

Length to tip of wings 14 millim. Alar expanse 27 millim.

Hab. Chicago (Osten Sacken).

7. L. submacula.

Leptocerus submacula Walk.! Catal. 70, 59.

Black, with black hair; antennæ extremely long; palpi hairy; tibiæ and tarsi testaceous; wings cinereous, the anterior ones sprinkled with white, and with three whitish spots, the one basal, the second discoidal, subcostal, and the third anal; veins black. (From the description of Walker.)

Length to tip of wings 14 millim. Alar expanse 25 millim.

Hab. St. Lawrence River. It is allied to *L. venosus* Ramb.; is it perhaps, *L. variegatus?*

8. L. mentiens.

Leptocerus mentiens Walk.! Catal. 71, 60.

Ferruginous, hairy; antennæ black, annulated with white; palpi hairy; tarsi banded with white; anterior wings cinereo-fuscous, with ferruginous pubescence, veins ferruginous; posterior wings cinereous. (From the description of Walker.)

Length to tip of wings 10 millim. Alar expanse 19 millim.

Hab. St. Martin's Falls, Albany River, Hudson's Bay (Barnston). Is this *L. lugens* Hagen?

9. L. incertus.

Leptocerus incertus Walk.! Catal. 71, 61.

Obscure testaceous, with golden hair, and more scarce black pile;

beneath whitish; antennæ extremely long, whitish; palpi hairy; apex of the abdomen ferruginous; feet whitish; wings cinereous, the anterior ones with golden pubescence. (From the description of Walker.)

Length to tip of wings 7 millim. Alar expanse 12 millim.

Hab. St. Martin's Falls, Albany River, Hudson's Bay (Barnston).

10. L. elegans.

Goëra elegans Walk.! Catal. 95, 5.

Testaceous, with testaceous pile; antennæ annulated with black; wings cinereous, the anterior ones with testaceous pubescence. (From the description of Walker.)

Length to tip of wings 12 millim. Alar expanse 23 millim.

Hab. North America?

11. L. indecisus.

Goëra indecisa Walk.! Catal. 95, 6.

Black, with black hair; feet ferruginous; antennæ extremely long; palpi very hairy; wings blackish, the anterior ones with fuscous pubescence. (From the description of Walker.)

Length to tip of wings 11 millim. Alar expanse 21 millim.

Hab. St. Martin's Falls, Albany River, Hudson's Bay (Barnston).

12. L. latifascia.

Notidobia latifascia Walk! Catal. 90, 3.

Testaceous, with testaceous hair; antennæ annulated with fuscous; anterior wings with a broad, oblique, fuscous band upon the middle; posterior wings cinereous. (From the description of Walker.)

Length to tip of wings 10 millim. Alar expanse 19 millim.

Hab. North America.

13. L. transversus!

Leptocerus transversus Hagen!

Grayish-fuscous, with snow-white hair; antennæ fuscous, annulated with white, the basal article fuscous; palpi fuscous, with gray hair; head and thorax fuscous, with white and fuscous hair; feet luteo-fuscous, with snow-white pile, tarsi spotted with fuscous; anterior wings fuscous, ciliated with fuscous, varied with cinereous, and with an anal cinereous spot; veins stout, fuscous; posterior wings cinereous; abdomen luteous. Male and female.

Length to tip of wings 7—9 millim. Alar expanse 13—17 millim.

Hab. Washington (Osten Sacken).

Leptocerus uwarowii Kol. Wien. Ent. Zeit. 1859, p. 58, is noticed only by name; it is entirely unknown to me.

SETODES Rambur.

Spurs arranged 0, 2, 2.

1. S. exquisita!

Leptocerus exquisitus Walk.! Catal. 72, 65.

Pale yellow, with snow-white hair; antennæ luteous, the base annulated with fuscous, the basal article yellow, with snow-white hair; head and thorax yellow, with snow-white hair; palpi and abdomen yellow; feet snow-white; anterior wings snow-white, with some transverse luteous bands, the apical ones maculose, imperfect; at the apex of the posterior margin are four black spots, and some obsolete black streaks; posterior wings snow-white. Male and female.

Length to tip of wings 8—13 millim. Alar expanse 15—25 millim.

Hab. Georgia (Abbot); Washington; St. Lawrence River, Canada (Osten Sacken). This is an extremely beautiful species.

2. S. candida!

Setodes candida Hagen!

Pale yellow, with snow-white hair; antennæ fuscous, the basal half yellowish, annulated with fuscous, the basal article yellow, with snow-white pile; head and thorax with snow-white hair; palpi, abdomen, and feet pale yellow; anterior wings snow-white, with luteous, sparse spots all over, which are sometimes obsolete; the posterior margin a little marked with black, the anal angle ciliated with black; posterior wings snow-white. Male and female. The female is more and deeper spotted upon the wings than the male.

Length to tip of wings 12—15 millim. Alar expanse 23—28 millim.

Hab. Georgia; Philadelphia, Pennsylvania (Zimmerman); Ohio River; Florida (Osten Sacken); South Carolina (Zimmerman).

3. S. nivea!

Setodes nivea Hagen!

Brownish-black, with snow-white hair; antennæ snow-white, the base subannulated with fuscous, the basal article yellow, with snow-white hair; head yellow, the disk brownish-black, with snow-white hair; thorax brownish-black, with snow-white hair; palpi and feet pale; abdomen luteous; anterior wings snow-white, with fuscous veins, at the apex transversely, obsoletely clouded; posterior wings snow-white. Male.

Length to tip of wings 15 millim. Alar expanse 28 millim.

Hab. St. Lawrence River, Canada (Osten Sacken).

4. S. ochracea!

Leptocerus ochraceus Curtis! Brit. Ent. II, pl. 57; Steph. Illust. VI, 195, 1.—*Phryganea hectica* Zetterst. Ins. Lapp. 1072, 48.—*Mystacides obsoleta* Ramb.! Neuropt. 509, 4.—*Leptocerus ochraceus* Walk.! Catal. 57, 1.

Pale ochreous; articles of the antennæ subfuscous; head, thorax, abdomen, palpi, and feet, pale ochreous,; anterior wings ochreous, with ochreous pile; veins a little deeper; posterior wings pale. Male and female.

Length to tip of wings 14 millim. Alar expanse 27 millim.

Hab. Georgia (Abbot); Europe everywhere.

I observed one specimen in the British Museum which was referred to *Leptocerus (Molanna) inconspicuus.*

5. S. ignita!

Leptocerus ignitus Walk.! Catal. 72, 64.

Pale testaceous, with testaceous hair; antennæ snow-white, the basal article testaceous; palpi with testaceous hair; head, thorax, abdomen, and feet, pale; anterior wings testaceous-yellow, with yellow hair and cilia, a point upon the middle of the posterior margin, and another anal one, black, with black almost elevated pile; posterior wings pale. Male.

Length to tip of wings 10 millim. Alar expanse 19 millim.

Hab. Georgia (Abbot); Washington (Osten Sacken); Mexico (Deppe).

6. S. pavida!
Setodes pavida Hagen!

Pale yellow, with yellow hair; antennæ pale, annulated obscurely; palpi, head, thorax, abdomen, and feet, pale yellow; anterior wings yellow, with yellow hair and veins, pointed with fuscous, the points small, longitudinally placed in series; posterior wings pale.

Length to tip of wings 7 millim. Alar expanse 13 millim.
Hab. Washington (Osten Sacken).
The specimen is damaged.

7. S. cinerascens!
Setodes cinerascens Hagen!

Pale fuscous, with cinereous hair; antennæ (? pale) at base, with cinereous hair; head, thorax, and palpi, fuscous, with cinereous hair; feet luteous; anterior wings cinereous, with cinereous hair, varied with fuscous; veins with dense and long cinereous and fuscous hair; cilia cinereous; posterior wings cinereous.

Length to tip of wings 10 millim. Alar expanse 19 millim.
Hab. Washington (Osten Sacken).
The specimen is mutilated.

8. S. flaveolata!
Setodes flaveolata Hagen!

Pale yellow, with yellow hair; antennæ whitish-yellow, a little annulated with fuscous, the basal article yellow; palpi, head, thorax, and feet, pale yellow; anterior wings yellow-ochreous, with yellow hair, veins, and cilia; posterior wings cinereous. Male and female.

Length to tip of wings 7 millim. Alar expanse 13 millim.
Hab. Washington (Osten Sacken); New Orleans.

9. S. resurgens.
Leptocerus resurgens Walk.! Catal. 70, 58.

Fuscous, with whitish hair; palpi and feet fulvous, a little covered with whitish hair; anterior wings fuscous, with white spots at the base, and at the disk and apex of the apical areoles; posterior wings cinereous. (From the description of Walker.)

Length to tip of wings 16 millim. Alar expanse 30 millim.

Hab. St. Martin's Falls, Albany River, Hudson's Bay (Barnston).

10. S. albida.

Leptocerus albidus Walk.! Catal. 71, 62.

Fuscous, with whitish hair; base of the antennæ annulated with white; palpi testaceous; feet whitish; wings whitish, with testaceous veins. (From the description of Walker.)

Length to tip of wings 13 millim. Alar expanse 25 millim.

Hab. St. Martin's Falls, Albany River, Hudson's Bay (Barnston).

Allied to *S. resurgens;*—may it not be immature?

11. S. injusta!

Setodes injusta Hagen!

Luteous, with luteous hair; antennæ luteous, subannulated with fuscous; palpi with luteo-fuscous pile; feet and abdomen pale luteous; anterior wings luteous, with ochreous pile and cilia, the anterior margin at base a little obscurer; the anal angle a little fuscous, and ciliated with fuscous hair; posterior wings luteous, with pale cilia. Male.

Length to tip of wings 12 millim. Alar expanse 23 millim.

Hab. St. Lawrence River, Canada (Osten Sacken); Chicago (id.).

12. S. immobilis!

Setodes immobilis Hagen!

Fuscous, with luteous hair; antennæ fuscous, the basal article luteous; palpi with fuscous hair; head and thorax fuscous; feet luteous; abdomen fusco-luteous; anterior wings fuscous, with luteous hair, the margin obsoletely spotted with fuscous, ciliated with fuscous; posterior wings brown-gray, with gray cilia. Male.

Length to tip of wings 7 millim. Alar expanse 13 millim.

Hab. St. Lawrence River, Canada (Osten Sacken).

13. S. micans!

Setodes micans Hagen!

Luteous, with fuscous hair; antennæ whitish-yellow, the basal article luteous; palpi with fuscous hair; head and abdomen luteous; feet whitish-yellow; anterior wings luteo-fuscous, subnude, the disk shining purple, anastomosis fuscous, cilia long, fuscous; posterior wings obscure; entirely shining purplish, with fuscous cilia.

Length to tip of wings 8 millim. Alar expanse 15 millim.

Hab. Washington (Osten Sacken); Mexico (Deppe).

Is this *L. incertus* Walker?

14. S. sagitta!

Setodes sagitta Hagen!

Luteous, with luteous hair; antennæ whitish, a little annulated with fuscous; palpi with fuscous hair; head and thorax luteous; feet whitish-yellow; anterior wings luteous, subnude, ciliated with luteous, anastomosis and apical margin spotted with fuscous; posterior wings gray, the apex long, acute, narrow, ciliated with gray. Male.

Length to tip of wings 11 millim. Alar expanse 21 millim.

Hab. Florida (Osten Sacken).

Sub-Fam. HYDROPSYCHIDES.

Ocelli none or three; the last article of the maxillary palpi very long, filiform, multiarticulate.

MACRONEMA Pictet.

Spurs arranged 2, 2, 4; ocelli absent; antennæ extremely long; the second article of the maxillary palpi longer than the first, the fifth extremely long; intermediate feet of the females dilated.

1. M. pallidum!

Leptonema pallida Guérin, Icon. Regn. Anim. Texte. 396; Walk. Catal. 78, 1.—*Macronema albovirens* Walk.! Catal. 76, 9.

Pale testaceous, almost unclothed; antennæ pale, slightly annulated with fuscous; palpi, head, thorax, abdomen and feet pale testaceous; wings pale, anterior ones hardly clothed with testaceous hair, veins pale. Male and female.

Length to tip of wings 18 millim. Alar expanse 34 millim.

Hab. Vera Cruz, Mexico (Sallé); Cordova (Saussure); Venezuela (Appun); Brazil (Classen).

2. M. chalybeum!

Macronema chalybeum Hagen!

Blackish-fuscous; antennæ black, the basal article orange; head orange, each side anteriorly with an oblique fuscous line; palpi black; thorax rufous, the disk fuscous; feet bright sulphureous; abdomen luteous; anterior wings blackish-fuscous, nude, with a steel-blue reflection, veins with golden hair; posterior wings fuscous. Male.

Length to tip of wings 13 millim. Alar expanse 25 millim.

Hab. Cuba (Poey).

3. M. aeneum!

Macronema aeneum Hagen!

Fuscous; antennæ, ? basal article fulvous; palpi fuscous; head fulvous; thorax fulvous, each side with a fuscous stripe; abdomen luteous; tibiæ fulvous, all the tarsi and the posterior tibiæ fuscous; anterior wings nude, fuscous, with a brilliant brazen reflection, veins fuscous; posterior wings fuscous. Female.

Length to tip of wings 12 millim. Alar expanse 23 millim.

Hab. Mexico (Sallé).

May it not be the female of the preceding? The specimen is mutilated.

4. M. flavum!

Macronema flavum Hagen!

Yellow, pale; antennæ yellow, slightly annulated with fuscous; palpi, head, thorax, feet, and abdomen pale yellow; anterior wings yellow, subnude, a little clothed with golden hair, veins and cilia yellow; posterior wings whitish-yellow, ciliated with pale. Male.

Length to tip of wings 9 millim. Alar expanse 17 millim.

Hab. St. Louis, Missouri (Osten Sacken).

5. M. zebratum!

Macronema zebratum Hagen!

Brassy-fuscous, spotted with yellow; antennæ black, head, thorax and abdomen brassy-fuscous; palpi yellow; feet yellow, the anterior tibiæ and base of the femora a little infuscated; posterior tibiæ with long, yellow spines; anterior wings subnude, yellow, with longitudinal stripes at base, and transverse ones on the disk, fuscous; the apex fuscous, with an orbicular, yellow spot; posterior wings cinereous, the anterior margin and pterostigma yellow. Male and female.

Var. Anterior wings less spotted, the basal stripes shorter, the disk spotted, and the apex with an incurved band, which has the open side inwards, fuscous.

Hab. St. Lawrence River, Canada; Washington; Virginia (Osten Sacken); Maryland; Niagara Falls; immensely common upon the foliage of trees on Goat Island (Uhler).

I possess a very small specimen from Washington, only 11 millim. long; but it is not different. Sometimes the bands of the wings are almost altogether confluent.

6. M. cupreum!

Macronema cuprea Walk. Catal. 76, 8.

Fuscous; antennæ fuscous, with the base luteous, the incisures fuscous; face, palpi and feet luteous; head and thorax fuscous, partly clothed with golden pile; anterior wings luteo-fuscous, with golden hair, before the apex clouded with black; posterior wings luteo-cinereous, the anterior margin luteous.

Length to tip of wings 17—20 millim. Alar expanse 32—34 millim.

Hab. Mexico (Deppe); Brazil.

I saw a male and female from Mexico in the Berlin Museum (immature specimens), the wings were luteo-fuscous, the golden pile was almost wanting or rubbed off; the other specimens from Brazil are not different.

Does *M. auripenne*, Rambur, differ from this species?

HYDROPSYCHE Pictet.

Spurs arranged 2, 4, 4; antennæ rather long, slender; ocelli absent; second article of the maxillary palpi long, the fifth equal to all of the others together; intermediate feet of the female dilated.

1. H. scalaris!

Hydropsyche scalaris Hagen!

Black-gray, with white hair; antennæ luteous, the base obliquely striated with black, the first article with snow-white hair; head grayish-fuscous, with snow-white hair; thorax grayish-fuscous, with a broad, medial stripe of white hair; eyes of the male larger, approximated; palpi luteo-fuscous; abdomen fuscous; feet pale luteous; anterior wings blackish-gray, densely flecked with white; veins black; posterior wings cinereous, luteous at base. Male and female.

Length to tip of wings 13 millim. Alar expanse 25 millim.

Hab. St. Lawrence River, Canada (Osten Sacken); Washington. I possess a male from N. Red River (Kennicott) which is extremely like this, but the eyes are larger, more approximate, the front hardly broader than the eyes. Is it different?

2. **H. morosa!**

Hydropsyche morosa Hagen!

Luteo-fuscous, with luteous hair; antennæ luteous yellow, annulated with fuscous; palpi fuscous; head and thorax luteo-fuscous, with luteous hair; feet luteous; abdomen fuscous; anterior wings luteo-fuscous, densely guttated with luteous, veins luteo-fuscous; posterior wings luteo-cinereous. Male and female.

Length to tip of wings 10—13 millim. Alar expanse 19—25 millim.

Hab. St. Lawrence River, Canada; Washington (Osten Sacken); N. Red River (Kennicott); Trenton Falls, New York (Osten Sacken).

3. **H. phalerata!**

Hydropsyche phalerata Hagen!

Fuscous, with luteous hair; antennæ fuscous, annulated with luteous; palpi and feet luteous; head and thorax fuscous, with luteous hair; anterior wings fuscous, guttated with luteous, with larger spots at the base, pterostigma and anal angle; veins fuscous; posterior wings blackish-gray. Male and female.

A variety has the anterior wings less spotted, the female obscurer.

Length to tip of wings 7—10 millim. Alar expanse 13—19 millim.

Hab. St. Lawrence River, Canada; Washington (Osten Sacken); Pennsylvania (Zimmerman).

4. H. alternans.

Philopotamus alternans Walk.! Catal. 104, 8.

Black, with hoary hair; base of the antennæ fulvous; feet and apices of the abdominal segments fulvous; anterior wings fuscous, closely irrorated with hoary; posterior wings cinereous. (From the description of Walker.)

Length to tip of wings 12 millim. Alar expanse 23 millim.

Hab. St. Martin's Falls, Albany River, Hudson's Bay (Barnston).

5. H. indecisa.

Philopotamus indecisus Walk.! Catal. 104, 9.

Blackish, beneath testaceous, antennæ testaceous, annulated with fuscous; palpi testaceous, fulvous at base; feet testaceous; anterior wings cinereous, closely guttated with yellow. (From the description of Walker.)

Length to tip of wings 12 millim. Alar expanse 23 millim.

Hab. St. Martin's Falls, Albany River, Hudson's Bay (Barnston); Nova Scotia (Redman).

Is this *H. morosa*?

6. H. reciproca.

Philopotamus reciprocus Walk.! Catal. 104, 10.

Blackish; antennæ and feet testaceous; palpi ferruginous, with the base black; anterior wings subfuscous, closely irrorated with yellow; posterior wings pale fuscous. (From the description of Walker.)

Length to tip of wings 14 millim. Alar expanse 27 millim.

Hab. North America?

It is very much like *H. indecisa*.

7. H. dubia.

Hydropsyche dubia Walk.! Catal. 112, 33.

Black, beneath testaceous; antennæ pale testaceous, annulated with fuscous, the apex fuscous; palpi ferruginous; feet testaceous; anterior wings subfuscous, obsoletely irrorated; posterior wings subcinereous. (From the description of Walker.)

Length to tip of wings 11 millim. Alar expanse 23 millim.

Hab. North America?

8. H. dubitans.

Hydropsyche dubitans Walk.! Catal. 113, 34.

Piceous, with pale hair; antennæ testaceous, the apex black; pectus ferruginous; palpi, feet and apices of the abdominal segments testaceous; wings cinereous, the anterior ones with fuscous hair and some paler spots, composed of yellow pile. (From the description of Walker.)

Length to tip of wings 11 millim. Alar expanse 23 millim.

Hab. North America (Doubleday).

9. H. maculicornis.

Hydropsyche maculicornis Walk.! Catal. 113, 36.

Blackish, hairy; antennæ testaceous, annulated with fuscous; palpi pale; pectus ferruginous; feet testaceous; anterior wings fusco-cinereous, with obsolete irrorations; posterior wings cinereous. (From the description of Walker.)

Length to tip of wings 8 millim. Alar expanse 15 millim.

Hab. St. Martin's Falls, Albany River, Hudson's Bay (Barnston).

10. H. robusta.

Hydropsyche robusta Walk.! Catal. 114, 37.

Ferruginous, hairy; antennæ, palpi and feet testaceous; thorax bivittated with piceous; wings cinereous, somewhat covered with yellow hair; the anterior wings with pale spots, which are clearer at the margin. (From the description of Walker.)

Length to tip of wings 8 millim. Alar expanse 17 millim.

Hab. North America?

11. H. transversa.

Hydropsyche transversa Walk.! Catal. 114, 38.

Testaceous; antennæ black, testaceous at base; abdomen black, apices of the segments pale; feet white; wings whitish, the anterior ones on the front margin and at the veins, yellow, with numerous, transverse cinereous spots, part of which are confluent; the apex subcinereous, spotted with pale; veins pale yellow. (From the description of Walker.)

Length to tip of wings 13 millim. Alar expanse 25 millim.

Hab. Georgia (Abbot).

12. H. chlorotica!

Hydropsyche chlorotica Hagen!

Pale ochreous, with ochreous hair; antennæ ochreous at base, annulated with fuscous, the apex fuscous; palpi fuscous; feet luteous; head and thorax luteo-fuscous, with luteous hair; abdomen luteous; anterior wings ochreous, the anal angle and apical margin ciliated with fuscous; posterior wings cinereous. Male and female.

Length to tip of wings 10—12 millim. Alar expanse 19—23 millim.

Hab. St. Lawrence River, Canada; Chicago; Trenton Falls (Osten Sacken); N. Red River (Kennicott).

13. H. depravata!

Hydropsyche depravata Hagen!

Blackish-fuscous; antennæ blackish-fuscous, the base annulated with luteous; palpi blackish-fuscous; head, thorax and abdomen fuscous; feet brownish-luteous; anterior wings blackish-fuscous, obsoletely irrorated with luteous; posterior wings blackish-gray. Female.

Length to tip of wings 12 millim. Alar expanse 23 millim.

Hab. Dalton, Georgia (Osten Sacken).

One specimen only, which is not fully unfolded.

14. H. sordida!

Hydropsyche sordida Hagen!

Blackish-fuscous; antennæ and palpi fuscous; head and thorax blackish-fuscous, with luteous hair; feet luteo-fuscous, femora fuscous; anterior wings blackish-fuscous, with fuscous hair; posterior wings blackish. Male and female.

Length to tip of wings 8 millim. Alar expanse 15 millim.

Hab. St. Lawrence River, Canada (Osten Sacken); Washington (id.).

15. H. incommoda!

Hydropsyche incommoda Hagen!

Luteous, with luteous hair; antennæ, palpi and feet luteous; head and thorax luteous, with luteous hair; anterior wings luteous, with luteous veins, and obsoletely irrorated with brownish-gray, especially at the pterostigma; posterior wings luteous; posterior tibiæ ciliated. Male.

Length to tip of wings 10 millim. Alar expanse 19 millim.

Hab. Georgia (Collection of Hagen).

16. H. bivittata!

Hydropsyche? bivittata Hagen!

Black, with black hair; antennæ pale whitish-yellow; palpi luteo-fuscous; feet whitish, the four posterior femora, tibiæ, and the apices of the tarsi brownish-black; wings black, the anterior ones with black hair, and two white, transverse streaks, the apical one interrupted.

Length to tip of wings 6 millim. Alar expanse 11 millim.

Hab. Panama. The specimen is mutilated;—does it belong to this genus?

PHILOPOTAMUS Leach.

Spurs arranged 2, 4, 4; ocelli three.

1. P. confusus.

Philopotamus confusus Walk.! Catal. 103, 7.

Black, with hoary pile; base of the antennæ annulated with testaceous; abdomen beneath, palpi and feet testaceous; wings cinereous, the anterior ones obsoletely irrorated with pale. (From the description of Walker.)

Length to tip of wings 12 millim. Alar expanse 23 millim.

Hab. Arctic America; Slave and Mackenzie Rivers (Richardson).

2. P. distinctus.

Philopotamus distinctus Walk.! Catal. 104, 11.

Black, with black and yellow hair; antennæ much longer than the body; palpi and feet testaceous; anterior wings brownish-gray, closely guttated with yellow. (From the description of Walker.)

Length to tip of wings 6 millim. Alar expanse 11 millim.

Hab. Trenton Falls, New York (Doubleday).

Does the apterous female of *Philopotamus* observed by Doubleday at the same place belong here? See Entomol. Mag. v. 279.

POLYCENTROPUS Curtis.

Spurs arranged 3, 4, 4; ocelli absent; female with the intermediate feet dilated; antennæ thick, rather short.

1. P. validus.

Polycentropus validus Walk.! Catal. 100, 10.

Blackish, with yellow hair, beneath ferruginous; maxillary palpi testaceous, the first article black; antennæ stout, fulvous; feet testaceous; wings cinereous, with yellow pubescence. (From the description of Walker.)

Length to tip of wings 8 millim. Alar expanse 15 millim.

Hab. United States (Doubleday).

2. P. crassicornis.

Polycentropus crassicornis Walk.! Catal. 101, 11.

Ferruginous, densely clothed with yellow hair, beneath testaceous; antennæ stout,. fulvous; palpi and feet testaceous; wings cinereous, the anterior ones with yellow pubescence and irroration. (From the description of Walker.)

Length to tip of wings 7—9 millim. Alar expanse 13—16 millim.

Hab. Georgia (Abbot).

A variety has the anterior wings immaculate.

3. P. invarius.

Polycentropus invarius Walk.! Catal. 101, 12.

Fulvous, with golden hair; vertex and disk of the thorax black; antennæ black, the base fulvous; feet testaceous; anterior wings subfuscous, with ferruginous veins; posterior wings cinereous. (From the description of Walker.)

Length to tip of wings 9 millim. Alar expanse 16 millim.

Hab. Nova Scotia (Redman).

4. P. crepuscularis.

Brachycentrus crepuscularis Walk.! Catal. 87, 6.

Black, with luteous hair; antennæ testaceous, obsoletely annulated with fuscous, the apex black; apices of the abdominal segments, and the legs testaceous; wings cinereous, the anterior ones with testaceous pubescence, veins fulvous. (From the description of Walker.)

Length to tip of wings 9 millim. Alar expanse 16 millim.

Hab. St. Martin's Falls, Albany River, Hudson's Bay (Barnston).

5. P. vestitus.

Polycentropus vestitus Hagen!

Luteo-fuscous, with fuscous hair; antennæ yellow, a little annulated with fuscous; palpi luteous; feet luteo-fuscous, the tarsi obsoletely annulated with yellow; head and thorax with fuscous hair; the disk with yellow hair; anterior wings fuscous, with fuscous hair; posterior wings black. Male.

Length to tip of wings 7 millim. Alar expanse 13 millim.

Hab. Washington (Osten Sacken).

6. P. cinereus!

Polycentropus cinereus Hagen!

Fuscous, with fuscous and whitish hair; antennæ fuscous, annulated with white; palpi luteous, head with white hair, occiput each side with fuscous hair; disk of the thorax with white hair; feet luteo-fuscous, the femora luteous; abdomen fuscous, beneath pale; anterior wings fuscous, with fuscous veins, and closely guttated with white; posterior wings blackish-gray, ciliated with black. Male and female.

Length to tip of wings 8—10 millim. Alar expanse 15—19 millim.

Hab. St. Lawrence River, Canada (Osten Sacken).

7. P. confusus!

Polycentropus confusus Hagen!

Fuscous, with luteous hair; antennæ yellow, annulated with fuscous; palpi fuscous, annulated with pale; disk of the head with luteous hair; feet luteo-fuscous; abdomen fuscous; the apex in the female triangular, acute; the anterior wings fuscous, closely guttated with yellow; posterior wings brownish-cinereous. Male and female.

Length to tip of wings 8—10 millim. Alar expanse 15—19 millim.

Hab. Trenton Falls (Osten Sacken); Washington (id.).

8. P. lucidus!

Polycentropus lucidus Hagen!

Luteous, subnude; antennæ luteo-fuscous, obsoletely annulated; palpi luteous; head and thorax luteo-fuscous, prothorax yellow; feet luteous; wings fusco-hyaline, with fuscous veins, the anterior ones subnude, in part a little clothed with luteous pile. Male.

Length to tip of wings 7 millim. Alar expanse 13 millim.

Hab. Trenton Falls (Osten Sacken); Pennsylvania (Zimmerman).

The specimen may have been defaced, and is possibly immature.

PSYCHOMYIA Latreille.

Spurs arranged 2, 4, 4; second, third and fourth articles of the maxillary palpi equal, longer than the first; wings rather acute, narrow; ocelli absent; apex of the abdomen of the female acute, recurved.

1. P. flavida!

Psychomyia flavida Hagen!

Yellow, with ochreous hair; antennæ whitish, with obsolete annulations; palpi and feet whitish; head and thorax luteous; anterior wings yellow, with dense ochreous hair and cilia; posterior wings cinereous, acute, with cinereous hair.

Length to tip of wings 5 millim. Alar expanse 9 millim.

Hab. St. Lawrence River, Canada (Osten Sacken); Washington (id.).

2. P. parva.

Hydroptila? *parva* Walk.! Catal. 134, 12.

Testaceous; dorsum of the abdomen piceous; wings whitish. (From the description of Walker.)

Length to tip of wings 4 millim. Alar expanse 6 millim.

Hab. St. Martin's Falls, Albany River, Hudson's Bay (Barnston).

The type is very much mutilated; it certainly is not an *Hydroptila*. Does it belong to this genus?

TINODES Stephens.

Spurs arranged 2, 4, 4; ocelli absent, the third article of the maxillary palpi longer than the others, almost equal to the fifth; apex of the abdomen of the female acute, recurved.

1. T. livida!

Tinodes? livida Hagen!

Luteous, with gray hair; antennæ luteous; palpi luteo-fuscous; feet pale, the anterior ones luteous; head and thorax luteo fuscous, with luteous hair; anterior wings gray, with gray hair and an anal luteous spot; posterior wings grayish hyaline. Female.

Length to tip of wings 8 millim. Alar expanse 15 millim.

Hab. St. Lawrence River, Canada (Osten Sacken).

Does it belong to this genus?

2. T. hirtipes.

Tinodes? hirtipes Curtis, Append. to Sir John Ross's Second Voyage. Wiegmann's Archiv. Zool. II, 1, 288.

Grayish-piceous; wings pale fuscous; it has the *habitus* of a *Tinodes*, but the reticulation is different; posterior tibiæ with only two spurs.

Alar expanse 19 millim.

Hab. Arctic America.

Is it a *Tinodes?*

Sub-Fam. RHYACOPHILIDES.

Maxillary palpi with the last article entire, straight, shorter than the rest.

RHYACOPHILA Pict.

Spurs arranged 3, 4, 4; three ocelli.

1. R. fuscula.

Neuronia fuscula Walk.! Catal. 10, 12.

Ferruginous, partly with black hair, beneath testaceous; thorax each side with a subfuscous spot; feet testaceous, apex of the anterior tibiæ fuscous; wings cinereous, the anterior ones irrorated with whitish and with many marginal guttæ. (From the description of Walker.)

Length to tip of wings 13 millim. Alar expanse 25 millim.

Hab. St. Martin's Falls, Albany River, Hudson's Bay (Barnston).

It is allied to *R. vulgaris* Pict.

2. R. torva!

Rhyacophila torva Hagen!

Rufo-fuscous; antennæ and palpi rufo-fuscous; head and thorax brownish-black; feet testaceous; abdomen luteous; wings fusco-hyaline, with fuscous veins; anterior ones with dense luteous guttæ. Male.

Length to tip of wings 10 millim. Alar expanse 19 millim.

Hab. Washington; Trenton Falls (Osten Sacken).

BERAEA Stephens.

Spurs arranged 2, 4, 4; palpi densely pilose; the first article of the antennæ thick, pilose; no ocelli.

1. B. maculata!

Beraea? maculata Hagen!

Black, with black hair; antennæ yellow, the base, middle and apex blackish-fuscous; palpi fuscous; feet whitish, annulated with black; abdomen pale beneath; anterior wings black, with black hair and cilia, with two white, transverse apical lines, and the apex pointed with white; posterior wings black, the anterior at the apex emarginated.

Length to tip of wings 4 millim. Alar expanse 7½ millim.

Hab. St. Lawrence River, Canada (Osten Sacken).

Does it belong to this genus?

2. B. viridiventris.

Phryganea viridiventris Say, West. Quart. Report. II, 160, 1.

Pale fuscous, with cinereous hair; antennæ pale fuscous, the base whitish; feet, head, and thorax beneath, white; abdomen green; the anterior wings blackish, ciliated, beyond the middle with a few whitish spots, somewhat arranged in two bands;

posterior wings black; intermediate tarsi dilated. (From the description of Say.)

Length to tip of wings 4 millim. Alar expanse 7½ millim.

Hab. Cincinnati, Ohio River, May; common (Say).

Is this not B. *maculata?*

CHIMARRHA Leach.

Spurs arranged 2, 4, 4; basal joint of the maxillary palpi short, the others longer, equal; three ocelli.

1. C. aterrima!

Chimarrha aterrima Hagen!

Deep black, with black hair; body, antennæ, palpi and feet black, the front with hardly hoary hair; anterior wings with black hair. Male and female.

Length to tip of wings 6—8 millim. Alar expanse 11—15 millim.

Hab. Pennsylvania; Washington; Dalton, Georgia; St. Lawrence River, Canada (Osten Sacken).

2. C. socia!

Chimarrha socia Hagen!

Blackish-fuscous, with fuscous hair; antennæ blackish-fuscous; palpi and feet luteous; head and thorax blackish-fuscous, with luteous hair; anterior wings blackish-fuscous, with fuscous hair, and black cilia; posterior wings blackish-hyaline.

Length to tip of wings 6 millim. Alar expanse 11 millim.

Hab. Washington (Osten Sacken).

3. C. obscura.

Beraea obscura Walk.! Catal. 121, 4.

Blackish, with fuscous hair; thorax and abdomen ferruginous; feet testaceous; antennæ black; wings brownish-black, ciliated. (From the description of Walker.)

Length to tip of wings 4¼ millim. Alar expanse 8 millim.

Hab. St. Martin's Falls, Albany River, Hudson's Bay (Barnston).

Does it belong to this genus?

4. C. pulchra!

Chimarrha pulchra Hagen!

Brownish-black, with golden hair; antennæ and palpi brownish-black; head and thorax orange, with golden hair; abdomen testaceous; feet brownish-black, the posterior femora testaceous; anterior wings brownish-black, with a longitudinal, broad, golden stripe, which is a little incurved towards the apex, at the anterior margin reaching to the pterostigma; posterior wings black.

Length to tip of wings 8—10 millim. Alar expanse 15—19 millim.

Hab. Cuba (Poey, Osten Sacken).

Ptilostomis kowalewskii Kol., from North America, Wien. Ent. Zeit. 1859, p. 21 (a new genus separated from *Rhyacophila*), is noticed only by name. It is unknown to me.

LIST

OF

SOUTH AMERICAN NEUROPTERA.

Fam. I. TERMITINA.

Calotermes Hagen.

castaneus! (Compare North Am. Neur.).
  Hab. Columbia, Venezuela; Brazil, Rio, St. Leopold; Chile.
nodulosus! *Calotermes nodulosus* Hagen, Linnæa, XII, 61, 11; pl. ii, fig. 4.
  Hab. Brazil, St. João del Rey.
rugosus! *Calotermes rugosus* Hagen, Linnæa, XII, 63, 12; pl. iii, fig. 4.
  Hab. Brazil, Constancia near Rio.
brevis! (See North Amer. Neur.).
  Hab. St. Fe de Bogota; Brazil.
serrifer! *Calotermes serrifer* Hagen, Linnæa, XII, 72, 19; pl. i. fig. 6.
  Hab. Santarem (Bates).

Hodotermes Hagen.

quadricollis! *Termes quadricollis* Rbr.! Neuropt. 304, 4. Linnæa, XII, 101, 12; pl. i. fig. 10. *Termes chilensis* Gay! Fn. Chil. Neuropt. pl. 1. fig. 1—3. *Termes pallidus* Walk.! Catal. Br. Mus. 504, 2.
  Hab. Chili (Gay).

Termes Linné.

dirus! *Termes dirus* Burm.! Hdb. II, 766, 8. Ramb.! Neuropt. 307, 13. Walk.! Catal. Br. Mus. 510, 9. Hagen! Peters' Reise Mozambique, II, 83; pl. iv, fig. 1—8. Linnæa! XII, 151, 14; pl. i. fig. 7; pl. ii, figs. 16, 17; pl. iii, figs. 17, 37—40. *T. flavicollis* Perty! Delect. 128, pl. xxv, figs. 11, 13. *T. fatalis* Perty! Delect. 127, pl. xxv, fig. 8. *Termes costatus* Ramb.! Neuropt. 305, 9. *Termes obscurum* Blanchard, Hist. Ins. pl. xlvii, fig. 1. Westwood! Introd. II, 12, fig. 58, 1. (*Soldier.*) *Termes spinosum* Latr.! Hist. Nat. XIII, 70, 8. Dictionn. d'hist. Nat. XXII, 63. *Termes dubius* Ramb.! Neuropt. 309, 17.
  Hab. Guiana; Brazil, Amazon, Carçara, Rio, Congonhas, Lagoa Santa (Burmeister).

grandis! *Termes grandis* RAMB.! Neuropt. 306, 10. WALK. Catal. Br. Mus. 519, 20. HAGEN! Linnæa, XII, 157, 15; pl. ii, fig. 10; pl. iii, fig. 16. *Termes decumanus* ERICHS.! Schomburgk, Reise Guiana, III, 582, 1. *Termes costatus* WALK. Catal. Br. Mus. 518, 19. *Termes fuscum* LATR.? Hist. Nat. XIII, 68, 2. Dictionn. d'hist. Nat. XXII, 60. HAB. Cayenne; British Guiana.

molestus! *Termes molestus* BURM.! Hdb. II, 766, 9. WALK. Catal. Br. Mus. 512, 10.. HAGEN! Linnæa, XII, 159, 16, pl. iii. fig. 19. HAB. Brazil; Amazon.

nigricans! *Termes nigricans* RAMB.! Neuropt. 308, 14. WALK. Catal. Br. Mus. 519, 23. HAGEN! Linnæa, XII, 162, 18. *Termes trinervius* ? HAGEN, Peters' Reise Mozamb. II, 85. *Termes destructor* FABR.? Entom. Syst. II, 89, 2. *Termes cephalotes* RAMB.? Neuropt. 309, 18. HAB. Brazil.

cumulans! *Termes cumulans* KOLLAR! Pohl's Reise Brazil. I, 111, fig. 9. KOLLAR! Brazil. laestige Insect. 13, fig. 9. HAGEN! Linnæa, XII, 165, 19; pl. ii, fig. 11; pl. iii, fig. 20. *Termes Americanus* RENGGER? Reise Paraguay. *Termes pallidipennis* BLANCHARD? Voyage d'Orbigny.
HAB. Brazil, Ypanema; Barra do Rio Negro (Natterer).

similis! *Termes similis* HAGEN! Linnæa, XII, 167, 20; pl. i, fig. 5; pl. iii, fig. 21.
HAB. Brazil, Lagoa Santa, Congonhas (Burmeister); Para.

striatus! *Termes striatus* HAGEN! Linnæa, XII, 171, 21. HAB. Brazil.

cingulatus! *Termes cingulatus* BURM.! Hdb. II, 767, 13. WALK. Catal. Br. Mus. 515, 14. HAGEN! Linnæa, XII, 187, 28; pl. i, fig. 13; pl. iii, fig. 24.
HAB. Brazil, Porto Allegro; British Guiana (Schomburgk).

marabitanas! *Termes marabitanas* HAGEN! Linnæa, XII, 191, 29; pl. i, fig. 4; pl. iii, fig. 25.
HAB. Brazil, St. Jose de Marabitanas (Natterer).

tenebrosus! *Termes tenebrosus* HAGEN! Linnæa, XII, 193, 30. HAB. Brazil, Ypanema, New Friburg, near Rio.

ater! *Termes ater* HAGEN! Linnæa, XII, 195, 31; pl. iii, fig. 26. *Termes morio* WALK.! Catal. Br. Mus. 514, 12.
HAB. Brazil, New Friburg (Burmeister); Columbia.

opacus! *Termes opacus* HAGEN! Linnæa, XII, 196, 32; pl. iii, fig. 27; pl. i, fig. 19.
HAB. Brazil, Lagoa Santa, Congonhas (Burmeister); Para; Cassapava.

testaceus! *Hemerobius testaceus* LINNÉ! Syst. Nat. X, 550, 6; XII, 912, 8; XIII, 2641, 8. *Termes testaceus* BURM.! Hdb. II, 767, 10. HAGEN! Linnæa, XII, 198, 33; pl. ii, fig. 12; pl. iii, fig. 28. *Termes morio* FABR. Entom. Syst. II, 90, 3. RAMB.! Neuropt. 305, 7. ERICHS.! Reise Guiana Schomburgk. III, 582, 2. *Termes nasutus* WALK.! Catal. Br. Mus. 506, 5. *Perla fusca* DEGEER! Mém. III, 567, 1; pl. xxvii, figs. 4, 5. RETZIUS, 60, 205.
HAB. Surinam; Cayenne; British Guiana; Venezuela, Puerto Cabello; Brazil, Para; Chili, Valparaiso; Santarem.

morio! (See Catal. North Amer. Neuropt.)
   HAB. Venezuela; Brazil, Santarem (Bates).
simplicinervis! *Termes simplicinervis* HAGEN! Linnæa, XII, 204, 35.
   HAB. Brazil, Santarem (Bates).
debilis! (See North Amer. Neuropt.)
   HAB. Brazil, Congonhas (Burmeister).
exiguus! *Termes exiguus* HAGEN! Linnæa, XII, 208, 39.
   HAB. Brazil, Santarem (Bates).
trispinosus! *Termes trispinosus* HAGEN! Linnæa, XII, 210, 41; pl. i, fig. 11.
   HAB. Brazil, Santarem (Bates) Miles.
rippertii! (See North Amer. Neuropt.)
   HAB. Columbia; Brazil, New Friburg; Ypanema.
arenarius! *Termes arenarius* HAGEN! Linnæa, XII, 222, 50. *Termes testaceus* WALK.! Catal. Br. Mus. 513, 11.
   HAB. Brazil, Santarem (Bates).
albidus! *Termes albidus* HAGEN! Linnæa, XII, 225, 51; pl. iii. 34.
   HAB. Brazil, Santarem (Bates).
devastans! *Termes devastans* KOLLAR! Pohl's Reise Brasil. I, fig. 8. KOLLAR! Brasil. laestig. Insect. 13, fig. 8. HAGEN! Linnæa, XII, 229, 54.
   HAB. Brazil, Rio.
tenuis! (See North Amer. Neuropt.)
   HAB. Brazil.
marginalis! *Hemerobius marginalis* LINNÉ! Syst. Nat. X, 550, 7; XII, 912, 9. *Termes marginalis* HAGEN! Linnæa, XII, 234. *Perla nasuta* DE GEER! Mém. III, 568; pl. xxvii, fig. 6, 7. RETZIUS, 60, 206. *Termes nasutum* LATR. Hist. Nat. XIII, 69, 4. Dictionn. d'hist. Nat. XXII, 61. BURM.! Hdb. II, 764, 4.
   HAB. Surinam.
nasutus! *Termes nasutum* PERTY! Delect. 127, pl. xxv, fig. 10. · HAGEN! Linnæa, XII, 237, 59, pl. ii, fig. 14; pl. iii, fig. 1.
   HAB. Brazil.

FAM. II. EMBIDINA.

Olyntha Gray.

brasiliensis. *Olyntha Brasiliensis* GRAY! Griff. Anim. Kingd. XV, 347; pl. lxxii, fig. 2. WESTW.! Trans. Linn. Soc. XVII, 373; pl. ii, fig. 3. BURM. Hdb. II, 770, 1. WALK.! Catal. Br. Mus. 532, 1.
   HAB. Brazil.
ruficapilla. *Olyntha ruficapilla* BURM. Hdb. II, 770, 2. WALK. Catal. Br. Mus. 532, 2.
   HAB. Brazil, Venezuela?
klugii. *Embia Klugii* RAMB. Neuropt. 313, 3. WALK. Catal. Br. Mus. 530, 3.
   HAB. Brazil.
   Olyntha staphilinoides WALK.! Catal. Br. Mus. 532, 3, from Brasil. Is it *Forficula?*

Fam. III. PSOCINA.

Thyrsophorus Burmeister.

speciosus! *Thyrsophorus speciosus* Burm.! Hdb. II, 782, 1. Walk. Catal. Br. Mus. 478, 1. *Thyrsophorus spinolae* Rbr.! Neuropt. 318, 1. Walk.! Catal. Br. Mus. 479, 3.
Hab. Brazil, Para.

pennicornis! *Thyrsophorus pennicornis* Burm.! Hdb. II, 782, 2. Walk. Catal. Br. Mus. 478, 2. *Thyrsophorus ramosus* Walk.! Catal. Br. Mus. 480, 5.
Hab. Brazil, Bahia, Para.

leucotelus. *Thyrsophorus leucotelus* Walk.! Catal. Br. Mus. 479, 4.
Hab. Brazil, Para.

anticus. *Thyrsophorus anticus* Walk.! Catal. Br. Mus. 480, 6.
Hab. Brazil, Para.

Psocus Latreille.

fuscipennis! *Psocus fuscipennis* Burm.! Hdb. II, 778, 9. Walk. Catal. Br. Mus. 484, 8.
Hab. Brazil.

opacus! *Psocus opacus* Hagen, Collect.
Hab. Brazil.

sticticus! *Psocus sticticus* Hagen, Collect.
Hab. Brazil.

albicinctus! *Psocus albicinctus* Hagen, Collect.
Hab. Brazil.

lepidus! *Psocus lepidus* Hagen, Collect.
Hab. Brazil.

quadrisignatus! *Psocus quadrisignatus* Hagen, Collect.
Hab. Brazil.

pictus! *Psocus pictus* Hagen, Collect.
Hab. Brazil.

marginatus! *Psocus marginatus* Hagen, Collect.
Hab. Brazil.

Fam. IV. PERLINA.

Perla Geoffroy.

nubes. *Perla nubes* Pict. Perl. 174, 9; pl. ix, fig. 7, 8. Walk. Catal. Br. Mus. 145, 14.
Hab. America.

braziliensis. *Perla braziliensis* Pict. Perl. 216, 24; pl. xviii, fig. 3. Walk. Catal. Br. Mus. 151, 36.
Hab. Brazil.

intermixta. *Perla intermixta* Walk.! Catal. Br. Mus. 153, 42.
Hab. Venezuela.

luteicollis. *Perla luteicollis* Walk.! Catal. Br. Mus. 154, 46.
Hab. Venezuela.

repanda! *Perla repanda* HAGEN, Collect.
HAB. Chili.
bifasciata! *Perla bifasciata* PICT.! Perl. 229, 30; pl. xx, fig. 5. WALK. Catal. Br. Mus. 156, 51.
HAB. Columbia.
signata. *Perla signata* Walk.! Catal. Br. Mus. 157, 54.
HAB. Venezuela.
gayi. *Perla gayi* PICT. Perl. 238, 33; pl. x, fig. 3. WALK. Catal. Br. Mus. 158, 55.
HAB. Chili.
longicauda! *Perla longicauda* PICT. Perl. 236, 34; pl. xxii, fig. 5—8. WALK. Catal. Br. Mus. 158, 57.
HAB. Brazil, New Friburg.
dilaticollis! (See North Amer. Neuropt.)
HAB. Columbia.
hyalina. *Perla hyalina* PICT. Perl. 247, 39; pl. xxi, fig. 5—10. WALK. Catal. Br. Mus. 159, 61.
HAB. Brazil.
annulicauda. (See North Amer. Neuropt.)
HAB. Brazil.
annularis. *Perla annularis* PICT. Perl. 252, 42; pl. xxv, fig. 3—5. WALK. Catal. Br. Mus. 160, 63.
HAB. Brazil.
debilis. *Perla debilis* PICT. Perl. 255, 44; pl. xxvi, fig. 4. WALK. Catal. Br. Mus. 161, 66.
HAB. Brazil.
klugii. *Perla klugii* PICT. Perl. 267, 50; pl. xxv, fig. 1—2. WALK. Catal. Br. Mus. 162, 72.
HAB. Brazil.
obscura. *Perla obscura* PICT. Perl. 269, 51; pl. xxviii, fig. 1—4. WALK. Catal. Br. Mus. 163, 73.
HAB. Brazil.
polita. *Perla polita* Burm. Hdb. II, 879, 6. PICT. Perl. 271, 52; pl. xxviii, fig. 5—9. WALK. Catal. Br. Mus. 163, 74.
HAB. Brazil.
morio! *Perla morio* PICT.! Perl. 272, 53; pl. xxx, fig. 1—5. WALK. Catal. Br. Mus. 163, 75.
HAB. Columbia.
fenestrata! *Perla fenestrata* PICT.! Perl. 281, 57; pl. xxxi, fig. 1—4. WALK. Catal. Br. Mus. 167, 85.
HAB. Columbia.

Capnia Pictet.

cancellata. *Capnia cancellata* PICT. Perl. 328, 4; pl. xli. Walk. Catal. Br. Mus. 175, 4.
HAB. Brazil.
gracilis! *Capnia gracilis* PICT.! Perl. 330, 5; pl. xlii, fig. 1—3. WALK. Catal. Br. Mus. 175, 5.
HAB. Brazil.

Fam. V. EPHEMERINA.

Ephemera Linné.
colombiæ. *Ephemera colombiae* WALK. Catal. 537, 6.
  HAB. Columbia.

Palingenia Burmeister.
albicans. *Ephemera albicans* PERCHERON, Gen. Ins. Livr. VI, Neuropt. pl. vi. *Palingenia albicans* BURM. Hdb. II, 803. PICT. Ephemer. 149, 4; vol. xiii, fig. 1—3. WALK. Catal. 548, 4.
  HAB. Brazil.
dorsalis! *Palingenia dorsalis* BURM. Hdb. II, 803, 3. PICTET. Ephemer. 153, 6, tab. xiii, fig. 5. WALK. Catal. 549, 5.
  HAB. Brazil.
atrostoma. *Ephemera atrostoma* WEBER. Obs. Entom. 99, 1. PICTET. Ephemer. 157. WALK. Catal. 550, 9.
  HAB. Brazil.
albifilum. *Palingenia albifilum* WALK.! Catal. 554, 19.
  HAB. Para.
curta. *Palingenia curta* HAGEN. *Palingenia albifilum* WALK.! var. Catal. 554, 19.
  HAB. Para.
latipennis. *Palingenia latipennis* WALK.! Catal. 554, 20.
  HAB. Para.
umbrata! *Palingenia umbrata* HAGEN, Collect.
  HAB. Amazon.
dorsigera! *Palingenia dorsigera* HAGEN, Collect.
  HAB. Montevideo.

Baëtis Leach.
albivitta. *Baëtis albivitta* Walk. Catal. 566, 33.
  HAB. Para.

Cloë Leach.
fasciata! *Cloë fasciata* PICTET. Ephemer. 262, 9; tab. xli, fig. 4. WALK. Catal. 575, 9.
  HAB. Brazil.

Oligoneuria Pictet.
anomala! *Oligoneuria anomala* PICT.! Ephemer. 291, tab. xlvi et xlvii. HAGEN! Stett. Ent. Zeit. XVI, 269, 2. WALK. Catal. 585, 1.
  HAB. Brazil.

FAM. VI. ODONATA.

Tribe I. AGRIONINA.

Sub-Fam. I. CALOPTERYGINA.

Lais HAGEN.

globifer! *Lais globifer* HAGEN! Monogr. Calopt. 88, 28; tab. x, fig. 1. SELYS! Synops. 27, 28. WALK. Catal. 613, 1.
HAB. Brazil, New Friburg.

aenea! *Lais aenea* SELYS! Monogr. Calopt. 91, 29; tab. x, fig. 2. SELYS! Synops. 28, 29. WALK. Catal. 613, 2.
HAB. Para.

cuprea! *Lais cuprea* SELYS! Monogr. Calopt. 92, 30; SELYS! Synops. 28, 30. WALK.! Catal. 613, 3.
HAB. Brazil, Para.

hyalina! *Lais hyalina* HAGEN! Monogr. Calopt. 92, 31. SELYS! Synops. 28, 31. WALK. Catal. 613, 4.
HAB. Brazil.

pruinosa! *Lais pruinosa* HAGEN! Monogr. Calopt. 93, 32; tab. x, fig. 3. SELYS! Synops. 28, 32. WALK. Catal. 615, 5.
HAB. Brazil.

pudica! *Lais pudica* HAGEN! Monogr. Calopt. 95, 33; tab. x, fig. 4. SELYS! Synops. 29, 33. WALK. Catal. 615, 6.
HAB. Brazil, Ypanema.

Hetaerina Hagen.

simplex! *Hetaerina simplex* SELYS! Monogr. Calopt. 98, 34; tab. x, fig. 5. SELYS! Synops. 30, 34. WALK. Catal. 616, 7.
HAB. Brazil, Minas Geraës.

sanguinea! *Hetaerina sanguinea* SELYS! Monogr. Calopt. 100, 35; tab. x, fig. 6. SELYS! Synops. 31, 35. WALK. Catal. 617, 8.
HAB. Para.

rosea! *Hetaerina rosea* SELYS! Monogr. Calopt. 102, 36; tab. x, fig. 7. SELYS! Synops. 31, 36. WALK. Catal. 617, 9.
HAB. Brazil, Minas Geraës; Chili.

caja! *Libellula caja* DRURY, II, 82; tab. xlv, fig. 2. *Calopteryx caja* BURM.! Hdb. II, 826, 5. *Hetaerina caja* SELYS! Monogr. Calopt. 104. 37; tab. x, fig. 8. SELYS! Synops. 32, 37. WALK. Catal. 618, 10.
HAB. Columbia, Venezuela, Porto Cabello (Appun).

dominula! *Hetaerina dominula* HAGEN! Monogr. Calopt. 107, 38; tab. xi, fig. 1. SELYS! Synops. 33, 38. *Calopteryx caja* ERICHS.! Voyag. Schomburgk, III. WALK. Catal. 619, 11.
HAB. Guiana, Surinam; Brazil.

auripennis! *Calopteryx auripennis* BURM.! Hdb. II, 827, 10. RAMB. Neuropt. 225, 13. *Hetaerina auripennis* SELYS! Monogr. Calopt. 109, 39; tab. xi, fig. 2. SELYS! Synops. 33, 39. WALK. Catal. 619, 12.
HAB. Brazil, Bahia, Rio.

hebe! *Hetaerina hebe* SELYS! Monogr. Calopt. 112, 40; tab. xi, fig. 3. SELYS! Synops. 34, 40. WALK. Catal. 620, 13.
HAB. Brazil.

sanguinolenta! *Hetaerina sanguinolenta* HAGEN! Monogr. Calopt. 115, 41; tab. xi, fig. 4. SELYS! Synops. 35, 41. WALK. Catal. 621, 14.
HAB. Brazil, Bahia.

mortua! *Hetaerina mortua* HAGEN! Monogr. Calopt. 117, 42; tab. xi, fig. 5. SELYS! Synops. 35, 42. WALK. Catal. 621, 15.
HAB. Guiana.

laesa! *Hetaerina laesa* HAGEN! Monogr. Calopt. 119, 44. SELYS! Synops. 36, 44. WALK. Catal. 622, 17.
HAB. Surinam.

longipes! *Hetaerina longipes* HAGEN! Monogr. Calopt. 121, 45; tab. xi, fig. 7. SELYS! Synops. 37, 45. WALK. Catal. 623, 18.
HAB. Brazil.

carnifex! *Hetaerina carnifex* HAGEN! Monogr. Calopt. 123, 46; tab. xi, fig. 8. SELYS! Synops. 37, 46. WALK. Catal. 624, 19.
HAB. Brazil, New Friburg, Minas Geraës.

proxima! *Hetaerina proxima* SELYS! Monogr. Calopt. 125, 47; tab. xi, fig. 9. SELYS! Synops. 38, 47. WALK. Catal. 624, 20.
HAB. Brazil, Ypanema.

cruentata! (See North American Neuropt.)
HAB. Venezuela, Merida, Paranas de St. Urban; Surinam.

vulnerata! (See North American Neuropt.)
HAB. Columbia, Brazil.

americana! (See North American Neuropt.)
HAB. Brazil.

moribunda! *Hetaerina moribunda* HAGEN! Monogr. Calopt. 134, 154; tab. xii, fig. 4. SELYS! Synops. 42, 51. WALK. Catal. 628, 24.
HAB. Cayenne; Brazil, Para.

occisa! *Hetaerina occisa* HAGEN! Monogr. Calopt. 143, 55; tab. xii, fig. 6. SELYS! Synops. 44, 55. WALK. Catal. 631, 28.
HAB. Columbia, Venezuela, Porto Cabello, Laguayra, Paranas de St. Urban.

brightwelli! *Agrion brightwelli* KIRBY, Trans. Linn. Soc. XIV, 107; tab. iii, fig. 5. *Calopteryx brightwelli* BURM. Hdb. II, 826, 5. *Hetaerina brightwelli* SELYS! Monogr. Calopt. 148, 57; tab. xii, fig. 8. SELYS! Synops. 46, 57. WALK. Catal. 633, 30.
HAB. Brazil, Rio, New Friburg, Irisauga.

majuscula! *Hetaerina majuscula* SELYS! Monogr. 151, 58; tab. xiii, fig. 1. SELYS! Synops. 47, 58. WALK. Catal. 634, 31.
HAB. Columbia; Surinam.

Heliocharis Selys.

amazona! *Heliocharis amazona* SELYS! Monogr. Calopt. 188, 1; tab. xiv, fig. 5. SELYS! Synops. 55, 71. WALK. Catal. 642, 1.
HAB. Brazil, Ega (Bates), Amazon River.

brasiliensis! *Heliocharis brasiliensis* HAGEN! addit. Synops. Calopt. 9, 71, bis.
HAB. Brazil, Bahia.

Dicterias Selys.

atrosanguinea! *Dicterias atrosanguinea* SELYS! Monogr. Calopt. 191, 72; tab. xiv, fig. 6. SELYS! Synops. 56, 72. WALK. Catal. 643, 2.
HAB. Amazon River (Bates).

procera! *Dicterias procera* HAGEN! addit. Synops. Calopt. 10, 72, bis.
HAB. Amazon River, Santarem (Bates).

Amphipteryx Selys.

agrioides! *Amphipteryx agrioides* SELYS! Monogr. Calopt. 241, 92. SELYS! Synops. 66, 1. WALK. Catal. 654, 1.
HAB. Colombia.

Chalcopteryx Selys.

rutilans! *Chalcopteryx rutilans* SELYS! Monogr. Calopt. 251, 94; tab. ix, fig. 7. SELYS! Synops. 68, 94. WALK. Catal. 655, 1. *Rhinocypha rutilans* RAMB.! Neuropt. 233, 1.
HAB. Brazil, Para.

Thore Hagen.

gigantea! *Thore gigantea* SELYS! Monogr. Calopt. 254, 1. SELYS! Synops. 69, 95. WALK. Catal. 656, 2.
HAB. Colombia, Bogota.

picta! *Euphaea picta* RAMB. Neuropt. 231, 4. *Thore picta* SELYS! Monogr. Calopt. 256, 96. SELYS! Synops. 70, 96. WALK. Catal. 656, 3.
HAB. Cayenne; Para.

saundersii! *Thore saundersii* SELYS! Monogr. Calopt. 257, 97. SELYS! Synops. 70, 97. WALK. Catal. 657, 4.
HAB. Amazon River; Para.

fasciata! *Thore fasciata* HAGEN! Monogr. Calopt. 259, 98; tab. ix, fig. 8. SELYS! Synops. 70, 98. WALK. Catal. 657, 5.
HAB. Colombia, Venezuela, Porto Cabello (Appun).

hyalina! *Thore hyalina* SELYS! Monogr. Calopt. 261, 99. SELYS! Synops. 71, 99. WALK. Catal. 658, 8.
HAB. Bahia.

fastigiata! *Thore fastigiata* SELYS! addit. Synops. 16, 99, bis.
HAB. Colombia, Bogota.

Cora Selys.

cyane! *Cora cyane* SELYS! Monogr. Calopt. 263, 100. SELYS! Synops. 71, 100. WALK. Catal. 658, 7.
HAB. Venezuela, Porto Cabello (Appun).

Sub-Fam. II. AGRIONINA.

Megaloprepus Rambur.

caerulatus! (See the North American Neuropt.) Var. *bolivar* SELYS.
HAB. Colombia, Bogota.

Microstigma Rambur.

anomalum! *Microstigma anomalum* RBR. Neuropt. 289, 1. *Microstigma proximum* RBR. Neuropt. 289, 2.
    HAB. Amazon River, Santarem, Para (Bates), Cayenne.
rotundatum! *Microstigma rotundatum* SELYS! Var. *M. exustum* SELYS! Var. *M. lunatum* SELYS!
    HAB. Peru; Amazon River; Para (Bates).
maculatum! *Microstigma maculatum* HAGEN!
    HAB. Cayenne; Amazon River, Santarem (Bates); Essequibo.

Pseudostigma Selys.

accedens! *Pseudostigma accedens* SELYS! (See North Amer. Neuropt.)
    HAB. Colombia.

Mecistogaster Rambur.

ornatus! (See North American Neuropt.)
    HAB. Venezuela, Caraccas; Surinam; Lima.
astictus! *Mecistogaster astictus* HAGEN!
    HAB. Brazil, New Friburg.
linearis! *Agrion linearis* FABR. Entom. Syst. II, 388, 5. *Mecistogaster filigerus* RBR.! Neuropt. 287, 10, mas. *Mecistogaster signatus* RBR. Neuropt. 286, 9, fem. *Mecistogaster flavistigma* RAMB. Neuropt. 287, 11? fem.
    HAB. Guiana; Surinam; Amazon River; Para; Santarem, Colombia.
lucretia! (See North American Neuropt.)
    HAB. Brazil, Amazon River.
marchali! *Mecistogaster marchali* RBR. Neuropt. 283, 2. *Mecistogaster filum* RAMB.! Neuropt. 284, 3. *Mecistogaster pedicellatus* RAMBR.! Neuropt. 284, 5.
    HAB. Guiana; Surinam; Amazon River; Para.

Lestes Leach.

grandis! (See North American Neuropt.)
    HAB. Colombia.
forficula! (See North American Neuropt.)
    HAB. Brazil.
undulata! *Lestes undulata* SAY, Journ. Acad. Philad. VIII, 35. *Lestes vittata* HAGEN! Revue des Odonat. d'Europe, 331.
    HAB. Montevideo; Buenos Ayres; Valdivia.
picta! *Lestes picta* HAGEN.
    HAB. Brazil.
tricolor! *Lestes tricolor* ERICHS.! Voyag. Schomburgk, III.
    HAB. Guiana; Bahia; Pernambuco.
contorta! *Lestes contorta* HAGEN!
    HAB. Brazil, New Friburg.
striata. *Lestes striata* SELYS.
    HAB. Venezuela, Cayenne (not seen by me).
minuta. *Lestes minuta* SELYS.
    HAB. Brazil (not seen by me).

NEONEURA.

Hyponeura SELYS.

funckii! *Hyponeura funckii* SELYS!
   HAB. Colombia.

Euclea Selys.

terminalis. *Euclea terminalis* SELYS.
   HAB. Amazon River (not seen by me).

Podagrion Selys.

oscillans. *Podagrion oscillans* SELYS.
   HAB. Bogota (not seen by me).
megalopus. *Podagrion megalopus* SELYS.
   HAB. Amazon River (not seen by me).
macropus. *Podagrion macropus* SELYS.
   HAB. Venezuela, Merida (not seen by me).
flavovittatum! *Podagrion flavovittatum* SELYS!
   HAB. Brazil, Minas Geraës.
venale! *Podagrion venale* HAGEN!
   HAB. Colombia.

Leptogaster Selys.

ovatus. *Leptogaster ovatus* SELYS.
   HAB. Bahia (not seen by me).
aurantiacus! *Leptogaster aurantiacus* HAGEN!
   HAB. Brazil.
cinnamomeus! *Leptogaster cinnamomeus* HAGEN!
   HAB. Bahia.
sordidus. *Leptogaster sordidus* SELYS.
   HAB. Santarem (not seen by me).
angustus. *Leptogaster angustus* SELYS.
   HAB. Santarem (not seen by me).

Neoneura Selys.

ciliaris! *Neoneura ciliaris* SELYS!
   HAB. Brazil; perhaps *N. ancilla*.
bilinearis! *Neoneura bilinearis* SELYS!
   HAB. Para.
rubriventris! *Neoneura rubriventris* SELYS!
   HAB. Para.
fragilis! *Agrion fragile* HAGEN!
   HAB. Brazil, New Friburg.

Sub-gen. *Notosticta* DE SELYS.

melanostigma! *Neoneura melanostigma* HAGEN!
   HAB. Venezuela.

Protoneura Selys.

sancta! *Protoneura sancta* HAGEN!
  HAB. Columbia.
tenuis. *Protoneura tenuis* SELYS.
  HAB. Para.

Agrion Fabricius.

Sub-gen. *Ischnura* CHARPENTIER.

gracile! *Agrion gracile* RAMB.! Neuropt. 260, 4.
  HAB. Brazil, Venezuela.
truncatum. *Agrion truncatum* SELYS.
  HAB. Minas Geraës, Brazil.
chelifer. *Agrion chelifer* SELYS.
  HAB. Minas Geraës, Brazil.
tuberculatum! (See North American Neuroptera.)
  HAB. Cayenne.
versutum! *Agrion versutum* HAGEN!
  HAB. Chili.
simile! *Agrion simile* SELYS!
  HAB. Venezuela, Merida.
rusticum! *Agrion rusticum* HAGEN!
  HAB. Bahia.
debile! *Agrion debile* HAGEN!
  HAB. Rio, Brazil.
cinctum! *Agrion cinctum* HAGEN!
  HAB. Quillota, Chili.
floridum! *Agrion floridum* HAGEN!
  HAB. Lima.
hastatum! (See North American Neuroptera.)
  HAB. Merida.
capreolus! (See North American Neuroptera.)
  HAB. Brazil.

Sub-genus (new).

macilentum. *Agrion macilentum* RBR. Neuropt. 259, 4.
  HAB. Brazil.
bicorne. *Agrion bicorne* SELYS.
  HAB. Para.
bitaeniatum. *Agrion bitaeniatum* SELYS.
  HAB. Brazil.
longissimum! *Agrion longissimum* SELYS.
  HAB. Brazil.

Sub-genus (new).

briseis! *Agrion briseis* HAGEN!
  HAB. Brazil.
elongatum. *Agrion elongatum* SELYS.
  HAB. Brazil.

porrectum! *Agrion porrectum* HAGEN.
    HAB. Brazil.
glaucopis! *Agrion glaucopis* HAGEN!
    HAB. Bahia.
iris! *Agrion iris* HAGEN!
    HAB. Bahia.
thetis! *Agrion thetis* HAGEN!
    HAB. Bahia.
andromache! *Agrion andromache* HAGEN!
    HAB. Brazil.
macrurum! *Agrion macrurum* BURM.! Hdb. II, 819, 4.
    HAB. Brazil.

Sub-gen. *Pyrrhosoma* CHARPENTIER.

flavipes. *Agrion flavipes* SELYS.
    HAB. Brazil.
corallinum. *Agrion corallinum* SELYS.
    HAB. Brazil.
coccineum. *Agrion coccineum* SELYS.
    HAB. Brazil, Minas Geraës.
erythrinum. *Agrion erythrinum* SELYS.
    HAB. Brazil, Minas Geraës.
rubellum. *Agrion rubellum* SELYS.
    HAB. Brazil.
rubidum. *Agrion rubidum* RAMB. Neuropt. 261, 8.
    HAB. Buenos Ayres.
haematinum! *Agrion haematinum* SELYS!
    HAB. Brazil, Minas Geraës.
terminale. *Agrion terminale* SELYS.
    HAB. Brazil, Minas Geraës.
vulneratum! (See N. American Neuroptera.)
    HAB. Guiana.
sulphuratum! *Agrion sulphuratum* HAGEN!
    HAB. Bahia.
croceum! *Agrion croceum* BURM.! Hdb. II, 819, 6.
    HAB. Surinam.
rubens. *Agrion rubens* SELYS.
    HAB. Brazil.
basale. *Agrion basale* SELYS.
    HAB. Brazil.
angustipenne. *Agrion angustipenne* SELYS.
    HAB. Brazil, Minas Geraës.
dispar! *Agrion dispar* HAGEN!
    HAB. Brazil, Minas Geraës.
filiola! *Agrion filiola* PERTY, Delect. Anim. 125; tab. xxv, fig. 4.
    HAB. Brazil, Minas Geraës, Pernambuco, Bahia.
pavidum! *Agrion pavidum* HAGEN!
    HAB. Brazil, New Friburg.
rufovittatum. *Agrion rufovittatum* BLANCHARD, Voyag. d'Orbigny.
    HAB. Bolivia.

Sub-gen. *Agrion* CHARPENTIER.

dorsale! *Agrion dorsale* BURM.! Hdb. II, 819, 5.
HAB. Brazil.
modestum. *Agrion modestum* SELYS.
HAB. Brazil, Minas Geraës.
sordidum! *Agrion sordidum* HAGEN!
HAB. Brazil, New Friburg.
fissum. *Agrion fissum* SELYS.
HAB. Columbia.
impurum. *Argya impura* RAMB. Neuropt. 255, 1.
HAB. Para.
claussenii! *Agrion claussenii* SELYS!
HAB. Brazil.
oculatum! *Agrion oculatum* HAGEN!
HAB. Venezuela; Pernambuco.
infumatum! *Agrion infumatum* SELYS!
HAB. Para.
serva! *Agrion serva* HAGEN!
HAB. Brazil.
insipidum! *Agrion insipidum* HAGEN!
HAB. Guiana.
incultum! *Agrion incultum* HAGEN!
HAB. Lima.
torvum! *Agrion torvum* HAGEN!
HAB. Quillota.
nuptum! *Agrion nuptum* HAGEN!
HAB. Quillota.
cupreum! (See North American Neuroptera.)
HAB. Venezuela.

Tribe II. **AESCHNINA.**

Sub-Fam. III. GOMPHINA.

Gomphus Leach.

crotalinus! (See North American Neuropt.)
HAB. Brazil.
paludosus! *Epigomphus paludosus* HAGEN! Gomphin. 85, 22.
HAB. Brazil.
molestus! *Hemigomphus molestus* HAGEN! Gomphin. 183, 65.
HAB. Chili.

Gomphoides Selys.

gracilis! *Progomphus gracilis* HAGEN! Gomphin. 189, 67.
HAB. Brazil, New Friburg.
complicata! *Progomphus complicata* SELYS! Gomphin. 198, 68.
HAB. Brazil, Bahia.
costalis! *Progomphus costalis* HAGEN! Gomph. 200, 69.
HAB. Brazil.

intricata! *Progomphus intricatus* HAGEN! Gomphin. 421, 68, bis.
HAB. Amazon.
infumata! *Diastatomma infumatum* RAMB.! Neuropt. , 4. *Gomphoides infumata* SELYS! Gomphin. 210, 73.
HAB. Brazil.
fuliginosa! *Gomphoides fuliginosa* HAGEN! Gomphin. 211, 74.
HAB. British Guiana, Essequibo.
audax! *Gomphoides audax* HAGEN! Gomphin. 213, 75..
HAB. Brazil.
diphylla! *Cyclophylla diphylla* SELYS! Gomphin. 217, 77.
HAB. Brazil.
gladiata! *Cyclophylla gladiata* HAGEN! Gomphin. 219, 78.
HAB. Brazil, Pernambuco.
signata! *Cyclophylla signata* HAGEN! Gomphin. 220, 79.
HAB. Brazil, Venezuela.
sordida! *Cyclophylla sordida* SELYS! Gomphin. 223, 80.
HAB. Para.
brevipes! *Aphylla brevipes* SELYS! Gomphin. 227, 82.
HAB. Para.
producta! (See North American Neuropt.)
HAB. British Guiana; Surinam; Brazil, Bahia.
dentata! *Aphylla dentata* SELYS! addit. Synops. 21, 81, bis.
HAB. Amazon (Bates).
campanulata! *Diastatomma campanulata* BURM.! Hdb. II, , 4. *Conophora campanulata* SELYS! Gomphin. 234, 84.
HAB. Brazil.
angustipennis! *Diaphlebia angustipennis* SELYS! Gomphin. 237, 85.
HAB. Amazon, Para.
brevistylus! (See North American Neuropt.)
HAB. Colombia.

Ictinus Rambur.

latro! *Ictinus latro* ERICHS.! Schomburgk, Reise Guiana, III. SELYS! Gomphin. 294, 102.
HAB. British Guiana.

Cordulegaster Leach.

diastatops! *Thecaphora diastatops* SELYS! Gomphin. 320, 105.
HAB. Colombia.

Petalia Hagen.

punctata! *Petalia punctata* HAGEN! Gomphin. 353, 117.
HAB. Chili, Ouchacay.
stictica! *Phyllopetalia stictica* HAGEN! Gomphin. 357, 118.
HAB. Chili, Valdivia.
apicalis! *Phyllopetalia apicalis* SELYS! Gomphin. 359, 119.
HAB. Chili, Valdivia.

Phenes Rambur.

raptor! *Phenes raptor* RAMB.! Neuropt. 176, 1. SELYS! Gomphin. 377, 123.
HAB. Chili, Valparaiso.

Sub-Fam. IV. AESCHNINA.

Anax Leach.

amazili! (See North American Neuropt.)
HAB. Venezuela, Brazil, Pernambuco.

Aeschna Fabricius.

variegata. *Aeschna variegata* FABR. Entom. Syst. II, 384, 2.
HAB. Terra del Fuego (Banks).
costalis! *Aeschna costalis* BURM.! Hdb. II, 837, 3. *Gynacantha ferox* ERICHS.! Schomburgk. Guiana, III.
HAB. Guiana; Bahia.
luteipennis! *Aeschna luteipennis* BURM.! Hdb. II, 837, 4.
HAB. Brazil; St. Leopoldo.
reticulata! *Aeschna reticulata* BURM.! Hdb. II, 837, 5.
HAB. Brazil; Venezuela.
virens! *Aeschna virens* RBR.! Neuropt. 193, 3. (See North American Neuroptera.)
HAB. St. Cruz de Bolivia; Venezuela.
marchali. *Aeschna marchali* RAMB. Neuropt. 203, 14.
HAB. Columbia.
diffinis! *Aeschna diffinis* RBR. Neuropt. 203, 15.
HAB. Chili.
bonariensis! *Aeschna Bonariensis* RBR. Neuropt. 204, 16.
HAB. Buenos Ayres; St. Leopoldo.
confusa. *Aeschna confusa* RAMB. Neuropt. 205, 17.
HAB. Buenos Ayres.
angusta! *Aeschna angusta* HAGEN!
HAB. Brazil.(?)
jucunda! *Aeschna jucunda* HAGEN!
HAB. Montevideo, New Friburg; Venezuela.
prasina! *Aeschna prasina* HAGEN!
HAB. Pernambuco.
configurata! *Aeschna configurata* HAGEN!
HAB. Valparaiso.
depravata! *Aeschna depravata* HAGEN!
HAB. Brazil; New Friburg.
lobata! *Aeschna lobata* HAGEN!
HAB. Brazil. New Friburg.
brevifrons! (See North American Neuropt.)
HAB. Valparaiso.
rufina! *Aeschna rufina* HAGEN!
HAB. Brazil, Minas Geraës.

faunaria! *Aeschna faunaria* HAGEN!
Hab. Brazil, Rio.

Gynacantha Rambur.

gracilis! *Aeschna gracilis* BURM.! Hdb. II, 837. 6. *Gynacantha nervosa* RAMB. Neuropt. 213, 7.
Hab. Brazil, St. Cruz de Bolivia, Surinam, Pernambuco, Rio.
trifida! (See North American Neuropt.)
Hab. Brazil.
septima. (See North American Neuropt.)
Hab. Brazil.
lanceolata! *Gynacantha lanceolata* HAGEN.
Hab. Pernambuco.
elata! *Gynacantha elata* HAGEN!
Hab. Brazil, New Friburg.
obscuripennis! *Aeschna obscuripennis* BLANCHARD, Voyag. d'Orbigny.
Hab. Bolivia; Venezuela.
tenuis! *Gynacantha tenuis* HAGEN!
Hab. Brazil.
conica! *Gynacantha conica* HAGEN!
Hab. Venezuela, Surinam.

Tribe III. LIBELLULINA.

Sub-Fam. V. CORDULINA.

Cordulia Leach.

valga! *Cordulia valga* HAGEN!
Hab. Brazil, New Friburg.
forcipula! *Cordulia forcipula* HAGEN!
Hab. Brazil, Mus. Berlin.
rustica! *Cordulia rustica* HAGEN!
Hab. Brazil, Mus. Berlin.
setifera! *Cordulia setifera* HAGEN!
Hab. Brazil, Mus. Berol.
chilensis! *Cordulia chilensis* HAGEN!
Hab. Chili; Brazil, Salto Grande.
tomentosa. *Libellula tomentosa* FABR. Entom. Syst. II, 381, 34.
Hab. America.
villosa. *Cordulia villosa* RBR. Neuropt. 144, 1.
Hab. Chili.

Sub-Fam. VI. LIBELLULINA.

Pantala Hagen.

flavescens! (See North American Neuropt.)
Hab. Venezuela; Surinam; Brazil.

Tramea Hagen.

basalis! *Libellula basalis* BURM. Hdb. II, 852, 25.
    HAB. Brazil.
binotata! *Libellula binotata* RBR.! Neuropt. 36, 7.
    HAB. Brazil, Minas Geraës.
cophysa! *Libellula cophysa* KOLLAR.
    HAB. Brazil.
marcella! *Libellula marcella* SELYS.
    HAB. Brazil.
argo! *Tramea argo* HAGEN!
    HAB. Rio, Brazil.

Libellula Linné.

appendiculata! *Libellula appendiculata* SELYS!
    HAB. Merida, Venezuela.
umbrata! (See North American Neuropt.)
    HAB. Venezuela, Porto Cabello; Guiana; Surinam; Essequibo; Brazil, Bahia, Rio; Buenos Ayres. Everywhere common.
cyanea. *Libellula cyanea* FABR. Entom. Syst. II, 381, 36.
    HAB. America.
    It is a species unknown to me; perhaps *L. quadrupla?*, but the "abdomen" is said to be "cylindrical."

Sub-gen. *Orthemis* HAGEN.

discolor! (See North American Neuropt.)
    HAB. Venezuela, Porto Cabello; Guiana; Surinam; Chili; Ecuador, Guayaquil; Brazil, Bahia, Pernambuco, Minas Geraës, Rio. Extremely common.

Lepthemis Hagen.

vesiculosa! (See North American Neuropt.)
    HAB. Guiana; Brazil, Pernambuco, Bahia, Rio.
haematogastra! (See North American Neuropt.)
    HAB. Surinam; Brazil, Pernambuco.
verbenata! (See North American Neuropt.)
    HAB. Venezuela, Porto Cabello; Surinam; Brazil.
picta! *Lepthemis picta* HAGEN!
    HAB. Brazil.
cardinalis! *Libellula cardinalis* ERICHS.! Schomburgk, Voyag. Guiana, III, 583.
    HAB. Guiana, Essequibo.
attenuata! *Libellula attenuata* ERICHS.! Schomburgk, Voyag. Guiana, III, 583.
    HAB. Guiana; Brazil.
extensa! *Lepthemis extensa* HAGEN!
    HAB. Brazil, Pernambuco.
cultriformis! *Lepthemis cultriformis* HAGEN!
    HAB. Brazil.

Dythemis Hagen.

pleurosticta! (See North American Neuroptera.)
   HAB. Brazil.
tenuis! *Dythemis tenuis* HAGEN!
   HAB. Brazil, New Friburg.
infamis! *Dythemis infamis* HAGEN!
   HAB. Brazil, Pernambuco.
marmorata! *Dythemis marmorata* HAGEN!
   HAB. Brazil, New Friburg.
hemichlora! *Libellula hemichlora* BURM.! Hdb. II, 849, 4.
   HAB. Venezuela, Porto Cabello; Brazil, Bahia.
tessellata! *Libellula tessellata* BURM.! Hdb. II, 849, 5.
   HAB. Brazil.
sterilis! *Dythemis sterilis* HAGEN! *Libellula tessellata* RAMB.! Neuropt. 89, 82.
   HAB. Venezuela; Brazil, Pernambuco, Rio; Surinam; Lima; Buenos Ayres.
lepida! *Dythemis lepida* HAGEN!
   HAB. Brazil, New Friburg.
gerula! *Dythemis gerula* HAGEN!
   HAB. Brazil, New Friburg.
liriope! *Dythemis liriope* HAGEN!
   HAB. Brazil.
apicalis! *Dythemis apicalis* HAGEN!
   HAB. Brazil, Rio; Surinam.
cydippe! *Dythemis cydippe* HAGEN!
   HAB. Brazil, Rio.
typographa! *Dythemis typographa!*
   HAB. Chili.
icterica! *Dythemis icterica* HAGEN!
   HAB. Brazil, Surinam.
phryne. *Libellula phryne* PERTY, Delectus Anim. 125; tab. xxv, fig. 3.
   HAB. Brazil, Piauhy.
columba! *Dythemis columba* HAGEN!
   HAB. Venezuela.
tabida! *Dythemis tabida* HAGEN!
   HAB. Brazil.
musiva! *Dythemis musiva* HAGEN!
   HAB. Brazil, Rio, Minas Geraës.
catenata! *Dythemis catenata* HAGEN!
   HAB. Brazil, Minas Geraës.
rapax! *Dythemis rapax* HAGEN.
   HAB. Venezuela.
nubecula! *Dythemis nubecula* RBR.! Neuropt. 122, 129.
   HAB. Brazil, New Friburg.

Erythemis Hagen.

furcata! (See North American Neuroptera.)
   HAB. Brazil, Bahia.

longipes! (See North American Neuroptera.)
   Hab. Brazil, Rio, Minas Geraës.
bicolor! (See North American Neuroptera.)
   Hab. Surinam; Guiana; Brazil.
peruviana. *Libellula peruviana* Rbr. Neuropt. 81, 69.
   Hab. Peru. (Perhaps *E. bicolor*.)
lavata! *Erythemis lavata* Hagen!
   Hab. Venezuela.
rubriventris! *Libellula rubriventris* Blanchard, Voyag. d'Orbigny.
   Hab. Corrientes. (Is it of this genus?)

Mesothemis Hagen.

gilva! *Mesothemis gilva* Hagen!
   Hab. Venezuela.
annulata! *Libellula annulata* Palis. de Beauv. Ins. Neur. 58, tab. iii, fig. 3. Rambur! Neuropt. 78, 65 (partly).
   Hab. Brazil.
plebeja! *Libellula plebeja* Ramb. Neuropt. 107, 106.
   Hab. Chili; Guillota.
connata! *Libellula connata* Burm.! Hbd. II, 855, 44.
   Hab. Valparaiso; Guillota.
communis. *Libellula communis* Rbr. Neuropt. 93, 88.
   Hab. Chili. (Is it of this genus?)
distinguenda. *Libellula distinguenda* Ramb. Neuropt. 81, 68. *Libellula incompta* Ramb. Neuropt. 119, 124 (fem.).
   Hab. Cayenne.
abbreviata. *Libellula abbreviata* Ramb. Neuropt. 119, 123.
   Hab. Cayenne. (Is it of this genus?)

Diplax Charpentier.

ochracea! (See North American Neuroptera.)
   Hab. Venezuela, Porto Cabello; Guiana; Surinam; Brazil; Bahia.
minuscula! (See North American Neuroptera.)
   Hab. Brazil.
credula! (See North American Neuroptera.)
   Hab. Brazil, Minas Geraës.
abjecta! (See North American Neuroptera.)
   Hab. Venezuela, Brazil.
obesa! *Diplax obesa* Hagen!
   Hab. Brazil.
unimaculata! *Libellula unimaculata* De Geer, Mém. III, 558, 4, tab. xxvi, fig. 5. Burm. Hdb. II, 855, 43.
   Hab. Surinam, Guiana; Brazil, Pernambuco.
famula! *Libellula famula* Erichs.! Schomburgk, Voyag. Guian. III, 584.
   Hab. Guiana.
fuscofasciata. *Libellula fuscofasciata* Blanchard, Voyag. d'Orbigny.
   Hab. Corrientes. (Is it of this genus?)
fusca! *Libellula fusca* Rbr.! Neuropt. 78, 64.
   Hab. Cayenne; Brazil.

apollina! *Libellula apollina* DE SELYS!
  HAB. Brazil.
catharina! *Libellula catharina* DE SELYS!
  HAB. Brazil.
indigna! *Diplax indigna* HAGEN!
  HAB. Brazil.
juliana! *Libellula juliana* DE SELYS!
  HAB. Brazil.
postica! *Diplax postica* HAGEN!
  HAB. Brazil.
fausta! *Libellula fausta* DE SELYS!
  HAB. Brazil.
faustina! *Libellula faustina* DE SELYS.
  HAB. Brazil.
contusa! *Libellula contusa* HAGEN!
  HAB. Brazil.
latimacula! *Libellula latimacula* DE SELYS!
  HAB. Brazil.
sobrina. *Libellula sobrina* RBR.! Neuropt. 114, 116.
  HAB. Brazil.
effrenata! *Libellula effrenata* HAGEN!
  HAB. Brazil.
familiaris! *Diplax familiaris* HAGEN!
  HAB. Brazil.
agricola! *Diplax agricola* HAGEN!
  HAB. Brazil.
luciana! *Libellula luciana* DE SELYS!
  HAB. Brazil.
flavilatera! *Diplax flavilatera* HAGEN!
  HAB. Brazil.
bilineata! *Libellula bilineata* HAGEN!
  HAB. Brazil, New Friburg.
venosa! *Libellula venosa* BURM.! Hdb. II, 848, 1.
  HAB. Brazil, Bahia.
oscularis! *Diplax oscularis* HAGEN!
  HAB. Brazil.
cyanifrons! *Libellula cyanifrons* HAGEN!
  HAB. Brazil.
pulla! *Libellula pulla* BURM.! Hdb. II, 855, 41.
  HAB. Surinam.
nigricans! *Libellula nigricans* RAMB. Neuropt. 97, 95.
  HAB. Buenos Ayres.
vilis. *Libellula vilis* RBR. Neuropt. 98, 96.
  HAB. Buenos Ayres.

Perithemis Hagen.

domitia! (See North American Neuropt.)
  HAB. Venezuela; Brazil, Bahia, St. Leopoldo.
lais! *Libellula lais* PERTY, Delect. Anim. 125, tab. xxv.
  HAB. Brazil, Pernambuco.

thais! *Perithemis thais* HAGEN!
  HAB. Amazon River.
cloe! *Perithemis cloë* HAGEN!
  HAB. Brazil.
bella! *Perithemis bella* HAGEN!
  HAB. Para.

Nannophya Rambur.

semiaurea! *Libellula semiaurea* Berlin Museum.
  HAB. Para.
prodita! *Libellula prodita* HAGEN.
  HAB. Brazil, Pernambuco.

Uracis Rambur.

imbuta! *Libellula imbuta* BURM.! Hdb. II, 850, 9. *Uracis quadra* RBR.!
  Neuropt. 31, tab. ii. fig. 5.
  HAB. Surinam; Brazil, Bahia.
fastigiata! *Libellula fastigiata* BURM.! Hdb. II, 850, 10.
  HAB. Bahia.
irrorata! *Uracis irrorata* HAGEN!
  HAB. Bahia.
ovata! *Uracis ovata* HAGEN!
  HAB. Bahia.

Sub-gen. (new).

guttata! *Libellula guttata* ERICHS.! Schomburgk, Voyag. Guiana, III, 584.
  HAB. Guiana.
infumata! *Libellula infumata* RBR. Neuropt. 74, 59.
  HAB. Brazil.
amphithea! *Libellula amphithea* DE SELYS.
  HAB. Brazil.
clymene! *Libellula clymene* HAGEN!
  HAB. Brazil, Pernambuco.

Palpopleura Rambur.

fasciata! *Libellula fasciata* LINNÉ, Syst. Nat. II, 903, 12. FABR. Entom.
  Syst. II, 378, 20. BURM. Hdb. II, 854, 37. RAMBUR, Neuropt. 134,
  8 (partly).
  HAB. Brazil; Surinam.
americana! *Libellula americana* LINNÉ, Syst. Nat. II, 904, 16. FABR.
  Entom. Syst. II, 378, 20. DEGEER, Mém. III, 559, 7; tab. xxvi, fig.
  7. SEBA, Thesaur. tab. lxxviii, fig. 11—12.
  HAB. Brazil.
circumcincta! *Palpopleura circumcincta* HAGEN!
  HAB. Brazil.

Diastatops Rambur.

dimidiata! *Libellula dimidiata* LINNE, Syst. Nat. II, 908, 14. DEGEER, Mémoir. III, 558; tab. xxvi, fig. 6. BURM. Hdb. II, 854, 36. RAMBUR, Neuropt. 129, 1. ERICHS. Voy. Schomburgk, III, 584.
HAB. Surinam; Essequibo, Guiana.

tincta! *Diastatops tincta* RAMB. Neuropt. 135, 1. ERICHS. Voy. Schomburgk, III, 584.
HAB. Brazil; St. Louis de Maranhon; Guiana.

pullata! *Libellula pullata* BURM.! Hdb. II, 854, 34. RAMB. Neuropt. 136, 2; tab. iii, fig. 4.
HAB. Brazil; Pernambuco; Peru; Moxos.

obscura! *Libellula obscura* FABR. Entom. Syst. 377, 15. BURM.! Hdb. II, 584, 35. RAMB. Neuropt. 137, 3.
HAB. Brazil.

FAM. VII. SIALINA.

Chauliodes Latreille.

chilensis! *Chauliodes chilensis* HAGEN, Collect.
HAB. Valparaiso, Valdivia.

Corydalis Latreille.

armata! *Corydalis armatus* HAGEN. *Corydalis cornuta* RAMB.! Neuropt. 440, 1. WALK.! Catal. Br. Mus. 208, 1.
HAB. Columbia, Venezuela.

affinis! *Corydalis affinis* BURM.! Hdb. II, 951, 2. *Corydalis cephalotes* RAMB.! Neuropt. 441, 2. WALK. Catal. Br. Mus. 208, 2.
HAB. Brazil, New Friburg.

armigera! *Corydalis armigera* HAGEN, Collect.
HAB. Brazil.

vetula! *Corydalis vetula* HAGEN, Collect.
HAB. Brazil.

ancilla! *Corydalis ancilla* HAGEN, Collect.
HAB. Paraguay.

nubila! *Corydalis nubila* ERICHS.! Schomburgk, Reise Guiana, III.
HAB. British Guiana; Venezuela.

hieroglyphica! *Neuromus hieroglyphicus* RBR.! Neuropt. 442, 2. WALK. Catal. Br. Mus. 206, 12.
HAB. Cayenne; Venezuela; Brazil; Buenos Ayres.

livida! *Corydalis livida* HAGEN, Collect.
HAB. Brazil.

illota! *Corydalis illota* HAGEN, Collect.
HAB. Brazil.

(Raphidia Linné.)

R. varia WALKER and the species described by Dr. Fischer, belong to *Mantispa*.

Fam. VIII. HEMEROBINA.

Hemerobius Linné.

lentus! *Hemerobius lentus* HAGEN, Collect.
HAB. Brazil.
signatus! *Hemerobius signatus* HAGEN, Collect.
HAB. Chili.

Mantispa Illiger.

semihyalina! *Mantispa semihyalina* SERVILLE, Encycl. Meth. X, 270. RAMB. Neuropt. 434, 7; pl. x, fig. 5. WESTWOOD, Trans. Ent. Soc. Lond. ser. 2, I, 253, 1. Walk.! Catal. Br. Mus. 214, 1. *Mantispa chalybea* ERICHS.! Germar Zeitschr. I, 160, 1. *Mantispa grandis* BURM. Hdb. II, 967, 4.
HAB. Brazil, Surinam.
ambusta. *Mantispa ambusta* ERICHS. Germar Zeitschr. I, 162, 4. WESTWOOD, Trans. Ent. Soc. Lond. ser. 2, I, 254, 4. WALK. Catal. Br. Mus. 215, 4.
HAB. Montevideo.
irrorata! *Mantispa irrorata* ERICHS.! Germar Zeitschr. I, 162, 5. WESTWOOD, Trans. Ent. Soc. Lond. ser. 2, I, 254, 5. WALK. Catal. Br. Mus. 215, 5. *Raphidia riedeliana* FISCHER, Bullet. Moscow, VII, 329; tab. vii, fig. 1.
HAB. Brazil.
decorata!. *Mantispa decorata* ERICHS.! Germar Zeitschr. I, 163, 6; pl. 2, fig. 5. WESTWOOD, Trans. Ent. Soc. Lond. ser. 2, I, 254, 6. WALK. Catal. Br. Mus. 215, 6.
HAB. Brazil.
prolixa! *Mantispa prolixa* ERICHS.! Germar Zeitschr. I, 163, 7. WESTWOOD, Trans. Ent. Soc. Lond. ser. 2, I, 254, 6.
HAB. Brazil.
costalis. *Mantispa costalis* ERICHS. Germar Zeitschr. I, 164, 9. WESTWOOD, Trans. Ent. Soc. Lond. ser. 2, I, 254, 9. WALK. Catal. Br. Mus. 216, 9.
HAB. Brazil.
flaveola! *Mantispa flaveola* ERICHS. Germar Zeitschr. I, 168, 13. WESTWOOD, Trans. Ent. Soc. Lond. ser. 2, I, 254, 13. WALK. Catal. Br. Mus. 216, 13.
HAB. Para.
gracilis! *Mantispa gracilis* ERICHS.! Germar Zeitschr. I, 169, 18. WESTWOOD, Trans. Ent. Soc. Lond. ser. 2, I, 255, 18. WALK. Catal. Br. Mus. 219, 18.
HAB. Brazil, Pernambuco.
viridula! *Mantispa viridula* ERICHS.! Germar Zeitschr. I, 170, 19. WESTWOOD, Trans. Ent. Soc. Lond. ser. 2, I, 255, 19. WALK. Catal. Br. Mus. 219, 19. *Raphidia margaritacea* FISCHER? Bullet. Moscow, VII, 330; tab. vii, fig. 1.
HAB. Brazil.

flavomaculata. *Mantispa flavomaculata* LATR. Gen. Crust. III, 94. ERICHS. Germar Zeitschr. 173, 24. WESTWOOD, Trans. Ent. Soc. Lond. ser. 2, 255, 28. WALK. Catal. Br. Mus. 220, 23. *Mantispa liliputana* OLIV. Encycl. Meth. VII, 640, 3. STOLL, Spectr. VII, pl. ii, fig. 7.
HAB. Surinam.

iridipennis. *Mantispa iridipennis* GUÉRIN, Icon. Regn. Anim. Ins. 392. *Mantispa gracilis* RAMB. Neur. 433, 6 ? WESTWOOD, Trans. Ent. Soc. Lond. ser. 2, I, 256, 30. WALK. Catal. Br. Mus. 222, 30.
HAB. Columbia.

areolaris. *Mantispa areolaris* WESTWOOD ! Trans. Ent. Soc. Lond. ser. 2, I, 265, 41 ; pl. xviii, fig. 3. WALK. Catal. Br. Mus. 226, 41.
HAB. Brazil.

chilensis ! *Mantispa chilensis* HAGEN ! Stett. Ent. Zeit. 1859, 708, 8.
HAB. Chili.

Trichoscelis Westwood.

notha ! *Mantispa notha* BURM.! Hdb. II, 968, 5. ERICHS.! Germ. Zeitschr. I, 170, 20 ; pl. ii, fig. 6. WESTWOOD, Trans. Ent. Soc. Lond. ser. 2, I, 255, 20. WALK. Catal. Br. Mus. 219, 20.
HAB. Brazil.

fenella. *Mantispa fenella* WESTWOOD ! Trans. Ent. Soc. Lond. ser. 2, I, 269, 46 ; pl. xviii, fig. 7. WALK. Catal. Br. Mus. 227, 46.
HAB. Para.

varia. *Raphidia varia* WALK.! Catal. Br. Mus. 212, 13.
HAB. Brazil.

Chrysopa Leach.

divisa ! *Chrysopa divisa* WALK.! Catal. Br. Mus. 242, 12.
HAB. Brazil.

hybrida ! *Chrysopa hybrida* SCHNEID. Chrys. 81, 10, pl. xvi. RAMB. Neuropt. 426, 7. WALK. Catal. Br. Mus. 245, 20.
HAB. Brazil.

brasiliensis. *Chrysopa brasiliensis* SCHNEID. Chrys. 83, 11, pl. xvii. WALK. Catal. Br. Mus. 246, 21.
HAB. Brazil.

cincta. *Chrysopa cincta* SCHNEID. Chrys. 86, 13, pl. xix. WALK. Catal. Br. Mus. 247, 24.
HAB. Brazil, Para.

circumfusa ! *Chrysopa circumfusa* SCHNEID.! Chrys. 87, 14, pl. xx. BURM. Hdb. II, 980, 3. WALK. Catal. Br. Mus. 247, 25.
HAB. Brazil.

cruentata ! *Chrysopa cruentata* SCHNEID.! Chrys. 89, 15, pl. xxi. WALK. Catal. Br. Mus. 248, 26.
HAB. Brazil.

costalis ! *Chrysopa costalis* SCHNEID.! Chrys. 90, 16, pl. xxii. WALK. Catal. Br. Mus. 248, 27.
HAB. America.

intermedia ! *Chrysopa intermedia* SCHNEID. Chrys. 106, 27, pl. xxxiii. WALK. Catal. Br. Mus. 252, 40.
HAB. Brazil.

internata! *Chrysopa internata* WALK.! Catal. Br. Mus. 252, 41.
  HAB. Brazil.
nigrovaria. *Chrysopa nigrovaria* WALK. Catal. Br. Mus. 253, 42.
  HAB. Venezuela.
elegans! *Hemerobius elegans* GUÉR. Icon. Règn. Anim. 388. SCHNEID.!
  Chrys. 134, 42, pl. xlii. WALK. Catal. Br. Mus. 261, 59.
  HAB. Brazil.
varia. *Chrysopa varia* SCHNEID. Chrys. 154, 52; pl. 1, viii. WALK. Catal.
  Br. Mus. 268, 71.
  HAB. Brazil, Para.
longicornis. *Hemerobius longicornis* GRAY, Griff. Anim. Kingd. XV, 331;
  pl. lxxii, fig. 3. SCHNEID. Chrys. 156, 53; pl. lix. WALK. Catal.
  Br. Mus. 270, 75.
  HAB. Brazil.
iridea. *Hemerobius irideus* OLIV. Encyc. Meth. VII, 50, 4. SCHNEID. Chrys.
  161. WALK. Catal. Br. Mus. 274, 84.
  HAB. Surinam.
conformis. *Hemerobius conformis* RAMB. Neuropt. 426, 8. SCHNEID. Chrys.
  163. WALK. Catal. Br. Mus. 275, 88.
  HAB. Colombia.
valida! *Hemerobius validus* ERICHS.! Schomburgk, Reise Guiana, 586.
  SCHNEID. Chrysop. 164. WALK. Catal. Br. Mus. 275, 89.
  HAB. British Guiana; Brazil, Pernambuco.
ternata! *Chrysopa ternata* HAGEN, Collect.
  HAB. Pernambuco.
marionella! *Hemerobius marionella* GUÉR. Revue. WALK.! Catal. Br.
  Mus. 271, 78.
  HAB. Para.
  Schneider, Mongr. Chrysop. p. 69, affirms that *Chr. vulgaris*, a very
  abundant European species, is found in Brazil. I have never seen
  an American specimen.

Belonoptera Gerstaecker.

spec. nov.
  HAB. Cassapava, Brazil. (Mus. Berlin.)

Acanthaclisis Rambur.

striata! *Acanthaclisis striata* HAGEN.
  HAB. Colombia (Saussure).
fallax! (See North American Neuropt.)
  HAB. Colombia; Guiana; Brazil.

Myrmeleon LINNÉ.

immitis. *Myrmeleon immitis* WALK. Catal. Br. Mus. 331, 50.
  HAB. Brazil, Santarem.
anomalus. *Myrmeleon anomalus* RAMB. Neuropt. 388, 6. WALK. Catal.
  Br. Mus. 333, 54.
  HAB. Colombia.

ingeniosus. *Myrmeleon ingeniosus* WALK. Catal. Br. Mus. 337, 63.
HAB. Brazil.
cautus. *Myrmeleon cautus* WALK. Catal. Br. Mus. 349, 79.
HAB. Brazil.
dolosus. *Myrmeleon dolosus* WALK. Catal. Br. Mus. 383, 144.
HAB. Brazil, Santarem.
metuendus. *Myrmeleon metuendus* WALK. Catal. Br. Mus. 387, 149.
HAB. Venezuela.
efferus. *Myrmeleon efferus* WALK. Catal. Br. Mus. 387, 150.
HAB. Para.
praedator. *Myrmeleon praedator* WALK. Catal. Br. Mus. 391, 156.
HAB. Brazil, Santarem.
elegans. *Myrmeleon elegans* PERTY, Delect. 125; pl. xxv. RAMB. Neuropt. 409, 43. WALK. Catal. Br. Mus. 395, 163.
HAB. Brazil.
subdolus! *Myrmeleon subdolus* WALK.! Catal. Br. Mus. 395, 164.
HAB. Lima.
sticticus. *Myrmeleon sticticum* BLANCH. Orbigny Voy. 218, 753; pl. xxviii, fig. 17. WALK. Catal. Br. Mus. 404, 187.
HAB. Chiquibos, Bolivia.
tarsalis. *Formicaleo tarsalis* GUILDING, Trans. Linn. Soc. Lond. XVI, 51, 2. WALK. Catal. Br. Mus. 410, 215.
HAB. Demerara?
chilensis! *Myrmeleon chilensis* HAGEN, Collect.
HAB. Chili.
corax! *Myrmeleon corax* HAGEN, Collect.
HAB. Venezuela.
impar! *Myrmeleon impar* HAGEN, Collect.
HAB. Chili.
ornatus! *Myrmeleon ornatus* KLUG! HAGEN, Collect.
HAB. Brazil.
sericeus! *Myrmeleon sericeus* HAGEN!
HAB. Chili.
leprosus! *Myrmeleon leprosus* HAGEN!
HAB. Chili.
compensus! *Myrmeleon compensus* HAGEN
HAB. Chili.
ereptus! *Myrmeleon ereptus* HAGEN!
HAB. Venezuela.
congruus! *Myrmeleon congruus* HAGEN
HAB. Amazon River.
arcuatus! *Myrmeleon arcuatus* HAGEN.
HAB. Bahia.
sanctus! *Myrmeleon sanctus* HAGEN.
HAB. Pernambuco.
mucoreus! *Myrmeleon mucoreus* HAGEN.
HAB. Pernambuco.
nervosus! *Myrmeleon nervosus* HAGEN!
HAB. Amazon River.

centurio! *Myrmeleon centurio* HAGEN!
  HAB. Pernambuco.
infantilis! *Myrmeleon infantilis* HAGEN!
  HAB. Columbia.
aequalis! *Myrmeleon aequalis* HAGEN!
  HAB. Columbia.

Ascalaphus Fabricius.

* *Eyes sulcated.*

loquax. *Ascalaphus loquax* WALK. Catal. 434, 48.
  HAB. Brazil.
subvertens. *Ascalaphus subvertens* WALK. Catal. 437, 55.
  HAB. St. Lucia.
inhonestus! *Ascalaphus inhonestus* WALK.! Catal. 437, 56.
  HAB. Brazil.
subripiens. *Ascalaphus subripiens* WALK. Catal. 443, 64.
  HAB. Venezuela.
impavidus. *Ascalaphus impavidus* WALK. Catal. 443, 65.
  HAB. Brazil, Santarem.
intempestivus. *Ascalaphus intempestivus* WALK. Catal. 444, 66.
  HAB. Brazil, Santarem.
sepultus. *Ascalaphus sepultus* WALK. Catal. 445, 67.
  HAB. Brazil.
nobilis! *Ascalaphus nobilis* HAGEN!
  HAB. Columbia.
apicalis! *Ascalaphus apicalis* LEFEB.! (Mus. Berlin.)
  HAB. Brazil.
calidus! *Ascalaphus calidus* HAGEN!
  HAB. Brazil, Pernambuco.
limbatus! (See North American Neuropt.)
  HAB. Brazil.
modestus! *Ascalaphus modestus* HAGEN!
  HAB. Venezuela; Surinam; Paramaribo.
chlorops. *Ascalaphus chlorops* BLANCH. Voyag. d'Orbigny, 218, 754; tab. xxviii, fig. 8. WALK. Catal. 453, 81.
  HAB. St. Cruz, Bolivia.
cayennensis. *Ascalaphus cayennensis* FABR. Entom. Syst. II, 96, 6.
  HAB. Cayenne.
macrocerus! *Ascalaphus macrocerus* BURM.! Hdb. II, 1000, 3.
  HAB. Brazil, Bahia.
  Perhaps *A. impavidus* WALK.?
versicolor! *Ascalaphus versicolor* BURM.! Hdb. II, 1000, 4. *Ascalaphus appendifer* LEFEBVRE! Mus. Berlin. WALK. Catal. 420, 23. *Calobopterus leptocerus* RBR.! (mas.) Neuropt. 361, 1. WALK. Catal. 440, 59. *Calobopterus nematocerus* RBR.! (fem.) Neuropt. 361, 2. WALK. Catal. 441, 60.
  HAB. Brazil.
surinamensis! *Ascalaphus surinamensis* FABR. Entom. Syst. App. 207, 4—5. *Cordulecerus surinamensis* RAMB. Neuropt. 360, tab. ix, fig. 1.

Ascalaphus vulpecula Burm.! Hdb. II, 1001, 6 (mas., wings immaculate). *Ascalaphus garrulus* Walk.! Catal. 441, 61 (mas.). *Ascalaphus alopecinus* Burm.! Hdb. II, 1000, 5 (fem.). *Ascalaphus litigiosus* Walk. Catal. 441, 62.
Hab. Surinam, Brazil, Bahia.

vetula. *Ulula vetula* Ramb. Neuropt. 358, 2. Walk. Catal. 436, 52.
Hab. Brazil, Campos Geraës.

* * *Eyes entire.*

costatus! *Ascalaphus costatus* Burm.! Hdb. II, 1000, 1. *Ascalaphus contrarius* Walk.! Catal. 452, 79. *Ascalaphus imperator* Lefeb.! (Mus. Berlin.)
Hab. Surinam; Brazil, Bahia, Para.
(Perhaps *Byas microcerus* Rhr. ?)

subcostatus! *Ascalaphus subcostatus* Burm.! Hdb. II, 1000, 2. *Ascalaphus injurius* Walk.! Catal. 447, 72. *Ascalaphus impediens* Walk.! Catal. 449, 74. *Ascalaphus damnosus* Walk. Catal. 449, 75 ? *Ascalaphus luteus* Walk.! Catal. 450, 77.
Hab. Brazil, Amazon River, Santarem, Para.

albistigma! *Ascalaphus albistigma* Walk.! Catal. 452, 80. *Ascalaphus circumflexus* Walk.! Catal. 451, 79.
Hab. Venezuela; Brazil, Santarem, Para.

iniquus. *Ascalaphus iniquus* Walk. Catal. 448, 73.
Hab. Brazil.

arenosus. *Ascalaphus arenosus* Walk. Catal. 450, 76.
Hab. Brazil.

appendiculatus. *Ascalaphus appendiculatus* Fabr. Ent. Syst. II, 96, 4. *Haploglenius appendiculatus* Ramb. Neuropt. 363. Walk. Catal. 446, 69.
Hab. Brazil.
Perhaps the male of *A. costatus*?

Fam. IX. PANORPINA.

Bittacus Latr.

brasiliensis! *Bittacus brasiliensis* Klug! Acad. Berol. 1836, 98, 3. Walk. Catal. Br. Mus. 466, 4.
Hab. Brazil, Cassapava.

femoralis. *Bittacus femoralis* Klug! Acad. Berol. 1836, 98, 5. Walk. Catal. Br. Mus. 466, 5.
Hab.

flavescens! *Bittacus flavescens* Klug! Acad. Berol. 1836, 99, 7. Walk. Catal. Br. Mus. 466, 7. *Bittacus affinis* Westw. Trans. Ent. Soc. Lond. IV, 196, 1. Walk. Catal. Br. Mus. 468, 12.
Hab. Brazil, Para.

chilensis. *Bittacus chilensis* Klug! Acad. Berol. 1836, 100, 9; pl. fig. 6. Walk. Catal. Br. Mus. 467, 9.
Hab. Chili.

blancheti! *Bittacus blancheti* PICT. Mém. Genève. VII, 403, fig. 3. KLUG! Acad. Berol. 1836, 100, 10. RAMB.! Neuropt. 327, 3; pl. viii. fig. 6. WALK. Catal. Br. Mus. 467, 10.
HAB. Brazil.

FAM. X. PHRYGANINA.

Barypenthus Burmeister.

concolor. *Barypenthus concolor* BURM.! Hdb. II, 929, 2. WALK. Catal. Br. Mus. 54, 1.
HAB. Brazil.

* **rufipes.** *Barypenthus rufipes* BURM.! Hdb. II, 929, 2. WALK. Catal. Br. Mus. 55, 2.
HAB. Brazil.

Sericostoma Latreille.

tropica! *Sericostoma? tropica* HAGEN, Collect.
HAB. Brazil.

Macronema Pictet.

hyalinum. *Macronemum hyalinum* PICT. Mém. Genève. VII. BURM. Hdb. II, 916, 3. WALK. Catal. Br. Mus. 75, 3.
HAB. Brazil.

speciosum. *Macronemum speciosum* BURM. Hdb. II, 916, 1. WALK. Catal. Br. Mus. 74, 1.
HAB. Brazil.

lineatum. *Macronema lineata* PICT. Mém. Genève. VII. BURM. Hdb. 916, 2. WALK. Catal. Br. Mus. 74, 2.
HAB. Brazil.

auripenne! *Macronema auripenne* RAMB.! Neuropt. 507, 2. WALK. Catal. Br. Mus. 75, 4.
HAB. Brazil.

rubiginosum. *Macronema rubiginosa* GUÉR. Icon. Règn. Anim. Texte, 395. WALK. Catal. Br. Mus. 75, 5.
HAB. Brazil.

oculatum. *Macronema oculata* WALK.! Catal. Br. Mus. 75, 6.
HAB. Venezuela.

cupreum. *Macronema cupreum* WALK.! Catal. Br. Mus. 76, 7.
HAB. Brazil. (Perhaps *M. auripenne?*)

apicale. *Macronema apicalis* WALK.! Catal. Br. Mus. 78, 15.
HAB. Venezuela.

pallida! (See North American Neuropt.)
HAB. Venezuela, Brazil.

vicarium. *Hydropsyche vicaria* WALK.! Catal. Br. Mus. 114, 39.
HAB. Venezuela.

agraphum. *Macronema agraphum* KOLEN. Wien. Ent. Zeits. 1859, p. 57.
HAB. Brazil.

arcuatum! *Macronema arcuatum* ERICHS.! Schomburgk, Reise Guiana, III.
HAB. British Guiana.

Hydropsyche Pictet.

australis! *Hydropsyche australis* HAGEN, Collect.
 HAB. Brazil.

Leptocerus Leach.

albicornis. *Mystacides albicornis* BURM. Hdb. II, 918, 1. WALK. Catal. Br. Mus. 69, 54.
 HAB. Brazil.
gracilis. *Mystacides gracilis* BURM. Hdb. II, 921, 12. WALK. Catal. Br. Mus. 69, 55.
 HAB. Brazil.
princeps. *Mystacides princeps* BURM. Hdb. II, 921, 13. WALK. Catal. Br. Mus. 69, 56.
 HAB. Brazil.
maculatus. *Phryganea maculata* PERTY, Delect. 129, pl. xxv, fig. 16. WALK. Catal. Br. Mus. 74, 70.
 HAB. Brazil, St. Paul.
diaphanus. *Blepharopus diaphanus* KOL. Wien. Ent. Zeit. 1859, p. 58.
 HAB. South America.

Chimarrha Leach.

morio! *Chimarrha morio* BURM. Hdb. II, 911, 2. WALK. Catal. Br. Mus. 81, 2.
 HAB. Brazil.
maculata! *Chimarrha? maculata* HAGEN, Collect.
 HAB. Brazil.

LIST OF THE NEUROPTERA DESCRIBED IN THE SYNOPSIS OF NORTH AMERICAN SPECIES.

	GENERA.	Species.	New species.	Species not examined.	United States.	Canada, Greenland, Arct. Amer.	Russian Colonies.	Mexico, Central America.	West Indies.	Species found also in S. Am.	Species found also in Europe.	Species found also in Asia, Africa, or Polynesia.
1	Calotermes	4	..	..	2	..	..	3	3	2	..	1?[2]
2	Termopsis	2	..	..	1	..	..	1	..	..	..	..
3	Termes	11	..	1	1	..	..	5	6	4	1[1]	1?[2]
4	Embia	1	1	..	..	..	..	..	1	..	..	..
5	Clothilla	1	1	..	1	..	..	..	..	..	..	..
6	Atropos	1	..	1	..	1	..	..	..	..	..	..
7	Psocus	16	13	..	15	1	..	2	2	..	..	..
8	Pteronarcys	6	1	1	5	3	..	..	..	..	..	..
9	Perla	40	9	21	25	9	1	9	..	2	..	..
10	Isopteryx	1	..	..	1	..	..	..	..	..	..	..
11	Capnia	4	..	..	2	2	..	..	..	..	..	..
12	Taeniopteryx	5	2	..	4	1	..	..	..	..	..	..
13	Nemoura	3	..	1	2	3	..	..	..	..	..	..
14	Leuctra	2	..	..	1	1	..	..	..	..	..	..
15	Ephemera	5	1	1	3	4	..	..	..	..	..	..
16	Palingenia	8	2	3	3	5	..	2	..	..	..	..
17	Baëtis	19	1	11	11	10	..	1	..	..	..	..
18	Potamanthus	3	..	2	2	2	..	..	..	..	..	..
19	Cloë	7	4	3	5	2	..	1	2	..	1?	..
20	Caenis	3	1	2	3	..	..	..	..	..	..	..
21	Calopteryx	6	..	1	6	1	..	..	..	..	1?	1?[3]
22	Hetaerina	10	..	..	5	..	..	7	1	3	..	..
23	Megaloprepus	1	..	..	..	..	..	1	..	1	..	..
24	Pseudostigma	2	2	..	..	..	..	2	..	1	..	..
25	Mecistogaster	3	1	..	..	..	..	2	1	2	..	..
26	Lestes	13	7	2	9	..	..	3	2	2	..	..
27	Paraphlebia	1	1	1	..	..	..	1	..	..	..	..
28	Palaemnema	1	..	1	..	..	..	1	..	..	..	..
29	Trichocnemis	2	..	2	1	..	..	..	1	..	..	..
30	Protoneura	2	..	2	1	..	..	..	1	..	..	..
31	Nehalennia	2	1	1	1	..	..	..	1	..	..	..
32	Ischnura	18	12	3	11	..	..	5	8	3	..	..
33	Pyrrhosoma	5	3	1	2	..	..	1	2	1	..	..
34	Agrion	23	19	1	14	1	1	9	..	1	..	..
35	Gomphus	19	1	5	19	2	..	..	..	..	..	..
36	Erpetogomphus	6	..	1	2	..	..	4	..	1	..	..
37	Ophiogomphus	1	..	..	..	1	..	..	..	..	..	..
38	Neogomphus	1	..	..	1	..	..	..	..	..	..	..
39	Progomphus	2	..	..	1	..	..	1	..	1	..	..
40	Gomphoides	7	1	2	1	..	..	5	1	1	..	..
41	Hagenius	1	..	..	1	..	..	..	..	1	..	..
42	Cordulegaster	4	..	1	3	..	1	..	..	..	..	..
43	Petalura	1	..	..	1	..	..	..	..	..	..	..
44	Anax	3	..	..	2	..	..	2	1	1	..	1[4]
45	Aeschna	25	13	7	12	4	2	5	5	2	2	2[5]
46	Gynacantha	2	..	1	..	..	..	..	2	2	..	..
47	Macromia	4	2	1	3	..	..	1	..	..	..	..
48	Epitheca	1	1	..	1	..	..	..	..	..	..	..
49	Didymops	2	..	..	2	..	..	..	..	..	..	..
50	Cordulia	15	12	10	5	10	..	..	..	..	..	..
51	Tetragoneuria	4	3	2	3	1	..	..	..	..	..	..
		329	115	92	194	64	5	74	40	30	5	6

[1] (Warmhouse.)   [2] Africa.   [3] Asia, Africa.   [4] Asia et Polynesia.   [5] Asia.

List of the Neuroptera of North America—Continued.

	GENERA.	Species.	New species.	Species not examined.	United States.	Canada, Greenland, Arct. Amer.	Russian Colonies.	Mexico, Central America.	West Indies.	Species found also in S. Am.	Species found also in Europe.	Species found also in Asia, Africa, or Polynesia.
		329	115	92	194	64	5	74	40	30	5	9
52	Pantala	2	..	..	2	..	..	2	1	1	..	1[1]
53	Tramea	7	3	..	4	..	..	4	4	..	..	1[2]
54	Celithemis	2	1	..	1	..	..	1	1	..	..	..
55	Plathemis	2	1	..	2	..	..	..	..	..	..	..
56	Libellula	22	6	..	18	1	..	6	3	2	1	1[2]
57	Lepthemis	3	1	..	1	..	..	1	2	3	..	..
58	Dythemis	13	9	..	3	..	..	5	8	1	..	..
59	Erythemis	3	2	..	..	..	..	2	2	3	..	..
60	Mesothemis	7	3	2	5	..	..	4	3	..	..	1[2]
61	Diplax	20	6	2	14	3	..	1	4	4	1	1[2]
62	Perithemis	1	..	..	1	..	..	1	1	1	..	..
63	Nannophya	3	2	1	3	..	..	..	..	..	..	..
64	Sialis	3	1	..	2	1	..	..	1	..	..	..
65	Chauliodes	7	1	1	7	..	..	..	..	..	..	..
66	Corydalis	5	3	..	2	1	..	3	..	1	..	..
67	Raphidia	4	4	..	4	..	..	..	..	..	1	..
68	Aleuronia	1	..	1	1	..	..	..	..	..	..	..
69	Coniopteryx	1	1	..	1	..	..	..	..	..	..	..
70	Sisyra	1	..	1	1	..	..	..	..	..	..	..
71	Megalomus	1	1	..	..	..	..	1	..	..	..	..
72	Micromus	5	3	1	5	..	..	..	..	..	..	..
73	Hemerobius	21	2	18	16	4	..	1	..	..	..	..
74	Polystoechotes	2	..	1	2	1	..	..	..	..	..	..
75	Mantispa	4	1	1	4	..	..	1	..	..	..	..
76	Meleoma	2	..	2	2	..	..	..	..	..	..	..
77	Chrysopa	37	4	16	26	3	..	5	6	1	1	1[2]
78	Acanthaclisis	3	1	1	2	..	..	1	1	1	..	..
79	Myrmeleon	25	10	8	19	..	..	4	3	1	..	..
80	Euptilon	1	..	1	1	..	..	..	..	..	..	..
81	Ascalaphus	7	1	1	2	..	..	3	3	1	..	..
82	Boreus	2	..	..	2	..	..	..	..	..	..	..
83	Panorpa	12	1	3	9	2	..	2	..	..	..	..
84	Bittacus	7	2	3	6	1	..	1	..	..	..	..
85	Merope	1	..	..	1	..	..	..	..	..	..	..
86	Neuronia	8	..	4	6	6	..	..	..	..	..	..
87	Phryganea	3	..	2	2	1	..	..	..	..	..	..
88	Limnophilus	30	6	18	10	18	2	..	..	..	5	2[2]
89	Anabolia	4	2	2	2	3	..	..	..	..	..	..
90	Hallesus	7	4	1	4	4	..	1	..	..	..	..
91	Enoicyla	7	2	2	3	5	..	..	..	..	..	..
92	Apatania	2	1	1	..	2	..	..	..	..	..	..
93	Sericostoma	2	..	2	2	..	..	..	..	..	..	..
94	Notidobia	3	2	..	2	1	..	..	1	..	..	..
95	Brachycentrus	2	1	1	1	1	..	..	..	..	..	..
96	Silo	2	2	..	2	..	..	..	..	..	..	..
97	Mormonia	1	1	..	1	1	..	..	..	..	..	..
98	Dasystoma	2	..	2	2	..	..	..	..	..	..	..
99	Hydroptila	3	2	1	..	3	..	..	..	..	..	..
100	Molanna	3	2	1	2	1	..	..	..	..	..	..
101	Leptocerus	13	5	7	7	6	..	..	..	..	1	..
102	Setodes	14	9	2	10	6	..	2	..	..	1	..
103	Macronema	6	4	..	2	1	..	4	1	3	..	..
		678	228	201	420	140	7	130	85	53	16	14

[1] Africa, Asia, Polynesia.   [2] Asia.

List of the Neuroptera of North America—Continued.

	GENERA.	Species.	New species.	Species not examined.	United States.	Canada, Greenland, Arct. Amer.	Russian Colonies.	Mexico, Central America.	West Indies.	Species found also in S. Am.	Species found also in Europe.	Species found also in Asia, Africa, or Polynesia.
		678	228	201	420	140	7	130	85	53	16	14
104	Hydropsyche	16	8	8	12	8	..	..	1	..	..	..
105	Philopotamus	2	..	2	1	1	..	..	..	..	..	..
106	Polycentropus	8	4	4	5	3	..	..	..	..	..	..
107	Psychomia	2	1	1	1	2	..	..	..	..	..	..
108	Tinodes	2	1	1	..	2	..	..	..	..	..	..
109	Rhyacophila	2	1	1	1	1	..	..	..	..	..	..
110	Beraea	2	1	1	1	1	..	..	..	..	..	..
111	Chimarrha	4	3	1	2	1	..	..	1	..	..	..
	Total	716	247	220	443	159	7	130	87	53	16	14

The number of species entirely unknown to me is considerably less than what is mentioned in the column of "species not examined;" this includes many species at one time seen in the British Museum, but which I have not since been able to re-examine.

	FAMILIES.	Genera.	Species.
1	Termitina	3	17
2	Embidina	1	1
3	Psocina	3	18
4	Perlina	7	61
5	Ephemerina	6	45
6	Odonata	43	273
7	Sialina	4	19
8	Hemerobina	14	111
9	Panorpina	4	22
10	Phryganina	26	150
		111	716

DISTRIBUTION OF SPECIES,
(AS FAR AS AT PRESENT KNOWN.)

	Species.		Species.		Species.
Massachusetts	27	Ohio	21	Alabama	1
Vermont	1	Michigan	1	Florida	35
New York	104	Indiana	22	Louisiana	83
Pennsylvania	65	Illinois	44	Texas	43
New Jersey	25	Missouri	16	California	82
Delaware	1	Wisconsin	5	North America, United States without locality	35
Maryland	42	N. W. Territory	9		
Dist. of Columbia	78	Carolina	29		
Virginia	24	Tennessee	3	Arkansas	2
Kentucky	9	Georgia	104	Mississippi	2
Greenland	6	Mexico	112	Martinique	8
Arctic America	29	Central America	22	St. Thomas	12
Russian Colonies	7	Cuba	61	Guadaloupe	3
Canada	100	St. Domingo	15	Barbadoes	1
Labrador	6	Porto Rico	7	St. Cruz	1
Nova Scotia	33	Jamaica	12	St. Vincent	1
Columbia, Venezuela	30	Guiana, Surinam, Cayenne	13	Brazil	38
				Chili	3
				Peru	1

LIST OF THE NEUROPTERA ENUMERATED IN THE CATALOGUE OF SOUTH AMERICAN SPECIES.

	GENERA.	Species.	New species.	Species not examined.	Species taken also in North America.	Brazil.	Guiana, Cayenne, Surinam.	Columbia, Venezuela.	Peru.	Chili.	Buenos Ayres and southern parts.
1	Calotermes	5	..	..	2	5	..	2	..	1	..
2	Hodotermes	1	..	..	..	..	..	..	..	1	..
3	Termes	25	..	..	4	23	5	3	..	1	..
4	Olyntha	3	..	3	..	3	..	1	..	..	..
5	Thyrsophorus	4	..	2	..	4	..	..	..	..	..
6	Psocus	8	7	..	..	8	..	..	..	..	..
7	Perla	19	1	13	2	10	..	7	..	2	..
8	Capnia	2	..	1	..	2	..	..	..	..	..
9	Ephemera	1	..	1	..	..	..	1	..	..	..
10	Palingenia	8	2	5	..	8	..	..	..	..	..
11	Baëtis	1	..	1	..	1	..	..	..	..	..
12	Cloë	1	..	..	..	1	..	..	..	..	..
13	Oligoneuria	1	..	..	..	1	..	..	..	..	..
14	Lais	6	..	..	..	6	..	..	..	..	..
15	Hetaerina	20	..	..	3	14	6	5	..	1	..
16	Heliocharis	2	..	..	..	2	..	..	..	..	..
17	Dicterias	2	..	..	..	2	..	..	..	..	..
18	Amphipteryx	1	..	..	..	..	..	1	..	..	..
19	Calopteryx	1	..	..	..	1	..	..	..	..	..
20	Thore	6	..	..	..	3	1	3	..	..	..
21	Cora	1	..	..	..	..	..	1	..	..	..
22	Megaloprepus	1	..	..	1	..	..	1	..	..	..
23	Microstigma	3	2	..	..	3	2	..	1	..	..
24	Pseudostigma	1	1	..	1	..	..	1	..	..	..
25	Mecistogaster	5	1	..	2	4	3	2	1	..	..
26	Lestes	8	4	2	2	6	2	2	..	1	1
27	Hyponeura	1	1	..	..	..	..	1	..	..	..
28	Euclea	1	1	1	..	1	..	..	..	..	..
29	Podagrion	5	5	3	..	3	..	2	..	..	..
30	Leptogaster	5	5	3	..	5	..	..	..	..	..
31	Neoneura	6	6	3	..	5	..	1	..	..	..
32	Protoneura	2	2	1	..	1	..	1	..	..	..
33	Agrion	56	42	20	5	39	2	5	2	4	1
34	Gomphus	3	..	..	1	2	..	..	..	1	..
35	Gomphoides	17	..	..	2	15	2	2	..	..	..
36	Ictinus	1	..	..	..	..	1	..	..	..	..
37	Cordulegaster	1	..	..	..	..	..	1	..	..	..
38	Petalia	3	..	..	..	..	..	..	..	3	..
39	Phenes	1	..	..	..	..	..	..	..	1	..
40	Anax	1	..	..	1	1	..	1	..	..	..
41	Aeschna	18	9	3	2	11	1	4	2	1	3
42	Gynacantha	8	4	1	2	5	1	2	..	..	..
43	Cordulia	7	5	1	..	6	..	..	..	2	..
44	Pantala	1	..	..	1	1	1	1	..	..	..
45	Tramea	5	2	..	..	5	..	..	..	..	..
46	Libellula	4	1	1	2	2	2	3	..	1	1
47	Lepthemis	8	3	..	3	7	5	1	..	..	..
48	Dythemis	21	15	1	1	18	3	4	1	1	..
49	Erythemis	6	3	2	3	4	1	1	1	..	..
50	Mesothemis	7	1	3	..	1	2	1	..	3	..
51	Diplax	31	19	4	4	26	5	2	..	..	2
		355	144	75	44	265	45	63	8	24	8

LIST OF SOUTH AMERICAN NEUROPTERA.

List of the Neuroptera of South America—Continued.

	GENERA.	Species.	New species.	Species not examined.	Species taken also in North America.	Brazil.	Guiana, Cayenne, Surinam.	Columbia, Venezuela.	Peru.	Chili.	Buenos Ayres and southern parts.
		355	144	75	44	265	45	63	8	24	8
52	Perithemis	5	3	..	1	5	..	1	..	..	..
53	Nannophya	2	2	..	..	2	..	..	..	..	..
54	Uracis	8	4	..	..	7	2	..	..	..	..
55	Palpopleura	3	1	..	..	3	1	..	..	..	..
56	Diastatops	4	..	..	..	3	2	..	1	..	..
57	Chauliodes	1	1	..	..	..	..	..	..	1	..
58	Corydalis	9	5	..	1	6	2	3	..	..	2
59	Hemerobius	2	2	..	..	1	..	..	..	1	..
60	Mantispa	13	..	5	..	10	1	1	..	1	..
61	Trichoscelis	3	..	2	..	3	..	..	..	..	..
62	Belonoptera	1	..	..	..	..	..	..	..	..	..
63	Chrysopa	18	1	7	1	15	2	2	..	..	..
64	Acanthaclisis	2	1	..	1	1	1	2	..	..	..
65	Myrmeleon	29	17	11	1	14	1	8	1	5	..
66	Ascalaphus	24	4	12	1	19	4	4	..	..	..
67	Bittacus	5	..	2	..	4	..	..	..	1	..
68	Barypenthus	2	..	2	..	2	..	..	..	..	..
69	Sericostoma	1	1	..	..	1	..	..	..	..	..
70	Macronema	12	..	9	3	8	1	4	..	..	..
71	Hydropsyche	1	1	..	..	1	..	..	..	..	..
72	Leptocerus	5	..	5	..	5	..	..	..	..	..
73	Chimarrha	2	1	..	..	2	..	..	..	..	..
		507	188	128	53	377	62	88	10	33	10

	FAMILIES.	Genera.	Species.
1	Termitina	3	31
2	Embidina	1	3
3	Psocina	2	12
4	Perlina	2	21
5	Ephemerina	5	12
6	Odonata	43	298
7	Sialina	2	10
8	Hemerobina	8	92
9	Panorpina	1	5
10	Phryganina	6	23
		73	507

SUMMARY.

North America contains	716 species.
South America contains	507 "
Total	1223 "

Deducting 53 species found in both North and South America, the whole continent of America contains 1170 species; of which 436 are new to science.

The actual number of "species not examined," 220 for North America and 128 for South America (total 348), is considerably less in reality; the species entirely unknown to me are 83 for North America and 29 for South America (total 112), mostly described by Say, Asa Fitch, and Pictet.

GLOSSARY.[1]

Abnormal. Deviating from the usual type.
Accessory subcostal vein. The vein given off from the *subcosta*, and branching towards the apex of the wing.
Acuminate. Furnished with a produced point.
Adult. The fully matured state of an insect.
Anal angle. The posterior interior corner of a wing.
Anal space. The area at the posterior base of the hind wings, which folds together when the wings are at rest, as in most *Phryganeæ*, &c.
Anastomosis. The thickened point of juncture of nervules.
Angulose. Constituting an angle or angles.
Annulated. Ringed; furnished with ring-like bands.
Annulus. A ring; a narrow, encircling band.
Antecubital. Pertaining to the space between the base of the wing and the *nodus*.
Antehumeral. Pertaining to the space immediately before the origin of the wings.
Antennæ. Two articulated feelers placed superiorly upon the head.
Anteocular. In front of the eyes.
Anterior. Before; forward part.
Anteriorly. Forwardly; in front.
Anus. The vent, or fundament.
Apex. The extremity, or smaller end opposite to the base.
Apical. Pertaining to the apex.
Apical sector. One of the longitudinal veins of the apex of a wing.
Approximated. Placed near; close together.
Arcuated. Curved, as a bow.
Article, or Articulation. A joint; or segment between two transverse sutures.
Areolate. Furnished with small areas.
Auricle. A small ear, or ear-like process.
Auriculated. Furnished with *auricles*.
Basal. Pertaining to the base.

---

[1] This Glossary has been prepared by Mr. UHLER, at the request of the Smithsonian Institution, with the view of furnishing an explanation of the technical terms employed in the present work.

Base. The foundation; as, Base of the head: that part of the head applied against the thorax.
Biarcuated. Twice-curved.
Bicolored. Two-colored.
Bidentate. Two-toothed.
Bifid. Two-branched.
Bifurcated. Two-forked.
Bi-impressed. Twice-impressed.
Bilineated. Marked with two lines.
Bilobed. Furnished with two lobes.
Bimaculated. Twice-spotted; having two spots.
Binotated. With two marks, or dots.
Biovate. Twice-ovate.
Biparted. Separated into two parts.
Biserrated. Provided with two small triangular teeth.
Bisetous. Furnished with two bristle-like appendages.
Bituberculated. Provided with two tubercles.
Bivittated. Marked with two longitudinal stripes.
Branchiæ. Breathing tubes analogous to gills.
Calcarated. Armed with spurs.
Carbonaceous. Resembling charcoal.
Carina. An elevated keel-like edge.
Carinate. Furnished with a *carina*.
Carpus. The *pterostigma*.
Caudal. Pertaining to the end of the abdomen.
Cellule. A little space surrounded by veins, on the wings.
Cerci. The superior processes at the end of the abdomen.
Chalybeous. Of a steel-blue color.
Cilia. Hairs set like a fringe; resembling eyelashes.
Ciliated. Furnished with *cilia*.
Cinereous. Of an ash-gray color.
Clavate. Furnished with a thickened extremity like a club.
Clypeus. That part of the head immediately above the *labrum*.
Compressed. Flattened together, as if by pressure applied at each side.
Confluent. Flowing together; united at the ends, as the veins of wings.
Connate. United; not separated by an articulated suture.
Cordiform. Shaped like a heart.
Coriaceous. Of a consistence resembling leather.
Costa. The same as *costal vein*.
Costal. Pertaining to the *costa*.
Costal area. A space between the *costa* and the next longitudinal vein.
Costal vein. The rib-like vein of the anterior margin of the wings, followed, in the section *Neuroptera*, by the *subcosta*, the *radius*, and the *cubitus*; the latter is frequently double (*cub. anticus, cub. posticus*).
Cultriform. Shaped like a pruning-knife.
Cuneiform. Shaped like a wedge.

Cupreous. Of a copper-color.
Deciduous. Casting off the wings.
Dentated. Furnished with teeth.
Denticle. A small tooth.
Depressed. Flattened down.
Dilated. Widened, expanded.
Discoidal. Pertaining to the disk or middle.
Discoidal areolets. Spaces of the middle of a wing; in the *Libellulina* they are placed beyond the triangle.
Disk. The middle surface.
Divaricated. Spreading apart, as two gradually separating branches.
Dolabriform. Shaped like a hatchet.
Dorsum. The superior surface of the thorax or abdomen.
Elliptical. Elongate-oval.
Emarginate, or Emarginated. Notched.
Ensiform. Sword-shaped; sharp on both edges, and tapering to a point.
Epistoma. That part of the face between the *front* and *labrum*.
Equal. Of the same size or length.
Excision. A cut out of an edge, not always of the same shape.
Facies. Aspect; appearance.
Falcate. Sickle-shaped; curved like a sickle.
Fascia. Used here as a stripe broader than a line.
Femora. The thighs.
Femur. A thigh.
Fenestrated. Marked with transparent spots surrounded by a darker color, somewhat like panes of glass in windows.
Ferruginous. Rust-colored.
Filiform. Slender and cylindrical, like a thread.
Flavescent. Somewhat yellow.
Flexuous. Almost zigzag, more acute at the angles than undulating.
Foliaceous. Leaf-like.
Forcipated. Furnished with two pieces approaching at the ends like pincers.
Fovea. A more or less rounded depression.
Foveolate. Furnished with cavities or depressions.
Free. Unrestrained in articulated movement; not soldered at the points of contact.
Front. The fore-face, bounded by the eyes, the vertex, and usually beneath by the *epistoma*.
Frontal. Pertaining to the *front*.
Fuliginous. Of the color of dark smoke.
Fulvo-aeneous. Brazen, with a tinge of brownish-yellow.
Fulvous. Tawny, color of the common deer.
Furcated. Forked; split into two separating ends.
Fuscescent. Measurably fuscous.
Fusco-ferruginous. Rust-colored, with a brownish tinge.

Fusco-testaceous. Dull reddish-brown.
Fuscous. Dark brown, approaching black.
Fusiform. Spindle-shaped; gradually tapering at each end.
Genital lobe. The bag-like appendage upon the second ventral segment of the male dragon-fly.
Genital accessory organs. The hooks, &c., situated beneath the second ventral segment of the male dragon-fly, &c.
Glaucous. Of a sea-green color.
Guttæ. Marks resembling dots or small spots.
Guttated. Marked with *guttæ*.
Gradate. Step by step; successive.
Granulated. Provided with minute, close prominences, like very small grains of sand, &c.
Hab. Abbreviation of *Habitat*.
Habitat. The place or region which an insect inhabits.
Habitus. Aspect; general appearance, or likeness.
Hamate. Furnished with hooks, or hook-like processes.
Hamule. A small hook.
Hastated. Halberd-shaped; excavated at the base and sides, but with spreading lobes or angles.
Hastiform. Shaped like a halberd.
Haustellate. Furnished with a proboscis-like mouth.
Hirsute. Clothed with shaggy hairs.
Humeral. Belonging to the *humerus* or shoulder.
Hyaline. Transparent; of the color of water.
Imagines. Plural of *imago*.
Imago. The insect in its last stage, after passing through *larva* and *pupa*.
Immarginare. Not furnished with a turned-up edge.
Incanous. Hoary; clothed with whitish hair or powder.
Incision. A slit-like cut.
Incisures. The impressed transverse lines between the segments of the abdomen, &c.
Incomplete. Not fully developed.
Inferiorly. Beneath; pertaining to the lower surface.
Infracted. Bent; suddenly bent.
Infumated. Clouded, as if with tobacco-smoke.
Infuscated. Darkened with a blackish tinge.
Interrupted. Suddenly stopped.
Involuted. Rolled inwards spirally.
Irrorated. Marked with spots like freckles.
Labium. The lower lip of an insect.
Labrum. The upper lip of an insect.
Lamelliform. Shaped like a plate of metal, &c.
Lamina. A plate or sheet-like piece.
Laminated. Provided with *laminæ*.
Lanceolate, or **Lanceolated.** Shaped like a spear.

Larva. The first stage of an insect after it is excluded from the egg.
Lateral. Pertaining to the sides.
Laterally. Sideways.
Linear. Shaped like a line; very narrow in form.
Lineated. Provided with line-like marks.
Lunule. A half-moon-shaped object or mark. .
Lurid. Bright colors obscured.
Luteous. Egg-yellow; clay-yellow.
Maculose. Spotted.
Mandibles. Jaws; two, generally horny pieces of the mouth, immediately under the labrum.
Mandibulate. Tarnished with mandibles.
Margined. Edged; provided with a margin.
Marmorated. Marbled; veined like marble.
Maxillæ. Pieces of the mouth which occupy the places of the jaw-bones.
Maxillary palpi. Jointed appendages attached to the *maxillæ*.
Median, or Medial. Of, or occupying the middle.
Median Nervule. The third basal nervule in *Calopterygina*, &c.
Median space. The posterior space at the base of the wings in *Calopteryx*, &c.
Membranaceous. Of a membrane-like character.
Membránule. The small triangular flap at the interior base of the wings in *Libellulina*, &c.
Meridional. Equatorial.
Mesothorax. Middle primary division of the thorax.
Metathorax. The posterior primary division of the thorax.
Mobile. Movable.
Moniliform. Shaped like a string of beads.
Multi-areolate. Composed of many small areas or spaces.
Multi-articulate. Composed of many articles or joints.
Mutic. Unarmed, *i. e.*, without spines, &c.
Nasus. A space directly above the labrum.
Nasute. Bearing a projection like a nose; said of certain workers, &c., amongst the *Termites*.
Nebula. A cloud-like spot.
Nodal. Pertaining to an oblique stout vein, called the *nodus*.
Nodulose. Clothed with knot-like small prominences.
Nodus. A stout, oblique, short vein in the *Odonata*, at the place where the anterior margin of the wings is somewhat drawn in.
Obovate. Inversely ovate, the smaller end turned towards the base.
Obsolete. Not distinct, or almost lost to view.
Obtected. Covered.
Ocelli. The simple eyes of insects; usually three amongst the *Neuroptera*.
Ochraceous, or Ochreous. Of a more or less deep ochre-color.
Occiput. The back part of the head behind the *vertex*.
Olivaceous. Of an olive-color.

Onychium. See *Plantula*.
Oval. Egg-shaped.
Ovate. More or less oval.
Palpi. The feelers attached to the mouth of insects.
Pectus. The breast, or inferior surface of the *thorax*.
Petiolated. Narrowed into a handle-like neck; as the base of the wings in *Agrion*.
Phalerated. Marked with stripes and bands like the harness of a horse.
Piceous. Color of pitch.
Pile. Hair; usually hair arranged somewhat in rows.
Pilose. Clothed with pile.
Plantula. A small lap or membranous appendage between the tarsal nails of insects; also called *Onychium*.
Plicated. Furnished with folds; folded.
Postcostal, or Postcubital. Pertaining to the space between the *nodus* and *pterostigma*.
Posteriorly. Behind; after.
Process. A prolongation of the surface, such as an ear-like elevation, &c.
Produced. Drawn out; prolonged.
Prothorax. The first segment of the *thorax*.
Pruinose. Clothed with bluish or white bloom or powder.
Pterostigma. A more or less colored mark upon the anterior margin before the apex of a wing, between the costal and the following longitudinal vein.
Pterostigmatical. Pertaining to the pterostigma, or its locality.
Pubescent. Clothed with short, soft, fine hair or down.
Punctiform. Shaped like a point or dot.
Pyriform. Shaped like a pear.
Quadrangular space. The space immediately beyond the basal one and in front of the median space of the wings.
Radius. The vein just behind the subcostal one.
Raptatorial. Adapted for seizing prey.
Recurved. Curved backwards.
Reniform. Kidney-shaped.
Reticulated. Furnished with veining or marking like network.
Reticulation. Veining, or marking like the meshes of a net.
Rhinarium. The nostril-piece; a portion of the *nasus*, or its equivalent when reduced in size.
Rhombical. Quadrangular, with two opposite angles acute and two obtuse.
Rhomboidal. Somewhat in the shape of a rhomb.
Rufescent. Somewhat reddish.
Rufous. Reddish.
Rugose. Wrinkled; furnished with numerous rough, small elevations like wrinkles.
Rugulæ. Minute wrinkles.
Rugulose. Minutely wrinkled.

Salient. Projecting; jutting out.
Sanguineous. Blood-red.
Sectors. Longitudinal nerves which strike the principal nerves at an angle, and usually reach the apex or hind margin of the wing.
Semihyaline. Half transparent.
Semilunar. Half-moon shaped.
Sericeous. Having the surface with a silk-like gloss, usually from minute, dense hairs.
Serrated. Having prominences like saw-teeth.
Seta. A bristle-like appendage, such as at the tail of *Ephemera*, &c.
Setaceous. Bristle-like; resembling a bristle.
Setæ. Plural of *Seta*.
Setiform. Bristle-shaped.
Sinuated. Scooped out, or broadly shallowly excavated on a margin.
Spurs. Stiff bristle-like appendages upon the *tibiæ*. In the Phryganeæ they are either at the tip or in the middle of the tibiæ; their number affords an important character for classification, and is expressed by three figures, meaning the three successive pairs of feet; thus 2, 4, 4, means two terminal spurs on the fore tibiæ, two terminal and two middle ones on the middle tibiæ, and two terminal and two middle ones on the hind tibiæ.
Stramineous. Straw-colored; yellow.
Stria. A line, usually depressed, sometimes composed of punctures.
Striæ. Plural of *stria*.
Striated. Charged with striæ.
Subaduncate. Somewhat hooked or curved.
Subcinereous. Somewhat gray.
Subcosta. The vein just behind the *costa*.
Subhyaline. Almost transparent, or water-colored.
Sublmago. A state of *Ephemera*, &c., wherein the wings, &c., are covered with a membrane, which is cast off when it becomes an *Imago*.
Submarginal. Just behind the margin.
Submedian nerve. The longitudinal large nerve just behind the *median*.
Subnude. Almost without clothing; without hairs, &c.
Subocular. Beneath the eyes.
Subrect. Almost straight.
Subscabrous. Indistinctly rough.
Subulate. Shaped like an awl.
Sulcus. A groove-like excavation.
Sulphureous. Of a color resembling sulphur.
Suture. A seam, or impressed line; usually between segments.
Tarsus (plural **Tarsi**). The terminal, almost always jointed divisions of the foot of an insect, immediately after the tibia.
Teneral. A state of the *imago* after exclusion, in which it has not fully completed its coloring, clothing, &c.
Testaceo-hyaline. Transparent, with a slight tinge of dull reddish.
Testaceous. Dull brick-color.

Tetragonal. Having four sides or angles.
Thorax. The second primary segment of the body, bearing the legs and wings.
Thyridium. A small pale or almost transparent spot near the anastomosis of the disk of the wings in *Phryganina*.
Tibia. The shanks; that part of the leg between the femur and tarsus.
Trapezoidal. Four-sided, with two sides unequal and parallel.
Triangle. A three-sided figure; found in the front wings of *Libellula* near the base.
Triarticulate. Composed of three joints or articles.
Trifid. Cleft into three ends.
Trifoveolated. Furnished with three pits or foveæ.
Trigonal. Triangular, three-sided.
Trilobed. Having three lobes.
Triquetral. Having three more or less long angles.
Trochanters. The joints of the legs situated between the *femora* and *coxæ*.
Truncated. Cut square off.
Tuberculoid. Resembling a tubercle.
Tuberculose. Covered with tubercle-like prominences.
Unguiculus. A nail, like that at the extremity of the *tarsus*.
Unguiculi. Plural of *Unguiculus*.
Unique. A single individual of a kind.
Vaginated. Covered with a sheath-like plate, or *vagina*.
Valvule. A small valve-like process.
Venter. The under surface of the *abdomen*.
Ventral. Pertaining to the under surface of the abdomen.
Verrucose. Covered with wart-like prominences.
Vertex. The upper part of the head, just above the *front*.
Vesicle of the penis. The bag-like appendage on the second ventral segment of the male dragon-fly.
Villose. Clothed with soft, rather long, hair.
Violaceous. Violet-colored.
Viridescent. Somewhat greenish.
Vulva. The orifice of the female genital tube.
Vulvar. Pertaining to the vulva.
Vulvar lamina. The scale or appendage upon the ventral surface of the eighth segment in the female dragon-fly.

To those desirous of becoming better acquainted with the terminology of Neuroptera, especially that of the neuration of the wings, the following inexpensive little work may be recommended: *Neuroptera austriaca*, by Friedr. Brauer and Franz Loew, Vienna, 1857, with five plates. Although written in German, it will prove useful, on account of its plates, even to those not familiar with that language.

INDEX.

Acanthaclisis, 223, 324
Aeschna, 119, 314
AESCHNINA, 98, 117, 312, 314
Agrion, 74, 87, 310, 312
AGRIONINA, 56, 62, 65, 305, 307
Aleuronia, 196
Amphipteryx, 307
Anabolia, 264
Anax, 117, 314
Apatania, 270
Ascalaphus, 237, 326
Atropos, 8

Baëtis, 44, 304
Barypenthus, 328
Belonoptera, 324
Beraea, 296
Bittacus, 246, 327
Boreus, 240
Brachycentrus, 272

Caenis, 54
CALOPTERYGINA, 56, 305
Calopteryx, 56
Calotermes, 1, 299
Capnia, 32, 303
Celithemis, 147
Chalcopteryx, 307
Chauliodes, 189, 321
Chimarrha, 297, 329
Chrysopa, 211, 323
Cloë, 52, 304
Clothilla, 7
Colpotaulius, 253
Coniopteryx, 197
Cora, 307
Cordulegaster, 115, 313
Cordulia, 136, 315
CORDULINA, 132, 315
Corydalis, 192, 321

Dasystoma, 273
Desmotaulius, 263
Diastatops, 321
Dicteriax, 307

Didymops, 135
Diplax, 173, 318
Dythemis, 162, 317

Embidina, xix, 7, 301
Enoicyla, 267
Ephemera, 38
Ephemerina, xix, 38, 304
Epitheca, 134
Erpetogomphus, 98
Erythemis, 168, 317
Euclea, 309
Euptilon, 237

GOMPHINA, 98, 312
Gomphoides, 111, 312
Gomphus, 98, 102, 312
Gynacantha, 131, 315

Hagenius, 114'
Hallesus, 265
Heliocharis, 306
Hemerobina, xx, 196, 322
Hemerobius, 200, 322
Hetaerina, 58, 305
Hodotermes, 299
Hydropsyche, 286, 329
HYDROPSYCHIDES, 284
Hydroptila, 274
Hyponeura, 309

Ictinus, 313
Ischnura, 75, 310
Isopteryx, 31 •

Lais, 305
Lepthemis, 160, 316
Leptogaster, 309
LEPTOCERIDES, 275
Leptocerus, 276, 329
Lestes, 65, 308
Leuctra, 37
Libellula, 150, 316
LIBELLULINA, 132, 141, 315

LIMNOPHILIDES, 253
Limnophilus, 253, 254
Macromia, 132
Macronema, 284, 328
Mantispa, 207, 322
Mecistogaster, 64, 308
Megalomus, 198
Megaloprepus, 62, 307
Meleoma, 210
Merope, 248
Mesothemis, 170, 318
Micromus, 198
Microstigma, 308
Molanna, 275
Mormonia, 273
Myrmeleon, 225, 324

Nannophya, 186, 320
Nehalennia, 74
Nemoura, 36
Neogomphus, 110
Neoneura, 309
Neuronia, 249
NEUROPTERA, xix, 187
Notidobia, 271
Notosticta, 309

Odonata, xix, 55, 305
Oligoneuria, 304
Olyntha, 7, 301
Ophiogomphus, 101
Orthemis, 160, 316

Palingenia, 40, 304
Palpopleura, 320
Panorpa, 241
Panorpina, xx, 240, 327
Pantala, 141, 315
Palaemnema, 72
Paraphlebia, 71
Perithemis, 185, 319
Perla, 17, 302
Perlina, xx, 14, 302
Petalia, 313
Petalura, 117
Phenes, 314
Philopotamus, 291

Phryganea, 252
PHRYGANIDES, 249
Phryganina, xx, 249, 328
Plathemis, 149
Podagrion, 309
Polycentropus, 292
Polystoechotes, 206
Potamanthus, 51
Progomphus, 110
Protoneura, 73, 310
PSEUDONEUROPTERA, xix, 1
Pseudostigma, 63, 308
PSEUDOSTIGMATA, 62

Psocina, xx, 7, 302
Psocus, 8, 302
Psychomyia, 294
Pteronarcys, 14
Pyrrhosoma, 85, 311

Raphidia, 194, 321
Rhyacophila, 295
RHYACOPHILIDES, 295

Sericostoma, 270, 328
SERICOSTOMIDES, 270
Setodes, 280
Sialina, xx, 187, 321
Sialis, 187

Silo, 272
Sisyra, 197
Taeniopteryx, 34
Termes, 3, 299
Termitina, xx, 1, 299
Termopsis, 3
Tetragoneuria, 140
Thyrsophorus, 302
Thore, 307
Tinodes, 295
Trameα, 143, 316
Trichocnemis, 72
Trichoscelis, 323

Uracis, 320

CORRECTIONS AND ADDITIONS.

Page 2, line 28, place semicolon instead of comma after *yellowish*.
" 4, line 2, add: "with a distinct fovea in the middle," which is occupied by a minute, elevated point.
" 5, line 7, dele last e in ferruginous; also on page 30, line 5, and wherever found so spelt.
" 60, bottom of page, dele diæresis from a in Hagen.
" 64, line 19, *for* Mecistogastur *read* Mecistogaster.
" 66, line 24, place a comma after the word *front*.
" 70, line 16, place a comma before the word *pruinose*.
" 76, line 21, remove the comma from behind the word *exteriorly*, and place it before.
" 78, line 21, add the word *with*, to the clause: a dorsal line, &c.
" 85, line 27, place a comma before and after *brassy-green*.
" 118, line 33, place a semicolon in the stead of comma before *beneath*.
" 131, line 30, place a comma after *narrowed*.
" 143, line 22, pl. xxxviii: change to pl. xlviii.
" 170, bottom of page, *for* Huastee *read* Huastec.
" 218, line 34, *for* little *read* dot.
" 223, line 19, place a comma after *side*.
" 224, line 1, place a comma after *beneath*.
" 256, place after description of *Limnophilus radiatus*, Hab. N. W. Territory (Say).

www.ingramcontent.com/pod-product-compliance
Lightning Source LLC
Chambersburg PA
CBHW020224240426

43672CB00006B/411